Knights of the Cross

Knights of the Cross
Translated by Sir Frank Morzials

Chronicle of the Fourth Crusade
and the Quest of Constantinople
Geoffrey de Villehardouin

Chronicle of the Crusade of St. Louis
Jean de Joinville

Knights of the Cross
Translated by Sir Frank Morzials
*Chronicle of the Fourth Crusade
and the Quest of Constantinople*
by Geoffrey de Villehardouin
and
Chronicle of the Crusade of St. Louis
by Jean de Joinville

First published under the titles
Memoirs of the Crusades

Leonaur is an imprint
of Oakpast Ltd

Copyright in this form © 2009 Oakpast Ltd

ISBN: 978-1-84677-816-2 (hardcover)
ISBN: 978-1-84677-815-5 (softcover)

http://www.leonaur.com

Publisher's Notes

In the interests of authenticity, the spellings, grammar and place names used have been retained from the original editions.

The opinions of the authors represent a view of events in which he was a participant related from his own perspective, as such the text is relevant as an historical document.

The views expressed in this book are not necessarily those of the publisher.

Contents

Introduction 7

Chronicle of the Fourth Crusade
and the Quest of Constantinople 39

Chronicle of the Crusade of St. Louis 163

Introduction

Preliminaries

Powerful and rich as English literature is, it has little to place in line against the superb array of French memoirs. Englishmen enough have done great things, or taken part in the doing of them, or seen them done; but only a scanty few have been moved to write—even fewer to write with any approach to style—of what they had done and seen. Among the French it has been otherwise. The French statesman, or leader, his life's greater battle being fought, has more often betaken himself to his pen, either—to use Guizot's image—for the purpose of fighting the old fights once more, with that weapon, in the smaller arena of letters, or simply for pure indulgence in the pleasures of memory. Villehardouin, Joinville—I exclude Froissart, beautiful as his work is, because he was a chronicler pure and simple and not an actor in the world's affairs—Commines, Sully, Retz, the "Grande Mademoiselle," Saint-Simon, Chateaubriand, Guizot,—here is a fine list of examples.

Of these French memoirs, the *Memoirs of Villehardouin and Joinville*, reproduced in an English form, are certainly not the least interesting. They are the first in date, those of Villehardouin having been written, probably, in the days of our King John, early in the thirteenth century; while those of Joinville were completed, about a century later, in October 1309, shortly after our Edward II. had begun to reign. Both are monuments of the French language, and of French prose, at an early stage of development—giant lispings, as one may say. Both are written by eyewitnesses who had taken an important part, in the case of Villehardouin a very important part, in what they describe. Both deal with stirring episodes in one of the most stirring chapters in human history, the chapter that tells how, for some three centuries, Christendom put forth its power to capture, and again recapture,

Those holy fields
Over whose acres walked those blessed feet
Which, fourteen hundred years ago, were nailed,
For our advantage, on the bitter cross. [1]

And both serve to illustrate the varied motives that went to the initiation and maintenance of that great movement.

VILLEHARDOUIN

Villehardouin's story opens with the closing years of the twelfth century. In those years, as he tells, Fulk of Neuilly, near Paris, a priest well known for his holiness and zeal, began to preach a new Crusade; and Fulk's words, so men thought, were confirmed by many signs and miracles; and even apart from such supernatural aid, it is not difficult, I think, to conjecture wherein lay the force of his appeal or to imagine its nature. But while he was descanting on the necessity for another attempt to recover the Holy Land, and setting forth the glories and spiritual advantages of the proposed adventure, did he ever dwell at all, one wonders, on the story of the Crusades that had already been undertaken? Did he unfold for his hearers that tragic and terrible scroll in the history of men—a scroll on which are recorded in strange, intermingled, fantastic characters, tales of saintly heroism, and fraud, and greed, and cruelty, and wrong—of sufferings at which one sickens, and foul deeds at which one sickens more, and acts of devotion and high courage that have found their place among the heirlooms and glories of mankind?

Did he tell them of the First Crusade—tell them how, a little more than a century before, the heart of Peter the Hermit had been moved to fiery indignation at the indignities offered to pilgrims at the sacred shrines, and he had made all Christendom resound to his angry eloquence; how at the Council of Clermont, in 1095, Pope Urban II. had re-echoed the hermit's cry; how the nations had responded to the call to arms in so holy a cause, the noble selling or mortgaging his land, the labourer abandoning his plough, the woman her hearth and distaff, the very children forsaking their play; how a great wave of humanity had thence been set rolling eastward—a wave of such mighty volume, and so impelled by fierce enthusiasm, that, notwithstanding every hindrance, dissension within, utter disorganisation, misrule, famine, plague, slaughter, wholesale desertions, treachery on every side,

---

1. The first part of King Henry IV., Act 1. Sc. 1.

wild fanatical hostility—notwithstanding all this, it had yet rolled right across Europe, rolled on across the deserts and defiles of Asia Minor, and swept the infidel from Jerusalem and the fastnesses of Judæa?

Did Fulk of Neuilly, one wonders, tell his hearers the story of that First Crusade, which, for all its miseries and horrors, accomplished the mission on which it started, and placed its great and saintly leader, Godfrey of Bouillon on the throne of Jerusalem, and founded a Christian kingdom in the Holy Land? (1099).

Did he tell them the story of the Second Crusade? That was the Crusade preached by one of very different mould from Peter the Hermit, by one who was in many ways the master-spirit of his time, St. Bernard. For to St. Bernard it seemed a scandal and intolerable that the Christian kingdom of Judæa, prayed for with so many prayers, purchased with so much blood, should be dissolved. He held it as not to be borne that the place where our Lord had been cradled in the manger, the fields where He had taught, the hill where He had died for men, the sepulchre in which He had lain, should fall once more in to the unholy possession of the infidel. And yet, ere fifty years had passed since the taking of Jerusalem, this seemed an approaching consummation, so weakened was the new kingdom by internal dissension, so fiercely attacked from without.

Already the Moslem were prevailing on every side. The important position of Edessa had fallen into their hands. So St. Bernard came to the rescue. By his paramount personal influence, he induced Louis VII. of France, and Conrad of Germany to take the cross. Again there was a march across Europe; again treachery on the part of the Greek Emperor at Constantinople; again most terrible slaughter in Asia Minor; again unheard-of sufferings; again folly, ineptitude, treachery. But not again the old ultimate success.

This time the great human wave, though it did indeed reach Jerusalem, yet reached it spent and broken. Edessa was not retaken. Damascus was besieged, only to show the utter want of unity among the Crusaders. Conrad returned to Germany. Louis, a year later, returned to France (1149); and of the Second Crusade there remained small immediate trace, save, in France and Germany, depopulated hamlets, and homes made desolate, and bones bleaching in the far Syrian deserts.

Could Fulk have turned, in the retrospect, with better heart to the Third Crusade?—Somewhat unquestionably. That Third Crusade is the one in which we Englishmen have most interest, for its central figure is our lion-hearted king, Richard. And it is, probably, the Crusade of which the main incidents are best known to the English reader, for they have been evoked from the past, and made, as it were, to re-enact themselves before us, by the magic of Sir Walter Scott. What boy has not read the *Talisman*?

And so it will not be necessary for me to dwell at length on the history of that Crusade: the rivalries of Richard and Philip Augustus; the siege and surrender of Acre; the return of Philip Augustus to France; the bitter feud with the Duke of Austria; the superb daring and personal prowess of Richard; the abortive march on Jerusalem—which must have been retaken save for the insane rivalries in the Christian host; the interchange of courtesies with the chivalrous Saladin; the abandonment of the Crusade; the return of the English king westward, and his imprisonment in an Austrian dungeon (1192).

Not a story of success, most certainly. Richard left the Holy Land pretty well where he found it. His object in going thither had been the recovery of Jerusalem, which, in 1187, after being nearly ninety years in Christian hands, had fallen a prey to Saladin. And that object was as far as ever from attainment. But still there rested about the Third Crusade a glamour of courage and heroic deeds, so that when scarce nine years after its conclusion, Fulk went about preaching new efforts for the expulsion of the Saracens, he may possibly have sought to raise the courage of his warlike hearers by dwelling on the doughty deeds of Richard and his knights.

Otherwise, if he referred to the past at all—or the latest German expedition of 1196-1197 had just come to an inglorious close,—his message can scarcely have been one of confidence as he addressed the nobles and lesser men assembled at Ecri, towards the end of November 1199, to take part in the great tournament instituted by Thibaut III., Count of Champagne. No, the past was against them. It spoke little of success, and much of misery, disorganisation, disaster; while as to the future, if Fulk and his hearers had seen into that, one doubts if they could have been moved to much enthusiasm. Whatever admixture of worldly motives there may have been, the Fourth Crusade was vehemently advocated by Pope Innocent III., proclaimed by Fulk, joined by multitudes of devout pilgrims, for the express purpose of recapturing Jerusalem, and driving the heathen out of Palestine.

But it never reached Palestine at all. It did far less than nothing towards the recovery of the Holy City. It delivered its blow with immense force and shattering effect upon a Christian, not a Moslem, State. It contributed not a little, in ultimate result, to break down

Europe's barrier against the Turk. Thus, from the Crusading point of view, it was a gigantic failure; and, as such, denounced again and yet again by the great Pope who had done so much to give it life.

How did this come about? What were the real influences that led the Fourth Crusade to change its objective from Jerusalem to Constantinople? The question has been many times debated. It is, as one may almost say, one of the stock questions of history; and I can scarcely altogether give it the go-by here—as I should like to do—because in that question is involved the more personal question of Villehardouin's own good faith as a historian.

If there were wire-pullers at work, almost from the beginning, who laboured to deflect the movement to their own ends; if the Venetians throughout played a double game,[2] and betrayed the Christian cause to the Saracens, then it is necessary, before we accept him altogether as a witness of truth, to inquire why he makes no mention of the Marquis of Montferrat's intrigues, or the Republic's duplicity. Did he write in ignorance? or did he, while possessing full knowledge, banish ugly facts from his narrative, and deliberately constitute himself, as has been said, the "official apologist" of the Crusade?

For, as he tells the story, all is simplicity itself. There is scarcely anything to explain. The Crusade has a purely religious origin: "Many took the cross because the indulgences were so great." Villehardouin himself, and his five brother delegates from the great lords assembled in parliament at Compiègne, go to Venice, and engage a fleet to take the host of the pilgrims "oversea"—an ambiguous term which meant Syria for the uninitiated, but "Babylon" or Cairo for the Venetian Council—"because it was in Babylon, rather than in any other land, that the Turks could best be destroyed."

Then comes the death of Count Thibaut of Champagne, who would have been the natural leader of the Crusade, and the selection, in his stead, of the Marquis of Montferrat, "a right worthy man, and one of the most highly esteemed that were then alive." Afterwards the pilgrims begin to assemble in Venice; but owing to numerous defections, their number is so reduced that the stipulated passage money is not forthcoming, and the Venetians naturally refuse to move.

The blame, up to this point, lies entirely with the pilgrims who had failed to keep their tryst. Meanwhile, what is to be done? Some,

---

2. "The unchristian cupidity of the banausically-minded Republic of St. Mark," is the quaint description given by Pope Innocent's latest biographer. *Innocent the Great*, by C. H. C. Pirie-Gordon, 1907.

who in their heart of hearts wish not well to the cause, would break up the host and return to their own land. Others, who are better affected, would proceed at all hazards. Then the Doge proposes a compromise. If, says he, addressing his own people, we insist upon our pound of flesh, we can, no doubt, claim to keep the moneys already received, as some consideration for our great outlay; but, so doing, we shall be greatly blamed throughout Christendom.

Let us rather agree to forego the unpaid balance and carry out our agreement, provided the pilgrims, on their part, will help us to recapture Zara, on the Adriatic, of which we have been wrongfully dispossessed by the King of Hungary. To this the Venetians consent, and likewise the Crusaders, notwithstanding the remonstrances of the evil-disposed party aforesaid. So the blind old Doge assumes the cross, with great solemnity, in the Church of St. Mark, and many Venetians assume it too, and all is got ready for departure.

Then, and not till then, do we get any hint of an attack on the Greek empire.

"Now listen," says Villehardouin, "to one of the greatest marvels and greatest adventures that ever you heard tell of," and he proceeds to narrate how the young Greek prince Alexius, having escaped from the hands of that wicked usurper, his uncle, and being at Verona on the way to the court of his brother-in-law, "Philip of Germany," makes overtures to the Crusaders, and how the latter are not unprepared to help him to recover his father's throne, provided he in turn will help them to reconquer Jerusalem. Whereupon envoys are sent to accompany the youth into Germany, for further negotiation with Philip, and the host, Crusaders and Venetians together, set sail for their attack on Christian Zara.

And here for the first time Villehardouin makes mention of the religious objection to the course that the Crusade is taking. The inhabitants of Zara are prepared to capitulate, but are dissuaded by the party which, according to Villehardouin, were anxious to break up the host, and while the matter is under discussion, the abbot of Vaux, of the order of the Cistercians, rises in his place and says, "Lords, on behalf of the Apostle of Rome, I forbid you to attack this city, for it is a Christian city, and you are pilgrims." Nevertheless the Doge insists that the Crusaders shall fulfil their contract, and Zara is besieged and taken.

While the host is waiting, after the capture, they are joined by the envoys from Philip, and from Philip's brother-in-law, Alexius, the son of the deposed Emperor of Constantinople. These envoys bring definite and very advantageous proposals. The Crusaders are to dispossess the treacherous and wicked emperor, also called Alexius, and reinstate the deposed Isaac; and in return for this great service, Alexius the younger promises, "in the very first place," that the Greek empire shall be brought back into obedience to Rome, and then—seeing that the pilgrims are poor—that they shall receive 200,000 marks of silver, and provisions for small and great, and further that substantial help shall be afforded towards the conquest of the "land of Babylon," oversea.

The hook was well baited. The reunion of Christendom, gold and stores in plenty, active co-operation from the near vantage ground of Constantinople in the dispossession of the infidel, a splendid adventure to be achieved—no wonder the Crusaders were tempted. Villehardouin himself never falters in his expressed conviction that the course proposed was the right course, that he and his companions did well in following, at this juncture, the fortunes of the younger Alexius.

Nevertheless it is clear, even from his narrative, that a great, almost overwhelming, party in the host were unconvinced and bitterly opposed to the deflection of the Crusade. Hotly was the question debated. The laymen were divided. The clergy, even of the same religious order, were at bitter strife. When it came to the ratification of the convention with Alexius, only twelve French lords could be induced to swear. Thereafter came defection on defection—the deserters, as Villehardouin is always careful to note, not without a certain complacency, coming mainly to evil ends.

"Now be it known to you, lords," says he, "that if God had not loved that host, it could never have kept together, seeing how many there were who wished evil to it." Even the Pope's forgiveness for the attack on Zara, and his exhortation to the pilgrims to remain united, did not avail to prevent further disintegration.

Nevertheless the host ultimately reaches Constantinople, routs the Greeks, who have no stomach for the fight, sends the usurping Emperor Alexius flying, reinstates the blinded Isaac, and seats the younger Alexius, by the side of Isaac, on the imperial throne. But naturally the position of Isaac and Alexius is precarious, and when the latter asks the Crusaders to delay their departure, the adverse party tries once more to obtain an immediate descent on Syria or Egypt. They are overborne.

Soon, however, it becomes clear that Isaac and Alexius either cannot, or will not, fulfil their promises. As a matter of fact Alexius has placed himself and his father in an impossible position, of which death, in cruel forms, is to be the outcome, and they become, in turn, the objects of attack, and their empire a field of plunder. Henceforward the die is cast. The Crusade ceases to be a Crusade, and becomes as purely an expedition of conquest as William's descent on England. Whatever may be their occasional qualms, Franks and Venetians have enough to do in the Greek Empire, without giving very much thought to Judæa.

But to all this there is another side. Thus, if we are to believe the chronicle[3] compiled in 1393, by order of Heredia, Grand Master of the Hospital of St. John of Jerusalem, Villehardouin first proposed the Crusade to his lord, the Count of Champagne, not on any specially religious grounds, but because, after the peace between the kings of France and England, there were a great many idle men-at-arms about, whom it would be desirable to employ.

So also Ernoul, a contemporary, after telling how the barons of France, who had sided with Richard against Philip Augustus, cast off their armour at the tournament at Ecri, and ran to take the cross, adds: "There are certain persons who say that they thus took the cross for fear of the King of France, and so that he might not punish them because they had sided against him." [4]

This, however, is relatively unimportant. Mixed motives may at once be conceded as probable and natural. What is of greater significance is the attitude of the Venetians and the question of their good faith. Villehardouin here hints no doubt. According to him, the Republic made a bargain to provide freight and food for an expedition to the Holy Land or to "Babylon," and provided both amply, and it was only on the failure of the pilgrims to carry out their side of the bargain that the Venetians fell back on Zara.

They were prepared to take the Crusade to its original destination. But the same Ernoul, from whom I have just quoted, tells another story. He relates how Saphardin, the brother of the deceased Saladin, hearing that the Crusaders had hired a fleet in Venice, sends envoys to the Venetians, with great gifts and promises of commercial advan-

---

3. *Libro de los Fechos et Conquistas del Principado de la Morea*, translated from Spanish into French by Alfred Morel-Fatio, and published at Geneva in 1885 for the Société de l'O'rient Latin. I am bound, however, to say that this chronicle, which assigns to Villehardouin a very important part in the organisation of the Crusade, was compiled long after date, and seems clearly apocryphal in many of its details.
4. *Chronique d'Ernoul et de Bernard le Trésorier*, published by M. L. de Mas Latrie for the Société de l'histoire de France. Paris, 1871

tage, and entreats them to "turn away the Christians," and how the Venetians accept the bribe, and use their influence accordingly;[5] while certain modern historians discover, or think they have discovered, that it was the Venetians who took the initiative in this act of treachery, and that after making the treaty with Villehardouin and his fellow delegates in 1201, they sent envoys to Saphardin and virtually gave the Crusaders away by a specific treaty—of which, however, the date, and with it the relevancy, has been contested.

So again, with regard to the evil influences at work within the host itself, certain historians have endeavoured to show that the misdirection of the Crusade was but an episode in the long struggle between Guelf and Ghibelline. For the Crusade was the pet child of Innocent III. It was the dearest object of his heart. It was to crown his pontificate. What more natural than that the Ghibelline, Philip of Swabia, the son of Barbarossa, himself just then lying under a solemn excommunication, should endeavour, by all the means in his power, to thwart the expedition, to turn it to his own ends—one of which was the conquest of Constantinople—for on Constantinople he had pretensions.

Thus, according to this view, when Villehardouin suggested the Marquis of Montferrat for the leadership, he was, indirectly indeed, acting as the mouthpiece of Philip. And the marquis, from the date of his election, did but become Philip's agent, and had in view only one object—an attack on the Greek emperor. (See note end of Introduction.)

All his actions and movements are to be explained on the grounds that he cared nothing about Jerusalem, and very much about Constantinople. To go at length into all the pros and cons of this controversy, would take, not the comparatively short space allotted to an introduction, but a very considerable volume. And, indeed, the latest historian who has dealt with the subject, the very learned M. Luchaire, of the French Institute,[6] declares that, on the available data, the questions involved are insoluble.

Having placed the two views before the reader, I shall not therefore go into the matter further here, beyond saying that after a great deal of reading, and research, I have come to the conclusion, Firstly, that the Venetians were not as bad as they have been painted. They were a commercial people, and they had made a bargain, and they kept to it. The Crusaders did not. To expect the Venetians, for the good of the

---

5. See *ibid*.
6. *Innocent III.: La Question d'Orient.* 1907.

cause, to forego repayment for the large sums expended on a superb fleet and what must have been, temporarily at least, a great disturbance of their commerce, is absurd. Why should the main expense of the expedition fall on them? As to the treacherous arrangements with the Saracens, they seem to me not proven.

Therefore I hold myself justified in asking the reader to look, without a smile of sarcasm and incredulity, at the great scene in which Dandolo, the grand old Doge, blind and bearing gallantly his ninety years, goes up into the reading-desk of St. Mark, and there, before all the people—who wept seeing him—places the sign of the cross in his bonnet. Surely his bearing in council, and afterwards in battle, was not that of a vulpine old impostor.

Secondly, I own to very great doubts as to the elaborate Machiavellian schemes of Philip of Swabia, and the Marquis of Montferrat, and the after-participation therein, to a greater or less degree, of the leaders of the Crusade. Web-spinning so successful would imply gifts of foresight verging on prophesy.

Let us "look at things more simply," as M. Luchaire says. And disbelieving, to a very great extent, in the plot, I am bound to exonerate Villehardouin from the charge of endeavouring to disguise its existence. Nay, I go further. What we see as the past was to Villehardouin the present and the future. We know that the Crusade came to nothing, ultimately "fizzled out," as one may say. But Villehardouin, looking forward from day to day, may quite honestly have believed that the course he consistently advocated was the course best calculated, all the circumstances being given, to ensure success. Shut up in the island of St. Nicholas, near Venice, without the necessary means for advance or retreat, or even for the provision of daily subsistence, the Crusading host was in helpless case. The advance on Zara had no alternative.

Afterwards, leaders and men were without the sinews of war. When Alexius came with his definite proposals, one cannot wonder that men of strong political instinct, like our hero, should have thought that the best coign of vantage for an attack on Jerusalem, was Constantinople. The ignorant commonalty were for a direct descent on the Holy Land. The wiser chiefs would have preferred to first break the power of the Saracens in Egypt. The politicians of still larger outlook might naturally hold that with the Greek empire at their back, and with coffers full of Greek gold, they had the best chance of re-establishing the Christian kingdom of Jerusalem.

Nay, shall I go further still? The Franks defeated the Greeks with ease, defeated them as Pizarro and Cortes defeated the Peruvians and Mexicans, as Clive defeated the armies of India. What if they had not only conquered Roumania, but had also revivified the Greek Empire; if, instead of giving themselves to the greed, and rapine, and unstatesmanlike oppression, which Villehardouin deplored, and so losing within sixty years (1261) what they had held unworthily—what if, instead of this, they had administered wisely and well, had mingled in blood and interest with the conquered, had breathed with the breath of a new life over the dry bones of that dead race and nationality, had created a virile state at this specially important point of the world's surface, and so barred the way against the entrance of the Turk into Europe? When the Frank fleet set sail from Venice, these things were on the knees of the gods. Should we have been misdoubting Villehardouin if they had come to pass?

And having said so much for Villehardouin's good faith and essential political honesty, one is the more free" to admire the force and effectiveness of the man. What was his exact age at the date of the tournament at Ecri (November 1199), is not known. Probably he was then about forty, and in the fullness of his strength, and, as one may fairly conjecture, well-knit, and possessing a frame fitted to endure hardship and fatigue. Even if we regard as doubtful the statement of Heredia's chronicler, that it was he who first proposed the Crusade to Count Thibaut,[7] yet it is clear that, from the very beginning, he took a leading part in the enterprise, and that, as one may conclude, on purely personal grounds, for the Villehardouins were of no imposing *noblesse*.

Thus he is chosen by the assembled chiefs as one of the six envoys sent to Venice to negotiate for the transport of the host; and it is he who stands forth as spokesman for the Crusaders in the first memorable assembly at St. Mark's. When Count Thibaut dies, he seems to take the most active part in the choice of a successor, and proposes the leader ultimately nominated. When, afterwards, the pilgrims begin to avoid Venice, and travel eastwards by other routes, he is one of the two delegates despatched to bring them to a better mind, succeeding, to some extent, by "comfort and prayers."

To him is entrusted the task of explaining to the restored Emperor Isaac what are the conditions on which the Crusaders have consented to come to his help at Constantinople. Again he is selected for the perilous office of bearing to the Emperors Isaac and Alexius, in full

---

7. See *ante*.

court, the haughty defiance of the host. He is selected once more for the particularly delicate mission of reconciling the Marquis of Montferrat with the Emperor Baldwin, and he is afterwards deputed to bring the Marquis to Constantinople.

Thus we see him king a prominent part wherever there is a task of difficulty or danger to be undertaken; and finally, in one of the darkest, direst hours of the expedition, he stands forth heroically, and masters circumstance. The Crusaders, contrary to all preconcerted plans, have left their ranks and followed the lightly-armed Comans into the field, whereupon the Comans attack in turn, and cut the Crusaders to pieces, killing Count Lewis of Blois, and taking the Emperor Baldwin prisoner.

A broken remnant of the host comes flying into the camp. "When he sees this, Geoffry, the Marshal of Champagne, who is keeping guard before one of the gates of the city, issues forth from the camp as quickly as he can, and with all his men, and sends word to Manasses of the Isle, who is keeping another gate, to follow."

One can almost see it all, as he tells the story: the advance in serried ranks, rapid but in strict order, and with all the pomp of war—*à grande allure,*—and the long line of mailed riders forming across the plain; the fugitives in full flight, for the most part too panic-stricken to stop short of the camp itself, but those of better heart staying to strengthen the immovable breakwater of men. Towards that breakwater, but still keeping a respectful distance, surges the scattered host of Comans, Wallachians, Greeks, who do such mischief as they can with bows and arrows.

It was between nones and vespers, as Villehardouin tells us, that the rout was stayed. It is not till nightfall that the enemy retire. Then, under cover of night, and in council with the Doge, he leads off the beaten remnant of the host, leaving, as he records with just pride, not one wounded man behind—and effects a masterly retreat to the sea and safety.

A man, evidently like Scott's William of Deloraine, "good at need"—a man trusted of all and trustworthy—honoured by the Doge, honoured by the Emperor Baldwin, honoured and beloved by the Marquis of Montferrat. Nor should it be imagined, because this is the impression left by a study of the chronicle, that Villehardouin's method of telling the story of the Crusade has in it anything of personal boastfulness or vainglory. When he speaks of himself, in the course of his narrative, he does so quite simply, and just as he speaks of others.

There is no attempt to magnify his own deeds or influence. If he has taken part in any adventure or deliberation, he mentions the fact without false modesty, but does not dwell upon it unduly. And, indeed, as I read the man's character, a certain honourable straightforwardness seems to me one of its most important traits. He is a religious man, no doubt. The purely religious side of the Crusade has its influence upon him. He is not unaffected by the greatness of the pardon offered by the Pope. He believes that the expedition is righteous, and that God approves of it. He holds that God looks with a favouring eye upon all who are doing their best for its furtherance.

"Listen," he cries after some great deliverance, "how great are the miracles of our Lord whenever it is his pleasure to perform them. Well may we say that no man can harm those whom God favours."

And he stands in no manner of doubt that the Divine justice will deal in a very exemplary manner with those who separate themselves from the host, and pursue their own paths to Palestine. But if he is a religious man, he is in no sense an enthusiast. He stands in marked contrast to such Crusaders as Godfrey of Bouillon and St. Louis. The worldly side of the whole thing—its policy and business, and fighting and conquests—these are very habitually present to his thoughts. And withal, as I have said—and notwithstanding the doubts referred to in the earlier pages of this introduction—there is a ring about him of honesty and sincerity. His utterances are such as may be counted honourable to all time. He never forbears to inveigh against dishonesty, double-dealing, covetousness. It is not only as a politician, but as an upright man that he denounces the rapacious mishandling to which the Greeks are subjected.

Of such a man, as I repeat, one hesitates to believe that he lent himself to a long course of intrigue, and afterwards constituted himself the "official apologist" of what he knew to be indefensible. And as the man is, so is his book. When judging that book, it has to be borne in mind that it is the first work of importance and sustained dignity written in the French tongue. At the time that he dictated it, therefore, Villehardouin had no precedents to go by, no models to imitate. He was in all respects—language, narrator's art, style—a pioneer. And this being so, it marks him as a born writer, and a writer of a very high order, that his narration should be so lucid and distinct.

He marshals his facts well, proceeds from point to point with order and method, brings important matters into due prominence, keeps accessories properly in the background. Nor, notwithstanding the usual sobriety of his method, is he incapable, on due occasion, of rendering the moral aspect of a scene, or even the physical aspect of what has passed before his eyes. In proof of this I may refer to the two great scenes in St. Mark's, to the account of the attack on Constantinople, to the story of the battle in which Baldwin was taken prisoner. (See Villehardouin's Chronicle.)

Still I admit that as a word-painter his powers are embryonic rather than fully developed—a fact which Sainte-Beuve, the great critic, accounts for by saying that "the descriptive style had not yet been invented." But here, I venture to think, Sainte-Beuve was nodding. For if Villehardouin himself depicts soberly, yet he had a contemporary and fellow-Crusader, Robert of Clan by name, who also wrote a chronicle, and Robert of Clan has left a description of the scene when the Crusading fleet set sail from Venice on the feast of St. Remigius, 1202, which is not wanting in picturesqueness and colour:

"The Doge," he says, "had with him fifty galleys, all at his own charges. The galley in which he himself sailed was all vermilion, and there was a pavilion of red satin stretched above his head. And there were before him four trumpets of silver that trumpeted, and cymbals that made joy and merriment. And all the men of note, as well clerks as lay, and whether of small condition or great, made such joy at our departure, that never before had such joy been made, or so fine a fleet been seen. And then the pilgrims caused all the priests and clerks there present to get up into the castles of the ships, and sing the *Veni Creator Spiritus*, and all, both the great and the small folk, wept for great joy and happiness. It seemed as if the whole sea swarmed with ants, and the ships burned on the water, and the water itself were aflame with the great joy that they had."[8]

It was in colours like these that Turner saw Venice suffused when he painted such pictures as the Sun of Venice going out to sea. It was in terms almost identical that Shakespeare described Cleopatra's barge "burning" upon the Nile. Surely when Robert of Clari, a writer not otherwise comparable with Villehardouin, mixed such hues upon his palette, it cannot be said that the descriptive style was unborn. And if Villehardouin makes use of it but soberly, the reason is rather, I conceive, to be found in this, that his interest was but little concerned with the outward shows of things. He was a politician and soldier who had played an important part in the drama of history.

---

8. The reader may compare this passage with Villehardouin's description of the same event, or of the departure from Corfu.

What he cared to remember, in after days, was the deeds of the men who had played their parts with him, their passions and objects. Their dress, the pomp and circumstance by which they were surrounded, the look of the stage, and appearance of the side-scenes, all this had, comparatively, faded from his memory. His chronicle is that of a statesman, like the chronicle in which, some two centuries and a half later, Philippe de Commines enthroned, or gibbeted, the craft of his master Louis XI.

As to his style, *why style is the man's own self*, according to Buffon's oft-quoted saying, and Villehardouin's style is simple, strong, and direct-like himself, and like his narration. Now and again, but very seldom, it bears a blossom, *puts forth a flower*, as the French say when some bright image, some smiling fancy, breaks like a crocus or snowdrop through the cold aridity of prose. Thus, when the fleet is leaving Abydos—these vessels in full sail seem wonderfully to have stirred the hearts of the pilgrim host—he says that the Straits of St. George were "in flower" with ships.

But expressions like this, which suffuse with imagination the plain statement of a fact, are rare with him. Usually he is sober in his use of image, as in his descriptions. He says what he has to say, and no more; and he says it in a short, plainly-constructed sentence which can be "construed," as a schoolboy would say, without difficulty. Compared with the sentence of most English and French writers of the fifteenth or sixteenth centuries, or even of most German writers of today, his sentence is simplicity itself.

"The modern literature of the West they might justly despise," says Gibbon, speaking of the Greeks of Villehardouin's time. Is that quite true? In Villehardouin we have a literature of the quite early spring—vigorous, full of sap, unforced, spontaneous, unsophisticated. Take, by way of contrast, and as illustrating the literature of autumn and decay, such a passage as the following from his contemporary, the Greek historian Nicetas:

> What shall I say of the statue of Helen, of the perfection of her form, the alabaster of her arms and of her breast, of her perfect limbs?—of that Helen who brought all Greece beneath the walls of Troy? Had she not softened the savage inhabitants of Laconia? All seemed possible to her whose looks enchained every heart. Her vesture was without artifice, but so ingeniously disposed that the greedy eye could see all the freshness of her

charms scarce hidden by her light tunic, her veil, her crown, and the tresses of her hair.

Her hair, bound only to her neck, floated according to the fancy of the winds, and fell to her feet in waving tresses; her mouth, half-opened like the calix of a young flower, seemed to offer a passage to the tender accents of her voice, and the sweet smile of her lips filled the soul of the spectator with delicious feeling.

Never will it be possible to express, and posterity will seek vainly to feel or depict, the grace overspreading this divine statue. But, O daughter of Tyndareus, O masterpiece of love, O rival of Venus, where is the omnipotence of thy charms? Why didst thou not exercise them to subdue those barbarians as thou didst exercise them amiably of yore?

Has Fate condemned thee to burn in the same fire with which thou wert wont to consume all hearts? Did the descendants of Æneas wish to condemn thee to the same flames that thou didst light erewhile in Ilion?[9]

Was Nicetas, the author of this artificial rhetoric, really in a position to "despise" Villehardouin? In this matter, and with all due respect for Gibbon, one may say that the Frank represents the twilight of dawn, and the Greek the twilight of night.

And what became of Villehardouin at last? How and when did he die? All here is obscurity. We know, as I have said, next to nothing about his birth and earlier years. We know next to nothing about his later life and end. He emerges into the half-light of history with the beginning of his chronicle. He passes back into the darkness of the years with its close.

Of what happened to him after the date in 1207, when, as he tells us—it is his latest record, as if his pen had faltered at that point—how the Marquis of Montferrat had been miserably slain—of what, I say, happened to him after that year we are almost ignorant.

He had left his wife, his, daughters, his two sons, to follow the cross. There is no. evidence to suggest that he ever rejoined them in his native Champagne. M. Bouchet conjectures [10] that, replete with honour and rewards, weary of life's battle, saddened by the loss of so many of

---

9. I am translating from a French version which I happen to have before me—*Bibliothèque des Croisades*, by M. Michaud, third part 1829, p. 428.

10. *La Conquête Constantinople, texte et traduction nouvelle*, 1891, Vol. 2., pp. 286 and following.

his old companions in arms, he retired to end his days in his castle of Messinopolis on the enemy's marches, and there composed his history; but much of this can be no more than conjecture.

That the man lived to any great age is improbable, and indeed the year 1213 has usually been assigned as the year of his death. That he wrote, or rather dictated, his Chronicles when the hand of time lay heavy upon him seems to me, from the internal evidence of style and spirit, to be quite unlikely. Rather do I fancy that he composed them, in the halls of Messinopolis indeed, but with spirit unsubdued, and during some brief lull in the great strife between the Greeks and their Frank conquerors.

JOINVILLE

With Joinville we pass into a different atmosphere. Joinville was born, it is believed, in 1224. He embarked with St. Louis for the Crusade on the 28th August 1248; he returned to France in the July of 1254. His *Memoirs*, as he himself tells us, were written, *i.e.* concluded, in the month of October,. 1309, that is to say, when he was eighty-five years of age, and more than half a century after the events he had set himself to narrate. Thus while Villehardouin writes as a middle-aged soldier, succinctly, soberly, with eye intent on important events, and only casually alive to the passing show of things, Joinville writes as an old man looking lovingly, lingeringly, at the past—garrulous, discursive, glad of a listener.

Nothing is beneath his attention. He lingers here, lingers there, picks up an anecdote as he goes along, tells how people looked, and what they wore, describes the manners and customs of the outlandish folk with whom he is brought into contact; has his innocent superstitions, his suspicions of spiritualistic influence, stops to tell you about a tumbler's tricks, about a strange fossil that has struck his fancy; illustrates, discusses, moralises; reports at length his conversations, especially with the king; and would have a tendency to repeat himself in any case, even if he had not adopted, to begin with, a defective plan of narration, that involved much repetition. And with such a charm in it all!

The man is so simple, so honest, so lovable. Fine fellow as he undoubtedly is, he makes claim to no heroic sentiments—tells you how he was afraid to turn his eyes towards his castle as he went away, leaving wife and children behind him—how he trembled, partly with fear, when he fell into the hands of the enemy. And his judgments upon his fellows are so essentially the judgments of a gentleman. Then he has the graphic gift: we see what he sees, and we know the people that he brings before us. All that world of the Crusade lives in his pages. Not even in Chaucer's immortal *Prologue* do we get so near to the life of the Middle Ages.

Yes, as one reads the chronicle, it is impossible not to love the chronicler. If a snob be, according to Thackeray's definition, one who meanly admires mean things, then surely one who grandly admires heroic things may be pronounced a hero. And Joinville had before him in St. Louis a high ideal of Christian manhood, and all his heart went out in love and veneration for the friend, long dead when he wrote, who had been to him king and saint. He looks back with pride at that great figure which had loomed so large in his earlier manhood. He sees him once more as he rode in the field among his knights, flashing in arms, overtopping them all, the goodliest presence there.[11]

He dwells upon his old chief's fearlessness, his courage before the enemy, his undaunted fortitude under the combined assault of disaster, defeat, and sickness unto death. He marks his refusal to selfishly abandon the people God had committed to his charge and secure his own safety. He notes that neither the prospect of death, nor torture, has power to move him one hair's breadth from what he holds to be right, and notes also how, in his unswerving rectitude, he will keep to his word, even though that word has been given to the infidel, and though the infidel are far from keeping a reciprocal faith.

Then, in more peaceful times, in the ordinary course of justice, he shows the king's determination that right shall be done, with no respect of persons, between man and man, and as between monarch and subject, and his passionate desire for a pure administration. And when, finally, St. Louis is canonised—when Rome sets its seal and mark upon him for all time—then the loyal, loving servant seems to utter a kind of *Nunc dimittis*. Joinville feels that he himself may now depart in peace.

Not that there is any Boswellism about him. All that St. Louis does is not of necessity good in Joinville's eyes. The servant keeps his own judgment quite clear even when judging of his master's acts, and is unduly swayed neither by love nor reverence. Thus, when the Abbot of

---

11. Joinville is here quite lyrical. He brings to mind Sir Richard Vernon's speech on the Royal Army, in the first part of King Henry IV.—
I saw young harry with his beaver on,
His cuisses on his thighs, gallantly arm'd,
Rise from the ground like feather'd Mercury, etc.

Cluny gives the king two costly palfreys as a preliminary to a discussion on certain business matters pending between them, Joinville does not hesitate to ask the king whether the gift had inclined him to listen with greater favour to what the abbot had to say, and to push home the obvious moral—a moral, be it said, in view of certain municipal facts, which the twentieth century might lay to heart with the same advantages as the contemporaries of St. Louis.

Again, when some fifteen years after the return from Palestine, St. Louis, prematurely old and broken in health, determines to turn Crusader once again (1270), Joinville not only refuses to accompany him, but evidently does all he can to dissuade his master from a policy so disastrous. "I thought that those committed a mortal sin who advised him to undertake that journey," says the upright counsellor, who was no parasite; and he thanks God he had no part or lot in that expedition.

And so too Joinville is not satisfied of the king's "good manners" in his relations with the queen. The queen, after being brought to bed of my lady Blanche, journeys by sea from Jaffa to rejoin the king at Sayette. Joinville goes to the shore to meet her—there is nothing to show why the king did not lovingly perform this office himself—and brings her up to the castle, reporting her arrival to the king, who is in his chapel. The king knew where Joinville was going, and has delayed the sermon till his return, and asks whether his wife and children are in good health.

"And I bring these things to your notice," says Joinville, "because I had been in his company five years, and never yet had he spoken a word to me about the queen, or about his children—nor to anyone else, so far as I ever heard. And, so it seems to me," adds the good chronicler, "there was some want of good manners" (*mores* in the Latin sense, I take it), "in being thus a stranger to one's wife and children."

To this the reader will, no doubt, be inclined to subscribe. Indeed, the want of more obviously cordial relations between the king and queen which may almost be inferred from Joinville's book, affords matter for surprise, seeing who and what that king and queen both were. For if Louis was a hero and a saint, Margaret of Provence, the "falcon-hearted dove" of Mrs. Hemans' poem, was a heroine, and not all unfit, as men and women go, for canonisation. When she figures in Joinville's narrative it is as a woman altogether brave and lovable, and possessing a sense of humour withal.

There are few more striking scenes in history than those in which she appears as a queen, about to become a mother, her husband and his host prisoners, the city in which she is, beleaguered and likely to fall-and kneels before the good old knight, and asks him to strike off her head or ever she falls into the enemy's hands; or that second scene, on the day after the birth of the child—Tristram they called him for sorrow—when she summons round her bed those who would basely surrender the city, and appealing to the babe's weakness and her own womanhood, seeks to inspire them with her own courage.

One might have thought, *primâ facie*, that there would be some record of the meeting between king and queen after scenes like these, some written word to show how the queen greeted the king when he came out of captivity and sore peril, and how the king acknowledged her proud bearing in extreme danger. But the chronicler, who loved them both, is silent. And yet he stays to give us the picture of an earlier time, and not so much earlier, when the relations between the royal couple had been more loverlike.

He tells how Blanche, the queen mother, had tyrannised over them, as the *maîtresse-femme*, the woman accustomed to authority, will tyrannise in all stations of life, and how, to secure some privacy of intercourse, they had arranged a meeting-place on a hidden stairway, each scuttling back like a rabbit at the approach of the maternal enemy. And he tells of the younger woman's passionate appeal—one of those appeals that are so human that they ring through the ages, like the appeal of Marie Antoinette to her motherhood—tells how Margaret lay after childbirth, as all thought dying, and the king hung over her, and the queen-mother ordered him away, and the wife cried: "Alas! whether dead or alive, you will not suffer me to see my lord!"

"Whereupon she fainted, and they thought she was dead, and the king, who thought she was dying, came back."[12]

It has been conjectured that politics came, to some extent, between the king and queen, and that the king wished to be unfettered by her influence in state affairs.[13] For Margaret was no lay-figure. She played a not unimportant part in the world's affairs. Failing the arbitration

---

12. I Should one smile or sigh? The same Margaret, in after years, tried to exercise her influence most unduly over her own son Philip, and induced him to swear that he would remain subject to her authority till be had attained the age of thirty—with other like stipulations. See p. 422, *Revue des Questions Historiques,* 1867. Vol. 3

13. See the extremely interesting article entitled *Marguerite de Provence, son caractère, son rôle politique,* in the *Revue des Questions Historiques,* Vol. 3., 1867, pp. 417-458.

of Louis himself, Henry III. and the English barons agreed to refer their differences to her. That arbitration proving abortive, she sided throughout and very actively with Henry, whose wife Eleanor was her younger sister.

All her life long she passionately maintained her claims on Provence as against the king's brother. Possibly, therefore, St. Louis may, while agreeing to allow her a certain independence of action, have preferred to remain outside the sphere of her activities. One cannot tell. The heart-relations between two human beings are always difficult to unravel—often too tangled to be unravelled even by the two persons most interested.

At the same time, as I said, one cannot but agree with Joinville, that the king's "good manners" in relation to the queen are somewhat open to question. For myself I confess that I should have thought it better" manners," if, when the ship struck on the sandbank, and death seemed imminent, he had gone to encourage his wife and children, instead of prostrating himself "crosswise, on the deck of the vessel . . . before the body of our Lord."

To a man of St. Louis's temperament, the cloister must have offered attractions well-nigh irresistible; and it is recorded that, on one occasion at least, he expressed a determination to seek its retirement, when the queen effectually combated his resolution by silently fetching his children, and placing them before him. Had such monkish ideals anything to do with his attitude towards his wife? Had he a kind of feeling that marriage acted as a restraint, not certainly on his passions, but on his piety? Was he swayed, in marriage, voluntarily or involuntarily, towards the celibate life? I scarcely think so. For the man, with all his religious fervour, was essentially sane of heart and head.

His ethics were those of a saint, but they were also those of a supremely honest and upright man. Nor was he in the least priest-ridden. When the assembled bishops of France came to him, and proposed a course which his own conscience did not approve, he unhesitatingly refused to acquiesce, and give them powers they might misuse. He offers the example, rare at all times, and under every form of government, whether monarchic, aristocratic, or democratic, of a ruler bent on ruling according to the moral law alone.

With such a guiding spirit, with pure religious zeal and honesty at the helm, there can be no question as to the aims and objects of the Crusade, nor any necessity, or indeed excuse, for such a disquisition as that with which I introduced Villehardouin's chronicle. Dandolo, Montferrat, Baldwin, even Henry, nearly all the leading actors on Villehardouin's stage, may have been swayed this way and that, by motives not all avowable. St. Louis had but one motive, and that open as the day, from the time when, in his sore sickness, and being then some thirty years of age (1244), he vowed to take the cross. Broadly, the condition of affairs in the Holy Land remained at that date pretty much what they had been when Montferrat's host embarked at Venice forty-two years before (1202).

True, the intervening years had been crowded with action. Apart from the constantly recurring local episodes of battle and siege, bloodshed and famine, and slaughter, there had been a descent into Egypt, with siege and sack of Damietta (1219), and a disastrous advance on Cairo, an expedition curiously similar in its incidents to that which St. Louis was about to undertake. There had been the expedition to the Holy Land of the brilliant and cultured Frederick II. of Germany, who by treaty had obtained possession of Jerusalem (1229)—curiously enough he was at the time under ban of excommunication—and had been crowned there as king.

There had been, also for a time, a recrudescence of Christian power and influence. But this had passed away. The tide had set against the West and against the Cross. A few strongholds on the shore of Judæa alone remained in Frank hands. As in 1202, so in 1248, when St. Louis sailed from Aigues-Mortes, the task of reconquering Jerusalem still remained to be accomplished. That was the task to which St. Louis set himself with all singleness of heart and aim,—and he failed. His generalship was clearly not on a level with his personal courage or self-devotion. Jerusalem had finally passed into Moslem hands. But the man himself, the story of him, the record of his loving follower and friend—these live for all time.

As to Joinville's style, why, I fear I have done him some wrong in speaking of his age and garrulity. No doubt he was eighty-five when he finished his book, and like most old men, he liked to hear himself talk. But those whom the gods love die young, and they die young not because their span of life is short: but because they carry into extreme age, nay to the very grave itself, the fresh youth of their spirit.

And, in this sense, Joinville was young at four score years and five. With all his garrulity, his readiness to turn aside and be beguiled from the forward path by incident or episode, his love for going over the past lingeringly—with all this, his outlook is as keen, as full of interest, as blithe, as the outlook of a boy. He sees clearly, he describes well, and his touch is light and bright—not perhaps, to speak with perfect accuracy, the touch of a writer in the French tradition, because the French tradition was scarcely formed, but of a writer who occupies his due place in the formation of that tradition. Here again *the style is the man himself.*

The nineteenth century, the present century, with their deeper feeling for the complexities of human life, are more tolerant. Here, for instance, is what that sober historian, Bishop Stubbs, says:

> The Crusades are not, in my mind, either the popular delusions that our cheap literature has determined them to be, nor papal conspiracies against kings and peoples, as they appear to the Protestant controversialist, nor the savage outbreaks of expiring barbarism thirsting for blood and plunder, nor volcanic explosions of religious intolerance. I believe them to have been, in their deep sources, and in the minds of their best champions, and in the main tendency of their results, capable of ample justification.
> They were the first great effort of mediæval life to go beyond the pursuit of selfish and isolated ambitions; they were the trial-feat of the young world, essaying to use, to the glory of God and the benefit of man, the arms of its new knighthood. That they failed in their direct object is only what may be alleged against almost, every design which the Great Disposer of events has moulded to help the world's progress; for the world has grown wise by the experience of failure, rather than by the winnings of high aims.
> That the good they did was largely leavened with evil may be said of every war that has ever been waged; that bad men rose by them while good men fell, is and must be true wherever and whenever the race is to the swift and the battle to the strong.
> But that, in the end, they were a benefit to the world no one who reads can doubt; and that in their course they brought out a love for all that is heroic in human nature—the love of freedom, the honour of prowess, sympathy with sorrow, perseverance to the last, and patient endurance without hope—the chronicles of the age abundantly prove; proving, moreover, that it was by the experience of those times that the former of those virtues were realised, and presented to posterity.... The history

of the Crusades has always had for me an interest that quite rivals all the interest I could take in the history of the Greeks and Romans. [14]

These are wise and sober words, and I quote them, partly because they carry weight, as coming from such an authority as Bishop Stubbs, and partly because they will, I think, provide the reader, as it were, with an atmosphere in which to study these fine old Chronicles of Villehardouin and Joinville.

Existing Translations and General Observations

It is scarcely necessary that I should enter here into a disquisition on the MSS. of Villehardouin and Joinville, and the various French editions of their chronicles.

Suffice it to say, that with regard to Villehardouin I have used, for the present translation, the learned and admirable editions of M. Natalis de Wailly[15] and the equally excellent edition of M. Emile Bouchet.[16] Both these editions contain an excellent text—that of M. de Wailly containing also notes of the various readings in the leading MSS., while L Bouchet's second volume embraces an elaborate and very valuable dissertation on the Crusade. With regard to Joinville, I have similarly used the edition of M. Natalis de Wailly, which is similar in form and character and excellence to that of his *Villehardouin*. [17]

As to English versions, a word more is necessary. Villehardouin's book has only, so far as I know, been once translated into English, and that was by a certain T. Smith, not otherwise known to me, whose version was published in 1829, by Pickering.[18] The book is comparatively rare, so that I think I may assume to be the first to place Villehardouin's

---

14. *Seventeen Lectures on the study of Mediæval and Modern History*, etc. by William Stubbs. Oxford, 1874.
15. *Geoffroi de Villehardouin, Conquête de Constantinople, avec la Continuation de Henri de Valenciennes, texte original, accompagné d' une traduction par* M. Natalis de Wailly, Membre de l'Institut. Seconde Edition, Paris, 1874.
16. *Geoffroi de Villehardouin. La Conquête de Constantinople. Texte et traduction nouvelle, avec notes, notice, et glossaire*, two vols. Paris, 1891.
17. *Jean, Sire de Joinville. Histoire de Saint Louis, Credo, et Lettre à Louis X. Texte original accompagné d' une traduction, par* M. Natalis de Wailly, Membre de l'Institut. Paris, 1874. The Credo and Letter to Louis X. I have not translated, They are beautiful in their own way, but scarcely of general interest.
18. The Chronicle of Geoffry de Villehardouin, Marshal of Champagne and Roumania, concerning the conquest of Constantinople by the French and Venetians, *anno* MCCIV., translated by T. Smith. London William Pickering, 1829.

Chronicle before the English reader in a popular form. T. Smith, whoever he may have been, was a scholar, and his work, subject to a slight criticism I shall have to make hereafter, was well done.

Joinville's Chronicle has, so far as I know, been translated three times. It was translated, in the early part of last century, by Johnes of Hafod.[19] Now Johnes of Hafod, though not an inspired translator, is a translator by no means to be despised. His version of Froissart has not the sixteenth-century charm, the old-world power and picturesqueness of Lord Berner's version, published in 1523-25; it is perforce less near to Froissart in language and spirit; but still it is a good translation.

When, however, he came to deal with Joinville, he was seriously handicapped. For the French version, on which he relied,[20] was that of Du Cange, published in 1668, which itself was founded on an earlier version, that of Ménard—Du Cange expressly regretting that he had had access to no MSS., and observing, with perfect candour, that he "finds a difficulty in believing that the Sire de Joinville had written in such polished language" as that which Ménard attributes to him. In other words Johnes' translation—which is that adopted in Bohn's series—is based on an edited and corrupt translation into modern French, and has, strictly, scant historical value.

For the translations published by James Hutton[21] in 1868, and Ethel Wedgwood[22] in 1906, I have no desire to speak with anything but civility. Both, however, possess what I cannot but regard as a defect, *viz.*, that they do not reproduce Joinville's book as he wrote it. In both there is abridgment, and, in Miss Wedgwood's book at least, rearrangement. Now I am not denying that for "editing" of this kind there is, in Joinville's case, considerable excuse.

Joinville, as I have already said, was garrulous; he dictated largely, freely, probably at intervals, as a great lord would; he divided his book

---

19. Memoirs of John, Lord de Joinville, Grand Mareschal of Champagne written by himself, etc.. the whole translated by Thomas Johnes, at the Hafod Press of James Henderson, 1807.
20. Though a far better version, for this purpose, was even then available *viz.* the version, founded on MSS. texts, published by Capperonnier in 1761. Anyone comparing the first parts, for instance, of Johnes' translation with that here published will see how seriously the original Joinville has been played with.
21. *Saint Lewis, King of France*, by the Sire de Joinville, translated by James Hutton. Sampson Low, Marston and Co. The sixth edition published in 1892 is before me.
22. *The Memoirs of the Lord of Joinville*, a new English version, by Ethel Wedgwood, 1906. John Murray.

into two parts, dealing, one, with the king's religious life and the other with the king's secular life—a division that even in more practised literary hands would have involved repetition, and he repeats himself without scruple. He had clearly never studied the art of composition in any polite academy. The most ordinary magazine writer of today could put him up to certain "tricks of the trade" of which he knew nothing.

But—and here is the real point—all this garrulity, literary nonchalance, naiveté, simplicity, absence of the author's pose—all this goes to make up the real Joinville, who was an old man with a boy's heart, and a *grand seigneur*, and a gentleman, and a Christian, and a very fellow. Even apart from the strict historical respect for a text, we lose by trying to improve upon the work of a man of this individuality and force. So I make no apology, nay, I claim credit, for presenting Joinville's Chronicle to the English reader, for the first time, as Joinville dictated it,[23] so far as the differences between the English and French languages will allow.

And this brings me to the question of translation. Now the translator, I take it, should endeavour to place himself, as it were, inside the author's mind, and reproduce the author's work in the same form which the author himself would use if he were writing in the language of the translation. But when the translator attempts to carry out this principle in dealing with such works as the chronicles of Villehardouin or Joinville, he is at once confronted with a great difficulty.

Villehardouin writes at the beginning of the thirteenth century, and Joinville at the beginning of the fourteenth, and to translate their old French into the language spoken in these islands circa 1209 and 1309, would—even if I could claim the ability for such a task, and this I am far indeed from doing—be a work of at least doubtful utility. The English reader of today would thank me very little for plunging him into a vernacular very much more archaic than that of Chaucer.

---

23. This, however, must be said with just a little qualification. Scribes in the days anterior to printing, and editors in the days after printing was invented, have rejuvenated and restored Joinville's text much as a succession of over-zealous rectors have dealt with some of our old parish churches. The first MSS. of the Chronicles, made at Joinville's own dictation, cannot be found. The earliest MSS. that can be found are not contemporary, and have been clearly doctored, so far as the language is concerned. The text on which the present translation is based is that of M. de Wailly, itself based on a careful comparison of the available sources. As regards all this question of MSS. and editions, I cannot do better than refer to the elaborate introduction to his edition of the Chronicle.

(*Canterbury Tales* circa 1383.) What, then, is the alternative? To frankly adopt the quite modern English in use among our contemporaries? I do not think so.

But in order to explain why I think otherwise, it will be necessary to go somewhat farther afield, and make an excursus into a question of literary æsthetics. Why do we read such books as the chronicles in question? For the facts recorded? Certainly, in a measure. Both Villehardouin and Joinville were eye and ear witnesses of much that they recorded, and in a general history of the great events they helped to fashion, they have a claim to be heard and considered.

But they did not know all that took place. No contemporary ever knows that. He sees what he sees, the strand, more or less slender, that he holds in his own hand, or that comes within his purview— not the other strands that the future will gather together and fashion into the great fabric of history. Villehardouin and Joinville were, in a sense, only the special war correspondents— though specially well-informed no doubt—of their own time. If we want a full account of the attack on the Greek empire, or St. Louis's Crusade, and want no more, we shall do better to go to one of the histories in which the whole story has been *quintessentiated* from all the chronicles and contemporary records.

Why, then, again, do we read such books as those of Villehardouin and Joinville? Partly, as I have said, for the facts, but much more for the spirit. These books take us back, and take us back delightfully, among "old forgotten far-off things;" and they take us back, not as a history, however graphic, takes us back, consciously, by effort, with inevitable modern sidelights, today perforce throwing some of its gleams and shadows back upon yesterday—but simply, naturally, by placing us in the company of the men who lived of old time, and enabling us, for the nonce, to see with their eyes and hear with their ears.

The very imperfection of those older writers has a charm. They repeat the same forms of expression freely. Their vocabulary is simple, often to monotony. Of adjectives they possess but a small provision. The literary tricks now performed quite freely by any tyro in journalism they have not acquired. They are essentially of their time—a lisping time—but the lisping time of giants. And to take their speech, their large and simple utterance, and mould it afresh into the language of modernity, dispels an illusion, jars us, brings us back too suddenly, like a diver rashly and over hastily coming out of the deep sea, into "the light of common day."

Let me briefly illustrate. Villehardouin returns from Venice, and gives an account of his mission to Thibaut of Champagne. These are his words, which I translate quite literally:

> So rode Geoffry the Marshal, day by day, that he came to Troyes in Champagne, and found his lord, the Count Thibaut, sick and languishing; and he (Count Thibaut) was greatly rejoiced at his coming. And when he (Geoffry) told him the news how they had fared, he was so rejoiced that he said he would mount horse, which he had not done of a long time; and he arose and rode forth. Alas! how great the pity! For never more did he mount horse, save that once.

Now this is how T. Smith, for whom, I repeat, I have every respect, translates the passage into the English of his generation:

> Geoffry the Marshal continued his journey until he arrived at Troyes in Champagne, where he found his lord, Count Thibaut sick and dispirited, but notwithstanding greatly rejoiced at his return. And when the count understood the good success of his embassy, he ,vas so elated that he called for his horse to ride forth which for a long time past he had not done. He arose from his bed and mounted his horse for the last time.

Here we have, no doubt, the substance. T. Smith tells us, practically, what Villehardouin tells us. But he gives us no more than dry bones. The soul, the thirteenth-century spirit, the feudatory's burst of sorrow over his beloved feudal lord, the predestined chief of a great expedition in which they were both to take part, the stern soldier's "Alas!"—for the "great pity" of it—all this has vanished. We are not with Villehardouin in the thirteenth century at all. We are, a very different thing for the present purpose, in the year 1829.

So the alternative is, unless I greatly deceive myself, a version that shall follow the old French idiom as closely as possible without ceasing to be genuinely English, and the use, in that version, of turns of speech, and a vocabulary, that are either archaic, or suggest archaism, and that in any case seek to avoid a too modern ring.

Whereupon I imagine that some

> *Brisk little somebody,*
> *Critic and whippersnapper, in a rage*
> *To set things right,—*

such an one as animadverted on Balaustion's recitation—will object, "such language as you suggest was not in use during the thirteenth or fourteenth centuries, nor has it ever been in use since. It is Wardour Street English"—that was, if I remember right, the term applied to William Morris's prose romances,—"it is a sham, or at best a convention."

A sham—no. There is not any pretence about it. A convention—yes. But then how essentially convention underlies all art! We say of Shakespeare that he is natural. And so he is, if you will accept the convention that human beings speak in blank verse, and possess the imperial sway over language that he, the great word-monarch, attributes to his characters.

Leonardo da Vinci's Last Supper, now fading on the old wall in Milan, touches the highest truth, the supreme of nature, in the faces and forms of Christ and the Apostles. But is it to be supposed that our Lord and His Apostles sat at their meal in that superb rhythmic order, which is almost suggestive of music?

Did they even sit with as much arrangement as in M. Dagnan-Bouveret's fine picture of the same subject? If we possessed a photograph of the scene, as it actually took place in the upper chamber at Jerusalem, that photograph would have inestimable value historically and, maybe, devotionally. But its artistic value would probably be none at all.

Or take again another art: M. Coquelin is, to my mind, the most "natural" great actor living. But M. Coquelin, quite obviously, would not speak off the stage as he does on the stage—he would not speak so loud, nor with the same elaborateness of elocution; nor would his gestures possess the same point and emphasis. As an actor he adopts perforce the stage conventions, and succeeds, not because he is really natural—which would entail failure—but because he produces the illusion of nature.

And so I contend that the translator of such old chronicles as those of Villehardouin and Joinville should aim at producing, in a similar way, an illusion of the past. He should place his readers in a congenial atmosphere—a conventional atmosphere, if you like, but one in which, if his work has been well done, there is nothing to jar and distract—no obtrusion of the winds and zephyrs, nay, possibly the fogs and miasma, of today.

While if precedents be wanted, are they not to hand? Rightly understood, is not Spenser's *Shepherd's Calendar* a series of poems in which the poet has reproduced, not the past, but its *simulacrum*? Kingsley's admirable *Greek Heroes* come exactly within my meaning.[24] So do William Morris's prose romances, and very large portions of his verse. So does Lady Gregory's *Cuchulain of Muirthemne*. So, to pass to another literature, does Balzac's *Contes Drolatiques*, very foolishly attacked, from the linguistic side, by certain pedants of his generation. Nay, *Esmond* itself—fully as Thackeray, by study, by the character of his own genius, had identified himself with the days of Queen Anne, so that he was all but the contemporary of Addison, and Steele, and Swift—are there not parts of *Esmond* itself when the modern speaks a speech that is not really that of the Augustinian age, but only—I am far from complaining—give us its illusion?

Or, going further still, that monument of the English tongue, the authorised version of the Bible—let every Englishman salute at the mention of it!—does it represent the language as spoken and written in Great Britain when James I. was king? No doubt it approaches nearer to that language than it approaches to ours. But even then, with Tyndale at the back of it, it had, more or less, an archaic form. It obtained force and solemnity by being somewhat out of date. It was, if you like to call it so, written in the English of "Wardour Street," or of whatever street it was that displayed objects of doubtful antiquity in King James's London!

But here my precedents are clearly overwhelming. Who am I to stand in such company? And if the reader says, "Your arguments are sound, your principles cannot be impeached, your intentions are excellent, but—your version is deplorable," I can only reply, "Don't visit my shortcomings on Villehardouin and Joinville. They are worthy of any reader's regard."

Frank T. Marzials.

London, February 1908.

Note

See M. Riant's articles quoted below. The curious reader who would follow this controversy is referred to the following works among many others, French and German. I place them, as will be seen, in the chronological order of publication:—

Histoire de l'Isle de Chypre sous le Règne des Princes de la Maison de

---

24. It is interesting from the point of view under discussion to compare Kingsley's book with Hawthorne's *Tanglewood Tales*. Hawthorne was a man of genius, no doubt, but the modern note injures his book. It will not stand beside Kingsley's.

Lusignan, par M. L. de Mas Latrie, etc. Paris, 1861, Vol. 1. pp. 161-165.—*Geoffroy de Villehardouin, Conquête de Constantinople,* etc., par M. Natalis de Wailly, etc. Second edition, Paris, 1874, pp. 429-439.

Up to this point only the conduct of Venice is in question. With the following enters as protagonist Philip of Swabia, and we are asked to consider the part which he took in deflecting the Crusade from Egypt or the Holy Land to Constantinople, and the action taken, under his influence, by the Marquis Boniface of Montferrat.

Innocent III., Philippe de Swabe et Boniface de Montferrat. Examen des Causes qui modifièrent au détriment de l'Empire Grec, le plan primitive de la 4e Croisade, published in *Revue des Questions Historiques,* Vol. 17., April 1875, pp. 321-374, and Vol. 18., July 1875, pp. 5-75. Signed, Comte Riant.

These two articles contain an elaborate and most learned indictment against Philip of Swabia and the Marquis of Montferrat, and, in a minor degree, against Villehardouin, as their accomplice and apologist. Comte Riant is most careful in giving reference to chapter and verse to support his conclusions, and so enable the student to verify and control, and—on occasion—to dissent.

A short note, signed M. de Wailly, on the above articles of Comte Riant, expressing dissent. *Revue des Questions Historiques,* Vol. 18., October 1875, pp. 578 and 579 (not p. 576 as stated in index).

Quatrième Croisade. La diversion sur Zara et Constantinople, par Jules Tessier, *professeur à la faculté des lettres de Caen.* Paris, 1884. In this volume, with an equal learning, M. Tessier contests the position taken up by M. Riant, and defends Philip of Swabia and Venice.

The Fall of Constantinople, by Edwin Pears. London, 1885.

The Notice, extending to 309 pages in Vol. 2. of M. Emile Bouchet's *Geoffroi de Villehardouin. La Conquête de Constantinople, texte et traduction nouvelle, avec notice, notes, et glossaire, par* Emile Bouchet. Paris, 1891.

M. Bouchet mainly accepts Comte Riant's facts and conclusions with regard to Philip and Venice, but exonerates Villehardouin, and defends him from the charge of having constituted himself the official apologist of the Crusade—pp. 289-297 and pp. 308, 309. M. Bouchet's manner is rather that of the historical narrator than of the erudite dissertator, and his notes are few. In this he differs from M. Riant and M. Tessier.

M. Luchaire, as I have noted in the text (1907) declares the questions raised to be insoluble on the available data. The matter is referred to, but with no additional evidence or further discussion, in Sir Rennell Rodd's *The Principalities of Achaia and the Chronicles of Morea*, 1907, Chap. 1, and Mr. Pirie-Gordon's *Innocent the Great, an Essay on his Life and Times*, 1907, Chap. 4.

Chronicle of the Fourth Crusade and the Quest of Constantinople

The First Preaching of the Crusade[1]

Be it known to you that eleven hundred and ninety-seven years after the Incarnation of our Lord Jesus Christ, in the time of Innocent Pope of Rome, and Philip King of France, and Richard King of England, there was in France a holy man named Fulk of Neuilly—which Neuilly is between Lagni-sur-Marne and Paris—and he was a priest and held the *cure* of the village. And this said Fulk began to speak of God throughout the Isle of France, and the other countries round about; and you must know that by him the Lord wrought many miracles.

Be it known to you further, that the fame of this holy man so spread, that it reached the Pope of Rome, Innocent;[2] and the Pope sent to France, and ordered the right worthy man to preach the cross (the Crusade) by his authority.

And afterwards the Pope sent a cardinal of his, Master Peter of Capua, who himself had taken the cross, to proclaim the Indulgence of which I now tell you, *viz.*, that all who should take the cross and serve in the host for one year, would be delivered from all the sins they had committed, and acknowledged in confession. And because this indulgence was so great, the hearts of men were much moved, and many took the cross for the greatness of the pardon.

Of those who took the Cross

---

1. In these divisions and headings I mainly follow, but not slavishly, M. N. de Neuilly.
2. Elected Pope on the 8th January 1198, at the early age of thirty-seven, Innocent III. was one of the leading spirits of his time—in every sense a strong man and great Pope. From the beginning of his pontificate he turned his thoughts and policy to the recovery of Jerusalem. M. Achille Luchaire has recently published four volumes dealing respectively with Innocent in his relations to *Rome and Italy*, *The Crusade against the Albigenses*, *The Papacy and the Empire*, *The Eastern Question*. Mr. Pirie-Gordon has also just published a volume entitled *Innocent the Great, an Essay on his Life and Times*.

The other year after that right worthy man Fulk had so spoken of God, there was held a tourney in Champagne, at a castle called Ecri, and by God's grace it so happened that Thibaut, Count of Champagne and Brie, took the cross, and the Count Louis of Blois and Chartres likewise; and this was at the beginning of Advent (28th November 1199). Now you must know that this Count Thibaut was but a young man, and not more than twenty-two years of age, and the Count Louis not more than twenty-seven. These two counts were nephews and cousins-german to the King of France, and, on the other part, nephews to the King of England.

With these two counts there took the cross two very high and puissant barons of France, Simon of Montfort,[3] and Renaud of Montmirail. Great was the fame thereof throughout the land when these two high and puissant men took the cross.

In the land of Count Thibaut of Champagne took the cross Garnier, Bishop of Troyes, Count Walter of Brienne, Geoffry of Joinville,[4] who was seneschal of the land, Robert his brother, Walter of Vignory, Walter of Montbèliart, Eustace of Conflans, Guy of Plessis his brother, Henry of Arzillières, Oger of Saint-Chéron, Villain of Neuilly, Geoffry of Villehardouin, Marshal of Champagne, Geoffry his nephew, William of Nully, Walter of Fuligny, Everard of Montigny, Manasses of l'Isle, Macaire of Sainte-Menehould, Miles the Brebant, Guy of Chappes, Clerembaud his nephew, Reginald of Dampierre, John Foisnous, and many other right worthy men whom this book does not here mention by name.

With Count Louis took the cross Gervais of Châtel, Hervée his son, John of Virsin, Oliver of Rochefort, Henry of Montreuil, Payen of Orléans, Peter of Bracieux, Hugh his brother, William of Sains, John of Friaize, Walter of Gaudonville, Hugh of Cormeray, Geoffry his brother, Hervée of Beauvoir, Robert of Frouville, Peter his brother, Orri of l'Isle, Robert of the Quartier, and many more whom this book does not here mention by name.

In the Isle of France took the cross Nevelon, Bishop of Soissons, Matthew of Montmorency, Guy the Castellan of Coucy, his nephew, Robert of Ronsoi, Ferri of Yerres, John his brother, Walter of Saint-Denis, Henry his brother, William of Aunoi, Robert Manvoisin, Dreux

---

3. This was the Simon de Montfort who afterwards ruthlessly crushed the Albigenses. It was his son who led the barons against Henry III. defeated the royal army at Lewes, and was killed at Evesham (1265).

4. This was the father of the Joinville whose Chronicle forms the second portion of this volume.

of Cressonsacq, Bernard of Moreuil, Enguerrand of Boves, Robert his brother, and many more right worthy men with regard to whose names this book is here silent.

At the beginning of the following Lent, on the day when folk are marked with ashes (23rd February 1200), the cross was taken at Bruges by Count Baldwin of Flanders and Hainault, and by the Countess Mary his wife, who was sister to the Count Thibaut of Champagne. Afterwards took the cross, Henry his brother, Thierri his nephew, who was the son of Count Philip of Flanders, William the advocate of Béthune, Conan his brother, John of Nêle Castellan of Bruges, Reginald of Trit, Reginald his son, Matthew of Wallincourt, James of Avesnes, Baldwin of Beauvoir, Hugh of Beaumetz, Girard of Mancicourt, Odo of Ham, William of Gommegnies, Dreux of Beaurain, Roger of Marek, Eustace of Sobruic, Francis of Colemi, Walter of Bousies, Reginald of Mons, Walter of the Tombes, Bernard of Somergen, and many more right worthy men in great number, with regard to whom this book does not speak further.

Afterwards took the cross, Count Hugh of St. Paul. With him took the cross, Peter of Amiens his nephew, Eustace of Canteleu, Nicholas of Mailly, Anseau of Cayeaux, Guy of Houdain, Walter of Nêle, Peter his brother, and many other men who are unknown to us.

Directly afterwards took the cross Geoffry of the Perche, Stephen his brother, Rotrou of Montfort, Ives of la Jaille, Aimery of Villeroi, Geoffry of Beaumont, and many others whose names I do not know.

The Crusaders Send Six Envoys to Venice

Afterwards the barons held a parliament at Soissons, to settle when they should start, and whither they should wend. But they could come to no agreement, because it did not seem to them that enough people had taken the cross. So during all that year (1200) no two months passed without assemblings in parliament at Compiègne.

There met all the counts and barons who had taken the cross. Many were the opinions given and considered; but in the end it was agreed that envoys should be sent, the best that could be found, with full powers, as if they were the lords in person, to settle such matters as needed settlement.

Of these envoys, Thibaut, Count of Champagne and Brie, sent two; Baldwin, Count of Flanders and Hainault, two; and Lewis, Count of Blois and Chartes, two. The envoys of the Count Thibaut were Geoffry of Villehardouin, Marshal of Champagne, and Miles the Brebant;

the envoys of Count Baldwin were Conon of Béthune, and Alard Maquereau, and the envoys of Count Louis were John of Friaise, and Walter of Gaudonville.

To these six envoys the business in hand was fully committed, all the barons delivering to them valid charters, with seals attached, to the effect that they would undertake to maintain and carry out whatever conventions and agreements the envoys might enter into, in all sea ports, and whithersoever else the envoys might fare.

Thus were the six envoys despatched, as you have been told; and they took counsel among themselves, and this was their conclusion: that in Venice they might expect to find a greater number of vessels than in any other port. So they journeyed day by day, till they came thither in the first week of Lent (February 1201).

The Envoys Arrive in Venice, and Proffer Their Request

The Doge of Venice, whose name was Henry Dandolo,[5] and who was very wise and very valiant, did them great honour, both he and the other folk, and entertained them right willingly, marvelling, however, when the envoys had delivered their letters, what might be the matter of import that had brought them to that country. For the letters were letters of credence only, and declared no more than that the bearers were to be accredited as if they were the counts in person, and that the said counts would make good whatever the six envoys should undertake.

So the Doge replied:

> *Signors,* I have seen your letters; well do we know that of men uncrowned your lords are the greatest, and they advise us to put faith in what you tell us, and that they will maintain whatsoever you undertake. Now, therefore, speak, and let us know what is

---

5. That Henry Dandolo was a very old man is certain, but there is doubt as to his precise age, as also as to the cause of his blindness. According to one account he had been blinded, or all but blinded. by the Greeks, and in a treacherous manner, when sent, at an earlier date, on an embassage to Constantinople—whence his bitter hostility to the Greek Empire. I agree, however, with Sir Rennell Rodd that, if this had been so, Villehardouin would scarcely have refrained from mentioning such an act of perfidy on the part of the wicked Greeks. (See p. 41 of Vol. 1. of Sir Rennell Rodd's *Princes of Achaia*.) It is hardly to be imagined that he would keep the matter dark because, if he mentioned it, people would think Dandolo acted throughout from motives of personal vengeance. This would be to regard Villehardouin as a very astute controversial historian indeed.

your pleasure.

And the envoys answered:

Sire, we would that you should assemble your council; and before your council we will declare the wishes of our lords; and let this be tomorrow, if it so pleases you.

And the Doge replied asking for respite till the fourth day, when he would assemble his council, so that the envoys might state their requirements. The envoys waited then till the fourth day, as had been appointed them, and entered the palace, which was passing rich and beautiful; and found the Doge and his council in a chamber. There they delivered their message after this manner:

Sire, we come to thee on the part of the high barons of France, who have taken the sign of the cross to avenge the shame done to Jesus Christ, and to reconquer Jerusalem, if so be that God will suffer it. And because they know that no people have such great power to help them as you and your people, therefore we pray you by God that you take pity on the land oversea, and the shame of Christ, and use diligence that our lords have ships for transport and battle.

"And after what manner should we use diligence?" said the Doge. "After all manners that you may advise and propose," rejoined the envoys, "in so far as what you propose may be within our means."

"*Certes*," said the Doge, "it is a great thing that your lords require of us, and well it seems that they have in view a high enterprise. We will give you our answer eight days from today. And marvel not if the term be long, for it is meet that so great a matter be fully pondered."

Conditions Proposed by the Doge

When the term appointed by the Doge was ended, the envoys returned to the palace. Many were the words then spoken which I cannot now rehearse. But this was the conclusion of that parliament:

"*Signors*," said the Doge, "we win tell you the conclusions at which we have arrived, if so be that we can induce our great council and the commons of the land to allow of them; and you, on your part, must consult and see if you can accept them and carry them through.

"We will build transports [6] to carry four thousand five hundred horses, and nine thousand squires, and ships for four thousand five hundred knights, and twenty thousand sergeants of foot. And we will agree also to purvey food for these horses and people during nine months. This is what we undertake to do at the least, on condition that you pay us for each horse four marks, and for each man two *marks*.

"And the covenants we are now explaining to you, we undertake to keep, wheresoever we may be, for a year, reckoning from the day on which we sail from the port of Venice in the service of God and of Christendom. Now the sum total of the expenses above named amounts to 85,000 *marks*.

"And this will we do moreover. For the love of God, we will add to the fleet fifty armed galleys on condition that, so long as we act in company, of all conquests in land or money, whether at sea or on dry ground, we shall have the half, and you the other half. Now consult together to see if you, on your parts, can accept and fulfil these covenants."

The envoys then departed, and said that they would consult together and give their answer on the morrow. They consulted, and talked together that night, and agreed to accept the terms offered. So the next day they appeared before the Doge, and said: "Sire, we are ready to ratify this covenant." The Doge thereon said he would speak of the matter to his people, and, as he found them affected, so would he let the envoys know the issue.

On the morning of the third day, the Doge, who was very wise and valiant, assembled his great council, and the council was of forty men of the wisest that were in the land. And the Doge, by his wisdom and wit, that were very clear and very good, brought them to agreement and approval. Thus he wrought with them; and then with a hundred others, then two hundred, then a thousand, so that at last all consented and approved. Then he assembled well ten thousand of the people in the chapel of St. Mark, the most beautiful chapel that there is, and bade them hear a mass of the Holy Ghost, and pray to God for counsel on the request and messages that had been addressed to them. And the people did so right willingly.

---

6. The old French term is *Vuissiers*, and denotes a kind of vessel, flat-bottomed, with large ports, specially constructed for the transport of horses. T. Smith translates "palanders," but I don't know that "palander" conveys any very clear idea to the English reader.

Conclusion of the Treaty, and Return of the Envoys

When mass had been said, the Doge desired the envoys to humbly ask the people to assent to the proposed covenant. The envoys came into the church. Curiously were they looked upon by many who had not before had sight of them. Geoffry of Villehardouin, the Marshal of Champagne, by will and consent of the other envoys, acted as spokesman and said unto them:

> Lords, the barons of France, most high and puissant, have sent us to you; and they cry to you for mercy, that you take pity on Jerusalem, which is in bondage to the Turks, and that, for God's sake, you help to avenge the shame of Christ Jesus. And for this end they have elected to come to you, because they know full well that there is none other people having so great power on the seas, as you and your people. And they commanded us to fall at your feet, and not to rise till you consent to take pity on the Holy Land which is beyond the seas.

Then the six envoys knelt at the feet of the people, weeping many tears. And the Doge and all the others burst into tears of pity and compassion, and cried with one voice, and lifted up their hands, saying: "We consent, we consent!" Then was there so great a noise and tumult that it seemed as if the earth itself were falling to pieces.

And when this great tumult and passion of pity—greater did never any man see—were appeased, the good Doge of Venice, who was very wise and valiant, went up into the reading-desk, and spoke to the people, and said to them:

> *Signors*, behold the honour that God has done you; for the best people in the world have set aside all other people, and chosen you to join them in so high an enterprise as the deliverance of our Lord!

All the good and beautiful words that the Doge then spoke, I cannot repeat to you. But the end of the matter was, that the covenants were to be made on the following day; and made they were, and devised accordingly.

When they were concluded, it was notified to the council that we should go to Babylon (Cairo), because the Turks could better be destroyed in Babylon than in any other land; but to the folk at large it was only told that we were bound to go overseas. We were then in Lent (March 1201), and by St. John's Day, in the following year—

which would be twelve hundred and two years after the Incarnation of Jesus Christ—the barons and pilgrims were to be in Venice, and the ships ready against their coming.

When the treaties were duly indited and sealed, they were brought to the Doge in the grand palace, where had been assembled the great and the little council. And when the Doge delivered the treaties to the envoys, he knelt greatly weeping, and swore on holy relics faithfully to observe the conditions thereof, and so did all his council, which numbered fifty-six persons. And the envoys, on their side, swore to observe the treaties, and in an good faith to maintain their oaths and the oaths of their lords; and be it known to you that for great pity many a tear was there shed. And forthwith were messengers sent to Rome, to the Pope Innocent, that he might confirm this covenant—the which he did right willingly.

Then did the envoys borrow five thousand marks of silver, and gave them to the Doge so that the building of the ships might be begun. And taking leave to return to their own land, they journeyed day by day till they came to Placentia in Lombardy.

There they parted. Geoffry, the Marshal of Champagne and Alard Maquereau went straight to France, and the others went to Genoa and Pisa to learn what help might there be had for the land oversea.

When Geoffry, the Marshal of Champagne, passed over Mont Cenis, he came in with Walter of Brienne, going into Apulia, to conquer the land of his wife, whom he had married since he took the cross, and who was the daughter of King Tancred. With him went Walter of Montbéliard, and Eustace of Conflans, Robert of Joinville, and a great part of the people of worth in Champagne who had taken the cross.

And when he told them the news how the envoys had fared, great was their joy, and much did they prize the arrangements made. And they said, "We are already on our way; and when you come, you will find us ready." But events fall out as God wills, and never had they power to join the host. This was much to our loss; for they were of great prowess and valiant. And thus they parted, and each went on his way.

So rode Geoffry the Marshal, day by day, that he came to Troyes in Champagne, and found his lord the Count Thibaut sick and languishing, and right glad was the count of his coming. And when he had told the count how he had fared, the count was so rejoiced that he said he would mount horse, a thing he had not done of a long time.

So he rose from his bed and rode forth. But alas, how great the pity! For never again did he bestride horse but that once.

His sickness waxed and grew worse, so that at the last he made his will and testament, and divided the money which he would have taken with him on pilgrimage among his followers and companions, of whom he had many that were very good men and true—no one at that time had more. And he ordered that each one, on receiving his money, should swear on holy relics, to join the host at Venice, according as he had promised. Many there were who kept that oath badly, and so incurred great blame. The count ordered that another portion of his treasure should be retained, and taken to the host, and there expended as might seem best.

Thus died the count; and no man in this world made a better end. And there were present at that time a very great assemblage of men of his lineage and of his vassals. But of the mourning and funeral pomp it is unmeet that I should here speak. Never was more honour paid to any man. And right well that it was so, for never was man of his age more beloved by his own men, nor by other folk. Buried he was beside his father in the church of our lord St. Stephen at Troyes.

He left behind him the Countess, his wife, whose name was Blanche, very fair, very good, the daughter of the King of Navarre. She had borne him a little daughter, and was then about to bear a son.

THE CRUSADERS LOOK FOR ANOTHER CHIEF

When the Count was buried, Matthew of Montmorency, Simon of Montfort, Geoffry of Joinville who was seneschal, and Geoffry the Marshal, went to Odo, Duke of Burgundy, and said to him,

Sire, your cousin is dead. You see what evil has befallen the land oversea. We pray you by God that you take the cross, and succour the land oversea in his stead. And we will cause you to have all his treasure, and will swear on holy relics, and make the others swear also, to serve you in all good faith, even as we should have served him.

Such was his pleasure that he refused. And be it known to you that he might have done much better. The envoys charged Geoffry of Joinville to make the self-same offer to the Count of Bar-le-Duc, Thibaut, who was cousin to the dead count, and he refused also.

Very great was the discomfort of the pilgrims, and of all who were about to go on God's service, at the death of Count Thibaut of Champagne; and they held a parliament, at the beginning of the month, at Soissons, to determine what they should do.

There were present Count Baldwin of Flanders and Hainault, the Count Lewis of Blois and Chartres, the Count Geoffry of Perche, the Count Hugh of Saint-Paul, and many other men of worth.

Geoffry the Marshal spake to them and told them of the offer made to the Duke of Burgundy, and to the Count of Bar-le-Duc, and how they had refused it.

"My lords," said he, "listen, I will advise you of somewhat if you will consent thereto. The Marquis of Montferrat[7] is very worthy and valiant, and one of the most highly prized of living men. If you asked him to come here, and take the sign of the cross, and put himself in place of the Count of Champagne, and you gave him the lordship of the host, full soon would he accept thereof."

Many were the words spoken for and against; but in the end all agreed, both small and great. So were letters written, and envoys chosen, and the marquis was sent for. And he came, on the day appointed, through Champagne and the Isle-de-France, where he received much honour, and specially from the King of France, who was his cousin.

BONIFACE, MARQUIS OF MONTFERRAT, BECOMES CHIEF OF THE CRUSADE-NEW CRUSADERS-DEATH OF GEOFFRY COUNT OF PERCHE

So he came to a parliament assembled at Soissons; and the main

---

7. Boniface, Marquis of Montferrat, was one of the most accomplished men of the time, and an approved soldier. His little court at Montferrat was the resort of artist and troubadour. His family was a family of Crusaders. The father, William of Montferrat, had gone oversea, and fought valiantly against the infidel. Boniface's eldest brother, William of the Long Sword, married a daughter of the titular King of Jerusalem, and their son became titular king in turn. Another brother, Conrad, starting for the Holy Land, stopped at Constantinople, and did there such good service that the Greek emperor gave his sister to him in marriage; but afterwards, fearing the perfidy of his brother-in-law, Conrad fled to Syria, and there battled against Saladin. Yet another brother, Renier, also served in the Greek Empire, married an Emperor's daughter, and received for guerdon of his deeds the kingdom of Salonica. Boniface himself had fought valiantly against Saladin, been made prisoner, and afterwards liberated on exchange. It was no mean and nameless knight that Villehardouin was proposing as chief to the assembled Crusaders, but a princely noble, the patron of poets, versed in state affairs, and possessing personal experience of Eastern warfare. I extract these details from M. Bouchet's *Notice*.

part of the counts and barons and of the other Crusaders were there assembled. When they heard that the marquis was coming, they went out to meet him, and did him much honour. In the morning the parliament was held in an orchard belonging to the abbey of our Lady of Soissons.

There they besought the marquis to do as they had desired of him, and prayed him, for the love of God, to take the cross, and accept the leadership of the host, and stand in the place of Thibaut Count of Champagne, and accept of his money and of his men. And they fell at his feet, with many tears; and he, on his part, fell at their feet, and said he would do it right willingly.

Thus did the marquis consent to their prayers, and receive the lordship of the host. Whereupon the Bishop of Soissons, and Master Fulk, the holy man, and two white monks whom the marquis had brought with him from his own land, led him into the Church of Notre Dame, and attached the cross to his shoulder. Thus ended this parliament, and the next day he took leave to return to his own land and settle his own affairs—telling them all to settle their own affairs likewise, for that he would meet them at Venice.

Thence did the marquis go to attend the Chapter at Cîteaux, which is held on Holy Cross Day in September (14th September 1041). There he found a great number of abbots, barons and other people of Burgundy; and Master Fulk went thither to preach the Crusade. And at that place took the cross Odo the Champenois of Champlitte, and William his brother, Richard of Dampierre, Odo his brother, Guy of Pesmes, Edmund his brother, Guy of Conflans, and many other good men of Burgundy, whose names are not recorded.

Afterwards took the cross the Bishop of Autun, Guignes Count of Forez, Hugh of Bergi (father and son), Hugh of Colemi. Further on in Provence took the cross Peter Bromont, and many others whose names are unknown to us.

Thus did the pilgrims make ready in all lands. Alas! a great mischance befell them in the following Lent (March 1202) before they had started, for the Count Geoffry of Perche fell sick, and made his will in such fashion that he directed that Stephen, his brother, should have his goods, and lead his men in the host. Of this exchange the pilgrims would willingly have been quit, had God so ordered. Thus did the count make an end and die; and much evil ensued, for he was a baron high and honoured, and a good knight. Greatly was he mourned throughout all his lands.

First Starting of the Pilgrims for Venice, and of Some Who Went Not Thither

After Easter and towards Whitsuntide (June 1202) began the pilgrims to leave their own country. And you must know that at their departure many were the tears shed for pity and sorrow, by their own people and by their friends. So they journeyed through Burgundy, and by the mountains of Mont-Joux (? Jura) by Mont Cenis, and through Lombardy, and began to assemble at Venice, where they were lodged on an island which is called St. Nicholas in the port.

At that time started from Flanders a fleet that carried a great number of good men-at-arms. Of this fleet were Captains John of Nêle, Castellan of Bruges, Thierri, who was the son of Count Philip of Flanders, and Nicholas of Mailly. And these promised Count Baldwin, and swore on holy relics, that they would go through the straits of Morocco, and join themselves to him, and to the host of Venice, at whatsoever place they might hear that the count was faring.

And for this reason the Count of Flanders and Henry his brother had confided to them certain ships loaded with cloth and food and other wares.

Very fair was this fleet, and rich, and great was the reliance that the Count of Flanders and the pilgrims placed upon it, because very many of their good sergeants were journeying therein. But ill did these keep the faith they had sworn to the count, they and others like them, because they and such others of the same sort became fearful of the great perils that the host of Venice had undertaken.

Thus did the Bishop of Autun fail us, and Guignes the Count of Forez, and Peter Bromont, and many people besides, who were greatly blamed therein; and of little worth were the exploits they performed there where they did go. And of the French failed us Bernard of Moreuil, Hugh of Chaumont, Henry of Araines, John of Villers, Walter of Saint-Denis, Hugh his brother, and many others, who avoided the passage to Venice because of the danger, and went instead to Marseilles—whereof they received shame, and much were they blamed—and great were the mishaps that afterwards befell them.

Of the Pilgrims Who Came to Venice, and of Those Who Went to Apulia

Now let us for this present speak of them no further, but speak of the pilgrims, of whom a great part had already come to Venice. Count

Baldwin of Flanders had already arrived there, and many others, and thither were tidings brought to them that many of the pilgrims were travelling by other ways, and from other ports. This troubled them greatly, because they would thus be unable to fulfil the promise made to the Venetians, and find the moneys that were due.

So they took counsel together, and agreed to send good envoys to meet the pilgrims, and to meet Count Louis of Blois and Chartres, who had not yet arrived, and to put them in good heart, and beseech them to have pity of the Holy Land beyond the sea, and show them that no other passage, save that from Venice, could be of profit.

For this embassage they made choice of Count Hugh of Saint-Paul and Geoffry the Marshal of Champagne, and these rode till they came to Pavia in Lombardy. There they found Count Louis with a great many knights and men of note and worth; and by encouragements and prayers prevailed on many to proceed to Venice who would otherwise have fared from other ports, and by other ways.

Nevertheless from Placentia many men of note proceeded by other ways to Apulia. Among them were Villain of Neuilly, who was one of the best knights in the world, Henry of Arzillières, Renaud of Dampierre, Henry of Longchamp, and Giles of Trasegnies, liegeman to Count Baldwin of Flanders and Hainault, who had given him, out of his own purse, five hundred *livres* to accompany him on this journey. With these went a great company of knights and sergeants, whose names are not recorded.

Thus was the host of those who went by Venice greatly weakened; and much evil befell them therefrom, as you shall shortly hear.

The Pilgrims Lack Money Wherewith to Pay the Venetians

Thus did Count Louis and the other barons wend their way to Venice; and they were there received with feasting and joyfully, and took lodging in the Island of St. Nicholas with those who had come before. Goodly was the host, and right worthy were the men. Never did man see goodlier or worthier. And the Venetians held a market, rich and abundant, of all things needful for horses and men. And the fleet they had got ready was so goodly and fine that never did Christian man see one goodlier or finer; as well galleys as transports, and sufficient for at least three times as many men as were in the host.

Ah! the grievous harm and loss when those who should have come thither sailed instead from other ports! Right well, if they had kept their tryst, would Christendom have been exalted, and the land of the Turks abased! The Venetians had fulfilled all their undertakings, and above measure, and they now summoned the barons and counts to fulfil theirs and make payment, since they were ready to start.

The cost of each man's passage was now levied throughout the host; and there were people enough who said they could not pay for their passage, and the barons took from them such moneys as they had. So each man paid what he could. When the barons had thus claimed the cost of the passages, and when the payments had been collected, the moneys came to less than the sum due—yea, by more than one half.

Then the barons met together and said: "Lords, the Venetians have well fulfilled all their undertakings, and above measure. But we cannot fulfil ours in paying for our passages, seeing we are too few in number; and this is the fault of those who have journeyed by other ports. For God's sake therefore let each contribute all that he has, so that we may fulfil our covenant; for better is it that we should give all that we have, than lose what we have already paid, and prove false to our covenants; for if this host remains here, the rescue of the land oversea comes to naught."

Great was then the dissension among the main part of the barons and the other folk, and they said: "We have paid for our passages, and if they will take us, we shall go willingly; but if not, we shall inquire and look for other means of passage." And they spoke thus because they wished that the host should fall to pieces and each return to his own land. But the other party said, "Much rather would we give all that we have and go penniless with the host, than that the host should fall to pieces and fail; for God will doubtless repay us when it so pleases Him."

Then the Count of Flanders began to give all that he had and all that he could borrow, and so did Count Lewis, and the marquis, and the Count of Saint-Paul, and those who were of their party. Then might you have seen many a fine vessel of gold and silver borne in payment to the palace of the Doge. And when all had been brought together, there was still wanting, of the sum required, 34,000 marks of silver. Then those who had kept back their possessions and not brought them into the common stock, were right glad, for they thought now surely the host must fail and go to pieces. But God, who advises those who have been ill-advised, would not so suffer it.

The Crusaders Obtain a Respite by Promising to Help the Venetians Against Zara

Then the Doge spoke to his people, and said unto them:

Signors, these people cannot pay more; and in so far as they have paid at all, we have benefited by an agreement which they cannot now fulfil. But our right to keep this money would not everywhere be acknowledged; and if we so kept it we should be greatly blamed, both us and our land. Let us therefore offer them terms.

The King of Hungary has taken from us Zara in Sclavonia, which is one of the strongest places in the world; and never shall we recover it with all the power that we possess, save with the help of these people. Let us therefore ask them to help us to reconquer it, and we will remit the payment of the debt of 34,000 marks of silver, until such time as it shall please God to allow us to gain the moneys by conquest, we and they together.

Thus was agreement made. Much was it contested by those who wished that the host should be broken up. Nevertheless the agreement was accepted and ratified.

The Doge and a Number of Venetians Take the Cross

Then, on a Sunday, was assemblage held in the Church of St. Mark. It was a very high festival, and the people of the land were there, and the most part of the barons and pilgrims.

Before the beginning of High Mass, the Doge of Venice, who bore the name of Henry Dandolo, went up into the reading-desk, and spoke to the people, and said to them:

Signors, you are associated with the most worthy people in the world, and for the highest enterprise ever undertaken; and I am a man old and feeble, who should have need of rest, and I am sick in body; but I see that no one could command and lead you like myself, who am your lord. If you will consent that I take the sign of the cross to guard and direct you, and that my son remain in my place to guard the land, then shall I go to live or die with you and with the pilgrims.

And when they had heard him, they cried with one voice: "We

pray you by God that you consent, and do it, and that you come with us!"

Very great was then the pity and compassion on the part of the people of the land and of the pilgrims; and many were the tears shed, because that worthy and good man would have had so much reason to remain behind, for he was an old man, and albeit his eyes were unclouded, yet he saw naught, having lost his sight through a wound in the head. He was of a great heart. Ah! how little like him were those who had gone to other ports to escape the danger.

Thus he came down from the reading-desk, and went before the altar, and knelt upon his knees greatly weeping. And they sewed the cross on to a great cotton hat, which he wore, in front, because he wished that all men should see it. And the Venetians began to take the cross in great numbers, a great multitude, for up to that day very few had taken the cross. Our pilgrims had much joy in the cross that the Doge took, and were greatly moved, because of the wisdom and the valour that were in him.

Thus did the Doge take the cross, as you have heard. Then the Venetians began to deliver the ships, the galleys, and the transports to the barons, for departure; but so much time had already been spent since the appointed term, that September drew near (1202).

Message of Alexius, the Son of Isaac, the Dethroned Emperor of Constantinople—Death of Fulk of Neuilly—Arrival of the Germans

Now give ear to one of the greatest marvels, and most wonderful adventures that you have ever heard tell of. At that time there was an emperor in Constantinople, whose name was Isaac, and he had a brother, Alexius by name, whom he had ransomed from captivity among the Turks. This Alexius took his brother the emperor, tore the eyes out of his head, and made himself emperor by the aforesaid treachery.

He kept Isaac a long time in prison, together with a son whose name was Alexius. This son escaped from prison, and fled in a ship to a city on the sea, which is called Ancona. Thence he departed to go to King Philip of Germany, who had his sister for wife; and he came to Verona in Lombardy, and lodged in the town, and found there a number of pilgrims and other people who were on their way to join the host.

And those who had helped him to escape, and were with him, said:

"Sire, here is an army in Venice, quite near to us, the best and most valiant people and knights that are in the world, and they are going oversea. Cry to them therefore for mercy, that they have pity on thee and on thy father, who have been so wrongfully dispossessed. And if they be willing to help thee, thou shalt be guided by them. Perchance they will take pity on thy estate."

And Alexius said he would do this right willingly, and that the advice was good.

Thus he appointed envoys, and sent them to the Marquis Boniface of Montferrat, who was chief of the host, and to the other barons. And when the barons saw them, they marvelled greatly, and said to the envoys:

> We understand right well what you tell us. We will send an envoy with the prince to King Philip, whither he is going. If the prince will help to recover the land oversea, we will help him to recover his own land, for we know that it has been wrested from him and from his father wrongfully.

So were envoys sent into Germany, both to the heir of Constantinople and to King Philip of Germany.

Before this happened, of which I have just told you, there came news to the host which greatly saddened the barons and the other folk, *viz.*, that Fulk, the good man, the holy man, who first preached the Crusade, had made an end and was dead.

And after this adventure, there came to the host a company of very good and worthy people from the empire of Germany, of whose arrival they of the host were full fain. There came the Bishop of Halberstadt, Count Bertrand of Katzenelenbogen, Garnier of Borland, Thierri of Loos, Henry of Orme, Thierri of Diest, Roger of Suitre, Alexander of Villers, Ulric of Tone, and many other good folk, whose names are not recorded in this book.

The Crusaders Leave Venice to Besiege Zara

Then were the ships and transports apportioned by the barons. Ah, God! what fine war-horses were put therein. And when the ships were fulfilled with arms and provisions, and knights and sergeants, the shields were ranged round the bulwarks and castles of the ships, and the banners displayed, many and fair.

And be it known to you that the vessels carried more than three hundred petraries and mangonels, and all such engines as are needed for the taking of cities, in great plenty. Never did finer fleet sail from any port. And this was in the octave of the Feast of St. Remigius (October) in the year of the Incarnation of Jesus Christ twelve hundred and two.

Thus did they sail from the port of Venice, as you have been told. On the Eve of St. Martin (10th November) they came before Zara in Sclavonia, and beheld the city enclosed by high walls and high towers; and vainly would you have sought for a fairer city, or one of greater strength, or richer. And when the pilgrims saw it, they marvelled greatly, and said one to another, "How could such a city be taken by force, save by the help of God himself?"

The first ships that came before the city cast anchor, and waited for the others; and in the morning the day was very fine and very clear, and all the galleys came up with the transports, and the other ships which were behind; and they took the port by force, and broke the chain that defended it and was very strong and well-wrought; and they landed in such sort that the port was between them and the town.

Then might you have seen many a knight and many a sergeant swarming out of the ships, and taking from the transports many a good war-horse, and many a rich tent and many a pavilion.

Thus did the host encamp. And Zara was besieged on St. Martin's Day (11th November 1202). At this time all the barons had not yet arrived.

Thus the Marquis of Montferrat had remained behind for some business that detained him. And Stephen of the Perche had remained at Venice sick, and Matthew of Montmorency.

When they were healed of their sickness Matthew of Montmorency came to rejoin the host at Zara; but Stephen of the Perche dealt less worthily, for he abandoned the host, and went to sojourn in Apulia.

With him went Rotrou of Montfort and Ives of the Jaille, and many others, who were much blamed therein; and they journeyed to Syria in the following spring.[8]

THE INHABITANTS OF ZARA OFFER TO CAPITULATE, AND THEN DRAW BACK—ZARA IS TAKEN

On the day following the feast of St. Martin, certain of the people of Zara came forth, and spoke to the Doge of Venice, who was in his pavilion, and said to him that they would yield up the city and all their

---

8. Literally, "in the passage of March," *i.e.* among the pilgrims who periodically started for the Holy Land in March.

goods—their lives being spared—to his mercy. And the Doge replied that he would not accept these conditions, nor any conditions, save by consent of the counts and barons, with whom he would go and confer.

While he went to confer with the counts and barons, that party, of whom you have already heard, who wished to disperse the host, spoke to the envoys and said,

> Why should you surrender your city? The pilgrims will not attack you—have no care of them. If you can defend yourselves against the Venetians, you will be safe enough.

And they chose one of themselves, whose name was Robert of Boves, who went to the walls of the city, and spoke the same words. Therefore the envoys returned to the city, and the negotiations were broken off.

The Doge of Venice, when he came to the counts and barons, said to them:

> *Signors*, the people who are therein desire to yield the city to my mercy, on condition only that their lives are spared. But I will enter into no agreement with them—neither this nor any other—save with your consent.

And the barons answered: "Sire, we advise you to accept these conditions, and we even beg of you so to do." He said he would do so; and they all returned together to the pavilion of the Doge to make the agreement, and found that the envoys had gone away by the advice of those who wished to disperse the host.

Then rose the abbot of Vaux, of the order of the Cistercians, and said to them:

> Lords, I forbid you, on the part of the Pope of Rome, to attack this city; for those within it are Christians, and you are pilgrims.

When the Doge heard this, he was very wroth, and much disturbed, and he said to the counts and barons:

> *Signors*, I had this city, by their own agreement, at my mercy, and your people have
> broken that agreement, you have covenanted to help me to conquer it, and I summon you to do so.

Whereon the counts and barons all spoke at once, together with those who were of their party, and said: "Great is the outrage of those who have caused this agreement to be broken, and never a day has passed that they have not tried to break up the host. Now are we shamed if we do not help to take the city."

And they came to the Doge, and said: "Sire, we will help you to take the city in despite of those who would let and hinder us."

Thus was the decision taken. The next morning the host encamped before the gates of the city, and set up their petraries and mangonels, and other engines of war, which they had in plenty, and on the side of the sea they raised ladders from the ships. Then they began to throw stones at the walls of the city and at the towers.

So did the assault last for about five days. Then were the sappers set to mine one of the towers, and began to sap the wall. When those within the city saw this, they proposed an agreement, such as they had before refused by the advice of those who wished to break up the host.

The Crusaders Establish Themselves in the City—Affray Between the Venetians and the Franks

Thus did the city surrender to the mercy of the Doge, on condition only that all lives should be spared. Then came the Doge to the counts and barons, and said to them:

> *Signors,* we have taken this city by the grace of God, and your own. It is now winter, and we cannot stir hence till Eastertide; for we should find no market in any other place; and this city is very rich, and well furnished with all supplies. Let us therefore divide it in the midst, and we will take one half, and you the other.

As he had spoken, so was it done. The Venetians took the part of the city towards the port, where were the ships, and the Franks took the other part. There were quarters assigned to each, according as was right and convenient. And the host raised the camp, and went to lodge in the city.

On the third day after they were all lodged, there befell a great misadventure in the host, at about the hour of vespers; for there began a fray, exceeding fell and fierce, between the Venetians and the Franks, and they ran to arms from all sides. And the fray was so fierce that there were but few streets in which battle did not rage with swords and lances and cross-bows and darts; and many people were killed and wounded.

But the Venetians could not abide the combat, and they began to suffer great losses. Then the men of mark, who did not want this evil to befall, came fully armed into the strife, and began to separate the combatants; and when they had separated them in one place, they began again in another. This lasted the better part of the night. Nevertheless with great labour and endurance at last they were separated. And be it known to you that this was the greatest misfortune that ever befell a host, and little did it lack that the host was not lost utterly. But God would not suffer it.

Great was the loss on either side. There was slain a high lord of Flanders, whose name was Giles of Landas: he was struck in the eye, and with that stroke he died in the fray; and many another of whom less was spoken. The Doge of Venice and the barons laboured much, during the whole of that week, to appease the fray, and they laboured so effectually that peace was made. God be thanked therefore.

On What Conditions Alexius Proposes to Obtain the Help of the Crusaders for the Conquest of Constantinople

A fortnight after came to Zara the Marquis Boniface of Montferrat, who had not yet joined, and Matthew of Montmorency, and Peter of Bracieux, and many another man of note. And after another fortnight came also the envoys from Germany, sent by King Philip and the heir of Constantinople. Then the barons, and the Doge of Venice assembled in a palace where the Doge was lodged. And the envoys addressed them and said: "Lords, King Philip sends us to you, as does also the brother of the king's wife" the son of the Emperor of Constantinople.

"'Lords,' says the king, 'I will send you the brother of my wife; and I commit him into the hands of God—may He keep him from death!—and into your hands. And because you have fared forth for God, and for right, and for justice, therefore you are bound, in so far as you are able, to restore to their own inheritance those who have been unrighteously despoiled. And my wife's brother will make with you the best terms ever offered to any people, and give you the most puissant help for the recovery of the land oversea.

"'And first, if God grant that you restore him to his inheritance, he will place the whole empire of Roumania in obedience to Rome, from which it has long been separated. Further, he knows that you have spent of your substance, and that you are poor, and he will give you 200,000 *marks* of silver, and food for all those of the host, both small and great. And he, of his own person, will go with you into the land of Babylon, or, if you hold that that will be better, send thither 10,000 men, at his own charges.

"'And this service he will perform for one year. And all the days of his life he will maintain, at his own charges, five hundred knights in the land oversea, to guard that land.'"

"Lords, we have full power," said the envoys, "to conclude this agreement, if you are willing to conclude it on your parts. And be it known to you, that so favourable an agreement has never before been offered to anyone; and that he that would refuse it can have but small desire of glory and conquest."

The barons and the Doge said they would talk this over; and a parliament was called for the morrow. When all were assembled, the matter was laid before them.

Discord Among the Crusaders—of Those Who Accept the Proposals of the Young Alexius

Then arose much debate. The abbot of Vaux, of the order of the Cistercians, spoke, and that party that wished for the dispersal of the host; and they said they would never consent: that it was not to fall on Christians that they had left their homes, and that they would go to Syria.

And the other party replied:

Fair lords, in Syria you will be able to do nothing; and that you may right well perceive by considering how those have fared who abandoned us, and sailed from other ports. And be it known to you that it is only by way of Babylon, or of Greece, that the land oversea can be recovered, if so be that it ever is recovered. And if we reject this covenant we shall be shamed to all time.

There was discord in the host, as you hear. Nor need you be surprised if there was discord among the laymen, for the white monks of the order of Cîteaux were also at issue among themselves in the host. The abbot of Loos, who was a holy man and a man of note, and other abbots who held with him, prayed and besought the people, for pity's sake, and the sake of God, to keep the host together, and agree to the proposed convention, in that "it afforded the best means by which the land oversea might be recovered;" while the abbot of Vaux, on the other hand, and those who held with him, preached full oft, and declared that all this was naught, and that the host ought to go to the land of Syria, and there do what they could.

Then came the Marquis of Montferrat, and Baldwin Count of Flanders and Hainault, and Count Lewis, and Count Hugh of St. Paul, and those who held with them, and they declared that they would enter into the proposed covenant, for that they should be shamed if they refused. So they went to the Doge's hostel, and the envoys were summoned, and the covenant, in such terms as you have already heard, was confirmed by oath, and by charters with seals appended.

And the book tells you that only twelve persons took the oaths on the side of the Franks, for more (of sufficient note) could not be found. Among the twelve were first the Marquis of Montferrat, the Count Baldwin of Flanders, the Count Lewis of Blois and of Chartres, and the Count of St. Paul, and eight others who held with them. Thus was the agreement made, and the charters ,prepared, and a term fixed for the arrival of the heir of Constantinople; and the term so fixed was the fifteenth day after the following Easter.

OF THOSE WHO SEPARATED THEMSELVES FROM THE HOST TO GO TO SYRIA, AND OF THE FLEET OF THE COUNT OF FLANDERS

Thus did the host sojourn at Zara all that winter (1202-120 3) in the face of the King of Hungary. And be it known to you that the hearts of the people were not at peace, for the one party used all efforts to break up the host, and the other to make it hold together.

Many of the lesser folk escaped in the vessels of the merchants. In one ship escaped well-nigh five hundred, and they were all drowned, and so lost. Another company escaped by land, and thought to pass through Sclavonia; and the peasants of that land fell upon them, and killed many, so that the remainder came back flying to the host. Thus did the host go greatly dwindling day by day. At that time a great lord of the host, who was from Germany, Garnier' of Borlande by name, so wrought that he escaped in a merchant vessel, and abandoned the host, whereby he incurred great blame.

Not long afterwards, a great baron of France, Renaud of Montmirail by name, besought so earnestly, with the countenance of Count Louis, that he was sent to Syria on an embassage in one of the vessels of the fleet; and he swore with his right hand on holy relics, he and all the knights who went with him, that within fifteen days after they had arrived in Syria, and delivered their message, they would return to the host. On this condition he left the host, and with him Hervée of the Chastel, his nephew, William the *vidame* of Chartres, Geoffry of Beaumont, John of Frouville, Peter his brother, and many others. And the oaths that they swore were not kept; for they did not rejoin the host.

Then came to the host news that was heard right willingly, *viz.*, that the fleet from Flanders, of which mention has been made above, had arrived at Marseilles. And John of Nêle, Castellan of Bruges, who was captain of that host, and Thierri, who was the son of Count Philip of Flanders, and Nicholas of Mailly, advised the Count of Flanders, their lord, that they would winter at Marseilles, and asked him to let them know what was his will, and said that whatever was his will, that they would do.

And he told them, by the advice of the Doge of Venice and the other barons, that they should sail at the end of the following March, and come to meet him at the port of Moton in Roumania. Alas! they acted very evilly, for never did they keep their word, but went to Syria, where, as they well knew, they would achieve nothing.

Now be it known to you, lords, that if God had not loved the host, it could never have held together, seeing how many people wished evil to it!

The Crusaders Obtain the Pope's Absolution for the Capture of Zara

Then the barons spoke together and said that they would send to Rome, to the Pope, because he had taken the capture of Zara in evil part. And they chose as envoys such as they knew were fitted for this office, two knights, and two clerks. Of the two clerks one was Nevelon, Bishop of Soissons, and the other Master John of Noyon, who was chancellor to Count Baldwin of Flanders; and of the knights one was John of Friaize, the other Robert of Boves. These swore on holy relics that they would perform their embassage loyally and in good faith, and that they would come back to the host.

Three kept their oath right well, and the fourth evilly, and this one was Robert of Boves. For he executed his office as badly as he could, and perjured himself, and went away to Syria as others had done. But the remaining three executed their office right well, and delivered their message as the barons had directed, and said to the Pope: "The barons cry mercy to you for the capture of Zara, for they acted as people who could do no better, owing to the default of those who had gone to other ports, and because, had they not acted as they did, they could not have held the host together. And as to this they refer themselves to you, as to their good Father, that you should tell them what are your commands, which they are ready to perform."

And the Pope said to the envoys that he knew full well that it was through the default of others that the host had been impelled to do this great mischief, and that he had them in great pity. And then he notified to the barons and pilgrims that he sent them his blessing, and absolved them as his sons, and commanded and besought them to hold the host together, inasmuch as he well knew that without that host God's service could not be done. And he gave full powers to Nevelon, Bishop of Soissons, and Master John of Noyon, to bind and to unloose the pilgrims until the cardinal joined the host.

Departure of the Crusaders for Corfu—Arrival of the Young Alexius—Capture of Duras

So much time had passed, that it was now Lent, and the host prepared their fleet to sail at Easter. When the ships were laden on the day after Easter (7th April 1203), the pilgrims encamped by the port, and the Venetians destroyed the city, and the walls and the towers.

Then there befell an adventure which weighed heavily upon the host; for one of the great barons of the host, by name Simon of Montfort, had made private covenant with the King of Hungary, who was at enmity with those of the host, and went to him, abandoning the host. With him went Guy of Montfort his brother, Simon of Nauphle and Robert Mauvoisin, and Dreux of Cressonacq, and the abbot of Vaux, who was a monk of the order of the Cistercians, and many others. And not long after another great lord of the host, called Enguerrand of Boves, joined the King of Hungary, together with Hugh, Enguerrand's brother, and such of the other people of their country as they could lead away.

These left the host, as you have just heard; and this was a great misfortune to the host, and to such as left it a great disgrace.

Then the ships and transports began to depart; and it was settled that they should take port at Corfu, an island of Roumania, and that the first to arrive should wait for the last; and so it was done.

Before the Doge, the Marquis, and the galleys left Zara, Alexius, the son of the Emperor Isaac of Constantinople, had arrived thither.

He was sent by the King Philip of Germany, and received with great joy and great honour; and the Doge gave him as many galleys and ships as he required. So they left the port of Zara, and had a fair wind, and sailed onwards till they took port at Duras. And those of the land, when they saw their lord yielded up the city right willingly and sware fealty to him

And they departed thence and came to Corfu, and found there the host encamped before the city; and those of the host had spread their tents and pavilions, and taken the horses out of the transports for ease and refreshment.

When they heard that the son of the Emperor of Constantinople had arrived in the port, then might you have seen many a good knight and many a good sergeant leading many a good war-horse and going to meet him. Thus they received him with very great joy, and much high honour. And he had his tent pitched in the midst of the host; and quite near was pitched the tent of the Marquis of Montferrat, to whose ward he had been commended by King Philip, who had his sister to wife.

How the Chiefs of the Crusaders Held Back Those Who Wanted to Abandon the Host

The host sojourned thus for three weeks in that island, which was very rich and plenteous. And while they sojourned, there happened a misadventure fell and grievous. For a great part of those who wished to break up the host, and had aforetime been hostile to it, spoke together and said that the adventure to be undertaken seemed very long and very perilous, and that they, for their part, would remain in the island, suffering the host to depart, and that—when the host had so departed—they would, through the people of Corfu, send to Count Walter of Brienne, who then held Brandis, so that he might send ships to take them thither.

I cannot tell you the names of all those who wrought in this matter, but I will name some among the most notable of the chiefs, *viz*., Odo of Champlitte, of Champagne, James of Avesnes, Peter of Amiens, Guy the Castellan of Couey, Oger of Saint-Chéron, Guy of Chappes and Clerembeau his nephew, William of Aunoi, Peter Coiseau, Guy of Pesmes and Edmund his brother, Guy of Conflans, Richard of Dampierre, Odo his brother, and many more who had promised privily to be of their party, but who dared not for shame openly so to avow themselves; in such sort that the book testifies that more than half the host were in this mind.

And when the Marquis of Montferrat heard thereof, and Count Baldwin of Flanders, and Count Lewis, and the Count of St. Paul, and the barons who held with them, they were greatly troubled, and said:

> Lords, we are in evil case. If these people depart from us, after so many who have departed from us afore time, our host is doomed, and we shall make no conquests. Let us then go to them, and fall at their feet, and cry to them for mercy, and for God's sake to have compassion upon themselves and upon us, and not to dishonour themselves, and ravish. from us the deliverance of the land oversea.

Thus did the council decide; .and they went, all together, to a valley where those of the other part were holding their parliament; and they took with them the son of the Emperor of Constantinople, and all the bishops and all the abbots of the host. And when they had come to the place they dismounted and went forward, and the barons fell at the feet of those of the other part, greatly weeping, and said they would not stir till those of the other part had promised not to depart from them.

And when those of the other part saw this, they were filled with very great compassion; and they wept very bitterly at seeing their lords, and their kinsmen, and their friends, thus lying at their feet. So they said they would consult together, and drew somewhat apart, and there communed. And the sum of their communing was this: that they would remain with the host till Michaelmas, on condition that the other part would swear, loyally, on holy relics, that from that day and thenceforward, at whatever hour they might be summoned to do so, they would in all good faith, and without guile, within fifteen days, furnish ships wherein the non-contents might betake themselves to Syria.

Thus was covenant made and sworn to; and then was there great joy throughout all the host. And all gat themselves to the ships, and the horses were put into the transports.

Departure From Corfu—Capture of Andros and Abydos

Then did they sail from the port of Corfu on the eve of Pentecost (24th May), which was twelve hundred and three years after the Incarnation of our Lord Jesus Christ. And there were all the ships assembled, and all the transports, and all the galleys of the host, and many other ships of merchants that fared with them. And the day was fine and clear, and the wind soft and favourable, and they unfurled all their sails to the breeze.

And Geoffry, the Marshal of Champagne, who dictates this work, and has never lied therein by one word to his knowledge, and who was moreover present at all the councils held—he bears witness that never was yet seen so fair a sight. And well might it appear that such a fleet would conquer and gain lands, for, far as the eye could reach, there was no space without sails, and ships, and vessels, so that the hearts of men rejoiced greatly.

Thus they sailed over the sea till they came to Malea, to straits that are by the sea. And there they met two ships with pilgrims, and knights and sergeants returning from Syria, and they were of the parties that had gone to Syria by Marseilles. And when these saw our fleet so rich and well-appointed, they conceived such shame that they dared not show themselves. And Count Baldwin of Flanders sent a boat from his ship to ask what people they were; and they said who they were.

And a sergeant let himself down from his ship into the boat, and said to those in the ship, "I cry quits to you for any goods of mine that may remain in the ship, for I am going with these people, for well I deem that they will conquer lands." Much did we make of the sergeant, and gladly was he received in the host. For well may it be said, that even after following a thousand crooked ways a man may find his way right in the end.

The host fared forward till it came to Nigra (Negropont). Nigra is a very fair island, and there is on it a very good city called Negropont. Here the barons took council. Then went forward the Marquis Boniface of Montferrat, and Count Baldwin of Flanders and Hainault, with a great part of the transports and galleys, taking with them the son of the Emperor Isaac of Constantinople; and they came to an island called Andros, and there landed. The knights took their arms, and over-rode the country; and the people of the land came to crave mercy of the son of the Emperor of Constantinople, and gave so much of their goods that they made peace with him.

Then they returned to the ships, and sailed over the sea; when a great mishap befell, for a great lord of the host, whose name was Guy, Castellan of Coucy, died, and was cast into the sea.

The other ships, which had not sailed thitherward, had entered the passage of Abydos, and it is there that the straits of St. George (the Dardanelles) open into the great sea. And they sailed up the straits to a city caned Abydos, which lies on the straits of St. George, towards Turkey, and is very fair, and well situate. There they took port and landed, and those of the city came to meet them, and surrendered the city, as men without stomach to defend themselves. And such guard was established that those of the city lost not one *stiver* current.

They sojourned there eight days to wait for the ships transports and galleys that had not yet come up. And while they thus sojourned, they took corn from the land, for it was the season of harvest, and great was their need thereof, for before they had but little. And within those eight days all the ships and barons had come up. God gave them fair weather.

Arrival at St. Stephen—Deliberation as to Plan of Attack

All started from the port of Abydos together. Then might you have seen the Straits of St. George (as it were) in flower with ships and galleys sailing upwards, and the beauty thereof was a great marvel to behold. Thus they sailed up the Straits of St. George till they came, on St. John the Baptist's Eve, in June (23rd June 1203) to St. Stephen, an abbey that lay three leagues from Constantinople. There had those on board the ships and galleys and transports full sight of Constantinople; and they took port and anchored their vessels.

Now you may know that those who had never before seen Constantinople looked upon it very earnestly, for they never thought there could be in all the world so rich a city; and they marked the high walls and strong towers that enclosed it round about, and the rich palaces, and mighty churches—of which there were so many that no one would have believed it who had not seen it with his eyes—and the height and the length of that city which above all others was sovereign. And be it known to you, that no man there was of such hardihood but his flesh trembled; and it was no wonder, for never was so great an enterprise undertaken by any people since the creation of the world.

Then landed the counts and barons and the Doge of Venice, and a parliament was held in the church of St. Stephen. There were many opinions set forth, this way and that. All the words then spoken shall not be recorded in this book; but in the end the Doge rose on his feet and said:

Signors, I know the state of this land better than you do, for I have been here erewhile. We have undertaken the greatest enterprise, and the most perilous, that ever people have undertaken.

Therefore it behoves us to go to work warily. Be it known to you that if we go on dry ground, the land is great and large, and our people are poor and ill-provided. Thus they will disperse to look for food; and the people of the land are in great multitude, and we cannot keep such good watch but that some of ours will be lost. Nor are we in case to lose any, for our people are but few indeed for the work in hand.

Now there are islands close by which you can see from here, and these are inhabited, and produce corn, and food, and other things. Let us take port there, and gather the corn and provisions of the land. And when we have collected our supplies, let us go before the city, and do as our Lord shall provide. For he that has supplies, wages war with more certainty than he that has none.

To this counsel the lords and barons agreed, and all went back to their ships and vessels.

The Crusaders Land at Chalcedon and Scutari

They rested thus that night. And in the morning, on the day of the feast of our Lord St. John the Baptist in June (24th June 1203), the banners and pennants were flown on the castles of the ships, and the coverings taken from the shields, and the bulwarks of the ships garnished. Everyone looked to his arms, such as he should use, for well each man knew that full soon he would have need of them.

The sailors weighed the anchors, and spread the sails to the wind, and God gave them a good wind, such as was convenient to them. Thus they passed before Constantinople, and so near to the walls and towers that we shot at many of their vessels. There were so many people on the walls and towers that it seemed as if there could be no more people (in the world).

Then did God our Lord set to naught the counsel of the day before, and keep us from sailing to the islands: that counsel fell to naught as if none had ever heard thereof. For lo, our ships made for the mainland as straight as ever they could, and took port before a palace of the Emperor Alexius, at a place called Chalcedon.

This was in face of Constantinople, on the other side of the straits, towards Turkey. The palace was one of the most beautiful and delectable that ever eyes could see, with every delight therein that the heart of man could desire, and convenient for the house of a prince.

The counts and barons landed and lodged themselves in the palace; and in the city round about, the main part pitched their tents. Then were the horses taken out of the transports, and the knights and sergeants got to land with an their arms, so that none remained in the ships save the mariners only. The country was fair, and rich, and well, supplied with all good things, and the sheaves of corn (which had been reaped) were in the fields, so that all—and they stood in no small need—might take thereof.

They sojourned thus in that palace the following day; and on the third day God gave them a good wind, and the mariners raised their anchors, and spread their sails to the wind. They went thus up the straits, a good league above Constantinople, to a palace that belonged to the Emperor Alexius, and was called Scutari. There the ships anchored, and the transports, and all the galleys. The horsemen who had lodged in the palace of Chalcedon went along the shore by land.

The host of the French encamped thus on the straits of St. George, at Scutari, and above it. And when the Emperor Alexius saw this, he caused his host to issue from Constantinople, and encamp over against us on the other side of the straits, and there pitched his tents, so that we might not take land against him by force. The host of the French sojourned thus for nine days, and those obtained supplies who needed them, and that was everyone in the host.

The Foragers Defeat the Greeks

During this time, a company of good and trustworthy men issued (from the camp) to guard the host, for fear it should be attacked, and the foragers searched the country. In the said company were Odo of Champlitte, of Champagne, and William his brother, and Oger of Saint-Chéron, and Manasses of l'Isle, and Count Girard, a count of Lombardy, a retainer of the Marquis of Montferrat; and they had with them at least eighty knights who were good men and true.

And they espied, at the foot of a mountain, some three leagues distant from the host, certain tents belonging to the Grand Duke of the Emperor of Constantinople, who had with him at least five hundred Greek knights. When our people saw them, they formed their men into four battalions, and decided to attack. And when the Greeks saw this, they formed their battalions, and arrayed themselves in rank before their tents, and waited. And our people went forward and fell upon them right vigorously.

By the help of God our Lord, this fight lasted but a little while, and the Greeks turned their backs. They were discomfited at the first onset, and our people pursued them for a full great league. There they won plenty of horses and stallions, and palfreys, and mules, and tents and pavilions, and such spoil as is usual in such case. So they returned to the host, where they were right well received, and their spoils were divided, as was fit.

Message of the Emperor Alexius—Reply of the Crusaders

The next day after, the Emperor Alexius sent an envoy with letters to the counts and to the barons. This envoy was called Nicholas Roux, and he was a native of Lombardy. He found the barons in the rich palace of Scutari, where they were holding council, and he saluted them on the part of the Emperor Alexius of Constantinople, and tendered his letters to the Marquis of Montferrat—who received them. And the letters were read before all the barons; and there were in them words, written after various manners, which the book does not (here) relate, and at the end of the other words so written, came words of credit, accrediting the bearer of the letters, whose name was Nicholas Roux.

"Fair sir," said the barons, "we have seen your letters, and they tell us that we are to give credit to what you say, and we credit you right well. Now speak as it pleases you."

And the envoy was standing before the barons, and spoke thus:

"Lords," said he, "the Emperor Alexius would have you know that he is well aware that you are the best people uncrowned, and come from the best land on earth. And he marvels much why, and for what purpose, you have come into his land and kingdom. For you are Christians, and he is a Christian, and well he knows that you are on your way to deliver the Holy Land oversea, and the Holy Cross, and the Sepulchre. If you are poor and in want, he will right willingly give you of his food and substance, provided you depart out of his land. Neither would he otherwise wish to do you any hurt, though he has full power therein, seeing that if you were twenty times as numerous as you are, you would not be able to get away without utter discomfiture if so be that he wished to harm you."

By agreement and desire of the other barons, and of the Doge of Venice, then rose to his feet Conon of Béthune, who was a good knight, and wise, and very eloquent, and he replied to the envoy:

Fair sir, you have told us that your lord marvels much why our *signors* and barons should have entered into his kingdom and land. Into his land they have not entered, for he holds this land wrongfully and wickedly, and against God and against reason. It belongs to his nephew, who sits upon a throne among us, and is the son of his brother, the Emperor Isaac. But if he is willing to throw himself on the mercy of his nephew, and to give him back his crown and empire, then we will pray his nephew to forgive him, and bestow upon him as much as will enable him to live wealthily. And if you come not as the bearer of such a message, then be not so bold as to come here again.

So the envoy departed and went back to Constantinople, to the Emperor Alexius.

The Crusaders Show the Young Alexius to the People of Constantinople, and Prepare for the Battle

The barons consulted together on the morrow, and said that they would show the young Alexius, the son of the Emperor of Constantinople, to the people of the city. So they assembled all the galleys. The Doge of Venice and the Marquis of Montferrat entered into one, and took with them Alexius, the son of the Emperor Isaac; and into the other galleys entered the knights and barons, as many as would.

They went thus quite close to the walls of Constantinople and showed the youth to the people of the Greeks, and said,

Behold your natural lord; and be it known to you that we have not come to do you harm, but have come to guard and defend you, if so be that you return to your duty. For he whom you now obey as your lord holds rule by wrong and wickedness, against God and reason. And you know full well that he has dealt treasonably with him who is your lord and his brother, that he has blinded his eyes and reft from him his empire by wrong and wickedness. Now behold the rightful heir. If you hold with him, you will be doing as you ought; and if not we will do to you the very worst that we can.

But for fear and terror of the Emperor Alexius, not one person on the land or in the city made show as if he held for the prince. So all went back to the host, and each sought his quarters.

On the morrow, when they had heard mass, they assembled in parliament, and the parliament was held on horseback in the midst of the fields. There might you have seen many a fine war-horse, and many a good knight thereon. And the council was held to discuss the order of the battalions, how many they should have, and of what strength. Many were the words said on one side and the other.

But in the end it was settled that the advanced guard should be given to Baldwin of Flanders, because he had a very great number of good men, and archers and crossbowmen, more than any other chief that was in the host.

And after, it was settled that Henry his brother, and Matthew of Walincourt, and Baldwin of Beauvoir, and many other good knights of their land and country, should form the Second Division.

The Third Division was formed by Count Hugh of St. Paul, Peter of Amiens his nephew, Eustace of Canteleu, Anselm of Cayeux, and many good knights of their land and country.

The Fourth Division was formed by Count Lewis of Blois and Chartres, and was very numerous and rich and redoubtable; for he had placed therein a great number of good knights and men of worth.

The Fifth Division was formed by Matthew of Montmorency and the men of Champagne. Geoffry the Marshal of Champagne formed part of it, and Oger of Saint-Chéron, Manasses of l'Isle, Miles the Brebant, Macaire of Sainte-Menehould, John Foisnons, Guy of Chappes, Cleremband his nephew, Robert of Ronsoi: all these people formed part of the Fifth Division. Be it known to you that there was many a good knight therein.

The Sixth Division was formed by the people of Burgundy. In this division were Odo the Champenois of Champlitte, William his brother, Guy of Pesmes, Edmond his brother, Otho of la Roche, Richard of Dampierre, Odo his brother, Guy of Conflans, and the people of their land and country.

The Seventh Division, which was very large, was under the command of the Marquis of Montferrat. In it were the Lombards and Tuscans and the Germans, and all the people who were from beyond Mont Cenis to Lyons on the Rhone. All these formed part of the division under the marquis, and it was settled that they should form the rearguard.

The Crusaders Seize the Port

The day was fixed on which the host should embark on the ships and transports to take the land by force, and either live or die. And be it known to you that the enterprise to be achieved was one of the most redoubtable ever attempted. Then did the bishops and clergy speak to the people, and tell them how they must confess, and make each one his testament, seeing that no one knew what might be the will of God concerning him. And this was done right willingly throughout the host, and very piously.

The term fixed was now come; and the knights went on board the transports with their war-horses; and they were fully armed, with their helmets laced, and the horses covered with their housings, and saddled. All the other folk, who were of less consequence in battle, were on the great ships; and the galleys were fully armed and made ready.

The morning was fair a little after the rising of the sun; and the Emperor Alexius stood waiting for them on the other side, with great forces, and everything in order. And the trumpets sound, and every galley takes a transport in tow, so as to reach the other side more readily. None ask who shall go first, but each makes the land as soon as he can.

The knights issue from the transports, and leap into the sea up to their waists, fully armed, with helmets laced, and lances in hand; and the good archers, and the good sergeants, and the good crossbowmen, each in his company, land so soon as they touch ground.

The Greeks made a goodly show of resistance; but when it came to the lowering of the lances, they turned their backs, and went away flying, and abandoned the shore. And be it known to you that never was port more proudly taken. Then began the mariners to open the ports of the transports, and let down the bridges, and take out the horses; and the knights began to mount, and they began to marshal the divisions of the host in due order.

Capture of the Tower of Galata

Count Baldwin of Flanders and Hainault, with the advanced guard, rode forward, and the other divisions of the host after him, each in due order of march; and they came to where the Emperor Alexius had been encamped. But he had turned back towards Constantinople, and left his tents and pavilions standing. And there our people had much spoil.

Our barons were minded to encamp by the port before the tower of Galata, where the chain was fixed that closed the port of Constantinople. And be it known to you, that any one must perforce pass that chain before he could enter into the port. Well did our barons then perceive that if they did not take the tower, and break the chain, they were but as dead men, and in very evil case. So they lodged that night before the tower, and in the Jewry that is called Stenon, where there was a good city, and very rich.

Well did they keep guard during the night; and on the morrow, at the hour of tierce, those who were in the tower of Galata made a sortie, and those who were in Constantinople came to their help in barges; and our people ran to arms. There came first to the onset James of Avesnes and his men on foot; and be it known to you that he was fiercely charged, and wounded by lance in the face, and in peril of death. And one of his knights, whose name was Nicholas of Jenlain, gat to horse, and came to his lord's rescue, and succoured him right well, and so won great honour.

Then a cry was raised in the host, and our people ran together from all sides, and drove back the foe with great fury, so that many were slain and taken. And some of them did not go back to the tower, but ran to the barges by which they had come, and there many were drowned, and some escaped.

As to those who went back to the tower, the men of our host pressed them so hard that they could not shut the gate. Then a terrible fight began again at the gate, and our people took it by force, and made prisoners of all those in the tower. Many were there killed and taken.

Attack on the City by Land and Sea

So was the tower of Galata taken, and the port of Constantinople won by force. Much were those of the host comforted thereby, and much did they praise the Lord God; and greatly were those of the city discomforted. And on the next day, the ships, the vessels, the galleys and the transports were drawn into the port.

Then did those of the host take council together to settle what thing they should do, and whether they should attack the city by sea or by land. The Venetians were firmly minded that the scaling ladders ought to be planted on the ships, and all the attack made from the side by the sea.

The French, on the other hand, said that they did not know so well how to help themselves on sea as on land, but that when they had their horses and their arms they could help themselves on land right well. So in the end it was devised that the Venetians should attack by sea, and the barons and those of the host by land.

They sojourned thus for four days. On the fifth day, the whole host were armed, and the divisions advanced on horseback, each in the order appointed, along the harbour, till they came to the palace of Blachernæ; and the ships drew inside the harbour till they came over against the self-same place, and this was near to the end of the harbour. And there is at that place a river that flows into the sea, and can only be passed by a bridge of stone.

The Greeks had broken down the bridge, and the barons caused the host to labour all that day and all that night in repairing the bridge. Thus was the bridge repaired, and in the morning the divisions were armed, and rode one after the other in the order appointed, and came before the city. And no one came out from the city against them; and this was a great marvel, seeing that for every man that was in the host there were over two hundred men in the city.

Then did the barons decide that they should quarter themselves between the palace of Blachernæ and the castle of Boemond, which was an abbey enclosed with walls. So the tents and pavilions were pitched—which was a right proud thing to look upon; for of Constantinople, which had three leagues of front towards the land, the whole host could attack no more than one of the gates. And the Venetians lay on the sea, in ships and vessels, and raised their ladders, and mangonels, and petraries, and made order for their assault right well. And the barons for their part made ready their petraries and mangonels on land.

And be it known to you that they did not have their time in peace and quiet; for there passed no hour of the night or day but one of the divisions had to stand armed before the gate, to guard the engines, and provide against attack. And, notwithstanding all this, the Greeks ceased not to attack them, by this gate and by others, and held them so short that six or seven times a day the whole host was forced to run to arms.

Nor could they forage for provisions more than four bow-shots' distance from the camp. And their stores were but scanty, save of flour and bacon, and of those they had a little; and of fresh meat none at all, save what they got from the horses that were killed. And be it known to you that there was only food generally in the host for three weeks. Thus were they in very perilous case, for never did so few people besiege so many people in any city.

First Incidents of the Assault

Then did they bethink themselves of a very good device; for they enclosed the whole camp with good lists, and good palisades, and good barriers, and were thus far stronger and much more secure. The Greeks meanwhile came on to the attack so frequently that they gave them no rest, and those of the host drove them back with great force; and every time that the Greeks issued forth they lost heavily.

One day the Burgundians were on guard, and the Greeks made an attack upon them, with part of the best forces that they had. And the Burgundians ran upon the Greeks and drove them in very fiercely, and followed so close to the gate that stones of great weight were hurled upon them. There was taken one of the best Greeks of the city, whose name was Constantine Lascaris; William of Neuilly took him all mounted upon his horse. And there did William of Champlitte have his arm broken with a stone, and great pity it was, for he was very brave and very valiant.

I cannot tell you of all the good strokes that were there stricken, nor of all the wounded, nor all the dead. But before the fight was over, there came into it a knight of the following of Henry, the brother of Count Baldwin of Flanders and Hainault, and his name was Eustace of the Marchais; and he was armed only in padded vest and steel cap, with his shield at his neck; and he did so well in the fray that he won to himself great honour. Few were the days on which no sorties were made; but I cannot tell you of them all. So hardly did they hold us, that we could not sleep, nor rest, nor eat, save in arms.

Yet another sortie was made from a gate further up; and there again did the Greeks lose heavily. And there a knight was slain, whose name was William of the Gi; and there Matthew of Walincourt did right well, and lost his horse, which was killed at the drawbridge of the gate; and many others who were in that fight did right well. From this gate, which was beyond the palace of Blachernæ, the Greeks issued most frequently, and there Peter of Bracieux gat himself more honour than any, because he was quartered the nearest, and so came most often into the fray.

Assault of the City

Thus their peril and toil lasted for nearly ten days, until, on a Thursday morning (17th July 1203) all things were ready for the assault, and the ladders in trim; the Venetians also had made them ready by sea. The order of the assault was so devised, that of the seven divisions, three were to guard the camp outside the city, and other four to give the assault.

The Marquis Boniface of Montferrat guarded the camp towards the fields, with the division of the Burgundians, the division of the men of Champagne, and Matthew of Montmorency. Count Baldwin of Flanders and Hainault went to the assault with his people, and Henry his brother; and Count Lewis of Blois and Chartres, and Count Hugh of St. Paul, and those who held with them, went also to the assault.

They planted two ladders at a barbican near the sea; and the wall was well defended by Englishmen and Danes; and the attack was stiff and good and fierce. By main strength certain knights and two sergeants got up the ladders and made themselves masters of the wall; and at least fifteen got upon the wall, and fought there, hand to hand, with axes and swords, and those within redoubled their efforts, and cast them out in very ugly sort, keeping two as prisoners.

And those of our people who had been taken were led before the Emperor Alexius; much was he pleased thereat. Thus .did the assault leave matters on the side of the French. Many were wounded and many had their bones broken, so that the barons were very wroth.

Meanwhile the Doge of Venice had not forgotten to do his part, but had ranged his ships and transports and vessels in line, and that line was well three crossbow-shots in length; and the Venetians began to draw near to the part of the shore that lay under the walls and the towers. Then might you have seen the mangonels shooting from the ships and transports, and the crossbow bolts flying, and the bows letting fly their arrows deftly and well; and those within defending the walls and towers very fiercely; and the ladders on the ships coming so near that in many places swords and lances crossed; and the tumult and noise were so great that it seemed as if the very earth and sea were melting together. And be it known to you that the galleys did not dare to come to the shore.

Capture of Twenty-Five Towers

Now may you hear of a strange deed of prowess; for the Doge of Venice, who was an old man, and saw naught (seeing he was blind), stood, fully armed, on the prow of his galley, and had the standard of St. Mark before him; and he cried to his people to put him on land, or else that he would do justice upon their bodies with his hands. And so they did, for the galley was run aground, and they leapt therefrom, and bore the standard of St. Mark before him on to the land.

And when the Venetians saw the standard of St. Mark on land, and the galley of their lord touching ground before them, each held himself for shamed, and they all gat to the land; and those in the transports leapt forth, and landed; and those in the big ships got into barges, and made for the shore, each and all as best they could, Then might you have seen an assault, great and marvellous; and to this bears witness Geoffry of Villehardouin, who makes this book, that more than forty people told him for sooth that they saw the standard of St. Mark of Venice at the top of one of the towers, and that no man knew who bore it thither.

Now hear of a strange miracle: those who are within the city fly and abandon the walls, and the Venetians enter in, each as fast and as best he can, and seize twenty-five of the towers, and man them with their people. And the Doge takes a boat, and sends messengers to the barons of the host to tell them that he has taken twenty-five towers, and that they may know for sooth that such towers cannot be retaken. The barons are so overjoyed that they cannot believe their ears; and the Venetians begin to send to the host in boats the horses and palfreys they have taken.

When the Emperor Alexius saw that our people had thus entered into the city, he sent his people against them in such numbers that our people saw they would be unable to endure the onset. So they set fire to the buildings between them and the Greeks; and the wind blew from our side, and the fire began to wax so great that the Greeks could not see our people, who retired to the towers they had seized and conquered.

The Emperor Alexius Comes Out for Battle, but Retires Without Attacking

Then the Emperor Alexius issued from the city, with all his forces, by other gates which were at least a league from the camp; and so many began to issue forth that it seemed as if the whole world were there assembled. The emperor marshalled his troops in the plain, and they rode towards the camp; and when our Frenchmen saw them coming, they ran to arms from all sides.

On that day Henry, the brother of Count Baldwin and Flanders, was mounting guard over the engines of war before the gate of Blachernæ, together with Matthew of Walincourt, and Baldwin of Beauvoir, and their followers. Against their encampment the Emperor Alexius had made ready a great number of his people, who were to issue by three gates, while he himself should fall upon the host from another side.

Then the six divisions issued from our camp as had been devised, and were marshalled in ranks before the palisades: the sergeants and squires on foot behind the horses, and the archers and crossbowmen in front. And there was a division of the knights on foot, for we had at least two hundred who were without horses. Thus they stood still before the palisades. And this showed great good sense, for if they had moved to the attack, the numbers of the enemy were such that they must have been overwhelmed and, (as it were,) drowned among them.

It seemed as if the whole plain was covered with troops, and they advanced slowly and in order. Well might we appear in perilous case, for we had but six divisions, while the Greeks had full forty, and there was not one of their divisions but was larger than any of ours. But ours were ordered in such sort that none could attack them save in front. And the Emperor Alexius rode so far forward that either side could shoot at the other. And when the Doge of Venice heard this, he made his people come forth, and leave the towers they had taken, and said he would live or die with the pilgrims. So he came to the camp, and was himself the first to land, and brought with him such of his people as he could.

Thus, for a long space, the armies of the pilgrims and of the Greeks stood one against the other; for the Greeks did not dare to throw themselves upon our ranks, and our people would not move from their palisades. And when the Emperor Alexius saw this, he began to withdraw his people, and when he had rallied them, he turned back. And seeing this, the host of the pilgrims began to march towards him with slow steps, and the Greek troops began to move backwards, and retreated to a palace called Philopas.

And be it known to you, that never did God save any people from such peril as He saved the host that day; and be it known to you further that there was none in the host so hardy but he had great joy thereof. Thus did the battle remain for that day. As it pleased God nothing further was done. The Emperor Alexius returned to the city, and those of the host to their quarters—the latter taking off their armour, for they were weary and overwrought; and they ate and drank little, seeing that their store of food was but scanty.

ALEXIUS ABANDONS CONSTANTINOPLE—HIS BROTHER
ISAAC IS REPLACED ON THE THRONE—THE CRUSADERS

Send Him a Message

Now listen to the miracles of our Lord—how gracious are they whithersoever it pleases Him to perform them! That very night the Emperor Alexius of Constantinople took of his treasure as much as he could carry, and took with him as many of his people as would go, and so fled and abandoned the city. And those of the city remained astonied, and they drew to the prison in which lay the Emperor Isaac, whose eyes had been put out. Him they clothed imperially, and bore to the great palace of Blachernæ, and seated on a high throne; and there they did to him obeisance as their lord. Then they took messengers, by the advice of the Emperor Isaac, and sent them to the host, to apprise the son of the Emperor Isaac, and the barons, that the Emperor Alexius had fled, and that they had again raised up the Emperor Isaac as emperor.

When the young man knew of this he summoned the Marquis Boniface of Montferrat, and the marquis summoned the barons throughout the host. And when they were met in the pavilion of the Emperor Isaac's son, he told them the news. And when they heard it, their joy was such as cannot be uttered, for never was greater joy in all this world. And greatly and most devoutly was our Lord praised by all, in that He had succoured them within so short a term, and exalted them so high from such a low estate. And therefore well may one say: "Him whom God will help can no man injure."

Then the day began to dawn, and the host to put on their armour; and all gat them to their arms throughout the host, because they did not greatly trust the Greeks. And messengers began to come out from the city, two or three together, and told the same tale.

The barons and counts, and the Doge of Venice had agreed to send envoys into the city, to know how matters really stood; and, if that was true which had been reported, to demand of the father that he should ratify the covenants made by the son; and, if he would not, to declare that they on their part should not suffer the son to enter into the city. So envoys were chosen: one was Matthew of Montmorency, and Geoffry the Marshal of Champagne was the other, and two Venetians on the part of the Doge of Venice.

The envoys were conducted to the gate, and the gate was opened to them, and they dismounted from their horses. The Greeks had set Englishmen and Danes, with their axes, at the gate and right up to the palace of Blachernæ. Thus were the envoys conducted to the great palace.

There they found the Emperor Isaac, so richly clad that you would seek in vain throughout the world for a man more richly apparelled than he, and by his side the empress, his wife, a most fair lady, the daughter of the King of Hungary; and of great men and great ladies there were so many, that you could not stir foot for the press, and the ladies were so richly adorned that richer adornment might not be. And all those who, the day before, had been against the emperor were, on that day, subject in everything to his good pleasure.

The Emperor Isaac Ratifies the Covenants Entered into by His Son

The envoys came before the Emperor Isaac, and the emperor and all those about him did them great honour. And the envoys said that they desired to speak to him privily, on the part of his son, and of the barons of the host. And he rose and entered into a chamber, and took with him only the empress, and his chancellor, and his dragoman (interpreter) and the four envoys. By consent of the other envoys, Geoffry of Villehardouin, the Marshal of Champagne, acted as spokesman, and he said to the Emperor Isaac:

"Sire, thou seest the service we have rendered to thy son, and how we have kept our covenants with him. But he cannot come hither till he has given us surety for the covenants he has made with us. And he asks of thee, as thy son, to confirm those covenants in the same form, and the same manner, that he has done."

"What covenants are they?" said the emperor.

"They are such as we shall tell you;" replied the envoys: "In the first place to put the whole empire of Roumania in obedience to Rome, from which it has been separated this long while; further to give 200,000 *marks* of silver to those of the host, with food for one year for small and great; to send 10,000 men, horse and foot—as many on foot as we shall devise and as many mounted—in his own ships, and at his own charges, to the land of Babylon, and keep them there for a year; and during his lifetime to keep, at his own charges, five hundred knights in the land oversea, so that they may guard that land. Such is the covenant that your son made with us, and it was confirmed by oath, and charters with seals appended, and by King Philip of Germany who has your daughter to wife. This covenant we desire you to confirm."

"*Certes*," said the emperor, "this covenant is very onerous, and I do not see how effect can be given to it; nevertheless, you have done us such service, both to my son and to myself, that if we bestowed upon you the whole empire, you would have deserved it well."

Many words were then spoken in this sense and that, but, in the end, the father confirmed the covenants, as his son had confirmed them, by oath and by charters with gold seals appended. These charters were delivered to the envoys. Then they took their leave of the Emperor Isaac, and went back to the host, and told the barons that they had fulfilled their mission.

Entry of the Crusaders Into Constantinople—Coronation of the Young Alexius

Then did the barons mount their horses, and led the young man, with great rejoicings, into the city, to his father; and the Greeks opened the gate to him, and received him with very much rejoicing and great feasting. The joy of the father and of the son was very great, because of a long time they had not seen one another, and because, by God's help and that of the pilgrims, they had passed from so great poverty and ruin to such high estate. Therefore the joy was great inside Constantinople; and also without, among the host of the pilgrims, because of the honour and victory that God had given them.

And on the morrow the emperor and his son also besought the counts and the barons, for God's sake, to go and quarter themselves on the other side of the straits, toward Estanor and Galatas; for, if they quartered themselves in the city, it was to be feared that quarrels would ensue between them and the Greeks, and it might well chance that the city would be destroyed. And the counts and barons said that they had already served him in so many ways that they would not now refuse any request of his. So they went and quartered themselves on the other side, and sojourned there in peace and quiet, and with great store of good provisions.

Now you must know that many of those in the host went to see Constantinople, and the rich palaces and great churches, of which there were many, and all the great wealth of the city—for never was there city that possessed so much. Of relics it does not behove me to speak, for at that day there were as many there as in all the rest of the world. Thus did the Greeks and French live in good fellowship in all things, both as regards trafficking and other matters.

By common consent of Franks and Greeks, it was settled that the new emperor should be crowned on the feast of our Lord St. Peter (1st August 1203). So was it settled, and so it was done. He was crowned full worthily and with honour according to the use for Greek emperors at that time. Afterwards he began to pay the moneys due to the host; and such moneys were divided among the host, and each repaid what had been advanced in Venice for his passage.

Alexius Begs the Crusaders to Prolong Their Stay

The new emperor went oft to see the barons in the camp, and did them great honour, as much as he could; and this was but fitting, seeing that they had served him right well. And one day he came to the camp, to see the barons privily in the quarters of Count Baldwin of Hainault and Flanders. Thither were summoned the Doge of Venice, and the great barons, and he spoke to them and said:

> Lords, I am emperor by God's grace and yours, and you have done me the highest service that ever yet was done by any people to Christian man. Now be it known to you that there are folk enough who show me a fair seeming, and yet love me not; and the Greeks are full of despite because it is by your help that I have entered into my inheritance.
>
> Now the term of your departure is nigh, and your fellowship with the Venetians is timed only to last till the feast of St. Michael. And within so short a term I cannot fulfil our covenant. Be it known to you therefore, that, if you abandon me, the Greeks hate me because of you: I shall lose my land, and they will kill me.
>
> But now do this thing that I ask of you: remain here till March, and I will entertain your ships for one year from the feast of St. Michael, and bear the cost of the Venetians, and will give you such things as you may stand in need of till Easter. And within that term I shall have placed my land in such case that I cannot lose it again; and your covenant will be fulfilled, for I shall have paid such moneys as are due to you, obtaining them from all my lands; and I shall be ready also with ships either to go with you myself, or to send others, as I have covenanted; and you will have the summer from end to end in which to carry on the war against the Saracens.

The barons thereupon said they would consult together apart; knowing full well that what the young man said was sooth, and that it would be better, both for the emperor and for themselves, to consent unto him. But they replied that they could not so consent save with the common agreement of the host, and that they would therefore lay the matter before the host, and then give such answer as might be devised.

So the Emperor Alexius departed from them, and went back to Constantinople. And they remained in the camp and assembled a parliament the next day. To this parliament were summoned all the barons and the chieftains of the host, and of the knights the greater part; and in their hearing were repeated all the words that the emperor had spoken.

Debate Among the Crusaders—Death of Matthew of Montmorency

Then was there much discord in the host, as had been ofttimes before on the part of those who wished that the host should break up; for to them it seemed to be holding together too long. And the party that had raised the discord at Corfu reminded the others of their oaths, and said: "Give us ships as you swore to us, for we purpose to go to Syria."

And the others cried to them for pity and said: "Lords, for God's sake, let us not bring to naught the great honour that God has given us. If we go to Syria at this present, we shall come thither at the beginning of winter and so not be able to make war, and the Lord's work will thus remain undone. But if we wait till March, we shall leave this emperor in good estate, and go hence rich in goods and in food. Thus shall we go to Syria, and over-run the land of Babylon. And the fleet will remain with us till Michaelmas, yes, and onwards from Michaelmas to Easter, seeing it will be unable to leave us because of the winter. So shall the land oversea fall into our hands."

Those who wished the host to be broken up, cared not for reasons good or bad so long as the host fell to pieces. But those who wished to keep the host together, wrought so effectually, with the help of God, that in the end the Venetians made a new covenant to maintain the fleet for a year, reckoning from Michaelmas, the Emperor Alexius paying them for so doing; and the pilgrims on their side, made a new covenant to remain in the same fellowship as theretofore, and for the same term. Thus were peace and concord established in the host.

Then there befell a very great mischance in the host; for Matthew of Montmorency, who was one of the best knights in the kingdom of France, and of the most prized and most honoured, took to his bed for sickness, and his sickness so increased upon him that he died. And much dole was made for him, for great was the loss—one of the greatest that had befallen the host by any man's death. He was buried in a church of my Lord St. John, of the Hospital of Jerusalem.

Progress of the Young Alexius Through the Empire

Afterwards, by the advice of the Greeks and the French" the Emperor Alexius issued from Constantinople, with a very great company, purposing to quiet the empire and subject it to his will. With him went a great part of the barons; and the others remained to guard the camp. The Marquis Boniface of Montferrat went with him, and Count Hugh of St. Paul, and Henry, brother to Count Baldwin of Flanders and Hainault, and James of Avesnes, and William of Champlitte, and Hugh of Colemi, and many others whom the book does not here mention by name. In the camp remained Count Baldwin of Hainault and Flanders, and Count Lewis of Blois and Chartres, and the greater part of the pilgrims of lesser note.

And you must know that during this progress all the Greeks, on either side of the straits, came to the Emperor Alexius, to do his will and commandment, and did him fealty and homage as to their lord—all except John, who was King of Wallachia and Bulgaria. This John was a Wallachian, who had rebelled against his father and uncle, and had warred against them for twenty years, and had won from them so much land that he had became a very wealthy king. And be it known to you, that of the land lying on the west side of the Straits of St. George, he had conquered very nearly the half. This John did not come to do the will of the emperor, nor to submit himself to him.

Conflict Between the Greeks and Latins in Constantinople—Burning of the City

While the Emperor Alexius was away on this progress, there befell a very grievous misadventure; for a conflict .arose between the Greeks and the Latins who inhabited Constantinople, and of these last there were many. And certain people—who they were I know not—out of malice, set fire to the city; and the fire waxed so great and horrible that no man could put it out or abate it. And when the barons of the host, who were quartered on the other side of the port, saw this, they were sore grieved and filled with pity—seeing the great churches and the rich palaces melting and falling in, and the great streets filled with merchandise burning in the flames; but they could do nothing.

Thus did the fire prevail, and win across the port, even to the densest part of the city, and to the sea on the other side, quite near to the church of St. Sophia. It lasted two days and two nights, nor could it be put out by the hand of man. And the front of the fire, as it went flaming, was well over half a league broad. What was the damage then done, what the possessions and riches swallowed up, could no man tell—nor what the number of men and women and children who perished—for many were burned.

All the Latins, to whatever land they might belong, who were lodged in Constantinople, dared no longer to remain therein; but they took their wives and their children, and such of their possessions as they could save from the fire, and entered into boats and vessels, and passed over the port and came to the camp of the pilgrims.

Nor were they few in number, for there were of them some fifteen thousand, small and great; and afterwards it proved to be of advantage to the pilgrims that these should have crossed over to them. Thus was there division between the Greeks and the Franks; nor were they ever again as much at one as they had been before, for neither side knew on whom to cast the blame for the fire; and this rankled in men's hearts upon either side.

At that time did a tiling befall whereby the barons and those of the host were greatly saddened; for the Abbot of Laos died, who was a holy man and a worthy, and had wished well to the host. He was a monk of the order of the Cistercians.

THE YOUNG ALEXIUS RETURNS TO CONSTANTINOPLE— HE FAILS IN HIS PROMISES TO THE CRUSADERS

The Emperor Alexius remained for a long time on progress, till St. Martin's Day, and then he returned to Constantinople. Great was the joy at his home-coming, and the Greeks and ladies of Constantinople went out to meet their friends in great cavalcades, and the pilgrims went out to meet their friends, and had great joy of them. So did the emperor re-enter Constantinople and the palace of Blachernæ; and the Marquis of Montferrat and the other barons returned to the camp.

The emperor, who had managed his affairs right well and thought he had now the upper hand, was filled with arrogance towards the barons and those who had done so much for him, and never came to see them in the camp, as he had done aforetime. And they sent to him and begged him to pay them the moneys due, as he had covenanted. But he led them on from delay to delay, making them, at one time and another, payments small and poor; and in the end the payments ceased and came to naught.

The Marquis Boniface of Montferrat, who had done more for him than any other, and stood better in his regard, went to him oftentimes, and showed him what great services the Crusaders had rendered him, and that greater services had never been rendered to anyone. And the emperor still entertained them with delays, and never carried out such things as he had promised, so that at last they saw and knew clearly that his intent was wholly evil.

Then the barons of the host held a parliament with the Doge of Venice, and they said that they now knew that the emperor would fulfil no covenant, nor ever speak sooth to them; and they decided to send good envoys to demand the fulfilment of their covenant, and to show what services they had done him; and if he would now do what was required) they were to be satisfied; but, if not, they were to defy him, and fight well might he rest assured that the barons would. by all means recover their due.

THE CRUSADERS DEFY THE EMPERORS

For this embassage were chosen Canon of Béthune and Geoffry of Villehardouin, the Marshal of Champagne, and Miles the Brabant of Provins; and the Doge also sent three chief men of his council. So these envoys mounted their horses, and, with swords girt, rode together till they came to the palace of Blachernæ. And be it known to you that, by reason of the treachery of the Greeks, they went in great peril, and on a hard adventure.

They dismounted at the gate and entered the palace, and found the Emperor Alexius and the Emperor Isaac seated on, two thrones, side by side. And near them was seated the empress, who was the wife of the father, and stepmother of the son, and sister to the King of Hungary—a lady both fair and good. And there were with them a great company of people of note and rank, so that well did the court seem the court of a rich and mighty prince.

By desire of the other envoys Conon of Béthune, who was very wise and eloquent of speech, acted as spokesman:

> Sire, we have come to thee on the part of the barons of the host and of the Doge of Venice. They would put thee in mind of the great service they have done to thee—a service known to the people and manifest to all men. Thou hast sworn, thou and thy father, to fulfil the promised covenants, and, they have your

charters in hand. But you have not fulfilled those covenants well, as you should have done.

Many times have they called upon you to do so, and now again we call upon you, in the presence of all your barons, to fulfil the covenants that are between you and them. Should you do so, it shall be well. If not, be it known to you that from this day forth they will not hold you as lord or friend, but well endeavour to obtain their due by all the means in their power.

And of this they now give you warning, seeing that they would not injure you, nor anyone, without first defiance given; for never have they acted treacherously, nor in their land is it customary to do so. You have heard what we have said. It is for you to take counsel thereon according to your pleasure.

Much were the Greeks amazed and greatly outraged by this open defiance; and they said that never had anyone been so hardy as to dare defy the Emperor of Constantinople in his own hall. Very evil were the looks now cast on the envoys by the Emperor Alexius and by all the Greeks, who aforetime were wont to regard them very favourably.

Great was the tumult there within, and the envoys turned about and came to the gate and mounted their horses. When they got outside the gate, there was not one of them but felt glad at heart; nor is that to be marvelled at, for they had escaped from very great peril, and it held to very little that they were not all killed or taken. So they returned to the camp, and told the barons how they had fared.

The War Begins—The Greeks Endeavour To Set Fire To The Fleet Of The Crusaders

Thus did the war begin; and each side did to the other as much harm as they could, by sea and by land. The Franks and the Greeks fought often; but never did they fight, let God be praised therefor! that the Greeks did not lose more than the Franks. So the war lasted a long space, till the heart of the winter.

Then the Greeks bethought themselves of a very great device, for they took seven large ships, and filled them full of big logs, and shavings, and tow, and resin, and barrels, and then waited until such time as the wind should blow strongly from their side of the straits.

And one night, at midnight, they set fire to the ships, and unfurled their sails to the wind. And the flames blazed up high, so that it seemed as if the whole world were a-fire. Thus did the burning ships come towards the fleet of the pilgrims; and a great cry arose in the host, and all sprang to arms on every side. The Venetians ran to their ships, and so did all those who had ships in possession, and they began to draw them away out of the flames very vigorously.

And to this bears witness Geoffry the Marshal of Champagne, who dictates this work, that never did people help themselves better at sea than the Venetians did that night; for the): sprang into the galleys and boats belonging to the ships, and seized upon the fire ships, all burning as they were, with hooks, and dragged them by main force before their enemies, outside the port, and set them into the current of the straits, and left them to go burning down the straits. So many of the Greeks had come down to the shore that they were without end and innumerable, and their cries were so great that it seemed as if the earth and sea would melt together. They got into barges and boats, and shot at those on our side who were battling with the flames, so that some were wounded.

All the knights of the host, as soon as they heard the clam our, armed themselves; and the battalions marched out into the plain, each according to the order in which they had been quartered, for they feared lest the Greeks should also attack them on land.

They endured thus in labour and anguish till daylight; but by God's help those on our side lost nothing, save a Pisan ship, which was full of merchandise, and was burned with fire. Deadly was the peril in which we stood that night, for if the fleet had been consumed, all would have been lost, and we should never have been able to get away by land or sea. Such was the guerdon which the Emperor Alexius would have bestowed upon us in return for our services.

Mourzuphles Usurps the Empire—Isaac Dies, and the Young Alexius is Strangled

Then the Greeks, being thus embroiled with the Franks, saw that there was no hope of peace; so they privily took; counsel together to betray their lord. Now there was a Greek who stood higher in his favour than all others, and lad done more to make him embroil himself with the Franks than any other. This Greek was named Mourzuphles.

With the advice and consent of the others, one night towards midnight, when the Emperor Alexius was asleep in his chamber, those who ought to have been guarding him—and specially Mourzuphles—took him in his bed and threw urn into a dungeon in prison. Then Mourzuphles assumed the scarlet buskins with the help and by the counsel of the other Greeks (January 1204). So he made himself emperor. Afterwards they crowned him at St. Sophia. Now see if ever people were guilty of such horrible treachery!

When the Emperor Isaac heard that his son was taken and Mourzuphles crowned, great fear came upon him, and he fell into a sickness that lasted no long time. So he died. And the Emperor Mourzuphles caused the son, whom he had in prison, to be poisoned two or three times; but it did not please God that he should thus die. Afterwards the emperor went and strangled him, and when he had strangled him, he caused it to be reported everywhere that he had died a natural death, and had him mourned for, and buried honourably and as an emperor, and made great show of grief.

But murder cannot be hid. Soon was it clearly known. both to the Greeks and to the French, that this murder had been committed, as has just been told to you. Then did the barons of the host and the Doge of Venice assemble in parliament, and with them met the bishops and the clergy And all the clergy, including those who had powers from the Pope, showed to the barons and to the pilgrims that any one guilty of such a murder had no right to hold lands, and that those who consented thereto were abettors of the murder; and beyond all this, that the Greeks had withdrawn themselves from obedience to Rome.

"Wherefore we tell you," said the clergy, "that this war is lawful and just, and that if you have a right intention in conquering this land, to bring it into the Roman obedience, all those who die after confession shall have part in the indulgence granted by the Pope." And you must know that by this the barons and pilgrims were greatly comforted.

THE CRUSADERS CONTINUE THE WAR— DEFEAT OF MOURZUPHLES

Dire was the war between the Franks and the Greeks, for it abated not, but rather increased and waxed fiercer, so that few were the days on which there was not fighting by sea or land. Then Henry, the brother of Count Baldwin of Flanders rode forth, and took with him a great part of the good men in the host. With him went James of Avesnes, an(Baldwin of Beauvoir, Odo of Champagne of Champlitte William his brother, and the people of their country. They started at vesper time and rode all night, and on the morrow, when it was full day, they came to a good city, called Phile, and took it; and they had great gain, beasts, and prisoners, and clothing, and food, which they sent in boats down the straits to the camp, for the city lies on the sea of Russia.

So they sojourned two days in that city, with food in great plenty, enough and to spare. The third day they departed with the beasts and the booty, and rode back towards the camp. Now the Emperor Mourzuphles heard tell how they had issued from the camp, and he left Constantinople by night, with a great part of his people, and set himself in ambush at a place by which they must needs pass.

And he watched them pass with their beasts and their booty, each division, the one after the other, till it came to the rear- guard. The rear-guard was under the command of Henry, the brother of Count Baldwin of Flanders, and formed of his people, and the Emperor Mourzuphles fell upon them at the entrance to a wood; whereupon they turned against him. Very fiercely did the battle rage there.

By God's help the Emperor Mourzuphles was discomfited, and came near to being taken captive; and he lost his Imperial banner and an Eikon that was borne before him, in which he and the other Greeks had great confidence—it was an Eikon that figured our Lady—and he lost at least twenty knights of the best people that he had. Thus was discomfited the Emperor Mourzuphles, as you have just heard; and fiercely did the war rage between him and the Franks; and by this time a great part of the winter had already passed, I and it was near Candlemas (2nd February 1204), and Lent was approaching.

Of the Pilgrims Who had Gone to Syria

Now we will leave off speaking of the host before Contantinople, and speak of those who sailed from other ports than Venice, and of the ships of Flanders that had sojourned during the winter at Marseilles, and had all gone over in the summer to the land of Syria; and these were far more in number than the host before Constantinople. Listen now, and you shall hear what a great mischance it was that they had not joined themselves to the host, for in that case would Christendom have been for ever exalted. But because of their sins, God would not so have it, for some died of the sickness of the land, and some turned back to their own homes. Nor did they perform any great deeds, or achieve aught of good, in the land oversea.

And there started also a company of very good men to go to Antioch, to join Boemond, prince of Antioch and Count of Tripoli, who was at war with King Leon, the lord of the Armenians. This company was going to the prince to be in his pay; and the Turks of the land knew of it, and made an ambuscade there where the men of the company needs must pass. And they came thither, and fought, and the Franks were discomfited, so that not one escaped that was not killed or taken.

There were slain Villain of Neuilly, who was one of the best knights in the world, and Giles of Trasegnies, and many others; and were taken Bernard of Moreuil, and Renaud of Dampierre, and John of Villers, and William of Neuilly. And you must know that eighty knights were in this company, and everyone was either killed or taken. And well does this book bear witness, that of those who avoided the host of Venice, there was not one but suffered harm or shame. He therefore must be accounted wise who holds to the better course.

Agreement Between the Franks and Venetians Before Attacking Constantinople

Now let us leave speaking of those who avoided the host, and speak of those before Constantinople. Well had these prepared all their engines, and mounted their petraries, and mangonels on the ships and on the transports, and got ready all such engines of war as are needful for the taking of a city, and raised ladders from the yards and masts of the vessels, so high that they were a marvel to behold.[9]

And when the Greeks saw this, they began, on their side, to strengthen the defences of the city which was enclosed with high walls and high towers. Nor was any tower so high that they did not raise thereon two or three stages of wood to heighten it still more. Never was city so well fortified. Thus did the Greeks and the Franks bestir themselves on the one side and the other during the greater part of Lent.

Then those of the host spoke together, and took counsel what they should do. Much was advanced this way and that, but in the end, they devised that if God granted them entry into the city by force, all the booty taken ,vas to be brought together, and fittingly distributed; and further, if the city fell into their power, six men should b taken from among the Franks, and six from among the Venetians, and these twelve should swear, on holy relics, to elect as emperor the man who, as they deemed, would rule with most profit to the land.

And whosoever was thus elected emperor, would have one quarter of whatever was captured, whether within the city or without, and moreover would possess the palace of Bucoleon and that of Blachernæ; and the remaining three parts would be divided into two, and

---

9. This passage is obscure in the original.

one of the halves awarded to the Venetians and the other to those of the host.

And there should be taken twelve of the wisest and most experienced men among the host of the pilgrims, and twelve among the Venetians, and those twenty-four would divide fiefs and honours, and appoint the service to be done therefor to the emperor.

This covenant was made sure and sworn to on the one side and the other by the Franks and the Venetians; with provision that at the end of March, a year thence, any who so desired might depart hence and go their way, but that those who remained in the land would be held to the service of the emperor in such manner as might be ordained. Thus was the covenant devised and made sure; and such as should not observe it were excommunicated by the clergy.

Attack of the Crusaders Repulsed—They Make Ready for Another Assault

The fleet was very well prepared and armed, and provisions were got together for the pilgrims. On the Thursday after mid-Lent (8th April 1204), all entered into the vessels, and put their horses into the transports. Each division had its own ships, and all were ranged side by side; and the ships were separated from the galleys and transports. A marvellous sight it was to see; and well does this book bear witness that the attack, as it had been devised, extended over full half a French league.

On the Friday morning the ships and the galleys and the other vessels drew near to the city in due order, and then began an assault most fell and fierce. In many places the the pilgrims landed and went up to the walls, and in many places the scaling ladders on the ships approached so close, that those on the towers and on the walls and those on the ladders crossed lances, hand to hand. Thus lasted the assault, in more than a hundred places, very fierce, and very dour, and very proud, till near upon the hour of nones.

But, for our sins, the pilgrims were repulsed in that assault, and those who had landed from the galleys and transports were driven back into them by main force. And you I must know that on that day those of the host lost more than the Greeks, and much were the Greeks rejoiced thereat. And some there were who drew back from the assault, with the ships in which they were. And some remained with their ships at anchor so near to the city that from either side they shot at one another with petraries and mangonels.

Then, at vesper time, those of the host and the Doge of Venice called together a parliament, and assembled in a church on the other side of the straits—on the side where they had been quartered. There were many opinions given and discussed; and much were those of the host moved for the mischief that had that day befallen them. And many advised that they should attack the city on another side—the side where it was not so well fortified.

But the Venetians, who had fuller knowledge of the sea, said that if they went to that other side, the current would carry them down the straits, and that they would be unable to stop their ships. And you must know that there were those who would have been well pleased if the current had borne them down the straits, or the wind, they cared not whither, so long as they left that land behind, and went on their way. Nor is this to be wondered at, for they were in sore peril.

Enough was there spoken, this way and in that; but the conclusion of their deliberation was this: that they would repair and refit on the following day, which was Saturday, and during the whole of Sunday, and that on the Monday they would return to the assault; and they devised further that the ships that carried the scaling ladders should be bound together, two and two, so that two ships should be in case to attack one tower; for they had perceived that day how only one ship had attacked each tower, and that this had been too heavy a task for the ship, seeing that those in the tower were more in number than those on the ladder. For this reason was it well seen that two ships would attack each tower with greater effect than one. As had been settled, so was it done, and they waited thus during the Saturday and Sunday.

The Crusaders Take a Part of the City

Before the assault the Emperor Mourzuphles had come to encamp, with all his power, in an open space, and had there pitched his scarlet tents. Thus matters remained till the Monday morning, when those on the ships, transports, and galleys were all armed. And those of the city stood in much less fear of them than they did at the beginning, and were in such good spirits that on the walls and towers you could see nothing but people. Then began an assault proud and marvellous, and every ship went straight before it to the attack. The noise of the battle was so great that it seemed to rend the earth.

Thus did the assault last for a long while, till our Lord raised a wind called Boreas which drove the ships and vessels further up on to the shore. And two ships that were bound together, of which the one was called the *Pilgrim* and the other the *Paradise*, approached so near to a tower, the one on the one side and the other on the other—so as God and the wind drove them—that the ladder of the *Pilgrim* joined on to the tower.

Immediately a Venetian, and a knight of France, whose name was Andrew of Urboise, entered into the tower, and other people began to enter after them, and those in the tower were discomfited and fled.

(Note

I should like to quote here another feat of arms related by Robert of Clari, one of those feats that serve to explain how the Crusaders obtained mastery—the mastery of perfect fearlessness—over the Greeks. Robert of Clari, then, relates how a small body of the besiegers, ten knights and nine sergeants, had come before a postern which had been newly bricked up.

> Now there was there a clerk, Aleaume of Clari by name, who had shown his courage whenever there was need, and was always first in any assault at which he might be present; and when the tower of Galata was taken, this same clerk had performed more deeds of prowess with his body, man for man, than anyone in the host, save only the Lord Peter of Bracuel; for the Lord Peter it was who surpassed all others, whether of high or low degree, so that there was none other that performed such feats of arms, or acts of prowess with his body, as the Lord Peter of Bracuel.
>
> So when they came to the postern they began to hew and pick at it very hardily; but the bolts flew at them so thick, and so many stones were hurled at them from the wall, that it seemed as if they would be buried beneath the stones—such was the mass of quarries and stones thrown from above.
>
> And those who were below held up targes and shields to cover those who were picking and hewing underneath; and those above threw down pots of boiling pitch, and Greek fire, and large rocks, so that it was one of God's miracles that the assailants were not utterly confounded; for my Lord Peter and his men suffered more than enough of blows and grievous danger. However, so did they hack at the postern, both above and below, with their axes and good swords, that they made a great hole therein; and when the postern was broken through, they all swarmed to the aperture, but saw so many people above and

below, that it seemed as if half the world were there, and they dared not be so bold as to enter.

Now when Aleaume, the clerk, saw that no one dared to go in, he sprang forward, and said that go in he would. And there was there present a knight, a brother to the clerk (the knight's name was Robert of Clari), who forbade him, and said he should not go in. And the clerk said he would, and scrambled in on his hands and feet. And when the knight saw this, he took hold upon him, by the foot, and began to drag him back.

But in his brother's despite, and whether his brother would or not, the clerk went in. And when he was within, many were the Greeks who ran upon him, and those on the walls cast big stones upon him. And the clerk drew his knife, and ran at them; and he drave them before him as if they had been cattle, and cried to those who were without, to the Lord Peter of Amiens and his folk, 'Sire, come in boldly, I see that they are falling back discomfited and flying.'

When my Lord Peter heard this, he and his people who were without, they entered in; and there were no more than ten knights with him, but there were some sixty sergeants, and they were all on foot. And when those who were on the wall at that place saw them, they had such fear that they did not dare to remain there, but avoided a great space on the wall, and fled helter-skelter.

Now the Emperor Mourzuphles, the traitor, was nearby, at less than a stone's throw of distance, and he caused the silver horns to be sounded, and the cymbals, and a great noise to be made. And when he saw my Lord Peter, and his people, who had entered in on foot, he made a great show of falling upon them, and spurring forward, came about half-way to where they stood. But my Lord Peter, when he saw him coming, began to encourage his people, and to say: 'Now, Lord God, grant that we may do well, and the battle is ours. Here comes the emperor! Let no one dare to think of retreat, but each bethink himself to do well.' Then Mourzuphles, seeing that they would in no wise give way, stayed where he was, and then turned back to his tents.

After this, according to Robert of Clari, Lord Peter's men break open a gate, and the Crusaders enter into the city. See *Li Estoires de chiaus qui conquisent Constantinoble, de Robert de Clari en aminois, chevalier,* pp. 60-62. The volume in the British Museum is undated, and there is this note in the catalogue, "No more printed." The volume itself is noteless, though there are printed marks here and there which would suggest that notes were intended. The Chronicle of Robert of Clari will also be found in Hopf's *Chroniques Gréco-romanes inédites ou peu connues*, etc., pp. 1-85. Berlin, 1873.)

When the knights see this, who are in the transports, they land, and raise their ladders against the wall, and scale the top of the wall by main force, and so take four of the towers. And all begin to leap out of the ships and transports and galleys, helter-skelter, each as best he can; and they break in some three of the gates and enter in; and they draw the horses out of the transports; and the knights mount and ride straight to the quarters of the Emperor Mourzuphles. He had his battalions arrayed before his tents, and when his men see the mounted knights coming, they lose heart and fly; and so goes the emperor flying through the streets to the castle of Bucoleon.

Then might you have seen the Greeks beaten down; and horses and palfreys captured, and mules, and other booty. Of killed and wounded there was neither end nor measure. A great part of the Greek lords had fled towards the gate of Blachernæ. And vesper-time was already past, and those of the host were weary of the battle and of the slaying.

And they began to assemble in a great open space that was in Constantinople, and decided that they would take up their quarters near the walls and towers they had captured. Never had they thought that in a whole month they should be able to take the city, with its great churches, and great palaces, and the people that were in it.

Flight of Mourzuphles—Second Fire in Constantinople

As they had settled, so was it done, and they encamped before the walls and before the towers by their ships. Count Baldwin of Flanders and Hainault quartered himself in the scarlet tents that the Emperor Mourzuphles had left standing, and Henry his brother before the palace of Blachernæ; and Boniface, Marquis of Montferrat, he and his men, towards the thickest part of the city. So were the host encamped as you have heard, and Constantinople taken on the Monday after Palm Sunday (12th April 1204).

Now Count Louis of Blois and Chartres had languished all the winter with a quartan fever, and could not bear his armour. And you must know that this was a great misfortune to the host, seeing he was a good knight of his body; and he lay in one of the transports.

Thus did those of the host, who were very weary, rest that night. But the Emperor Mourzuphles rested not, for he assembled all his people, and said he would go and attack the Franks. Nevertheless he did not do as he had said, for he rode along other streets, as far as he could from those held by the host, and came to a gate which is called the Golden Gate, whereby he escaped, and avoided the city; and afterwards all who could fled also. And of all this those of the host knew nothing.

During that night, towards the quarters of Boniface, Marquis of Montferrat, certain people, whose names are unknown to me, being in fear lest the Greeks should attack them, set fire to the buildings between themselves and the Greeks. And the city began to take fire, and to burn very direfully; and it burned all that night and all the next day, till vesper-time. And this was the third fire there had been in Constantinople since the Franks arrived in the land; and more houses had been burned in the city than there are houses in any three of the greatest cities in the kingdom of France.

That night passed and the next day came, which was a Tuesday morning (13th April 1204); and all armed themselves throughout the host, both knights and sergeants, and each repaired to his post. Then they issued from their quarters, and thought to find a sorer battle than the day before, for no word had come to them that the emperor had fled during the night. But they found none to oppose them.

The Crusaders Occupy the City

The Marquis Boniface of Montferrat rode all along the shore to the palace of Bucoleon, and when he arrived there it surrendered, on condition that the lives of all therein should be spared.

At Bucoleon were found the larger number of the great ladies who had fled to the castle, for there were found the sister[10] of the King of France, who had been empress, and the sister[11] of the King of Hungary, who had also been empress, and other ladies very many. Of the treasure that was found in that palace I cannot well speak, for there was so much that it was beyond end or counting.

At the same time that this palace was surrendered to the Marquis Boniface of Montferrat, did the palace of Blachernæ surrender

---

10. Agnes, sister of Philip Augustus, married successively to Alexius II., to Andronicus, and to Theodore Branas.

11. Margaret, sister of Emeric, King of Hungary, married to the Emperor Isaac, and afterwards to the Marquis of Montferrat.

to Henry, the brother of Count Baldwin of Flanders, on condition that no hurt should be done to the bodies of those who were therein. There too was found much treasure, not less than in the palace of Bucoleon. Each garrisoned with his own people the castle that had been surrendered to him, and set a guard over the treasure.

And the other people, spread abroad throughout the city, also gained much booty. The booty gained was so great that, none could tell you the end of it: gold and silver, and vessels and precious stones, and samite, and cloth of silk, and robes vair and grey, and ermine, and every choicest thing found upon the earth. And well does Geoffry of Villehardouin, the Marshal of Champagne, bear witness, that never, since the world was created, had so much booty been won in any city.

Every one took quarters where he pleased, and of lodgings there was no stint. So the host of the pilgrims and of the Venetians found quarters, and greatly did they rejoice and give thanks because of the victory God had vouchsafed to them—or those who before had been poor were now in wealth and luxury. Thus they celebrated Palm Sunday and the Easter Day following (25th April 1204) in the joy and honour that God had bestowed upon them. And well might they praise our Lord, since in all the host there were no more than twenty thousand armed men, one with another, and with the help of God they had conquered four hundred thousand men, or more, and in the strongest city in all the world—yea, a great city—and very well fortified.

DIVISION OF THE SPOIL

Then was it proclaimed throughout the host by the Marquis Boniface of Montferrat, who was lord of the host, and by the barons, and by the Doge of Venice, that all the booty should be collected and brought together, as had been covenanted under oath and pain of excommunication. Three churches were appointed for the receiving of the spoils, and guards were set to have them in charge, both Franks and Venetians, the most upright that could be found.

Then each began to bring in such booty as he had taken, and to collect it together. And some brought in loyally, and some in evil sort, because covetousness, which is the root of all evil, let and hindered them. So from that time forth the covetous began to keep things back, and our Lord began to love them less. Ah God! how loyally they had borne themselves up to now! And well had the Lord God shown them that in all things He was ready to honour and exalt them above all people. But full oft do the good suffer for the sins of the wicked.

The spoils and booty were collected together, and you must know that all was not brought into the common stock, for not a few kept things back, maugre the excommunication of the Pope. That which was brought to the churches was collected together and divided, in equal parts, between the Franks and the Venetians, according to the sworn covenant. And you must know further that the pilgrims, after the division had been made, paid out of their share fifty thousand *marks* of silver to the Venetians, and then divided at least one hundred thousand *marks* between themselves, among their own people.

And shall I tell you in what wise? Two sergeants on foot counted as one mounted, and two sergeants mounted as one knight. And you must know that no man received more, either on account of his rank or because of his deeds, than that which had been so settled and ordered—save in so far as he may have stolen it.

And as to theft, and those who were convicted thereof, you must know that stern justice was meted out to such as were found guilty, and not a few were hung. The Count of St. Paul hung one of his knights, who had kept back certain spoils with his shield to his neck; but many there were, both great and small, who kept back part of the spoils, and it was never known. Well may you be assured that the spoil was very great, for if it had not been for what was stolen, and for the part given to the Venetians, there would have been at least four hundred thousand *marks* of silver, and at least ten thousand horses—one with another. Thus were divided the spoils of Constantinople, as you have heard.

Baldwin, Count of Flanders, Elected Emperor

Then a parliament assembled, and the commons of the host declared that an emperor must be elected, as had been settled aforetime. And they parliamented so long that the matter was adjourned to another day, and on that day would they choose the twelve electors who were to make the election. Nor was it possible that there should be lack of candidates, or of men covetous, seeing that so great an honour was in question as the imperial throne of Constantinople. But the greatest discord that arose was the discord concerning Count Baldwin of Flanders and Hainault and the Marquis Boniface of Montferrat; for all the people said that either of those two should be elected.

And when the chief men of the host saw that all held either for

Count Baldwin or for the Marquis of Montferrat, they conferred together and said: "Lords, if we elect one of these two great men, the other will be so filled with envy that he will take away with him all his people. And then the land that we have won may be lost, just as the land of Jerusalem came nigh to be lost when, after it had been conquered, Godfrey of Bouillon was elected king, and the Count of St. Giles became so fulfilled with envy that he enticed the other barons, and whomsoever he could, to abandon the host.

Then did many people depart, and there remained so few that, if God had not sustained them, the land of Jerusalem would have been lost. Let us therefore beware lest the same mischance befall us also, and rather bethink ourselves how we may keep both these lords in the host. Let the one on whom God shall bestow the empire so devise that the other is well content; let him grant to that other all the land on the further side of the straits, towards Turkey, and the Isle of Greece, and that other shall be his liegeman. Thus shall we keep both lords in the host."

As had been proposed, so was it settled, and both consented right willingly. Then came the day for the parliament, and the parliament assembled. And the twelve electors were chosen, six on one side and six on the other; and they swore on holy relics to elect, duly, and in good faith, whomsoever would best meet the needs of the host, and bear rule over the empire most worthily.

Thus were the twelve chosen, and a day appointed for the election of the emperor; and on the appointed day the twelve electors met at a rich palace, one of the fairest in the world, where the Doge of Venice had his quarters. Great and marvellous was the concourse, for every one wished to see who should be elected. Then were the twelve electors called, and set in a very rich chapel within the palace, and the door was shut, so that no one remained with them. The barons and knights stayed without in a great palace.

The council lasted till they were agreed; and by consent of all they appointed Névelon, Bishop of Soissons, who was one of the twelve, to act as spokesman. Then they came out to the place where all the barons were assembled, and the Doge of Venice. Now you must know that many set eyes upon them, to know how the election had turned. And the bishop, lifting up his voice—while all listened intently—spoke as he had been charged, and said: "Lords, we are agreed, let God be thanked! upon the choice of an emperor; and you have all sworn that he whom we shall elect as emperor shall be held by you to be emperor indeed, and that if anyone gainsay him, you will be his helpers. And we name him now at the self-same hour when God was born, The Count Baldwin of Flanders and Hainault!"

A cry of joy was raised in the palace, and they bore the count out of the palace, and the Marquis Boniface of Montferrat bore him on one side to the church, and showed him all the honour he could. So was the Count Baldwin of Flanders , and Hainault elected emperor, and a day appointed for his coronation, three weeks after Easter (16th May 1204). And you must know that many a rich robe was made for the coronation; nor did they want for the wherewithal.

BONIFACE WEDS ISAAC'S WIDOW, AND AFTER BALDWIN'S CORONATION OBTAINS THE KINGDOM FF SALONIKA

Before the time appointed for the coronation, the Marquis Boniface of Montferrat espoused the empress who had been the wife of the Emperor Isaac, and was sister to the King of Hungary. And within that time also did one of the most noble barons of the host, who bore the name of Odo of Champlitte of Champagne, make an end and die. Much was he mourned and bewept by William his brother, and by his other friends; and he was buried in the church of the Apostles with great honour.

The time for the coronation drew near, and the Emperor Baldwin was crowned with great joy and great honour in the Church of St. Sophia, in the year of the Incarnation of Jesus Christ one thousand twelve hundred and four. Of the rejoicings and feasting there is no need to speak further, for the barons and knights did all they could; and the Marquis Boniface of Montferrat and Count Louis of Blois and Chartres did homage to the emperor as their lord. After the great rejoicings and ceremonies of the coronation, he was taken in great pomp, and with a great procession, to the rich palace of Bucoleon. And when the feastings were over he began to discuss his affairs.

Boniface the Marquis of Montferrat called upon him to carry out the covenant made, and give him, as he was bound to do, the land on the other side of the straits towards Turkey and the Isle of Greece. And the emperor acknowledged that he was bound so to do, and said he would do it right willingly. And when the Marquis of Montferrat saw that the emperor was willing to carry out this covenant so debonairly, he besought him, in exchange for this land, to bestow upon him the kingdom of Salonika, because it lay near the land of the King of Hungary, whose sister he had taken to wife.

Much was this matter debated in various ways; but in the end the emperor granted the land of Salonika to the marquis, and the marquis did homage therefor. And at this there was much joy throughout the host, because the marquis was one of the knights most highly prized in all the world, and one whom the knights most loved, inasmuch as no one dealt with them more liberally than he. Thus the marquis remained in the land, as you have heard.

Baldwin Marches Against Mourzuphles

The Emperor Mourzuphles had not yet removed more than four days' journey from Constantinople; and he had taken with him the empress who had been the wife of the Emperor .Alexius, who aforetime had fled, and his daughter. This Emperor Alexius was in a city called Messinople, with all his people, and still held a great part of the land. And at that time the men of note in Greece departed, and a large number passed over the straits towards Turkey; and each one, for his own advantage, made himself master of such lands as he could lay hands upon; and the same thing happened also throughout the other parts of the Empire.

The Emperor Mourzuphles made no long tarrying before he took a city which had surrendered to my lord the Emperor Baldwin, a city called Tchorlu. So he took it and sacked it, and seized whatever he found there.

When the news thereof came to the Emperor Baldwin, he took counsel with the barons, and with the Doge of Venice, and they agreed to this, that he should issue forth, with all his host, to make conquest of the land, and leave a garrison in Constantinople to keep it sure, seeing that the city had been newly taken and was peopled with the Greeks.

So did they decide, and the host was called together, and decision made as to who should remain in Constantinople, and who should go in the host with the Emperor Baldwin. In Constantinople remained Count Lewis of Blois, and Chartres, who had been sick, and was not yet recovered, and the Doge of Venice.

And Conon of Béthune remained in the palaces of Blachernæ and Bucoleon to keep the city; and with him Geoffry the Marshal of Champagne, and Miles the Brabant of Provins, and Manasses of l'Isle, and all their people. All the rest made ready to go in the host with the emperor.

Before the Emperor Baldwin left Constantinople, his brother

Henry departed thence, by his command, with a hundred very good knights; and he rode from city to city, and in every city to which he came the people swore fealty to the emperor.

So he fared forward till he came to Adrianople, which was a good city, and wealthy; and those of the city received him right willingly and swore fealty to the emperor. Then he lodged in the city, he and his people, and sojourned there till the Emperor Baldwin came thither.

Mourzuphles Takes Refuge With Alexius, the Brother of Isaac, Who Puts Out His Eyes

The Emperor Mourzuphles, when he heard that they thus advanced against him, did not dare to abide their coming, but remained always two or three days' march in advance. So he fared forward till he came near Messinople, where the Emperor Alexius was sojourning, and he sent on messengers, telling Alexius that he would give him help, and do all his behests.

And the Emperor Alexius answered that he should be as welcome as if he were his own son, and that he would give him his daughter to wife, and make of him his son. So the Emperor Mourzuphles encamped before Messinople, and pitched his tents and pavilions, and Alexius was quartered within the city. So they conferred together, and Alexius gave him his daughter to wife.. and they entered into alliance, and said they should be as one.

They sojourned thus for I know not how many days, the one in the camp and the other in the city, and then did the Emperor Alexius invite the Emperor Mourzuplùes to come and eat with him, and to go with him to the baths. So were matters settled. The Emperor Mourzuphles came privately, and with few people, and when he was within the house, the Emperor Alexius called him into a privy chamber, and had him thrown on to the ground, and the eyes drawn out of his head.

And this was done in such treacherous wise as you have heard. Now say whether this people, who wrought such cruelty one to another, were fit to have lands in possession! And when the host of the Emperor Mourzuphles heard what had been done, they scattered, and fled this way and that; and some joined themselves to the Emperor Alexius, and obeyed him as their lord, and remained with him.

Baldwin Marches Against Alexius— He is Joined by Boniface

Then the Emperor Baldwin moved from Constantinople, with all his host, and rode forward till he came to Adrianople. There he found Henry his brother, and the men with him. All the people whithersoever the emperor passed, came to him, and put themselves at his mercy and under his rule. And while they were at Adrianople, they heard the news that the Emperor Alexius had pulled out the eyes of the Emperor Mourzuphles. Of this there was much talk among them; and well did all say that those who betrayed one another so disloyally and treacherously had no right to hold land in possession.

Then was the Emperor Baldwin minded to ride straight to Messinople, where the Emperor Alexius was. And the Greeks of Adrianople besought him, as their lord, to leave a garrison in their city because of Johannizza, King of Walachia. and Bulgaria, who ofttimes made war upon them. And the Emperor Baldwin left there Eustace of Saubruic, who was a knight of Flanders, very worthy and very valiant, together with forty right good knights, and a hundred mounted sergeants.

So departed the Emperor Baldwin from Adrianople, and rode towards Messinople, where he thought to find the Emperor Alexius. All the people of the lands through which he passed put themselves under his role and at his mercy; and when the Emperor Alexius saw this, he avoided Messinople and fled. And the Emperor Baldwin rode on till he came before Messinople; and those of the city went out to meet him and surrendered the city to his commandment.

Then the Emperor Baldwin said he would sojourn there, waiting for the arrival of Boniface, Marquis of Montferrat, who had not yet joined the host, seeing he could not move as fast as the emperor, because he was bringing with him the empress, his wife. However, he also rode forward till he came to Messinople, by the river, and there encamped, and pitched his tents and pavilions. And on the morrow he went to speak to the Emperor Baldwin, and to see him, and reminded him of his promise.

"Sire," said he, "tidings have come to me from Salonika that the people of the land would have me know that they are ready to receive me willingly as their lord. And I am your liegeman, and hold the land from you. Therefore, I pray you, let me go thither; and when I am in possession of my land and of my city, I will bring you out such supplies as you may need, and come ready prepared to do your behests. But do not go and ruin my land. Let us rather, if it so pleases you, march against Johannizza, the King of Walachia and Bulgaria, who holds a great part of the land wrongfully."

Rupture Between Baldwin and Boniface—The One Marches on Salonika, the Other on Demotica

I know not by whose counsel it was that the emperor replied that he was determined to march towards Salonika, and would afterwards attend to his other affairs. "Sire," said Boniface, Marquis of Montferrat, "I pray thee, since I am able without thee to get possession of my land, that thou wilt not enter therein; but if thou dost enter therein, I shall deem that thou art not acting for my good. And be it known to thee that I shall not go with thee, but depart from among you." And the Emperor Baldwin replied that, notwithstanding all this, he should most certainly go.

Alas! how ill-advised were they, both the one and the other, and how great was the sin of those who caused this quarrel! For if God had not taken pity upon them, now would they have lost all the conquests they had made, and Christendom been in danger of ruin. So by ill fortune was there division between the Emperor Baldwin of Constantinople and Boniface, Marquis of Montferrat,—and by ill-advice.

The Emperor Baldwin rode towards Salonika, as he devised, with all his people, and with all his power. And Boniface, the Marquis of Montferrat, went back, and he took with him a great number of right worthy people. With him went James of Avesnes, William of Champlitte, Hugh of Colemi, Count Berthold of Catzenellenbogen, and the greater part of those who came from the Empire of Germany and held with the marquis.

Thus did the marquis ride back till he came to a castle, very goodly, very strong, and very rich, which is called Demotica; and it was surrendered by a Greek of the city, and when the marquis had entered therein he garrisoned it. Then because of their knowledge of the empress (his wife), the Greeks began to turn towards him, and to surrender to his rule from all the country round about, within a day or two's journey.

The Emperor Baldwin rode straight on to Salonika, and came to a castle called Christopolis, one of the strongest in the world. And it surrendered, and those of the city did homage to him. Afterwards he came to another place called Blache, which was very strong and very rich, and this too surrendered, and the people did homage. Next he came to Cetros, a city strong and rich, and it also came to his rule and order, and did homage. Then he rode to Salonika, and encamped before the city, and was there for three days. And those within surrendered the city, which was one of the best and wealthiest in Christendom at that day, on condition that he would maintain the uses and customs theretofore observed by the Greek emperor.

MESSAGE OF THE CRUSADERS TO BONIFACE—HE SUSPENDS THE SIEGE OF ADRIANOPLE

While the Emperor Baldwin was thus at Salonika, and the land surrendering to his good pleasure and commandment, the Marquis Boniface of Montferrat, with all his people and a great quantity of Greeks who held to his side, marched to Adrianople and besieged it, and pitched his tents and pavilions round about. Now Eustace of Saubruic was therein, with the people whom the emperor had left there, and they mounted the walls and towers and made ready to defend themselves.

Then took Eustace of Saubruic two messengers and sent them, riding night and day, to Constantinople. And they came to the Doge of Venice, and to Count Louis, and to those who had been left in the city by the Emperor Baldwin, and told them that Eustace of Saubruic would have them know that the emperor and the marquis were embroiled together, and that the marquis had seized Demotica, which was one of the strongest castles in Roumania, and one of the richest, and that he was besieging them in Adrianople.

And when those in Constantinople heard this they were moved with anger, for they thought most surely that all their conquests would be lost.

Then assembled in the palace of Blachernæ the Doge of Venice, and Count Louis of Blois and Chartres, and the other barons that were in Constantinople; and much were they distraught, and greatly were they angered, and fiercely did they complain of those who had put enmity between the emperor and the marquis. At the prayer of the Doge of Venice and of Count Louis, Geoffry of Villehardouin, the Marshal of Champagne, was enjoined to go to the siege of Adrianople, and appease the war, if he could, because he was well in favour with the marquis, and therefore they thought he would have more influence than any other.

And he, because of their prayers, and of their great need, said he would go willingly; and he took with him Manasses of l'Isle, who was one of the good knights of the host, and one of the most honoured.

So they departed from Constantinople, and rode day by day till they came to Adrianople, where the siege was going on. And when the marquis heard thereof, he came out of the camp and went to meet them. With him came James of Avesnes, and William of Champlitte, and Hugh of Colemi, and Otho of la Roche, who were the chief counsellors of the marquis. And when he saw the envoys, he did them much honour and showed them much fair seeming.

Geoffry the Marshal, with whom he was on very good terms, spoke to him very sharply, reproaching him with the fashion in which he had taken the land of the emperor and besieged the emperor's people in Adrianople, and that without apprising those in Constantinople, who surely would have obtained such redress as was due if the emperor had done him any wrong. And the marquis disculpated himself much, and said it was because of the wrong the emperor had done him that he had acted in such sort.

So wrought Geoffry, the Marshal of Champagne, with the help of God, and of the barons who were in the confidence of the marquis, and who loved the said Geoffry well, that the marquis assured him he would leave the matter in the hands of the Doge of Venice, and of Count Louis of Blois and Chartres, and of Conon of Béthune, and of Geoffry of Villehardouin, the Marshal—all of whom well knew what was the covenant made between himself and the emperor. So was a truce established between those in the camp and those in the city.

And you must know that Geoffry the Marshal, and Manasses of l'Isle, were right joyously looked upon, both by those in the camp and those in the city, for very strongly did either side wish for peace.

And in such measure as the Franks rejoiced, so were the Greeks dolent, because right willingly would they have seen the Franks quarrelling and at war. Thus was the siege of Adrianople raised, and the marquis returned with all his people to Demotica, where was the empress his wife.

MESSAGE OF THE CRUSADERS TO BALDWIN—DEATH OF SEVERAL KNIGHTS

The envoys returned to Constantinople, and told what they had done. Greatly did the Doge of Venice, and Count Lewis of Blois, and all besides, then rejoice that to these envoys had been committed the negotiations for a peace; and they chose good messengers, and wrote a letter, and sent it to the Emperor Baldwin, telling him that the marquis had referred himself to them, with assurances that he would accept their arbitration, and that he (the emperor) was even more strongly bound to do the same, and that they besought him to do so—for they would in no wise countenance war—and promise to accept their arbitration, as the marquis had done.

While this was in progress the Emperor Baldwin had settled matters at Salonika and departed thence, garrisoning it with his people, and had left there as chief Renier of Mons, who was a good knight and a valiant. And tidings had come to him that the marquis had taken Demotica, and established himself therein, and conquered a great part of the land lying round about, and besieged the emperor's people in Adrianople.

Greatly enraged was the Emperor Baldwin when these tidings came to him, and much did he hasten so as to raise the siege of Adrianople, and do to the marquis all the harm that he could. Ah God! what mischief their discord might have caused! If God had not seen to it, Christendom would have been undone.

So did the Emperor Baldwin journey day by day. And a very great mischance had befallen those who were before Salonika, for many people of the host were stricken down with sickness. Many who could not be moved had to remain in the castles by which the emperor passed, and many were brought along in litters, journeying in sore pain; and many there were who died at Cetros (La Serre).

Among those who so died at Cetros was Master John of Noyon, chancellor to the Emperor Baldwin. He was a good clerk, and very wise, and much had he comforted the host by the word of God, which he well knew how to preach. And you must know that by his death the good men of the host were much discomforted.

Nor was it long ere another great misfortune befell the host, for Peter of Amiens died, who was a man rich and noble, and a good and brave knight, and great dole was made for him by Hugh of St. Paul, who was his cousin-german; and heavily did his death weigh upon the host. Shortly after died Gerard of Mancicourt, who was a knight much prized, and Giles of Aunoy, and many other good people. Forty knights died during this expedition, and by their death was the host greatly enfeebled.

BALDWIN'S REPLY TO THE MESSAGE OF THE CRUSADERS

The Emperor Baldwin journeyed so day by day that he met the

messengers sent by those of Constantinople. One of the messengers was a knight belonging to the land of Count Louis of Blois, and the count's liegeman; his name was Bigue of Fransures, and he was wise and eloquent. He spoke the message of his lord and the other barons right manfully, and said:

> Sire, the Doge of Venice, and Count Lewis, my lord, and the other barons who are in Constantinople send you health and greeting as to their lord, and they complain to God and to you of those who have raised discord between you and the Marquis of Montferrat, whereby it failed but little that Christendom was not undone; and they tell you that you did very ill when you listened to such counsellors. Now they apprise you that the marquis has referred to them the quarrel that there is between him and you, and they pray you, as their lord, to refer that quarrel to them likewise, and to promise to abide by their ruling. And be it known to you that they will in no wise, nor on any ground, suffer that you should go to war.

The Emperor Baldwin went to confer with his council, and said he would reply anon. Many there were in the emperor's council who had helped to cause the quarrel, and they were greatly outraged by the declaration sent by those at Constantinople, and they said:

> Sire, you hear what they declare to you, that they will not suffer you to take vengeance of your enemy. Truly it seems that if you will not do as they order, they will set themselves against you.

Very many big words were then spoken; but, in the end, the council agreed that the emperor had no wish to lose the friendship of the Doge of Venice, and Count Louis, and the others who were in Constantinople; and the emperor replied to the envoys:

> I will not promise to refer the quarrel to those who sent you, but I will go to Constantinople without doing aught to injure the marquis.

So the Emperor Baldwin journeyed day by day till he came to Constantinople, and the barons, and the other people, went to meet him, and received him as their lord with great honour.

Reconciliation of Baldwin and Boniface

On the fourth day the emperor knew clearly that he had been ill-advised to quarrel with the marquis, and then the Doge of Venice and

Count Louis came to speak to him and said: "Sire, we would pray you to refer this matter to us, as the marquis has done." And the emperor said he would do so right willingly. Then were envoys chosen to fetch the marquis, and bring him thither. Of these envoys one was Gervase of the Châtel, and the second Renier of Trit, and Geoffry, Marshal of Champagne the third, and the Doge of Venice sent two of his people.

The envoys rode day by day till they came to Demotica, and they found the marquis with the empress his wife, and a great number of right worthy people, and they told him how they had come to fetch him. Then did Geoffry the Marshal desire him to come to Constantinople, as he had promised, and make peace in such wise as might be settled by those in whose hands he had remitted his cause; and they promised him safe conduct, as also to those who might go with him.

The marquis took counsel with his men. Some there were who agreed that he should go, and some who advised that he should not go. But the end of the debate was such that he went with the envoys to Constantinople, and took full a hundred knights with him; and they rode day by day till they came to Constantinople. Very gladly were they received in the city; and Count Lewis of Blois and Chartres, and the Doge of Venice went out to meet the marquis, together with many other right worthy people, for he was much loved in the host.

Then was a parliament assembled, and the covenants were rehearsed between the Emperor Baldwin and the Marquis Boniface; and Salonika was restored to Boniface, with the land, he placing Demotica, which he had seized, in the hands of Geoffry the Marshal of Champagne, who undertook to keep it till he heard, by accredited messenger, or letters duly sealed, that the marquis was seized of Salonika, when he would give back Demotica to the emperor, or to whomsoever the emperor might appoint.

Thus was peace made between the emperor and the marquis, as you have heard. And great was the joy thereof throughout the host, for out of this quarrel might very great evil have arisen.

The Kingdom of Salonika is Restored to Boniface— Division of the Land Between the Crusaders

The marquis then took leave, and went towards Salonika with his people, and with his wife; and with him rode the envoys of the emperor; and as they went from castle to castle, each, with all its lordship, was restored to the marquis on the part of the emperor. So they came to Salonika, and those who held the place for the emperor surrendered it. Now the governor, whom the emperor had left there, and whose name was Renier of Mons, had died; he was a man most worthy, and his death a great mischance.

Then the land and country began to surrender to the marquis, and a great part thereof to come under his rule. But a Greek, a man of great rank, whose name was Leon Sgure, would in no wise come under the rule of the marquis, for he had seized Corinth and Napoli, two cities that lie upon the sea, and are among the strongest cities under heaven. He then refused to surrender, but began to make war against the marquis, and a very great many of the Greeks held with him.

And another Greek, whose name was Michael, and who had come with the marquis from Constantinople, and was thought by the marquis to be his friend, he departed, without any word said, and went to a city called Arthe (? Durazzo) and took to wife the daughter of a rich Greek, who held the land from the emperor, and seized the land, and began to make war on the marquis.

Now the land from Constantinople to Salonika was quiet and at peace, for the ways were so safe that all could come and go at their pleasure, and from the one city to the other there were full twelve long days' journey. And so much time had now passed that we were at the beginning of September (1204). And the Emperor Baldwin was in Constantinople, and the land at peace, and under his rule. Then died two right good knights in Constantinople, Eustace of Canteleu, and Aimery of Villeroi, whereof their friends had great sorrow.

Then did they begin to divide the land. The Venetians had their part, and the pilgrims the other. And when each one was able to go to his own land, the covetousness of this world, which has worked so great evil, suffered them not to be at peace, for each began to deal wickedly in his land, some more, and some less, and the Greeks began to hate them and to nourish a bitter heart.

Then did the Emperor Baldwin bestow on Count Louis the duchy of Nice, which was one of the greatest lordships in the land of Roumania, and situate on the other side of the straits, towards Turkey. Now all the land on the other side of the straits had not surrendered to the emperor, but was against him. Then afterwards he gave the duchy of Philippopolis to Renier of Trit.

So Count Louis sent his men to conquer his land—some hundred and twenty knights. And over them were set Peter of Bracieux and Pay en of Orleans. They left Constantinople on All Saints Day (1st November 1204), and passed over the Straits of St. George on ship-board, and me to Piga, a city that lies on the sea, and is inhabited by Latins. And they began to war against the Greeks.

Execution of Mourzuphles and Imprisonment of Alexius

In those days it happened that the Emperor Mourzuphles; whose eyes had been put out—the same who had murdered his lord, the Emperor Isaac's son, the Emperor Alexius, whom the pilgrims had brought with them to that land—it happened, I say, that the Emperor Mourzuphles fled privily, and with but few people, and took refuge beyond the straits, But Thierri of Loos heard of it, for Mourzuphles' flight was revealed to him, and he took Mourzuphles and brought him to the Emperor Baldwin at Constantinople. And the Emperor Baldwin rejoiced thereat, and took counsel with his men what he should do with a man who had been guilty of such a murder upon his lord.

And the council agreed to this: There was in Constantinople, towards the middle of the city, a column, one of the highest and the most finely wrought in marble that eye had ever seen; and Mourzuphles should be taken to the top of that column and made to leap down, in the sight of all the people, because it was fit that an act of justice so notable should be seen of the whole world. So they led the Emperor Mourzuphles to the column, and took him to the top, and all the people in the city ran together to behold the event. Then they cast him down, and he fell from such a height that when he came to the earth he was all shattered and broken.

Now hear of a great marvel! On that column from which he fell were images of divers kinds, wrought in the marble. And among these images was one, worked in the shape of an emperor, falling headlong; for of a long time it had been prophesied that from that column an emperor of Constantinople should be cast down. So did the semblance and the prophecy come true.

It came to pass, at this time also, that the Marquis Boniface of Montferrat, who was near Salonika, took prisoner the Emperor Alexius—the same who had put out the eyes of the Emperor Isaac—and the empress his wife with him. And he sent the scarlet buskins, and the Imperial vestments, to the Emperor Baldwin, his lord, at Constantinople, and the Emperor took the act in very good part. Shortly after the marquis sent the Emperor Alexius and the empress his wife, to Montferrat, there to be imprisoned.

Capture of Abydos, of Philippopolis, and of Nicomia— Theodore Lascaris Pretends to the Empire

At the feast of St. Martin after this (11th November 1204), Henry, the brother of the Emperor Baldwin, went forth from Constantinople, and marched down by the straits to the mouth of Abydos; and he took with him some hundred and twenty good knights. He crossed the straits near a city which is called Abydos, and found it well furnished with good things, with corn and meats, and with all things of which man has need.

So he seized the city, and lodged therein, and then began to war with the Greeks who were before him. And the Armenians of the land, of whom there were many, began to turn towards him, for they greatly hated the Greeks.

At that time Renier of Trit left Constantinople, and went towards Philippopolis, which the emperor had given him; and he took with him some hundred and twenty very good knights, and rode day by day till he passed beyond Adrianople, and came to Philippopolis. And the people of the land received him, and obeyed him as their lord, for they beheld his coming very willingly. And they stood in great need of succour, for Johannizza, the King of Wallachia, had mightily oppressed them with war. So Renier helped them right well, and held a great part of the land, and most of those who had sided with Johannizza, now turned to him. In those parts the war with Johannizza raged fiercely.

The emperor had sent some hundred knights over the straits of Saint George opposite Constantinople. Macaire of Sainte-Marehould was in command, and with him went Matthew of Wallincourt, and Robert of the Ronsoi. They rode to a city called Nicomedia, which lies on a gulf of the sea, and is well two days' journey from Constantinople. When the Greeks saw them coming, they avoided the city, and went away; so the pilgrims lodged therein, and garrisoned it, and enclosed it with walls, and began to wage war before them, on that side also.

The land on the other side of the straits had for lord a Greek named Theodore Lascaris. He had for wife the daughter of the Emperor Alexis, through whom he laid claim to the land—this was the Alexius whom the Franks had driven from Constantinople, and who had put out his brother's eyes. The same Lascaris maintained the war against the Franks on the other side of the straits, in whatsoever part they might be. In Constantinople remained the Emperor Baldwin and

Count Louis, with but few people, and the Count of St. Paul, who was grievously sick with gout, that held him by the knees and feet; and the Doge of Venice, who saw naught.

REINFORCEMENTS FROM SYRIA—DEATH OF MARY, THE WIFE OF BALDWIN

After this time came from the land of Syria a great company of those who had abandoned the host, and gone thither from other ports than Venice. With this company came Stephen of the Perche, and Reginald of Montmirail, who was cousin to Count Lewis, and they were by him much honoured; for he was very glad of their coming. And the Emperor Baldwin, and the rest of the people also received them very gladly, for they were of high rank, and very rich, and brought very many good people with them.

From the land of Syria came Hugh of Tabarie, and Raoul his brother, and Thierri of Tenremonde, and very many people of the land, knights and light horsemen, and sergeants. And the Emperor Baldwin gave to Stephen of the Perche the duchy of Philadelphia.

Among other tidings came news at this time to the Emperor Baldwin whereby he was made very sorrowful; for the Countess Mary [12] his wife, whom he had left in Flanders, seeing she could not go with him because she was with child—he was then but count—had brought forth a daughter—and afterwards, on her recovery, she started to go to her lord oversea, and passed to the port of Marseilles, and coming to Acre, she had but just landed, when the tidings came to her from Constantinople—told by the messengers whom her lord had sent—that Constantinople was taken, and her lord made emperor, to the great joy of all Christendom.

On hearing this the lady was minded to come to him forthwith. Then a sickness took her, and she made an end and died, whereof there was great dole throughout all Christendom, for she was a gracious and virtuous lady and greatly honoured. And those who came in this company brought the tidings of her death, whereof the Emperor Baldwin had sore affliction, as also the barons of the land, for much did they desire to have her for their lady.

DEFEAT OF THEODORE AND CONSTANTINE LASCARIS

At that time those who had gone to the city of Piga—Peter of Bra-

---

12. She was the daughter of Henry Count of Champagne and of Mary, daughter of Philip Augustus, King of France.

cieux and Payen of Orleans being the chiefs—fortified a castle called Palormo; and they left therein a garrison of their people, and rode forward to conquer the land. Theodore Lascaris had collected all the people he could, and on the day of the feast of our Lord St. Nicholas (6th December 1204), which is before the Nativity, he joined battle in the plain before a castle called Poemaninon.

The battle was engaged with great disadvantage to our people, for those of the other part were in such numbers as was marvellous; and on our side there were but one hundred and forty knights, without counting the mounted sergeants.

But our Lord orders battles as it pleases Him. By His grace and by His will, the Franks vanquished the Greeks and discomfited them, so that they suffered very great loss. And within the week, they surrendered a very large part of the land. They surrendered Poemaninon, which was a very strong castle, and Lopadion, which was one of the best cities of the land, and Polychna, which is seated on a lake of fresh water, and is one of the strongest and best castles that can be found. And you must know that our people fared very excellently, and by God's help had their will of that land.

Shortly after, by the advice of the Armenians, Henry, the brother of the Emperor Baldwin of Constantinople, started from the city of Abydos, leaving therein a garrison of his people, and rode to a city called Atramittium, which lies on the sea, a two days' journey from Abydos. This city yielded to him, and he lodged therein, and a great part of the land surrendered; for the city was well supplied with corn and meats, and other goods. Then he maintained the war in those parts against the Greeks.

Theodore Lasaris, who had been discomfited at Poemaninon, collected as many people as he could, and assembled a very great army, and gave the command thereof to Constantine, his brother, who was one of the best Greeks in Roumania, and then rode straight towards Atramittium. And Henry, the brother of the Emperor Baldwin, had knowledge, through the Armenians, that a great host was marching against him, so he made ready to meet them, and set his battalions in order; and he had with him some very good men, as Baldwin of Belvoir, and Nicholas of Mailly, and Anseau of Cayeux, and Thierri of Laos, and Thierri of Tenremonde.

So it happened that on the Saturday which is before mid-Lent (19th March 1205), came Constantine Lascaris with his great host, before Atramittium. And Henry, when he knew of his coming, took counsel, and said he would not suffer himself to be shut up in the city, but would issue forth. And those of the other part came on with all their host, in great companies of horse and foot, and those on our part went out to meet them, and began the onslaught.

Then was there a dour battle and fighting hand to hand; but by God's help the Franks prevailed, and discomfited their foes, so that many were killed and taken captive, and there was much booty. Then were the Franks at ease, and very rich, so that the people of the land turned to them, and began to bring in their rents.

Boniface Attacks Leon Sgure; He is Joined by Geoffry of Villehardouin, the Nephew

Now let us leave speaking further (for the nonce), of those at Constantinople, and return to the Marquis Boniface of Montferrat. The marquis had gone, as you have heard, towards Salonika, and then ridden forth against Leon Sgure, who held Napoli and Corinth, two of the strongest cities in the world. Boniface besieged both cities at once. James of Avesnes, with many other good men, remained before Corinth, and the rest encamped before Napoli, and laid siege to it.

Then befell a certain adventure in the land. For Geoffry of Villehardouin, who was nephew to Geoffry of Villehardouin, Marshal of Roumania and Champagne, being his brother's son, was moved to leave Syria with the company that came to Constantinople. But wind and chance carried him to the port of Modon, and there his ship was injured, so that, of necessity, it behoved him to winter in that country.

And a Greek, who was a great lord of the land, knew of it, and came to him, and did him much honour, and said:

> Fair sir, the Franks have conquered Constantinople, and elected an emperor. If thou wilt make alliance with me, I will deal with thee in all good faith, and we together will conquer much land.

So they made alliance on oath, the Greek and Geoffry of Villehardouin, and conquered together a great part of the country, and Geoffry of Villehardouin found much good faith in the Greek.

But adventures happen as God wills, and sickness laid hold of the Greek, and he made an end and died. And the Greek's son rebelled against Geoffry of Villehardouin, and betrayed him, and the castles in which Geoffry had set a garrison turned against him. Now he heard tell that the marquis was besieging Napoli, so he went towards him with as many men as he could collect, and rode through the land for some six days in very great peril, and thus came to the camp, where he was received right willingly, and much honoured by the marquis and all who were there. And this was but right, seeing he was very honourable and valiant, and a good knight.

Exploits of William of Champlitte and Geoffry of Villehardouin, the Nephew, in Morea

The marquis would have given him land and possessions so that he might remain with him, but he would not, and spoke to William of Champlitte, who was his friend, and said:

Sir, I come from a land that is very rich, and is called Morea. Take as many men as you can collect, and leave this host, and let us go and conquer that land by the help of God. And that which you will give me out of our conquests, I will hold from you, and I will be your liegeman.

And William of Champlitte, who greatly trusted and loved him, went to the marquis, and told him of the matter, and the marquis allowed of their going.

So William of Champlitte and Geoffry of Villehardouin (the nephew) departed from the host, and took with them about a hundred knights, and a great number of mounted sergeants, and entered into the land of Morea, and rode onwards till they came to the city of Modon. Michael heard that they were in the land with so few people, and he collected together a great number of people, a number that was marvellous, and he rode after them as one thinking they were an no better than prisoners, and in his hand.

And when they heard tell that he was coming, they refortified Modon, where the defences had long since been pulled down, and there left their baggage, and the lesser folk. Then they rode out a day's march, and ordered their array with as many people as they had. But the odds seemed too great, for they had no more than five hundred men mounted, whereas on the other part there were well over five thousand.

But events happen as God pleases; for our people fought with the Greeks, and discomfited and conquered them. And the Greeks lost very heavily, while those on our side gained horses and arms enough, and other goods in very great plenty, and so returned very happy, and very joyously, to the city of Modon.

Afterwards they rode to a city called Coron, on the sea: and besieged it. And they had not besieged it long before it surrendered, and William gave it to Geoffry of Villehardouin (the nephew) and he became his liegeman, and set therein a garrison of his men.

Next they went to a castle called Chalemate, which was very strong and fair, and besieged it. This castle troubled them for a very long space, but they remained before it till it was taken. Then did more of the Greeks of that land surrender than had done aforetime.

Siege of Napoli and Corinth; Alliance Between the Greeks and Johannizza

The Marquis of Montferrat besieged Napoli, but he could there do nothing, for the place was too strong, and his men suffered greatly. James of Avesnes, meanwhile, continued to besiege Corinth, where he had been left by the marquis. Leon Sgure, who was in Corinth, and very wise and wily, saw that James had not many people with him, and did not keep good watch. So one morning, at the break of day, he issued from the city in force, and got as far as the tents, and killed many before they could get to their armour.

There was killed Dreux of Estruen, who was very honourable and valiant, and greatly was he lamented. And James of Avesnes, who was in command, waxed very wroth at the death of his knight, and did not leave the fray till he was wounded in the leg right grievously. And well did those who were present bear witness that it was to his doughtiness that they owed their safety; for you must know that they came very near to being all lost. But by God's help they drove the Greeks back in to the castle by force.

Now the Greeks, who were very disloyal, still nourished treachery in their hearts. They perceived at that time that the Franks were so scattered over the land that each had his own matters to attend to. So they thought they could the more easily betray them.

They took envoys therefore privily, from all the cities in the land, and sent them to Johannizza, the King of Wallachia and Bulgaria, who was still at war with them as he had been aforetime. And they told Johannizza they would make him emperor, and give themselves wholly to him, and slay all the Franks. So they swore that they would obey him as their lord, and he swore that he would defend them as though they were his own people. Such was the oath sworn.

Uprising of the Greeks at Demotica and Adrianople; Their Defeat at Arcadioplis

At that time there happened a great misfortune at Constantinople, for Count Hugh of St. Paul, who had long been in bed, sick of the gout, made a end and died; and this caused great sorrow, and was a great mishap, and much was he bewept by his men and by his friends. He was buried with great honour in the church of our Lord St. George of Mangana.

Now Count Hugh in his lifetime had held a castle called Demotica, which was very strong and rich, and he had therein some of his knights and sergeants. The Greeks, who had made oath to the King of Wallachia that they would kill and betray the Franks, betrayed them in that castle, and slaughtered many and took many captive. Few escaped, and those who escaped went flying to a city called Adrianople, which the Venetians held at that time.

Not long after the Greeks in Adrianople rose in arms; and such of our men as were therein, and had been set to guard it, came out in great peril, and left the city. Tidings thereof came to the Emperor Baldwin of Constantinople, who had but few men with him, he and Count Louis of Blois. Much were they then troubled and dismayed. And thenceforth, from day to day, did evil tidings begin to come to them, that everywhere the Greeks were rising, and that wherever the Greeks found Franks occupying the land, they killed them.

And those who had left Adrianople, the Venetians and the others who were there, came to a city called Tzurulum, that belonged to the Emperor Baldwin. There they found William of Blanvel, who kept the place for the emperor. By the help and comfort that he gave them, and because he accompanied them with as many men as he could, they turned back to a city, some twelve leagues distant, called Arcadiopolis, which belonged to the Venetians, and they found it empty. So they entered in, and put a garrison there.

On the third day the Greeks of the land gathered together, and came at the break of dawn before Arcadiopolis; and then began, from all sides, an assault, great and marvellous. The Franks defended themselves right well, and opened their gates, and issued forth, attacking vigorously. As was God's will, the Greeks were discomfited, and those on our side began to cut them down and to slay them, and then chased them for a league, and killed many, and captured many horses and much other spoil.

So the Franks returned with great joy to Arcadiopolis, and sent tidings of their victory to the Emperor Baldwin, in Constantinople, who was much rejoiced thereat. Nevertheless they dared not hold the city of Arcadiopolis, but left it on the morrow, and abandoned it, and returned to the city of Tzurulum.

Here they remained in very great doubt, for they misdoubted the Greeks who were in the city as much as those who were without, because the Greeks in the city had also taken part in the oath sworn to the King of Wallachia, and were bound to betray, the Franks. And many there were who did not dare to abide in Tzurulum, but made their way back to Constantinople.

The Crusaders on the Other Side of the Straits are Recalled to March on Adrianople—Expedition of Geoffry of Villehardouin

Then the Emperor Baldwin and the Doge of Venice, and Count Louis took counsel together, for they saw they were losing the whole land. And they settled that the emperor should tell his brother Henry, who was at Adramittium, to abandon whatsoever conquests he had made, and come to their succour.

Count Lewis, on his side, sent to Payen of Orleans, and Peter of Bracieux, who were at Lopadium, and to all the people that were with them, telling them to leave whatsoever conquests they had made, save Piga only, that lay on the sea, where they were to set a garrison—the smallest they could—and that the remainder were to come to their succour.

The emperor directed Macaire of Sainte-Menehould, and Matthew of Wallincourt, and Robert of Ronsoi, who had some hundred knights with them in Nicomedia, to leave Nicomedia and come to their succour. By command of the Emperor Baldwin, Geoffry of Villehardouin, Marshal of Champagne and of Roumania, issued from Constantinople, with Manasses of l'Isle, and with as many men as they could collect, and these were few enough, seeing that all the land was being lost.

And they rode to the city of Tzurulum, which is distant a three days' journey. There they found William of Blanvel, and those that were with him, in very great fear, and much were these reassured at their coming. At that place they remained four days. The Emperor Baldwin sent after Geoffry the Marshal as many as he could, of such people as were coming into Constantinople, so that on the fourth day there were at Truzulum eighty knights.

Then did Geoffry the Marshal move forward, and Manasses of l'Isle, and their people, and they rode on, and came to the city of Arcadiopolis, and quartered themselves therein. There they remained a day, and then moved to a city called Bulgaropolis. The Greeks had avoided this city and the Franks quartered themselves therein.

The following day they rode to a city called Neguise, which was very fair and strong, and well furnished with all good things. And they found that the Greeks had abandoned it, and were all gone to Adrianople. Now Adrianople was distant nine French leagues, and therein were gathered all the great multitude of the Greeks. And the Franks decided that they should wait where they were till the coming of the Emperor Baldwin.

Renier of Trit Abandoned at Finepopolis by his Son and the Greater Part of his People

Now does this book relate a great marvel: for Renier of Trit, who was at Finepopolis, a good nine days' journey from Constantinople, with at least one hundred and twenty knights, was deserted by Renier his son, and Giles his brother, and James of Bandies, who was his nephew, and Achard of Verdun, who had his daughter to wife. And they had taken some thirty of his knights, and thought to come to Constantinople; and they had left him, you must know, in great peril.

But they found the country raised against them, and were discomfited; and the Greeks took them, and afterwards handed them over to the King of Wallachia, who had their heads cut off. And you must know that they were but little pitied by the people, because they had behaved in such evil sort to one whom they were bound to treat quite otherwise.

And when the other knights of Renier de Trit saw that he was thus abandoned by those who were much more bound to him than themselves, they felt the less shame, and some eighty together left him, and departed by another way. So Renier of Trit remained among the Greeks with very few men, for he had not more than fifteen knights at Philippopolis and Stanimac—which is a very strong castle which he held, and where he was for a long time besieged.

Baldwin Undertakes the Siege of Adrianople

We will speak no further now of Renier of Trit, but return to the Emperor Baldwin, who is in Constantinople, with but very few people, and greatly angered and much distracted. He was waiting for

Henry his brother, and all the people on the other side of the straits, and the first who came to him from the other side of the straits came from Nicomedia, *viz*.: Macaire of Sainte-Menehould, and Matthew of Wallincourt, and Robert of Ronsoi, and with them full a hundred knights.

When the emperor saw them, he was right glad, and he consulted with Count Louis, who was Count of Blois and Chartres. And they settled to go forth, with as many men as they had, to follow Geoffry the Marshal of Champagne, who had gone before. Alas! what a pity it was they did not wait till all had joined them who were on the other side of the straits, seeing how few people they had, and how perilous the adventure on which they were bound.

So they started from Constantinople, some one hundred and forty knights, and rode from day to day till they came to the castle of Neguise, where Geoffry the Marshal was quartered. That night they took counsel together, and the decision to which they came was, that on the morrow they should go before Adrianople, and lay siege to it. So they ordered their battalions, and did for the best with such people as they had.

When the morning came, and full daylight, they rode as had been arranged, and came before Adrianople. And they found it very well defended, and saw the flags of Johannizza, King of Wallachia and Bulgaria, on the walls and towers; and the city was very strong and very rich, and very full of people. Then they made an assault, with very few people, before two of the gates, and this was on the Tuesday of Palmtide (29th March 1205). So did they remain before the city for three days, in great discomfort, and but few in number.

The Siege of Adrianople Continued Without Result

Then came Henry Dandolo, the Doge of Venice, who was an old man and saw naught. And he brought with him as many people as he had, and these were quite as many as the Emperor Baldwin and Count Louis had brought, and he encamped before one of the gates. On the morrow they were joined by a troop of mounted sergeants, but these might well have been better men than they proved themselves to be. And the host[13] had small store of provisions, because the merchants could not come with them; nor could they go foraging because of the many Greeks that were spread throughout the land.

---

13. Meaning here a little obscure. I think, however, the intention of the original is to state that the host, and not only the sergeants, lacked supplies.

Johannizza, King of Wallachia, was coming to succour Adrianople with a very great host; for he brought with him Wallachians and Bulgarians, and full fourteen thousand Comans who had never been baptised.

Now because of the dearth of provisions, Count Louis of Blois and Chartres went foraging on Palm Sunday. With him went Stephen of the Perche, brother of Count Geoffry of the Perche, and Renaud of Montmirail, who was brother of Count Hervée of Nevers, and Gervase of the Châtel, and more than half of the host. They went to a castle called Peutace, and found it well garrisoned with Greeks, and assailed it with great force and fury; but they were able to achieve nothing, and so retreated without taking any spoils.

Thus they remained during the week of the two Easters (Palm Sunday to Easter Day), and fashioned engines of divers sorts, and set such miners as they had to work underground and so undermine the wall. And thus did they celebrate Easter (10th April) before Adrianople, being but few in number and scant of provisions.

Johannizza, King of Wallachia, Comes to Relieve Adrianople

Then came tidings that Johannizza, King of Wallachia, was coming upon them to relieve the city. So they set their affairs in order, and it was arranged that Geoffry the Marshal, and Manasses of l'Isle should guard the camp, and that the Emperor Baldwin and all the remainder of the host should issue from the camp if so be that Johannizza came and offered battle.

Thus they remained till the Wednesday of Easter week; and Johannizza had by that time approached so near that he encamped at about five leagues from us. And he sent his Comans running before our camp, and a cry was raised throughout the camp, and our men issued therefrom helter-skelter, and pursued the Comans for a full league very foolishly; for when they wished to return, the Comans began to shoot at them in grievous wise, and wounded a good many of their horses.

So our men returned to the camp, and the barons were summoned to the quarters of the Emperor Baldwin. And they took counsel, and all said that they had dealt foolishly in thus pursuing people who were so lightly armed. And in the end they settled that if Johannizza came on again, they would issue forth, and set themselves in array of battle before the camp, and there wait for him, and not move from thence.

And they had it proclaimed throughout the host that none should be so rash as to disregard this order, and move from his post for any cry or tumult that might come to his ears. And it was settled that Geoffry the Marshal should keep guard on the side of the city, with Manasses of l'Isle.

So they passed that night till the Thursday morning in Easter week, when they heard mass and ate their dinner. And the Comans ran up to their tents, and a cry arose, and they ran to arms, and issued from the camp with all their battalions in array, as had afore been devised.

Defeat of the Crusaders—Baldwin Taken Prisoner

Count Louis went out first with his battalion, and began to follow after the Comans, and sent to urge the emperor to come after him. Alas! how ill did they keep to what had been settled the night before! For they ran in pursuit of the Comans for at least two leagues, and joined issue with them, and chased them a long space. And then the Comans turned back upon them, and began to cry out and to shoot.

On our side there were battalions made up of other people than knights, people having too little knowledge of arms, and they began to wax afraid and be discomfited. And Count Louis, who had been the first to attack, was wounded in two places full sorely; and the Comans and Wallachians began to invade our ranks; and the count had fallen, and one of his knights, whose name was John of Friaise, dismounted, and set him on his horse. Many were Count Louis' people who said: "Sir, get you hence, for you are too sorely wounded, and in two places."

And he said: "The Lord God forbid that ever I should be reproached with flying from the field, and abandoning the emperor."

The emperor, who was in great straits on his side, recalled his people, and he told them that he would not fly, and that they were to remain with him: and well do those who were there present bear witness that never did knight defend himself better with his hands than did the emperor.

This combat lasted a long time. Some were there who did well, and some were there who fled. In the end, for so God suffers misadventures to occur, they were discomfited. There on the field remained the Emperor Baldwin, who never would fly, and Count Louis; the Emperor Baldwin was taken alive and Count Louis was slain.

Alas! how woeful was our loss! There was lost the Bishop Peter of Bethleem, and Stephen of the Perche, brother to Count Geoffry, and

Renaud of Montmirail, brother of the Count of Nevers, and Matthew of Wallincourt, and Robert of Ronsoi, John of Friaise, Walter of Neuilli, Ferri of Yerres, John his brother, Eustace of Heumont, John his brother, Baldwin of Neuville, and many more of whom the book does not here make mention. Those who were able to escape, they came back flying to the camp.

The Crusaders Raise the Siege of Adrianople

When Geoffry the Marshal of Champagne, who was keeping guard at one of the gates of the city, saw this he issued from the camp as soon as he could, with all the men that were with him, and gave command to Manasses of l'Isle, who was on guard at another gate, that he should follow after him. And he rode forth with all his force at full speed, and in full array, to meet the fugitives, and the fugitives all rallied round him. And Manasses of l'Isle followed as soon as he was able, with his men, and joined himself to him, so that together they formed a very strong body; and all those who came out of the rout, and whom they could stop, were taken into their ranks.

The rout was thus stayed between Nones and Vespers. But the most part of the fugitives were so affeared that they fled right before them till they came to the tents and quarters. Thus was the rout stayed, as you have heard; and the Comans, with the Wallachians and Greeks, who were in full chace, ceased their pursuit.

But these still galled our force with their bows and arrows, and the men of our force kept still with their faces turned towards them. Thus did both sides remain till nightfall, when the Comans and Wallachians began to retire.

Then did Geoffry of Villehardouin, the Marshal of Champagne and Roumania, summon to the camp the Doge of Venice, who was an old man and saw naught, but very wise and brave and vigorous; and he asked the Doge to come to him there where he stood with his men, holding the field; and the Doge did so. And when the Marshal saw him, he called him into council, aside, all alone, and said to him:

> Lord, you see the misadventure that has befallen us. v have lost the Emperor Baldwin and Count Louis, and the larger part of our people, and of the best. Now let us bethink ourselves how to save what is left. For if God does not take pity of them, we are but lost.

And in the end they settled it thus: that the Doge would return to the camp, and put heart into the people, and order that everyone should arm and remain quiet in his tent or pavilion; and that Geoffry the Marshal would remain in full order of battle before the camp till it was night, so that their enemies might not see the host move; and that when it was night all would move from before the city; the Doge of Venice would go before, and Geoffry the Marshal would form the rear-guard, with those who were with him.

Retreat of the Crusaders

Thus they waited till it was night; and when it was night the Doge of Venice left the camp, as had been arranged, and Geoffry the Marshal formed the rear-guard. And they departed at foot pace, and took with them all their people mounted and dismounted, the wounded as well those who were whole—they left not one behind.

And they journeyed towards a city that lies upon the sea, called Rodosto, and that was full three days' journey distant. So they departed from Adrianople, as you have heard; and this adventure befell in the year of the Incarnation of Jesus Christ twelve hundred and five.

And in the night that the host left Adrianople, it happened that a company started to get to Constantinople earlier, and by a more direct way; and they were greatly blamed therefor. In this company was a certain count from Lombardy named Gerard, who came from the land of the marquis, and Odo of Ham, who was lord of a castle called Ham in Vermandois, and John of Maseroles, and many others to the number of twenty-five knights, whom the book does not name.

And they went away so fast after the discomfiture, which had taken place on the Thursday evening, that they came to Constantinople on the Saturday night, though it was ordinarily a good five days' journey. And they told the news to the Cardinal Peter of Capua, who was there by the authority Innocent Pope of Rome, and to Conon of Bethune, who guarded the city, and to Miles the Brabant; and to the other good men in the city.

And you must know that these were greatly affeared, and thought of a certainty that all the rest, who had been left before Adrianople, were lost, for they had no news of them.

Peter of Bracieux and Payen of Orleans Meet the Retreating Host

Now will we say no more about those at Constantinople, who were in sore trouble, but go back to the Doge of Venice and Geoffry the Marshal, who marched all the night that they left Adrianople, till the dawn of the following day; and then they came to a city called Pamphyle.

Now listen and you shall hear how adventures befall as God wills: for in that city had lain during the night, Peter of Bracieux and Payen of Orleans and all the men belonging to the land of Count Louis, at least a hundred very good knights and one hundred and forty mounted sergeants, and they were coming from the other side of the straits to join the host at Adrianople.

When they saw the host coming, they ran to their arms right nimbly, for they thought we were the Greeks. So they armed themselves, and sent to know what people we were, when their messengers discovered that we were the host retreating after our discomfiture. So the messengers went back, and told them that the Emperor Baldwin was lost, and their lord Count Louis, of whose land and country they were, and of whose following.

Sadder news could they not have heard. There might you have seen many tears wept, and many hands wrung for sorrow and pity. And they went on, all armed as they were, till they came to where Geoffry, the Marshal of Champagne, was keeping guard in the rear, in very great anxiety and misease.

For Johannizza, the King of Wallachia and Bulgaria, had come at the point of day before Adrianople with all his host, and found that we had departed, and so ridden after us till it was full day; and when he found us not, he was full of grief; and well was it that he found us not, for if he had found us we must all have been lost beyond recovery.

"Sir," said Peter of Bracieux and Payen of Orleans to Geoffry the Marshal, "what would you have us do? We will do whatever you wish."

And he answered them:

> You see how matters stand with us. You are fresh and unwearied, and your horses also; therefore do you keep guard in the rear, and I will go forward and hold in hand our people, who are greatly dismayed and in sore need of comfort.

To this they consented right willingly. So they established the rearguard duly and efficiently, and as men who well knew how, for they were good knights and honourable.

The Host Reaches Rodosto

Geoffry the Marshal rode before and led the host, and rode till he came to a city called Cariopolis. Then he saw that the horses were weary with marching all night, and entered into the city, and put them up till noon. And they gave food to their horses, and ate themselves of what they could find, and that was but little.

So they remained all the day in that city until night. And Johannizza, the King of Wallachia, had followed them all the day with all his powers, and encamped about two leagues from them. And when it was night, those in the city all armed themselves and departed. Geoffry the Marshal led the van, and those formed the rear-guard who had formed it during the day. So they rode through that night, and the following day (16th April) in great fear and much hardship, till they came to the city of Rodosto, a city very rich and very strong, and inhabited by Greeks. These Greeks did not dare to defend themselves, so our people entered in and took quarters; so at last were they in safety.

Thus did the host escape from Adrianople, as you have heard. Then was a council held in the city of Rodosto; and it seemed to the council that Constantinople was in greater jeopardy than they were. So they took messengers, and sent them by sea, telling them to travel night and day, and to advise those in the city not to be anxious about them—for they had escaped—and that they would repair back to Constantinople as soon as they could.

Seven Thousand Pilgrims Leave the Crusaders

At the time when the messengers arrived, there were in Constantinople five ships of Venice, very large and very good, laden with pilgrims, and knights and sergeants, who were leaving the land and returning to their own countries. There were at least seven thousand men at arms in the ships, and one was William the advocate of Bethune, and there were besides Baldwin of Aubigny, and John of Virsin, who belonged to the land of Count Louis, and was his liegeman, and at least one hundred other knights, whom the book does not here name.

Master Peter of Capua, who was cardinal from the Pope of Rome, Innocent, and Conon of Bethune, who commanded in Constantinople, and Miles the Brabant, and a great number of other men of mark, went to the five ships, and prayed those who were in them, with sighs and tears, to have mercy and pity upon Christendom, and upon their liege lords who had been lost in battle, and to remain for the love of

God.

But they would not listen to a single word, and left the port. They spread their sails, and went their way, as God ordained, in such sort that the wind took them to the port of Rodosto; and this was on the day following that on which those who had escaped from the discomfiture came thither.

The same prayers, with tears and weeping, that had been addressed to them at Constantinople—those same prayers were now addressed to them at Rodosto; and Geoffry the Marshal, and those who were with him, besought them to have mercy and pity on the land, and remain, for never would they be able to succour any land in such dire need. They replied that they would consult together, and give an answer on the morrow.

And now listen to the adventure which befell that night in the city. There was a knight from the land of Count Louis, called Peter of Frouville, who was held in honour, and of great name. The same fled by night, and left all his baggage and his people, and gat himself to the ship of John of Virsin, who was from the land of Count Lewis of Blois and Chartres.

And those on board the five ships, who in the morning were to give their answer to Geoffry the Marshal and to the Doge of Venice, so soon as they saw the day, they spread their sails, and went their way without word said to anyone. Much and great blame did they receive, both in the land whither they went, and in the land they had left; and he who received most blame of all was Peter of Frouville. For well has it been said that he is but ill-advised who, through fear of death, does what will be a reproach to him forever.

Meeting of Many of the Crusaders—Henry, the Brother of Baldwin, is Made Regent

Now let us speak of these last no farther, but speak of Henry, brother to the Emperor Baldwin of Constantinople, who had left Atramittium, which he had conquered, and passed the straits at the city of Abydos, and was coming towards Adrianople to succour the Emperor Baldwin, his brother. And with him had come the Armenians of the land, who had helped him against the Greeks—some twenty thousand with all their wives and children—for they dared not remain behind.

Then came to him the news, by certain Greeks, who had escaped from the discomfiture, that his brother the Emperor Baldwin was lost, and Count Louis, and the other barons. Afterwards came the news of those who had escaped and were at Rodosto; and these asked him to make all the haste he could, and come to them.

And because he wanted to hasten as much as he could, and reach them earlier, he left behind the Armenians, who travelled on foot, and had with them chariots, and their wives and children; and inasmuch as these could not come on so fast, and he thought they would travel safely and without hurt, he went forward and encamped in a village called Cartopolis.

On that very day came thither the nephew of Geoffry the Marshal, Anseau of Courcelles, whom Geoffry had summoned from the parts of Macre, Trajanopolis, and the Baie, lands that had been bestowed upon him; and with Anseau came the people from Philippopolis, who had left Renier of Trit. This company held full a hundred good knights, and full five hundred mounted sergeants, who all were on their way to Adrianople to succour the Emperor Baldwin.

But tidings had come to them, as to the others, that the emperor had been defeated, so they turned to go to Rodosto, and came to encamp at Cartopolis, the village where Henry, the brother of the Emperor Baldwin, was then encamped. And when Baldwin's men saw them coming, they ran to arms, for they thought they were Greeks, and the others thought the same of Baldwin's men. And so they advanced till they became known to one another, and each was right glad of the other's coming, and felt all the safer; and they quartered themselves in the village that night until the morrow.

On the morrow they left, and rode straight towards Rodosto, and came that night to the city; and there they found the Doge of Venice and Geoffry the Marshal, and all who had escaped from the late discomfiture; and right glad were these to see them. Then were many tears shed for sorrow by those who had lost their friends. Ah, God! what pity it was that those men now assembled had not been at Adrianople with the Emperor Baldwin, for in that case would nothing have been lost. But such was not God's pleasure.

So they sojourned there on the following day, and the day after, and arranged matters; and Henry, the brother of the Emperor Baldwin, was received into lordship, as regent of the empire, in lieu of his brother.

And then misfortune came upon the Armenians, who were coming after Henry, the brother of the Emperor Baldwin, for the people of the land gathered together and discomfited the Armenians, so that they were all taken, killed or lost.

Return to Constantinople—Appeals for Help Sent to the Pope, and to France and to Other Lands—Death of the Doge

Johannizza, King of Wallachia and Bulgaria, had with him all his power, and he occupied the whole land; and the country, and the cities, and the castles held for him; and his Comans over-ran the land as far as Constantinople. Henry the regent of the empire, and the Doge of Venice, and Geoffry the Marshal, were still at Rodosto, which is a three days' journey from Constantinople.

And they took council, and the Doge of Venice set a garrison of Venetians in Rodosto—for it was theirs. And on the morrow they put their forces in array, and rode, day by day, towards Constantinople.

When they reached Salymbria, a city which is two days' journey from Constantinople, and belonged to the Emperor Baldwin, Henry his brother set there a garrison of his people, and they rode with the rest to Constantinople, where they were received right willingly, for the people were in great terror. Nor is that to be wondered at, for they had lost so much of the country, that outside Constantinople they only held Rodosto and Salymbria; the whole of the rest of the country being held by Johannizza, King of Wallachia and Bulgaria. And on the other side of the straits of St. George, they held no more than the castle of Spiga, while the rest of the land was in the hands of Theodore Lascaris.

Then the barons decided to send to the Apostle of Rome, Innocent, and to France and Flanders, and to other lands, to ask for succour. And for this purpose were chosen as envoys Nevelon, Bishop of Soissons, and Nicholas of Mailly, and John Bliaud. The rest remained in Constantinople, in great distress, as men who stood in fear of losing the land. So they remained till Pentecost (29th May 1205). And within this time a very great misfortune happened to the host, for Henry Dandolo was taken sick; so he made an end and died, and was buried with great honour in the Church of St. Sophia.

When Pentecost had come, Johannizza, the King of Wallachia and Bulgaria, had pretty well had his will of the land; and he could no longer hold his Comans together, because they were unable to keep the field during the summer; so the Comans departed to their own country.

And he, with all his host of Bulgarians and Greeks, marched against the marquis towards Salonica. And the marquis, who had heard the news of the discomfiture of the Emperor Baldwin, raised the siege of Napoli, and went to Salonica with as many men as he could collect, and garrisoned it.

The Regent Obtains Certain Advantages Over the Greeks

Henry, the brother of the Emperor Baldwin of Constantinople, with as many people as he could gather, marched against the Greeks to a city called Tzurulum, which is a three days' journey from Constantinople. This city surrendered, and the Greeks swore fealty to him—an oath which at that time men observed badly. From thence he marched to Arcadiapolis, and found it void, for the Greeks did not dare to await his coming. And from thence again he rode to the city of Bizye, which was very strong, and well garrisoned with Greeks; and this city too surrendered. Afterwards he rode to the city of Napoli (Apros) which also remained well garrisoned with Greeks.

As our people were preparing for an assault, the Greeks within the city asked to negotiate for capitulation. But while they thus negotiated, the men of the host effected an entrance into the city on another side, and Henry the Regent of the empire and those who were negotiating knew nothing of it. And this proved very disastrous to the Greeks.

For the Franks, who had effected an entrance, began to slaughter them, and to seize their goods, and to take all that they had. So were many killed and taken captive. In this wise was Napoli (Apros) captured; and the host remained there three days. And the Greeks were so terrified by this slaughter, that they abandoned all the cities and castles of the land, and fled for refuge to Adrianople and Demotica, which were very strong and good cities.

Seres Surrenders to Johannizza—He Forfeits His Word

At that time it happened that Johannizza, the King of Wallachia and Bulgaria, with all his host, marched against the marquis, towards a city called Seres. And the marquis had set a strong garrison of his people in the city, for he had set there Hugh of Colemi, who was a very good knight, and high in rank, and William of Arles, who was his marshal, and great part of his best men. And Johannizza, the King of Wallachia besieged them; nor had he been there long before he took the burgh by force. And at the taking of the burgh a great misfortune befell, for Hugh of Colemi was killed; he was struck through the eye.

When he was killed, who was the best of them all, the rest of the garrison were greatly affeared. They drew back into the castle, which was very strong; and Johannizza besieged them, and erected his petraries and mangonels. Nor had he besieged them long before they began to talk about surrendering, for which they were afterwards blamed, and incurred great reproach. And they agreed to yield up the castle to Johannizza, and Johannizza on his side caused twenty-five of the men of highest rank that he had to swear to them that they should be taken, safe and sound, with all their horses, and all their arms, and all their baggage, to Salonica, or Constantinople, or Hungary—whichever of the three it liked them best.

In this manner was Seres surrendered, and Johannizza! caused the besieged to come forth from the castle and encamp near him in the fields; and he treated them with much fair seeming, and sent them presents. So he kept them for three days, and then he lied and foreswore his promises; for he had them taken, and spoiled of their goods, and led away to Wallachia, naked, and unshod, and on foot.

The poor and the mean people, who were of little worth, he sent into Hungary; and as for the others, he caused their heads to be cut off. Of such mortal treachery was the King of Wallachia guilty, as you have heard. Here did the host suffer grievous loss, one of the most dolorous that ever it suffered. And Johannizza had the castle and city razed, and went on after the marquis.

The Regent Besieges Adrianople in Vain

Henry, the Regent of the empire, with all his power, rode towards Adrianople, and laid siege to it; and he was in great peril, for there were many, both within and without the city who so hemmed him in, he and his people, that they could scantly buy provisions, or go foraging. Therefore they enclosed their camp with palisades and barriers, and told off part of their men to keep guard within the palisades and barriers, while the others attacked the city.

And they devised machines of divers kinds, and scaling ladders, and many other engines, and wrought diligently to take the city. But they could not take it, for the city was very strong and well furnished for defence. So matters went ill with them, and many of their people were wounded; and one of their good knights, Peter of Bracieux, was struck on the forehead from a mangonel, and brought near to death; but he recovered, by the will of God, and was taken away in a litter.

When they saw that they could in no wise prevail against the city, Henry the Regent of the empire, and the French host departed. And greatly were they harassed by the people of the land and by the Greeks; and they rode from day to day till they came to a city called Pamphylia, and lodged there, and sojourned in it for two months. And they made thence many forays towards Demotica and the country round about, where they captured much cattle, and other booty. So the host remained in those parts till the beginning of winter; and supplies came to them from Rodosto, and from the sea.

Destruction of Philippopolis by Johannizza

Now let us leave speaking of Henry, the Regent of the empire, and speak of Johannizza, the King of Wallachia and Bulgaria, who had taken Seres, as you have already heard, and killed by treachery those who had surrendered to him. Afterwards he had ridden towards Salonica, and sojourned thereby a long while, and wasted a great part of the land. The Marquis Boniface of Montferrat was at Salonica, very wroth, and sorrowing greatly for the loss of his lord the Emperor Baldwin, and for the other barons, and for his castle of Seres that he had lost, and for his men.

And when Johannizza saw that he could do nothing more, he retired towards his own land, with all his force. And the people in Philippopolis—which belonged to Renier of Trit, for the Emperor Baldwin had bestowed it upon him—heard tell how the Emperor Baldwin was lost, and many of his barons, and that the marquis had lost Seres; and they saw that the relatives of Renier of Trit, and his own son and his nephew, had abandoned him, and that he had with him but very few people; and they deemed that the Franks would never be in power again. So a great part of the people, who were Paulicians,[14] betook themselves to Johannizza, and surrendered themselves to him, and said: "Sire, ride to Philippopolis, or send thither thy host, and we will deliver the whole city into thy hands."

When Renier of Trit, who was in the city, knew of this, he doubted not that they would yield up the city to Johannizza. So he issued forth with as many people as he could collect, and left at the point of day, and came to one of the outlying quarters of the city where dwelt the Pauliclans who had repaired to Johannizza, and he set fire to that quarter of the city, and burned a great part of it.

---

14. An Eastern sect. They believed, among other things, that all matter is evil, and that Christ suffered in appearance only.

Then he went to the castle of Stanimac, which was at three leagues' distance, and garrisoned by his people, and entered therein. And in this castle he lay besieged for a long while, some thirteen months, in great distress and great poverty so that for famine they ate their horses. He was distant a nine days' journey from Constantinople, and could neither obtain tidings therefrom, nor send tidings thither.

Then did Johannizza send his host before Philippopolis; nor had he been there long before those who were in the city surrendered it to him, and he promised to spare their lives.

And after he had promised to spare their lives, he first caused the archbishop of the city to be slain, and the men of rank to be flayed alive, and certain others to be burned, and certain others to have their heads cut off, and the rest he caused to be driven away in chains.

And the city he caused to be pulled down, with its towers and walls; and the high palaces and rich houses to be burned and utterly destroyed.

Thus was destroyed the noble city of Philippopolis, one of the three finest cities in the empire of Constantinople.

The Regent Sets Garrisons in Such Places as He Still Held

Now let us leave off speaking of those who were at Philippopolis, and of Renier of Trit, who is shut up in Stanimac, and return to Henry, the brother of the Emperor Baldwin, who had sojourned at Pamphylia till the beginning of winter. Then he took council with his men and with his barons; and they decided to set a garrison in a city called Rusium, which was situate at a place rich and fertile in the middle of the land; and the chiefs placed over this garrison were Thierri of Laos, who was seneschal, and Thierri of Tenremonde, who was constable. And Henry, the Regent of the empire, gave to them at least seven score knights, and a great many mounted sergeants, and ordered them to maintain the war against the Greeks, and to guard the marches.

And he himself went with the rest of his people to the city of Bizye, and placed a garrison there; and left in command Anseau of Cayeux, and confided to him at least six score knights, and a great many mounted sergeants. Another city, called Arcadiopolis was garrisoned by the Venetians.

And the city of Napoli was restored by the brother of the Emperor Baldwin to Vernas, who had to wife the sister[15] of the King of France,

15. Agnes, sister to Philip Augustus, King of France.

and was a Greek who sided with us; and except he, no other Greek was on our part. And those who were in these cities maintained the war against the Greeks, and made many forays. Henry himself returned to Contantinople with the rest of his men.

Now Johannizza, the King of Wallachia and Bulgaria, though rich and of great possessions, never forgat his own interests, but raised a great force of Comans and Wallachians. And when it came to three weeks after Christmas, he sent these men into the land of Roumania to help those at Adrianople and Demotica; and the latter, being now in force, grew bolder and rode abroad with the greater assurance.

Defeat of the Franks Near Rusium

Thierri of Tenremonde, who was chief and constable, made a foray on the fourth day before the feast of St. Mary Candlemas (30th January 1206); and he rode all night, having six score knights with him, and left Rusium with but a small garrison. When it was dawn, he came to a village where the Comans and Wallachians were encamped, and surprised them in such sort that those who were in the village were unaware of their coming. They killed a good many of the Comans and Wallachians, and captured some forty of their horses; and when they had done this execution, they turned back towards Rusium.

And on that very night the Comans and Wallachians had ridden forth to do us hurt; and there were some seven thousand of them. They came in the morning before Rusium, and were there a long space; and the garrison, which was but small, closed the gates, and mounted the walls; and the Comans and Wallachians turned back. They had not gone more than a league and a half from the city, when they met the company of the French under the command of Thierri of Tenremonde. So soon as the French saw them advancing, they formed into their four battalions, with intent to draw into Rusium in slow time; for they knew that if, by God's grace, they could come thither, they would then be in safety.

The Comans, and the Wallachians, and the Greeks of the land rode towards them, for they were in very great force. And they came upon the rear-guard, and began to harass it full sorely. Now the rear-guard was formed of the men of Thierri of Loos, who was seneschal, and had returned to Constantinople, and his brother Villain was now in command.

And the Comans and Wallachians and Greeks pressed them very hard, and wounded many of their horses. Loud were the cries and fierce the onslaught, so that by main force and pure distress they drove the rear-guard back on the battalion of Andrew of Urboise and John of Choisy; and in this manner the Franks retreated, suffering greatly

The enemy renewed their onslaught so fiercely that they drove the Franks who were nearest to them back on the battalion of Thierri of Tenremonde, the constable. Nor was it long before they drove them back still further on to the battalions led by Charles of the Frêne. And now the Franks had retreated, sore harassed, till they were within half a mile of Rusium. And the others ever pressed upon them more hardily; and the battle went sore against them, and many were wounded, and of their horses. So, as God will suffer misadventures, they could endure no further, but were discomfited; for they were heavily armed, and their enemies lightly; and the latter began to slaughter them.

Alas! well might Christendom rue that day! For of all those six score knights did not more than ten escape who were not killed or taken; and those who escaped came flying into Rusium, and rejoined their own people. There was slain Thierri of Tenremonde, the constable, Orri of l'Isle, who was a good knight and highly esteemed, and John of Pompone, Andrew of Urboise, John of Choisy, Guy of Conflans, Charles of the Frêne, Villain the brother of Thierri the seneschal. Nor can this book tell the names of all who were then killed or taken. On that day happened one of the greatest mishaps, and the most grievous that ever befell to the Christendom of the land of Roumania, and one of the most pitiful.

The Comans and Greeks and Wallacruans retired, having done according to their will in the land, and won many good horses and good hawberks.

And this misadventure happened on the day before the eve of our Lady St. Mary Candlemas (31st January 1206). And the remnant who had escaped from the discomfiture, together with those who had been in Rusium, escaped from the city, so soon as it was night, and went an night flying, and came on the morrow to the city of Rodosto.

New Invasion of Johannizza; Ruin of Napoli

This dolorous news came to Henry the Regent of the empire, while he was going in procession to the shrine of our Lady of Blachernæ, on the day of the feast of our Lady St. Mary Candlemas. And you must know that many were then dismayed in Constantinople, and they thought of a truth that the land was but lost. And Henry, the Regent of the empire, decided that he would place a garrison in

Salymbria, which was a two days' journey from Constantinople, and he sent thither Macaire of Sainte-Menehould, with fifty knights to garrison the city.

Now when tidings came to Johannizza, King of Wallachia, as to how his people had fared, he was very greatly rejoiced; for they had killed or taken a very great part of the best men in the French host. So he sent throughout all his lands to collect as many people as he could, and raised a great host of Comans, and Greeks and Wallachians, and entered into Roumania. And the greater part of the cities held for him, and all the castles; and he had so large a host that it was a marvel.

When the Venetians heard tell that he was coming with so great a force, they abandoned Arcadiopolis. And Johannizza rode with all his hosts till he came to Napoli, which was garrisoned by Greeks and Latins, and belonged to Vernas, who had to wife the empress, the sister of the King of France; and of the Latins was chief Bègue of Fransures, a knight of the land of the Beauvaisais. And Johannizza, the King of Wallachia, caused the city to be assaulted, and took it by force.

There was so great a slaughter of people killed that it was a marvel. And Bègue of Fransures was taken before Johannizza, who had him killed incontinently, together with all, whether Greek or Latin, who were of any account; and all the meaner folk, and women and children, he caused to be led away captive to Wallachia. Then did he cause all the city—which was very good and very rich, and in a good land, to be cast down and utterly destroyed. Thus was the city of Napoli rased to the ground as you have heard.

Destruction of Rodosto

Twelve leagues thence lay the city of Rodosto, on the sea. It was very strong, and rich, and large, and very well garrisoned by Venetians. And besides all this, there had come thither a body of sergeants, some two thousand strong, and they had also come to guard the city. When they heard that Napoli had been taken by force, and that Johannizza had caused all the people that were therein to be put to death, they fell into such terror that they were utterly confounded and foredone.

As God suffers misadventures to fall upon men, so the Venetians rushed to their ships, helter-skelter, pell-mell, and in such sort that they almost drowned one another; and the mounted sergeants, who came from France and Flanders, and other countries, went flying through the land.

Now listen and hear how little this served them, and what a misadventure was their flight; for the city was so strong., and so well enclosed by good walls and good towers, that no one would ever have ventured to assault it, and that Johannizza had no thought of going thither.

But when Johannizza, who was full half a day's journey distant, heard tell that they had fled, he rode thither. The Greeks who had remained in the city, surrendered, and he incontinently caused them to be taken, small and great—save those who escaped—and led captive into Wallachia; and the city he ordered to be destroyed and rased to the ground. Ah! the loss and damage! for the city was one of the best in Roumania, and of the best situated.

Johannizza Continues His Conquests and Ravages

Near there was another city called Panedor, which surrendered to him; and he caused it to be utterly destroyed, and the people to be led captive to Wallachia like the people of Rodosto. Afterwards he rode to the city of Heraclea, that lay by a good seaport, and belonged to the Venetians, who had left in it but a weak garrison; so he assaulted it, and took it by force. There again was a mighty slaughter, and the remnant that escaped the slaughter he caused to be led captive to Wallachia, while the city itself he destroyed, as he had destroyed the others.

Thence he marched to the city of Daonium, which was very strong and fine; and the people did not dare to defend it. So he caused it to be destroyed and rased to the ground. Then he marched to the city of Tzurulum, which had already surrendered to him, and caused it to be destroyed and rased to the ground, and the people to be led away captive. And thus he dealt with every castle and city that surrendered; even though he had promised them safety, he caused the buildings to be destroyed, and the men and women to be led away captive; and no covenant that he made did he ever keep.

Then the Comans and Wallachians scoured the land up to the gates of Constantinople, where Henry the Regent then was, with as many men as he could command; and very dolorous was he and very wroth, because he could not get men enough to defend his land. So the Comans seized the cattle off the land, and took captive men, women, and children, and destroyed the cities and castles, and caused such ruin and desolation that never has man heard tell of greater.

So they came to a city called Athyra, which was twelve leagues from Constantinople, and had been given to Payen of Orleans by Henry, the emperor's brother. This city held a very great number of people, for the dwellers in the country round about had fled thither; and the Comans assaulted it, and took it by force. There the slaughter was so great, that there had been none such in any city where they had been. And you must know that all the castles and all the cities that surrendered to Johannizza under promise of safety were destroyed and rased to the ground, and the people led away captive to Wallachia in such manner as you have heard.

And you must know that within five days' journey from Constantinople there remained nothing to destroy save only the city of Bizye, and the city of Salymbria, which were garrisoned by the French. And in Bizye abode Anseau of Cayeux, with six score knights, and in Salymbria abode Macaire of Sainte-Menehould with fifty knights; and Henry the brother of the Emperor Baldwin remained in Constantinople with the remainder of the host. And you may know that their fortunes were at the lowest, seeing that outside of Constantinople they had kept possession of no more than these two cities.

The Greeks are Reconciled to the Crusaders— Johannizza Besieges Demotica

When the Greeks who were in the host with Johannizza—the same who had yielded themselves up to him, and rebelled against the Franks—when they saw how he destroyed their castles and cities, and kept no covenant with them, they held themselves to be but dead men, and betrayed. They spoke one to another, and said that as Johannizza had dealt with other cities, so would he deal with Adrianople and Demotica, when he returned thither, and that if these two cities were destroyed, then was Roumania for ever lost.

So they took messengers privily, and sent them to Vernas in Constantinople. And they besought Vernas to cry for pity to Henry, the brother of the Emperor Baldwin, and to the Venetians, so that they might make peace with them; and they themselves, in turn, would restore Adrianople and Demotica to the Franks; and the Greeks would all turn to Henry; and the Greeks and Franks dwell together in good accord.

So a council was held, and many words were spoken this way and that, but in the end it was settled that Adrianople and Demotica, with all their appurtenances, should be bestowed on Vernas and the empress his wife, who was sister to the King Philip of France, and that they should do service therefor to the emperor and to the empire. Such was the convention made and concluded, and so was peace established between the Greeks and the Franks.

Johannizza, the King of Wallachia and Bulgaria, who had sojourned long in Roumania, and wasted the country during the whole of Lent, and for a good while after Easter (2nd April 1206), now retired towards Adrianople and Demotica, and had it in mind to deal with those cities as he had dealt with the other cities of the land. And when the Greeks who were with him saw that he turned towards Adrianople, they began to steal away, both by day and by night, some twenty, thirty, forty, a hundred, at a time.

When he came to Adrianople, he required of those that were within that they should let him enter, as he had entered elsewhere. But they said they would not, and spoke thus: "Sire, when we surrendered to thee, and rebelled against the Franks, thou didst swear to protect us in all good faith, and to keep us in safety. Thou hast not done so, but hast utterly ruined Roumania; and we know full well that thou wilt do unto us as thou hast done unto others." And when Johannizza heard this, he laid siege to Demotica, and erected round it sixteen large petraries, and began to construct engines of every kind for the siege, and to waste all the country round.

Then did those in Adrianople and Demotica take messengers, and send them to Constantinople, to Henry, the Regent of the empire, and to Vernas, and prayed them, for God's sake, to rescue Demotica, which was being besieged. And when those at Constantinople heard these tidings, they decided to succour Demotica. But some there were who did not dare to advise that our people should issue from Constantinople, and so place in jeopardy the few Christian folk that remained. Nevertheless, in the end, as you have heard, it was decided to issue forth, and move on Salymbria.

The cardinal, who was there as legate on the part of the Pope of Rome, preached thereon to the people, and promised a full indulgence to all such as should go forth, and lose their lives on the way.

So Henry issued from Constantinople with as many men as he could collect, and marched to the city of Salymbria; and he encamped before the city for full eight days. And from day to day came messengers from Adrianople praying him to have mercy upon them, and come to their relief, for if he did not come to their relief, they were but lost.

The Crusaders March to the Relief of Demotica

Then did Henry take council with his barons, and their decision was that they would go to the city of Bizye, which was a fair city, and strong. So they did as they had devised, and came to Bizye, and encamped before the city on the eve of the feast of our Lord St. John the Baptist, in June (23rd June 1206). And on the day that they so encamped came messengers from Adrianople, and said to Henry, the brother of the Emperor Baldwin:

> Sire, be it known to thee that if thou dost not relieve the city of Demotica, it cannot hold out more than eight days, for Johannizza's petraries have breached the walls in four places, and his men have twice got on to the walls.

Then he asked for counsel as to what he should do. Many were the words spoken, to and fro; but in the end they said:

> Lord, we have come so far that we shall be forever shamed if we do not succour Demotica. Let every man now confess and receive the communion; and then let us set our forces in array.

And it was reckoned that they had with them about four hundred knights, and of a certainty no more. So they summoned the messengers who had come from Adrianople, and asked them how matters stood, and what number of men Johannizza had with him. And the messengers answered that he had with him at least forty thousand men-at-arms, not reckoning those on foot, of whom they had no count.

Ah God! what a perilous battle—so few against so many! In the morning, on the day of the feast of our Lord St. John the Baptist, all confessed and received the communion, and on the following day they marched forward. The van was commanded by Geoffry, the Marshal of Roumania and Champagne, and with him was Macaire of Sainte-Menehould. The Second Division was under Conon of Bethune and Miles the Brabant; the Third under Payen of Orleans and Peter of Bracieux; the Fourth was under Anseau of Cayeux; the Fifth under Baldwin of Beauvoir; the Sixth under Hugh of Beaumetz; the Seventh under Henry, brother of the Emperor Baldwin; the Eighth, with the Flemings, under Walter of Escornai; Thierri of Loos, who was seneschal, commanded the rear-guard.

So they rode for three days, all in order; nor did any host ever advance seeking battle so perilously. For they were in peril on two accounts; first because they were so few, and those they were about to attack so many; and secondly, because they did not believe the Greeks, with whom they had just made peace, would help them heartily. For they stood in fear lest, when need arose, the Greeks would go over to Johannizza, who, as you have already heard, had been so near to taking Demotica.

Johannizza Retreats, Followed by the Crusaders

When Johannizza heard that the Franks were coming, he did not dare to abide, but burned his engines of war, and broke up his camp. So he departed from Demotica; and you must know that this was accounted by all the world as a great miracle. And Henry, the Regent of the empire, came on the fourth day (28th June) before Adrianople, and pitched his camp near the river of Adrianople, in the fairest meadows in the world. When those who were within the city saw his host coming, they issued forth, bearing all their crosses, and in procession, and showed such joy as had never been seen. And well might they rejoice for they had been in evil case.

Then came tidings to the host that Johannizza was lodged at a castle called Rodosto. So in the morning they set forth and marched to those parts to seek battle; and Johannizza broke up his camp, and marched back towards his own land. The host followed after him for five days, and he as constantly retired before them. On the fifth day they encamped at a very fair and pleasant place by a castle called Fraim; and there they sojourned three days.

And at this place there was a division in the host, and a company of valiant men separated themselves therefrom because of a quarrel that they had with Henry, the brother of the Emperor Baldwin. Of this company Baldwin of Beauvoir was chief; and Hugh of Beaumetz went with him, and William of Gommegnies and Dreux of Beaurain. There were some fifty knights who departed together in that company; and they never thought the rest would dare to remain in the land in the midst of their enemies.

Renier of Trit Relieved and Delivered

Then did Henry, the Regent of the empire, take council with the barons that were with him; and they decided to ride forward. So they rode forward for two days, and encamped in a very fair valley, near a castle called Moniac. The castle yielded itself to them, and they remained there five days; and then said they would go and relieve Renier of Trit, who was besieged in Stanimac, and had been shut up therein for thirteen months. So Henry the Regent of the empire, remained in the camp, with a great part of the host, and the remainder went forward to relieve Renier of Trit at Stanimac.

And you must know that those who went forward went in very great peril, and that any rescue so full of danger has but seldom been undertaken, seeing that they rode for three days through the land of their enemies. In this rescue took part Conon of Bethune, and Geoffry of Villehardouin, Marshal of Roumania and Champagne, and Macaire of Sainte-Menehould, and Miles the Brabant, and Peter of Bracieux, and Payen of Orleans, and Anseau of Cayeux, and Thierri of Laos, and William of the Perchoi, and a body of Venetians under command of Andrew Valère. So they rode forward till they came to the castle of Stanimac, and approached so near that they could now see it.

Renier of Trit was on the walls, and he perceived the advanced guard, which was under Geoffry the Marshal, and the other battalions, approaching in very good order; and he knew not what people they might be. And no wonder that he was in doubt, for of a long time he had heard no tidings of us; and he thought we were Greeks coming to besiege him.

Geoffry the Marshal of Roumania and Champagne took certain Turcoples[16] and mounted cross-bowmen and sent them forward to see if they could learn the condition of the castle; for they knew not if those within it were alive or dead, seeing that of a long time they had heard no tidings of them. And when these came before the castle, Renier of Trit and his men knew them; and you may well think what joy they had! They issued forth and came to meet their friends, and all made great joy of each other.

The barons quartered themselves in a very good city that lay at the foot of the castle, and had aforetime besieged the castle. Then said the barons that they had often heard tell that the Emperor Baldwin had died in Johannizza's prison, but that they did not believe it. Renier of Trit, however, told them of a truth that the emperor was dead, and then they believed it. Greatly did many then grieve; alas! if only their grief had not been beyond remedy!

So they lay that night in the city; and on the morrow they departed, and abandoned Stanimac. They rode for two days, and on the third they came to the camp, below the castle of Moniac, that lies on the River Arta, where Henry, the Emperor's brother, was waiting for them. Greatly did those of the host rejoice over Renier of Trit, who had thus been rescued from durance, and great was the credit given

---

16. Soldiers born of a Turkish father and a Greek mother.

to those who had brought him back, for they had gone for him in great peril.

HENRY CROWNED EMPEROR—JOHANNIZZA RAVAGES THE COUNTRY AGAIN—THE EMPEROR MARCHES AGAINST HIM

The barons now resolved that they would go to Constantinople, and crown Henry, the brother of the Emperor Baldwin as emperor, and leave in the country Vernas, and all the Greeks of the land, together with forty knights, whom Henry, the Regent of the empire, would leave with him. So Henry, the Regent of the empire, and the other barons, went towards Constantinople, and they rode from day to day till they came thither, and right well were they received.

They crowned Henry as emperor with great joy and great honour in the Church of St. Sophia, on the Sunday (20th August) after the festival of our Lady St. Mary, in August. And this was in the year of the Incarnation of our Lord Jesus Christ twelve hundred and six.

Now when Johannizza, the King of Wallachia and Bulgaria, heard that the emperor had been crowned in Constantinople, and that Vernas had remained in the land of Adrianople and Demotica, he collected together as large a force as he could. And Vernas had not rebuilt the walls of Demotica where they had been breached by Johannizza with his petraries and mangonels, and he had set but a weak garrison therein. So Johannizza marched on Demotica, and took it, and destroyed it, and rased the walls to the ground, and over-ran the whole country, and took men, women, and children for a prey, and wrought devastation. Then did those in Adrianople beseech the Emperor Henry to succour them, seeing that Demotica had been lost in such cruel sort.

Then did the Emperor Henry summon as many people as he could, and issued from Constantinople, and rode day by day towards Adrianople, with all his forces in order. And Johannizza, the King of Wallachia who was in the land, when he heard that the emperor was coming, drew back into his own land. And the Emperor Henry rode forward till he came to Adrianople, and he encamped outside the city in a meadow.

Then came the Greeks of the land, and told him that Johannizza, the King of Wallachia, was carrying off men and women and cattle, and that he had destroyed Demotica, and I wasted the country round; and that he was still within day's march. The emperor settled that he would follow after, and do battle—if so be that Johannizza would abide his coming—and deliver the men and women who were being led away captive. So he rode after Johannizza, and Johannizza retired as the emperor advanced, and the emperor followed him for four days. Then they came to a city called Veroi.

When those who were in the city saw the host of the Emperor Henry approaching, they fled into the mountains and abandoned the city. And the emperor came with all his host, and encamped before the city, and found it well furnished with corn and meat, and such other things as were needful. So they sojourned there for two days, and the emperor caused his men to overrun the surrounding country, and they obtained a large booty in beeves and cows and buffaloes, and other beasts in very great plenty.

Then he departed from Veroi with all his booty, and rode to another city, a day's journey distant, called Blisnon. And as the other Greeks had abandoned Veroi, so did the dwellers in Blisnon abandon their city; and he found it furnished with all things necessary, and quartered himself there.

The Emperor Meets Johannizza, and Recaptures His Prisoners

Then came tidings that in a certain valley, three leagues distant from the host, were the men and women whom Johannizza was leading away captive, together with all his plunder, and all his chariots. Then did Henry appoint that the Greeks from Adrianople and Demotica should go and recover the captives and the plunder, two battalions of knights going with them; and as had been arranged, so was this done on the morrow. The command of the one battalion was given to Eustace, the brother of the Emperor Henry of Constantinople, and the command of the other to Macaire of Sainte-Menehould.

So they rode, they and the Greeks, till they came to the valley of which they had been told; and there they found the captives. And Johannizza's men engaged the Emperor Henry's men, and men and horses were killed and wounded on either side; but by the goodness of God, the Franks had the advantage, and rescued the captives, and caused them to turn again, and brought them away.

And you must know that this was a mighty deliverance; for the captives numbered full twenty thousand men, women, and children; and there were full three thousand chariots laden with their clothes and baggage, to say nothing of other booty in good quantity. The line of the captives, as they came to the camp, was two great leagues in length, and they reached the camp that night. Then was the Emperor

Henry greatly rejoiced, and all the other barons; and they had the captives lodged apart, and well guarded, with their goods, so that they lost not one pennyworth of what they possessed. On the morrow the Emperor Henry rested for the sake of the people he had delivered. And on the day after he left that country, and rode day by day till he came to Adrianople.

There he set free the men and women he had rescued; and each one went whithersoever he listed, to the land where he was born, or to any other place. The booty, of which he had great plenty, was divided in due shares among the host. So the Emperor Henry sojourned there five days, and then rode to the city of Demotica, to see how far it had been destroyed, and whether it could again be fortified. He encamped before the city, and saw, both he and his barons, that in the state in which it then was, it were not well to refortify it.

Projected Marriage Between the Emperor and the Daughter of Boniface—The Crusaders Ravage the Lands of Johannizza

Then came to the camp, as envoy, a baron, Otho of La Roche by name, belonging to the Marquis Boniface of Montferrat. He came to speak of a marriage that had been spoken of aforetime between the daughter of Boniface, the Marquis of Montferrat, and the Emperor Henry; and brought tidings that the lady had come from Lombardy, whence her father had sent to summon her, and that she was now at Salonica. Then did the emperor take council, and it was decided that the marriage should be ratified on either side. So the envoy, Otho of La Roche, returned to Salonica.

The emperor had reassembled his men, who had gone to place in safe holding the booty taken at Veroi. And he marched day by day from Adrianople till he came to the land of Johannizza, the King of Wallachia and Bulgaria. They came to a city called Fenne, and took it, and entered in, and won much booty. They remained there for three days, and overran all the land, got very much spoil, and destroyed a city called Aquilo.

On the fourth day they departed from Ferme, which was a city fair and well situated, with hot water springs for bathing, the finest in the world; and the emperor caused the city to be burned and destroyed, and they carried away much spoil, in cattle and goods. Then they rode day by day till they came back to the city of Adrianople; and they sojourned in the land till the feast of All Saints (1st November 1206), when they could no longer carry on the war because of the winter. So Henry and all his barons, who were much aweary of campaigning, turned their faces towards Constantinople; and he left at Adrianople, among the Greeks, a man of his named Peter of Radinghem, with ten knights.

The Emperor Resumes the War Against Theodore Lascaris

At that time Theodore Lascaris, who held the land on the other side of the straits towards Turkey, was at truce with the Emperor Henry; but that truce he had not kept well, having broken and violated it. So the emperor held council, and sent to the other side of the straits, to the city of Piga, Peter of Bracieux, to whom land had been assigned in those parts, and with him Payen of Orleans, and Anseau of Cayeux, and Eustace, the emperor's brother, and a great part of his best men to the number of seven score knights. These began to make war in very grim and earnest fashion against Theodore Lascaris, and greatly wasted his land.

They marched to a land called Skiza, which was surrounded by the sea except on one side. And in old days the way of entry had been defended with walls and towers, and moats, but these were now decayed. So the host of the French entered in, and Peter of Bracieux, to whom the land had been devised, began to restore the defences, and built two castles, and made two fortified ways of entry.

From thence they overran the land of Lascaris, and gained much booty and cattle, and brought such booty and cattle into their island. Theodore Lascaris, on the other hand, harked back upon Skiza, so that there were frequent battles and skirmishes, and losses on the one side and on the other; and the war in those parts was fierce and perilous.

Now let us leave speaking of those who were at Skiza, and speak of Thierri of Loos, who was seneschal, and to whom Nicomedia should have belonged; and Nicomedia lay a day's journey from Nice the Great, the capital of the land of Theodore Lascaris. Thierri then went thither, with a great body of the emperor's men, and found that the castle had been destroyed. So he enclosed an fortified the Church of St. Sophia, which was very large and fair, and maintained the war in that place.

Advantages Obtained by Boniface—Marriage of His Daughter With the Emperor

At that time the Marquis Boniface of Montferrat departed from Salonica, and went to Seres, which Johannizza had destroyed; and he rebuilt it; and afterwards rebuilt a castle called Drama in the valley of Philippi. All the country round about surrendered to him, and came under his rule; and he wintered in the land.

Meanwhile, so much time had gone by, that Christmas was now past. Then came messengers from the marquis to the emperor at Constantinople to say that the marquis had sent his daughter in a galley to the city of Abydos. So the Emperor Henry sent Geoffry the Marshal of Roumania and Champagne, and Miles the Brabant, to bring the lady; and these rode day by day till they came to Abydos.

They found the lady, who was very good and fair, and saluted her on behalf of their lord Henry, the emperor, and brought her to Constantinople in great honour. So the Emperor Henry was wedded to her in the Church of St. Sophia, on the Sunday after the feast of our Lady St. Mary Candlemas (4th February 1207), with great joy and in great pomp; and they both wore a crown; and high were the marriage-feastings in the palace of Bucoleon. Thus, as you have just heard, was the marriage celebrated between the emperor and the daughter of the Marquis Boniface, Agnes the empress by name.

Theodore Lascaris Forms an Alliance With Johannizza

Theodore Lascaris, who was warring against the Emperor Henry, took messengers and sent them to Johannizza, the King of Wallachia and Bulgaria. And he advised Johannizza that all the forces of the Emperor Henry were fighting against him (Lascaris) on the other side of the straits towards Turkey; that the emperor was in Constantinople with but very few people; and that now was the time for vengeance, inasmuch as he himself would be attacking the emperor on the one side, and Johannizza on the other, and the emperor had so few men that he would not be able to defend himself against both.

Now Johannizza had already engaged a great host of Comans, who were on their way to join his host; and had collected together as large a force of Wallachians and Bulgarians as ever he could. And so much time had now gone by, that it was the beginning of Lent (7th March 1207).

Macaire of Sainte-Menehould had begun to build a castle at Charax, which lies on a gulf of the sea, six leagues from Nicomedia, towards

Constantinople. And William of Sains began to build another castle at Cibotos, that lies on the gulf of Nicomedia, on the other side, towards Nice. And you must know that the Emperor Henry had as much as he could do near Constantinople; as also the barons who were in the land. And well does Geoffry of Villehardouin, the Marshal of Champagne and Roumania, who is dictating this work, bear witness, that never at any time were people so distracted and oppressed by war; this was by reason that the host were scattered in so many places.

SIEGE OF ADRIANOPLE BY JOHANNIZZA—SIEGE OF SKIZA AND CIBOTOS BY LASCARIS

Then Johannizza left Wallachia with all his hosts, and with a great host of Comans who joined themselves to him, and entered Roumania. And the Comans overran the country up to the gates of Constantinople; and he himself besieged Adrianople, and erected there thirty-three great petraries, which hurled stones against the walls and the towers. And inside Adrianople were only the Greeks and Peter of Radinghem, who had been set there by the emperor, with ten knights. Then the Greeks and the Latins together sent to tell the Emperor Henry how Johannizza had besieged them, and prayed for succour.

Much was the emperor distraught when he heard this; for his forces on the other side of the straits were so scattered, and were everywhere so hard pressed that they could do no more than they were doing, while he himself had but few men in Constantinople. None the less he undertook to take the field with as many men as he could collect, in the Easter fortnight; and he sent word to Skiza, where most of his people were, that they should come to him. So these began to come to him by sea; Eustace, the brother of the Emperor Henry, and Anseau of Cayeux, and the main part of their men, and thus only Peter of Bracieux, and Payen of Orleans, with but few men, remained in Skiza.

When Theodore Lascaris heard tidings that Adrianople was besieged, and that the Emperor Henry, through utter need, was recalling his people, and did not know which way to turn□whether to this side or to that—so heavily was he oppressed by the war, then did Lascaris with the greater zeal gather together all the people he could, and pitched his tents and pavilions before the gates of Skiza; and many were the battles fought before Skiza, some lost and some won.

And when Theodore Lascaris saw that there were few people remaining in the city, he took a great part of his host, and such ships as he could collect on the sea, and sent them to the castle of Cibotos, which William of Sains was fortifying; and they set siege to the castle by sea and land, on the Saturday in mid-Lent (31st March 1207).

Within were forty knights, very good men, and Macaire of Sainte-Menehould was their chief; and their castle was as yet but little fortified, so that their foes could come at them with swords and lances. The enemy attacked them by land and by sea very fiercely; and, the assault lasted during the whole of Saturday, and our people defended themselves very well. And this book bears witness that never did fifty knights defend themselves at greater disadvantage against such odds. And well may this appear, for of the knights that were there, all were wounded save five only; and one was killed, who was nephew to Miles the Brabant, and his name was Giles.

The Emperor Attacks the Fleet of Theodore Lascaris, and Rescues Cibotos

Before this assault began, on the Saturday morning, there came a messenger flying to Constantinople. He found the Emperor Henry in the palace of Blachernæ, sitting at meat, and spoke to him thus: "Sire, be it known to you that those at Cibotos are being attacked by land and sea; and if you do not speedily deliver them, they will be taken, and but dead men."

With the emperor were Conon of Bethune, and Geoffry the Marshal of Champagne, and Miles the Brabant, and but very few people. And they held a council, and the council was but short, and the emperor went down to the shore, and entered into a galleon; and each one was to take ship such as he could find. And it was proclaimed throughout the city that all were to follow the emperor in the utter need wherein he stood, to go and rescue his men, seeing that without help they were but lost.

Then might you have seen the whole city of Constantinople all a-swarm with Venetians and Pisans and other seafaring folk, running to their ships, helter-skelter and pell-mell; and with them entered into the ships the knights, fully armed; and whosoever was first ready, he first left port to go after the emperor.

So they went rowing hard all the evening, as long as the light lasted, and all through the night till the dawn of the following day. And the emperor had used such diligence, that a little after sun-rising he came in sight of Cibotos, and of the host surrounding it by sea and land. And those who were within the castle had not slept that night, but had kept guard through the whole night, however sick or wounded they might be, as men who expected nothing but death.

The emperor saw that the Greeks were close to the walls and about to assault the city. Now he himself had but few of his people with him—among them were Geoffry the Marshal in another ship, and Miles the Brabant, and certain Pisans, and other knights, so that he had some sixteen ships great and small, while on the other side there were full sixty. Nevertheless they saw that if they waited for their people, and suffered the Greeks to assault Citobos, then those within must be all killed or taken; and when they saw this they decided to sail against the enemy's ships.

They sailed thitherward therefore in line; and all those on board the ships were fully armed, and with their helms laced. And when the Greeks, who were about to attack the castle, saw us coming, they perceived that help was at hand for the besieged, and they avoided the castle, and came to meet us; and all this great host, both horse and foot, drew up on the shore. And the Greeks on ship-board [17] when they saw that the emperor and his people meant to attack them in any case, drew back towards those on shore, so that the latter might give them help with bows and darts.

So the emperor held them close with his seventeen ships, till the shouts of those coming from Constantinople began to reach him; and when the night fell so many had come up that the Franks were everywhere in force upon the sea; and they lay all armed during the night, and cast anchor. And they settled that as soon as they saw the day, they would go and do battle with the enemy on the shore, and also seize their ships. But when it came to about midnight, the Greeks dragged all their ships to land, and set fire to them, and burned them all, and broke up their camp, and went away flying.

The Emperor Henry and his host were right glad of the victory that God had given them, and that they had thus been able to succour their people. And when it came to be morning, the emperor and his barons went to the castle of Cibotos, and found those who were therein very sick, and for the most part sore wounded. And the emperor and his people looked at the castle, and saw that it was so weak as not to be worth the holding. So they gathered all their people into the ships, and left the castle and abandoned it. Thus did the Emperor Henry return to Constantinople.

---

17. The meaning here is a little obscure in the original.

Johannizza Raises the Siege of Adrianople

Johannizza, the king of Wallachia, who had besieged Adrianople, gave himself no rest, for his petraries, of which he had many, cast stones night and day against the walls and towers, and damaged the walls and towers very greatly. And he set his sappers to mine the walls, and made many assaults.

And well did those who were within, both Greeks and Latins, maintain themselves, and often did they beg the Emperor Henry to succour them, and warn him that, if he did not succour them, they were utterly undone. The emperor was much distraught; for when he wished to go and succour his people at Adrianople on the one side, then Theodore Lascaris pressed upon him so straitly on the other side, that of necessity he was forced to draw back.

So Johannizza remained during the whole month of April (1207) before Adrianople; and he came so near to taking it that in two places he beat down the walls and towers to the ground, and his men fought hand to hand, with swords and lances, against those who were within. Also he made assaults in force, and the besieged defended themselves well; and there were many killed and wounded on one side and on the other.

As it pleases God that adventures should be ordered, so it befell that the Comans who had overrun the land, and gained much booty, and returned to the camp before Adrianople, with all their spoils, now said they would remain with Johannizza no longer, but go back to their own land. Thus the Comans abandoned Johannizza. And without them he dared not remain before Adrianople. So he departed from before the city, and left it.

And you must know that this was held to be a great miracle: that the siege of a city so near to the taking should be abandoned, and by a man possessed of such power. But as God wills, so do events befall. Those in Adrianople made no delay in begging the emperor, for the love of God, to come o them as soon as he could; for sooth it was that if Johannizza, the King of Wallachia returned, they would all be killed or taken.

Skiza Again Besieged by Theodore Lascaris—
The Emperor Delivers the City

The emperor, with as many men as he possessed, had prepared to go to Adrianople, when tidings came, very grievous, that Escurion, who was admiral of the galleys of Theodore Lascaris, had entered with seventeen galleys into the straits of Abydos, in the channel of St. George, and come before Skiza, where Peter of Bracieux then was, and Payen of Orleans; and that the said Escurion was besieging the city by sea, while Theodore Lascaris was besieging it by land. Moreover, the people of the land of Skiza had rebelled against Peter of Bracieux, as also those of Marmora, and had wrought him great harm, and killed many of his people.

When these tidings came to Constantinople, they were greatly dismayed. Then did the Emperor Henry take council with his men, and his barons, and the Venetians also; and they said that if they did not succour Peter of Bracieux, and Payen of Orleans, they were but dead men, and the land would be lost. So they armed fourteen galleys in all diligence, and set in them the Venetians of most note, and all the barons of the emperor.

In one galley entered Conon of Bethune and his people; in another Geoffry of Villehardouin and his people; in the third Macaire of Sainte-Menehould and his people; in the fourth Miles the Brabant; in the fifth Anseau of Cayeux; in the sixth Thierri of Loos, who was seneschal of Roumania; in the seventh William of the Perchoi; and in the eighth Eustace the emperor's brother. Thus did the Emperor Henry put into all these galleys the best people that he had; and when they left the port of Constantinople, well did all say that never had galleys been better armed, nor manned with better men. And thus, for this time, the march on Adrianople was again put off.

Those who were in the galleys sailed down the straits, right towards Skiza. How Escurion, the admiral of Theodore Lascaris' galleys, heard of it, I know not; but he abandoned Skiza, and went away, and fled down the straits. And the others chased him two days and two nights, beyond the straits of Abydos, forty miles. And when they saw they could not come up with him, they turned back, and came to Skiza, and found there Peter of Bracieux and Payen of Orleans; and Theodore Lascaris had dislodged from before the city and repaired to his own land. Thus was Skiza relieved, as you have just heard; and those in the galleys turned back to Constantinople, and prepared once more to march on Adrianople.

The Emperor Twice Delivers Nicomedia, Besieged by Theodore Lascaris

Theodore Lascaris sent the most part of his force into the land of Nicomedia. And the people of Thierri of Loos, who had fortified the Church of St. Sophia, and were therein, besought their lord and the emperor to come to their relief; for if they received no help they could not hold out, especially as they had no provisions. Through sheer distress and sore need, the Emperor Henry and his people agreed that they must once more abandon thought of going to Adrianople, and cross the straits of St. George, to the Turkish side, with as many people as they could collect, and succour Nicomedia.

And when the people of Theodore Lascaris heard that the emperor was coming, they avoided the land, and retreated towards Nice the Great. And when the emperor knew of it, he took council, and it was decided that Thierri of Loos, the seneschal of Roumania, should abide in Nicomedia, with all his knights, and all his sergeants, to guard the land; and Macaire of Sainte-Menehould should abide at Charax, and William of the Perchois in Skiza; and each defend the land where he abode.

Then did the Emperor Henry, and the remainder of his people return to Constantinople, and prepare once again to go towards Adrianople. And while he was so preparing, Thierri of Loos the seneschal, who was in Nicomedia, and William of the Perchoi, and all their people, went out foraging on a certain day. And the people of Theodore Lascaris knew of it, and surprised them, and fell upon them. Now the people of Theodore Lascaris were very many, and our people very few. So the battle began, and they fought hand to hand, and before very long the few were not able to stand against the many.

Thierri of Loos did right well, as also his people; he was twice struck down, and by main strength his men remounted him. And William of the Perchoi was also struck down, and remounted and rescued. But numbers hemmed them in too sore, and the Franks were discomfited. There was taken Thierri of Loos, wounded in the face, and in peril of death. There, too, were most of his people taken, for few escaped. William of the Perchois fled on a hackney, wounded in the hand. Those that escaped from the discomfiture rallied in the Church of St. Sophia.

He who dictates this history heard blame attached in this affair—whether rightly or wrongly he knows not—to a certain knight named Ànseau of Remi, who was liegeman of Thierri of Laos the seneschal, and chief of his men; and who abandoned him in the fray.

Then did those who had returned to the Church of St. Sophia in Nicomedia, *viz.* William of the Perchoi and Anseau of Remi, take a messenger, and send him flying to Constantinople, to the Emperor Henry; and they told the emperor what had befallen, how the seneschal had been taken with his men; how they themselves were besieged in the Church of St. Sophia, in Nicomedia., and how they had food for no more than five days; and they told him he must know of a certainty that if he did not succour them they must be killed or taken. The emperor, as one hearing a cry of distress, passed over the straits of St. George, he and his people, each as best he could, and pell-mell, to go to the relief of those in Nicomedia. And so the march to Adrianople was put off once more.

When the emperor had passed over the straits of St. George, he set his troops in array, and rode day by day till he came to Nicomedia. When the people of Theodore Lascaris, and his brothers, who formed the host, heard thereof, they drew back, and passed over the mountain on the other side, towards Nice. And the emperor encamped by Nicomedia in a very fair field that lay beside the river on this side of the mountain. He had his tents and pavilions pitched; and caused his men to overrun and harry the land, because the people had rebelled when they heard that Thierri of Loos, the seneschal, was taken; and the emperor's men captured much cattle and many prisoners.

Truce With Theodore Lascaris—the Emperor Invades the Lands of Johannizza

The Emperor Henry sojourned after this manner for five days in the meadow by Nicomedia. And while he was thus sojourning, Theodore Lascaris took messengers, and sent them to him, asking him to make a truce for two years, on condition that the emperor would suffer him to demolish Skiza and the fortress of the church of St. Sophia of Nicomedia, while he, on his side, would yield up all the prisoners taken in the last victory, or at other times—of whom he had a great many in his land.

Now the emperor took council with his people; and they said that they could not maintain two wars at the same time, and that it was better to suffer loss as proposed than suffer the loss of Adrianople, and the land on the other side of the straits; and moreover that they would (by agreeing to this truce) cause division between their enemies, *viz.* Johannizza, the King of Wallachia and Bulgaria and Theodore Lascaris, who were now friends, and helped one another in the war.

The matter was thus settled, and agreed to. Then the Emperor Henry summoned Peter of Bracieux from Skiza; and he came to him; and the Emperor Henry so wrought with him that he gave up Skiza into his hands, and the emperor delivered it to Theodore Lascaris to be demolished, as also the Church of St. Sophia of Nicomedia. So was the truce established, and so were the fortresses demolished. Thierri of Loos was given up, and all the other prisoners.

Then the Emperor Henry repaired to Constantinople, and undertook once more to go to Adrianople with as many men as he could collect. He assembled his host at Selymbria; and so much time had already passed that this did not take place till after the feast of St. John, in June (1207). And he rode day by day till he came to Adrianople, and encamped in the fields before the city. And those within the city, who had greatly desired his coming, went out to meet him in procession, and received him very gladly. And all the Greeks of the land came with them.

The emperor remained only one day before the city to see all the damage that Johannizza had done to the walls and towers, with mines and petraries; and these had worked great havoc to the city. And on the morrow he departed, and marched towards the country of Johannizza, and so marched for four days. On the fifth day he came to the foot of the mountain of Wallachia, to a city called Euloi, which Johannizza had newly repeopled with his folk. And when the people of the land saw the host coming, they abandoned the city, and fled into the mountains.

The Emperor's Foragers Suffer Loss

The Emperor Henry and the host of the French encamped before the city; and the foraging parties overran the land, and captured oxen, and cows, and beeves in great plenty, and other beasts. And those from Adrianople, who had brought their chariots with them, and were poor and ill-furnished with food, loaded their chariots with corn and other grain; and they found also provisions in plenty and loaded with them, in great quantities, the other chariots that they had captured. So the host sojourned there for three days; and every day the foraging parties went foraging throughout the land; but the land was full of mountains, and strong defiles, and the host lost many foragers, who adventured themselves madly.

In the end, the Emperor Henry sent Anseau of Cayeux to guard the foragers, and Eustace his brother, and Thierri of Flanders, his nephew, and Walter of Escornai, and John Bliaud. Their four battalions went to guard the foragers, and entered into a land rough and mountainous. And when their people had overrun the land, and wished to return, they found the defiles very well guarded. For the Wallachians of the country had assembled, and fought against them, and did them great hurt, both to men and horses. Hardly were our men put to it to escape discomfiture; and the knights had, of necessity, to dismount and go on foot. But by God's help they returned to the camp, though not without great loss and damage.

On the morrow the Emperor Henry, and the host of the French departed thence, and marched day by day till they came to Adrianople; and they stored therein the corn and other provisions that they brought with them. The emperor sojourned in the field before the city some fifteen days.

HOMAGE RENDERED BY BONIFACE TO THE EMPEROR, AND BY GEOFFRY OF VILLEHARDOUIN TO BONIFACE

At that time Boniface, the Marquis of Montferrat, who was at Seres, which he had fortified, rode forth as far as Messinopolis, and all the land surrendered to his will. Then he took messengers, and sent them to the Emperor Henry and told him that he would right willingly speak with him by the river that runs below Cypsela. Now they two had never been able to speak together face to face since the conquest of the land, for so many enemies lay between them that the one had never been able to come to the other. And when the emperor and those of his council heard that the Marquis Boniface was at Messinopolis, they rejoiced greatly; and the emperor sent back word by the messengers that he would speak with the marquis on the day appointed.

So the emperor went thitherward, and he left Conon of Bethune to guard the land near Adrianople, with one hundred knights. And they came on the set day to the place of meeting in a very fair field, near the city of Cypsela. The emperor came from one side, and the marquis from the other, and they met with very great joy; nor is that to be wondered at, seeing they had not, of a long time, beheld one another. And the marquis asked the emperor for tidings of his daughter Agnes; and the emperor told him she was with child, and the marquis was glad thereof and rejoiced.

Then did the marquis become liegeman to the emperor, and held from him his land, as he had done from the Emperor Baldwin, his brother. And the marquis gave to Geoffry of Villehardouin, Marshal of Roumania and Champagne, the city of Messinopolis, and all its appurtenances, or else that of Ceres, whichever he liked best; and the marshal became his liegeman, save in so far as he owed fealty to the emperor of Constantinople. They sojourned thus in that field for two days, in great joy, and said that, as God had granted that they should come together, so might they yet again defeat their enemies.

And they made agreement to meet at the end of the summer, in the month of October, with all their forces, in the meadow before the city of Adrianople, and make war against the King of Wallachia. So they separated joyous and well content. The marquis went to Messinopolis, and the Emperor Henry towards Constantinople.

Boniface is Killed in a Battle Against the Bulgarians

When the marquis had come to Messinopolis, he did not remain there more than five days before he rode forth, by the advice of the Greeks of the land, on an expedition to the mountain of Messinopolis, which was distant a long day's journey. And when he had been through the land, and was about to depart, the Bulgarians of the land collected and saw that the marquis had but a small force with him.

So they came from all parts and attacked the rear-guard. And when the marquis heard the shouting, he leapt on a horse, all unarmed as he was, with a lance in his hand. And when he came thither, where the Bulgarians were fighting with the rear-guard, hand to hand, he ran in upon them, and drove them a great way back.

Then was the Marquis Boniface of Montferrat wounded with an arrow, in the thick of the arm, beneath the shoulder, mortally, and he began to lose blood. And when his men saw it, they began to be dismayed, and to lose heart, and to bear themselves badly. Those who were round the marquis held him up, and he was losing much blood; and he began to faint.

And when his men perceived that he could give them no farther help, they were the more dismayed, and began to desert him. So were they discomfited by misadventure; and those who remained by him—and they were but few—were killed.

The head of the Marquis Boniface of Montferrat was cut off, and the people of the land sent it to Johannizza; and that was one of the greatest joys that ever Johannizza had. Alas! what a dolorous mishap for the Emperor Henry, and for all the Latins of the land of Roumania, to lose such a man by such a misadventure—one of the best barons and most liberal, and one of the best knights in the world!

And this misadventure befell in the year of the Incarnation of Jesus Christ, twelve hundred and seven.

Chronicle of
the Crusade of St. Louis

Dedication and Division of the Work

To his good Lord Louis,[1] son of the King of France,[2] and, by the grace of God, King of Navarre, Count Palatine of Champagne and of Brie, John, Lord of Joinville, his seneschal of Champagne, gives greeting, and love, and honour, and loyal service.

Dear Sire, I would have you know that our lady, the queen, your mother,[3] who loved me much—may God have her in His grace!—prayed me, as earnestly as she could, to cause a book to be written for her, containing the holy words and good deeds of our King St. Louis; and I covenanted to do so; and, with God's help, the book is now completed, in two parts The first part tells how he governed himself, at all times, according to the will of God and the Church, and for the good of his kingdom. The second part speaks of his chivalrous deeds, and of his great feats of arms.

Sire, because it is written: "Do first that which appertaineth to God, and He shall direct thee in all thine other doings,"[4] therefore have I first caused to be written that which appertaineth to the three things above named, *viz.* that which appertaineth to the good of the soul and the good of the body, and that which appertaineth to the government of the people.

And these things have I caused to be written also in honour of this true saint, because by such things will men be able to see clearly that no layman in our time lived so holily all his days, even from the beginning of his reign to the end of his life When the end of his life came I myself was not present; but Count Peter of Alençon, his son—who loved me much—was there, and told me what a good end he made, as you will find written at the end of this book.

---
1 Louis, afterwards Louis X., King of France.
2 Philip, called Philippe le Bel.
3. Joan of Navarre, then deceased.
4. The reference seems to be to Matt. chap. 6. ver. 33.

And as to this, meseems that those honoured him insufficiently who did not place him among the martyrs, seeing the great pains that he endured on the pilgrimage of the cross during the six years that I was in his company, and seeing in especial that he followed our Lord in the . matter of the cross. For if God died on the cross, so, did he, for he was a Crusader wearing the cross when he died at Tunis.

The second book will speak to you of his great deeds of chivalry, and acts of hardihood, which were such that I saw him four times put his body in peril of death—as you shall be told hereinafter—to spare his people from hurt.

Examples of the Devotion of St. Louis

The first time he put his body in peril of death was when we arrived before Damietta. And all his councillors, as I heard tell, advised him to remain on board his ship till he saw how his knights fared, who were going on land. The reason why they so advised was that if he landed with them, and they were slain and he likewise, the whole expedition must come to naught; whereas if he remained on his ship, he would, of himself, be able to recommence the conquest of Egypt. But he would not listen, and leapt into the sea, all armed, with his shield at his neck, and his spear in his hand, and was one of the first to reach the shore.

The second time he put his body in peril of death, was when, on his departure from Mansourah to come to Damietta, his councillors advised, as I have been given to understand, that he should go to Damietta in a galley. And this advice was given, as I have been told, because, if any mischance happened to his people, he might thus, of himself, deliver them from captivity. And also, in particular, because of the condition of his body, which was afflicted by several diseases, for he had a double tertian fever, and a very sore dysentery, and the special sickness of the host in his mouth and legs. But he would listen to none, and said he should never leave his people, and should make such end as they made. So it happened that owing to the dysentery that he had upon him, it became necessary to cut off the lower part of his drawers; and through the sore pain of the sickness of the host, he fainted several times in the evening, as shall be told to you hereinafter.

The third time he put his body in peril of death was when he remained four years in the Holy Land after his brothers had returned to France. Then were we in great peril of death, for during the time that the king was lodged in Acre he had but one man-at-arms in his company for every thirty that the people of Acre had in after time when the city was taken by the Saracens. And I know of no reason why the Turks did not then come and take us in the city, save for the love that God had for the king, putting fear into the hearts of our enemies so that they did not dare to attack us, as it is written: *If thou fearest God, all will fear thee.* And the king thus sojourned in the Holy Land against the advice of his councillors, as you shall hear, putting his body in peril to defend the people of the land, who would have been lost if he had not remained with them.

The fourth time he put his body in peril of death was when we were returning from the land oversea and came before the island of Cyprus, and our vessel struck in such perilous sort that the rock carried away three yards of the keel on which the vessel was built. Then the king sent for fourteen master mariners, who belonged either to that ship or the others in its company, to advise what he should do. And all advised him, as you shall be told hereafter, to enter into another ship, for they did not see how the ship would be able to stand the blows of the waves; inasmuch as the nails with which her timbers were attached had all been loosened.

And they showed the king by example in what peril the ship stood, telling him how, when we were sailing to the land oversea, one of the ships had perished in like case (and I myself had seen, at the Count of Joigny's, a woman and child who alone had escaped out of that ship). To this the king made answer:

"Lords, I see that if I leave this ship, it will be condemned; and I see that there are now in it eight hundred persons and more; and in that each man loves his life as much as I do mine, no one will dare to stay in the ship if I abandon it, but all will remain in Cyprus. For this reason, please God, I shall not place so many people as there are here in peril of death, but shall remain where I am, to save my) people."

So he remained; and God, in whom he trusted, kept us safe for six weeks from the dangers of the sea; and we came at last to a fair haven, as you shall hear. Now it chanced that Oliver of Termes, who had behaved well and valiantly oversea, abandoned the king, and stayed in Cyprus; and we saw him no more by the space of a year and a half. Thus did the king save from harm the eight hundred persons that were in the ship.

In the last part of this book we shall speak of his end, and how he died in saintly wise.

Now I tell you, my lord the King of Navarre, that I promised my lady the queen, your mother—to whom may God show grace and mercy!—that I should write this book; and in order to acquit myself of my promise, I have caused it to be written. And inasmuch as I see no one who has so much right to it as you, who are her heir, I send it to you, so that you and your brothers—and whosoever else shall hear it read—may take examples therefrom, and put such examples to good use, and thereby obtain the favour of God.

First Book

Beginning of the First Book—Principal Virtues of St. Louis

In the name of God Almighty, I, John, Lord of Joinville, seneschal of Champagne, dictate the life of our holy King Lewis; that which I saw and heard by the space of six years that I was in his company on pilgrimage oversea, and that which I saw and heard after we returned. And before I tell you of his great deeds, and of his prowess, I will tell you what I saw and heard of his good teachings and of his holy words, so that these may be found here set in order for the edifying of those who shall hear thereof.

This holy man loved God with all his heart, and followed Him in His acts; and this appeared in that, as God died for the love He bore His people, so did the king put his body in peril, and that several times, for the love he bore to his people; and such peril he might well have avoided, as you shall be told hereafter.

The great love that he bore to his people appeared in what he said during a very sore sickness that he had at Fontainebleau, unto my Lord Louis, his eldest son. "Fair son," he said, "I pray thee to make thyself beloved of the people of thy kingdom; for truly I would rather that a Scot should come out of Scotland and govern the people of the kingdom well and equitably than that thou shouldest govern it ill in the sight of all men." The holy king so loved truth, that, as you shall hear hereafter, he would never consent to lie to the Saracens as to any covenant that he had made with them.

Of his mouth he was so sober, that on no day of my life did I ever hear him order special meats, as many rich men are wont to do; but he ate patiently whatever his cooks had made ready, and was set before him. In his words he was temperate; for on no day of my life did I ever hear him speak evil of anyone; nor did I ever hear him name the

Devil—which name is very commonly spoken throughout the kingdom, whereby God, as I believe, is not well pleased.

He put water into his wine by measure, according as he saw that the strength of the wine would suffer it. At Cyprus he asked me why I put no water into my wine; and I said this was by order of the physicians, who told me I had a large head and a cold stomach, so that I could not get drunk. And he answered that they deceived me; for if I did not learn to put water into my wine in my youth, and wished to do so in my old age, gout and diseases of the stomach would take hold upon me, and I should never be in health; and if I drank pure wine in my old age, I should get drunk every night, and that it was too foul a thing for a brave man to get drunk.

He asked me if I wished to be honoured in this world, and to go into paradise at my death? And I said "Yes."

And he said: "Keep yourself then from knowingly doing or saying anything which, if the whole world heard thereof, you would be ashamed to acknowledge, saying 'I did this,' or 'I said that.'"

He told me to beware not to contradict or impugn anything that was said before me—unless indeed silence would be a sin or to my own hurt—because hard words often move to quarrelling, wherein men by the thousand have found death.

He said that men ought to clothe and arm their bodies in such wise that men of worth and age would never say, this man has done too much, nor young men say, this man has done too little. And I repeated this saying to the father of the king that now is, when speaking of the embroidered coats of arms that are made nowadays; and I told him that never, during our voyage oversea, had I seen embroidered coats, either belonging to the king or to anyone else. And the king that now is told me that he had such suits, with arms embroidered, as had cost him eight hundred pounds *parisis*. And I told him he would have employed the money to better purpose if he had given it to God, and had had his suits made of good taffeta (satin) ornamented with his arms, as his father had done.

St. Louis's Horror of Sin—His Love for the Poor

He called me once to him and said: "Because of the subtle mind that is in you I dare not speak to you of the things relating to God; so I have summoned these two monks that are here, as I want to ask you a question."

Now the question was this: "Seneschal," said he, "what manner of thing is God?"

And I said: "Sire, it is so good a thing that there cannot be better."

"Of a truth," said he, "you have answered well; for the answer that you have given is written in this book that I hold in my hand."

"Now I ask you," said he, "which you would the better I like, either to be a leper, or to have committed a mortal sin?"

And I, who never lied to him, made answer that I would rather have committed thirty mortal sins than be a leper. And when the monks had departed, he called me to him alone, and made me sit at his feet, and said, "How came you to say that to me yesterday?" And I told him that I said it again.

And he answered, "You spoke hastily and as a fool. For you should know that there is no leprosy so hideous as the being in mortal sin, inasmuch as the soul that is in mortal sin is like unto the Devil; wherefore no leprosy can be so hideous. And sooth it is that, when a man dies, he is healed of the leprosy in his body; but when a man who has committed mortal sin dies, he cannot know of a certainty that he has, during his lifetime, repented in such sort that God has forgiven him; wherefore he must stand in great fear lest that leprosy of sin should last as long as God is in paradise. So I pray you," said he, "as strongly as I can, for the love of God, and for the love of me, so to set your heart that you prefer any evil that can happen to the body, whether it be leprosy, or any other sickness rather than that mortal sin should enter into your soul."

He asked me if I washed the feet of the poor on Holy Thursday.[1]

"Sire," said I, "it would make me sick! The feet of these villains will I not wash."

In truth," said he, "that was ill said; for you should never disdain what God did for our teaching. So I pray you, for the love of God first, and then for the love of me, that you accustom yourself to wash the feet of the poor."

REGARD OF ST. LOUIS FOR WORTH AND UPRIGHTNESS

He so loved all manner of people who had faith in God and loved Him, that he gave the constableship of France to my Lord Giles Le Brun, who was not of the kingdom of France, because men held him in so great repute for his faith and for love to God. And verily I believe that his good repute was well deserved.

He caused Master Robert of Sorbon to eat at his table, because of

---

1. Literally "the day of great Thursday."

the great repute in which he was held as a man of uprightness and worth. One day it chanced that Master Robert was eating at my side, and we were talking to one another. The king took us up, and said: "Speak out, for your companions think you are speaking ill of them. If you talk at table of things that can give us pleasure, speak out, and, if not, hold your peace."

When the king would be mirthful he would say to me: "Seneschal, tell me the reasons why a man of uprightness and worth (*prud'-homme* [2]) is better than a friar?" Then would begin a discussion between me and Master Robert.

When we had disputed for a long while, the king would give sentence and speak thus: "Master Robert, willingly would I bear the title of upright and worthy (*prod'-homme*) provided I were such in reality-and all the rest you might have. For uprightness and worth are such great things and such good things that even to name them fills the mouth pleasantly."

On the contrary, he said it was an evil thing to take other people's goods. "For," said he, "to restore is a thing so grievous, that even in the speaking the word restore scratches the throat by reason of the rs that are in it, and these rs are like so many rakes with which the Devil would draw to himself those who wish to 'restore' what they have taken from others. And very subtly does the Devil do this; for he works on great usurers and great robbers in such sort that they give to God what they ought to 'restore' to men."

He told me to warn King Thibaut, from him, to beware of the house of the Preachers of Provins, which he was building, lest he should encumber his soul on account of the great sums he was spending thereon. "For wise men," said he, "should, while they live, deal with their possessions as executors ought to do. Now the first thing a

---

2. This word *prud'-homme*, which is in constant use both by Villehardouin and Joinville, is one of the words that are the despair of the translator; they stand for so much that it is impossible to provide a full equivalent. Sainte-Beuve returns to the term more than once. Thus he says: "*Prud'-homme* represented for Joinville, and for St. Lewis what the beautiful and the good represented for the Greeks, what the word *honnête-homme* was to stand for in the seventeenth century. It was a term large and of floating outline, coming into constant use, and made to include the most beautiful meanings." And again: "The word *prud'-homme* includes all the virtues, wisdom, prudence, courage, craft within the measure which faith allows, civil worth, and what is right and fitting in human intercourse as that race of old Christians understood the terms." See *Causertes du Lundi*.", art. on Joinville, Vol. 8. of edition of 1855, pp. 420 and 423-424.

good executor does is to satisfy all the claims upon the dead, and pay back to others what is due to them, and it is only after having done this that he should spend in alms what remains of the dead man's possessions."

How St. Louis Thought Men Ought to Clothe Themselves

The holy king was at Corbeil one Pentecost day, and there were there eighty knights. The king came down after dinner into the court below the chapel, and was talking, at the entrance of the door, to the Count of Brittany, the father of the count that now is—whom may God preserve!—when Master Robert of Sorbon came to fetch me thither, and took me by the skirt of my mantle and led me to the king; and all the other knights came after us. Then I said to Master Robert, "Master Robert, what do you want with me?"

He said, "I wish to ask you whether, if the king were seated in this court, and you were to seat yourself on his bench, and at a higher place than he, ought you to be greatly blamed?"

And I said, "Yes."

And he said, "Then are you to be blamed when you go more nobly apparelled than the king, for you dress yourself in fur and green cloth, and the king does not do so."

And I replied: "Master Robert, saving your grace, I do nothing blameworthy when I clothe myself in green cloth and fur, for this garment was left to me by my father and mother. But you are to blame, for you are the son of a common man and a common woman, and you have abandoned the vesture worn by your father and mother, and wear richer woollen cloth than the king himself."

Then I took the skirt of his surcoat, and of the surcoat of the king, and said, "See if I am not speaking sooth."

Then the king set himself to defend Master Robert with all his power.

After this my lord the king called my Lord Philip, his son, the father of the king that now is, and King Thibaut, and sat himself at the entrance to his oratory, and put his hand to the ground and said: "Sit yourselves down here, quite close to me, so that we be not overheard."

"Ah! sire," they replied, "we should not dare to sit so close to you."

And he said to me, "Seneschal, sit you here."

And I did so—so close that my robe touched his. And he made

them sit after me, and said to them: "You have done very ill, seeing you are my sons, and have not, at the first word, done what I commanded you. See, I pray you, that this does not happen again."

And they said it should not so happen.

Then he said to me that he had so called us together to confess that he had wrongly defended Master Robert against me.

"But," said he, "I saw that he was so discouraged that he had great need of my help. Nevertheless, you must not attach import to anything I may have said to defend Master Robert; for, as the seneschal says, you ought to clothe yourselves well and suitably, so that your wives may love you the better, and your people hold you in the greater honour. For, as the sage tells us, our garments should be of such fashion as neither to cause the aged and worthy to say that too much has been spent upon them, nor the young to say that too little has been spent."

The Warnings of God—How They are to be Turned to Advantage

You shall be told here of one of the lessons he taught me at sea, when we were returning from the lands oversea. It chanced that our ship struck before the island of Cyprus, when a wind was blowing which is called *garban*; and this wind is not one of the four great winds. And at the shock that our ship received, the mariners so despaired that they rent their garments and tore their beards.

The king sprang from his bed, barefoot, for it was night, and having on no more than his tunic, and went and placed himself cross-wise before the body of our Lord, as one who expected nothing but death. The day after this happened, the king called me to him alone, and said: "Seneschal, God has just showed us a portion of His great power; for one of these little winds, a wind so little that one can scarcely give it a name, came near to drown the King of France, his children, his wife, and his men. Now St. Anselm says that such are warnings from our Lord, as if God meant to say to us, 'See how easily I could have compassed your death, had it been my will.'

"'Lord God,' says the saint, 'why dost Thou thus threaten us? For when Thou dost threaten us, it is not for Thine own profit, nor for Thine advantage—seeing that if Thou hadst caused is all to be lost, Thou wouldst have been none the poorer, and if Thou hadst caused us all to be saved, Thou wouldst have been none the richer. Therefore, this Thy warning is lot for Thine own advantage, but for ours, if so be that we suffer it do its work.' Let us therefore take the warning that

God has given us in such sort that, if we feel that we have, in our hearts or bodies, anything displeasing to God, we shall remove it hastily; and if there be anything we think will please Him, let us try hastily to do it.

If we so act, then our Lord will give us blessings in this world, and in the next blessings greater than we can tell. And if we do not act thus, He will deal with us as the good lord deals with his wicked servant; for if the wicked servant will not amend after warning given, the lord punishes him with death, or with other great troubles that are worse than death."

Let the king that now is beware; for he has escaped from peril as great as that in which we then were, or greater. Therefore let him amend from his evil deeds in such sort that God smite him not grievously, either in himself or in his possessions.

What St. Louis Thought About Faith

The holy king endeavoured with all his power—as you shall here be told—to make me believe firmly in the Christian law, which God has given us. He said that we ought to believe so firmly the articles of faith that neither from fear of death, nor for any mischief that might happen to the body, should we be willing to go against them in word or deed. And he said that the Enemy is so subtle that, when people are dying, he labours all he can to make them die doubting as to some points of the faith. For he knows that he can in no wise deprive a man of the good works he has done; and he knows also that the man is lost to him if he dies in the faith.

Wherefore we should so guard and defend ourselves from this snare, as to say to the Enemy, when he sends such a temptation: "Away!" Yes, "Away!" must one say to the Enemy. "Thou shalt not tempt me so that I cease to believe firmly all the articles of the faith. Even if thou didst cause all my members to be cut off, yet would I live and die in the faith." And whosoever acts thus, overcomes the Enemy with the very club and sword that the Enemy desired to murder him withal.

He said that the Christian faith and creed were things in which we ought to believe firmly, even though we might not be certain of them except by hearsay. On this point he asked me what was my father's name? And I told him his name was Simon. And he asked how I knew it. And I said I thought I was certain of it, and believed it firmly, because my mother had borne witness thereto. Then he said, "So ought you to believe all the articles of the faith, to which the Apostles have borne witness, as also you chant of a Sunday in the Creed."

WILLIAM, BISHOP OF PARIS, COMFORTS A CERTAIN THEOLOGIAN

He told me that the bishop, William of Paris, had related how a great master of divinity had come to him and told him he desired to speak with him. And the bishop said to him: "Master, say on." And when the master thought to speak to the bishop, he began to weep bitterly.

And the bishop said: "Master, say on; be not discomfited; no one can sin so much but that God can forgive him more."

"And yet I tell you," said the master, "that I cannot choose but weep; for I fear me I am a miscreant, inasmuch as I cannot so command my heart as to believe in the sacrifice of the altar, like as holy Church teaches; and yet I know well that this is a temptation of the Enemy."

"Master," said the bishop, "pray tell me, when the Enemy sends you this temptation, does it give you pleasure?"

And the master said: "Sir, far from it; it troubles me as much as anything can trouble me."

"Now," said the bishop, "I will ask you whether, for gold or silver you would utter anything out of your mouth that was against the sacrament of the altar, or the other holy sacraments of the Church?"

Sir!" said the master, "be it known to you that there is nothing in the world that would induce me so to do; I would much rather that every member were torn from my body than that I should say such a thing."

"Now I will say something more," said the bishop. "You know that the King of France is at war with the King of England, and you know too that the castle that lies most exposed in the border-land between the two is the castle of la Rochelle in Poitou. Now I will ask you a question: If the king had set you to guard la Rochelle, which is in the dangerous border-land, and had set me to guard the castle of Montlhéri, which is in the heart of France, where the land is at peace, to whom, think you, would the king owe most at the end of the war—to you who had guarded la Rochelle without loss, or to me, who had guarded the castle of Montlhéri without loss?"

"In God's name, sir," said the master, "to me, who had guarded la Rochelle without losing it."

"Master," said the bishop, "my heart is like the castle of Montlhéri; for I have neither temptation nor doubt as to the sacrament of the altar. For which thing I tell you that for the grace that God owes to me because I hold this firmly, and in peace, He owes to you four-fold, because you have I guarded your heart in the war of tribulation, and have such goodwill towards Him that for no earthly good, nor for any harm done to the body, would you relinquish that faith. Therefore I tell you, be of good comfort, for in this your state is better pleasing to our Lord than mine."

When the master heard this, he knelt before the bishop, and held himself for well appeased.

Faith of the Count of Montfort—One Must Not Enter into Controversy with Jews

The sainted king told me that several people among the Albigenses came to the Count of Montfort, who was then guarding the land of the Albigenses for the king, and asked him to come and look at the body of our Lord, which had become blood and flesh in the hands of the priest.

And the Count of Montfort said, "Go and look at it yourselves, you who do not believe it. As for me, I believe it firmly, holding as holy Church teaches of the sacrament of the altar. And do you know what I shall gain," said the count, "in that during this mortal life I have believed as holy Church teaches? I shall have a crown in the heavens, above the angels, for the angels cannot but believe, inasmuch as they see God face to face."

He told me that there was once a great disputation between clergy and Jews at the monastery of Cluny. And there was at Cluny a poor knight to whom the abbot gave bread at that place for the love of God; and this knight asked the abbot to suffer him to speak the first words, and they suffered him, not without doubt. So he rose, and leant upon his crutch, and asked that they should bring to him the greatest clerk and most learned master among the Jews; and they did so.

Then he asked the Jew a question, which was this: "Master," said the knight, "I ask you if you believe that the Virgin Mary, who bore God in her body and in her arms, was a virgin mother, and is the mother of God?"

And the Jew replied that of all this he believed nothing. Then the knight answered that the Jew had acted like a fool when neither believing in her, nor loving her—he had yet entered into her monastery and house. "And verily," said the knight, "you shall pay for it!"

Whereupon he lifted his crutch and smote the Jew near the ear, and beat him to the earth. Then the Jews turned to flight, and bore away their master, sore wounded. And so ended the disputation.

The abbot came to the knight and told him he had committed a deed of very great folly. But the knight replied that the abbot had committed a deed of greater folly in gathering people together for such a disputation; for there were a great many good Christians there who, before the disputation came to an end, would have gone away misbelievers through not fully understanding the Jews.

"And I tell you," said the king, "that no one, unless he be a very learned clerk, should dispute with them; but a layman, when he hears the Christian law mis-said, should not defend the Christian law, unless it be with his sword, and with that he should pierce the mis-sayer in the midriff, o far as the sword will enter."

The Devotions of St. Louis—How He Did Justice in His Land

The rule of his land was so arranged that every day he heard the hours sung, and a *Requiem* mass without song; and then, if it was convenient, the mass of the day, or of the saint, with song. Every day he rested in his bed after having eaten, and when he had slept and rested, he said, privily in his chamber—he and one of his chaplains together—the office for the dead; and after he heard vespers. At night he heard complines.

A gray-friar (Franciscan) came to him at the castle of Hyères, there where we disembarked; and said in his sermon, for the king's instruction, that he had read the Bible, and the books pertaining to heathen princes, and that he had never found, either among believers or misbelievers, that a kingdom had been lost, or had changed lords, save there had first been failure of justice.

"Therefore let the king, who is going into France, take good heed," said he, "that he do justice well and speedily among his people, so that our Lord suffer his kingdom to remain in peace all the days of his life."

It is said that the right worthy man who thus instructed the king, lies buried at Marseilles, where our Lord, for his sake, performs many a fine miracle. He would never consent to remain with the king, however much the king might urge it, for more than a single day.

The king forgat not the teaching of the friar, but ruled his land very loyally and godly, as you shall hear. He had so arranged that my Lord of Nesle, and the good Count of Soissons, and all of us who were about him, should go, after we had heard our masses, and hear the pleadings at the gate which is now called the gate of Requests.

And when he came back from church, he would send for us and sit at the foot of his bed, and make us all sit round him, and ask if there were any whose cases could not be settled save by himself in person. And we named the litigants; and he would then send for such and ask: "Why do you not accept what our people offer?"

And they would make reply, "Sire, because they offer us very little."

Then would he say, "You would do well to accept what is proposed, as our people desire." And the saintly man endeavoured thus, with all his power, to bring them into a straight path and a reasonable.

Ofttimes it happened that he would go, after his mass, and seat himself in the wood of Vincennes, and lean against an oak, and make us sit round him. And all those who had any cause in hand came and spoke to him, without hindrance of usher, or any other person. Then would he ask out of his own mouth, "Is there anyone who has a cause in hand?"

And those who had a cause in hand stood up.

Then would he say, "Keep silence all, and you shall be heard in turn, one after the other."

Then he would call my Lord Peter of Fontaines and my Lord Geoffry of Villette, and say to one of them, "Settle me this cause."

And when he saw that there was anything to amend in the words of those who spoke on his behalf, or in the words of those who spoke on behalf of any other person, he would himself, out of his own mouth, amend what they had said. Sometimes have I seen him, in summer, go to do justice among his people in the garden of Paris, clothed in a tunic of camlet, a surcoat of tartan without sleeves, and a mantle of black taffeta about his neck, his hair well combed, no cap, and a hat of white peacock's feathers upon his head.

And he would cause a carpet to be laid down, so that we might sit round him, and all the people who had any cause to bring before him stood around. And then would he have their causes settled, as I have told you afore he was wont to do in the wood of Vincennes.

St. Louis Refuses an Unjust Demand Made by the Bishops

I saw him, yet another time, in Paris, when all the prelates of France had asked to speak with him, and the king went to the palace to give them audience. And there was present Guy of Auxerre, the son of my

Lord William of Mello, and he spoke to the king on behalf of all the prelates, after this manner: "Sire, the lords who are here present, archbishops and bishops, have directed me to tell you that Christendom, which ought to be guarded and preserved by you, is perishing in your hands."

The king crossed himself when he heard that word, and he said, "Tell me how that may be."

"Sire," said Guy of Auxerre, "it is because excommunications are at the present day so lightly thought of that people suffer themselves to die before seeking absolution, and will not give satisfaction to the Church. These lords require you therefore, for the sake of God, and because it is your duty to command your provosts and bailiffs to seek out all such as suffer themselves to remain excommunicated for a year and day, and constrain them, by seizure of their goods, to have themselves absolved."

And the king replied that he would issue such commands willingly whensoever it could be shown to him that the excommunicate persons were in the wrong. The bishops said they would accept this condition at no price whatever, as they contested his jurisdiction in their causes. Then the king told them he would do no other; for it would be against God and reason if he constrained people to seek absolution when the clergy were doing them wrong.

"And of this," said the king, "I will give you an example, *viz.*, that of the Count of Brittany, who, for seven years long, being excommunicated, pleaded against the prelates of Brittany, and carried his :cause so far that the Apostle (the Pope) condemned them all. Wherefore, if I had constrained the Count of Brittany, at the end of the first year, to get himself absolved, I should have sinned against God and against him." Then the prelates resigned themselves; nor did I ever hear tell that any further steps were taken in the aforesaid matters.

THE UPRIGHTNESS OF ST. LOUIS

The peace that he made with the King of England was made against the advice of his council, for the council said to him: "Sire, it seems to us that you are giving away the land that you make over to the King of England; [3] for he has no right thereto, seeing that his father lost it justly."

To this the king replied that he knew well that the King of Eng-

---

3. Henry III. Margaret, the wife of St. Louis, and Eleanor, the wife of Henry III., were sisters, the daughters of the Count of Provence.

land lad no right to the land, but that there was a reason why he should give it him, "for," said he, "we have two sisters to wife, and our children are cousins-german; wherefore it is fitting that there should be peace between us. Moreover a very great honour accrues to me through the peace that I have made with the King of England, seeing that he is now my liegeman, which he was not aforetime."

The uprightness of the king may be seen in the case of my Lord Renaud of Trie, who brought to the saintly man a charter stating that the king had given to the heirs of the Countess of Boulogne, lately deceased, the county of Dammartin in Gouelle. The seal on the charter was broken, so that naught remained save half the legs of the image on the king's seal, and the stool on which the king set his feet. And the king showed the seal to all those who were of his council, and asked us to help him to come to a decision. We all said, without a dissentient, that he was not bound to give effect to the charter. Then he told John Sarrasin, his chamberlain, to give him a charter which he had asked him to obtain. When he held this charter in his hands, he said: "Lords, this is the seal I used before I went overseas, and you can see clearly from this seal that the impression on the broken seal is like unto that of the seal that is whole; wherefore I should not dare, in good conscience, to keep the said county."

So he called to him my Lord Renaud of Trie, and said, "I give you back the county."

Second Book

Birth and Coronation of St. Louis

In the name of God Almighty, we have, hereinbefore, written out a part of the good words and of the good teachings of our saintly King Louis, so that those who read may find them set in order, the one after the other, and thus derive more profit therefrom than if they were set forth among his deeds.

And from this point we begin, in the name of God and in his own name, to speak of his deeds. As I have heard tell he was born on the day of St. Mark the Evangelist, after Easter (25th April 1214).

On that day crosses are, in many places, carried in procession, and, in France, these are called black crosses; and this was as it) were a prophecy of the great number of people who were to die in the two Crusades, *viz.*, that of Egypt, and the other, in which he himself died, at Carthage, whereby there were great mournings in this world, and many great rejoicings in paradise for such as in these two pilgrimages died true Crusaders.

He was crowned on the first Sunday in Advent (29th November 1226). The beginning of the mass for that Sunday runs: *Ad te levari animam meam,* and what follows after; and this means, "Fair Lord God, I shall lift up my soul to thee, I put my confidence in thee." In God had he great confidence from his childhood to his death; for when he died, in his last words, he called upon God and His saints, and specially upon my lord St. James and my lady St. Geneviève.

First Troubles in the Reign of St. Louis

God, in whom he put his trust, kept him all his days from his childhood unto the end; and specially, in his youth, did He keep him, when great need was, as you shall shortly hear. As to his soul, God kept it through the good teachings of his mother, who taught him to believe in God and to love Him, and to gather round himself all good people of religion. And, child as he was, she made him recite all the Hours, and listen to the sermons on festival days. He recorded that his mother had sometimes given him to understand that she would rather he were dead than have committed a mortal sin.

Good need had he of God's help in his youth, for his mother, who came from Spain, had neither relations nor friends in all the kingdom of France. And because the barons of France saw that the king was but a child, and the queen, his mother, a foreign woman, they made the Count of Boulogne, who was uncle to the king, their chief, and held him as their lord. After the king was crowned, there were certain barons who demanded of the queen that she should give them great lands, and because she would none of it, all the barons assembled at Corbeil.

And the saintly king told me that neither he, nor his mother, who were at Montlhéri, dared return to Paris till those in Paris came in arms to fetch them. And he told me that all the way, from Montlhéri to Paris, was filled with people, armed and unarmed, and that all cried to our Saviour to give him a good life, and a long, and to defend and guard him from his enemies. And this God did, as you shall presently hear.

In this parliament which the barons held at Corbeil, the barons there present decided, so it is said, that the good knight, the Count Peter of Brittany, should rebel against the king, and they agreed besides that they would each in person, and with two knights only, attend the count when he obeyed the summons which the king would address to him. And this they did to see if the Count of Brittany would be able to master the queen, who was a foreign woman, as you have heard. And many people say that the count would have mastered the queen, and the king too, if God had not helped the king in this his hour of need, as He never failed to do.

The help God gave him was such that Count Thibaut of Champagne, who was afterwards King of Navarre, came there to serve the king with three hundred knights; and through the help that the count gave to the king, the Count of Brittany had to yield to the king's mercy, and when making that peace, as it is said, to surrender to the king the county of Anjou and the county of the Perche.

Crusade of Richard Cœur-De-Lion—Rights of Alice, Queen of Cyprus, Over Champagne

Inasmuch as there are certain things of which you should have knowledge, I hold it fitting here to depart somewhat from my subject. We will tell you here, therefore, that the good Count Henry the Large had by the Countess Mary—who was sister to the King of France and sister to King Richard of England—two sons, of whom the elder was called Henry and the other Thibaut. This Henry, the elder, went as a Crusader on pilgrimage to the Holy Land at the time when King Philip and King Richard besieged Acre and took it.

So soon as Acre was taken, King Philip returned to France, for which he was greatly blamed; but King Richard remained in the Holy Land, and did there such mighty deeds that the Saracens stood in great fear of him; so much so, as it is written in the book of the Holy Land, that when the Saracen children cried, their mothers called out, "Wisht! here is King Richard," in order to keep them quiet.

And I when the horses of the Saracens and Bedouins started at tree or bush, their masters said to the horses, "Do you think that is King Richard?"

This King Richard wrought to such effect that he gave for wife to Count Henry of Champagne, who had remained with him, the Queen of Jerusalem, who was direct heiress to the kingdom. By the said queen Count Henry had two daughters, of whom the first was Queen of Cyprus, and the other did my Lord Everard of Brienne have to wife, and from them sprang a great lineage, as is known in France and Champagne. Of the wife of my Lord Everard of Brienne I will say nothing to you at this present; but I will speak to you of the Queen of Cyprus, seeing she is related to the matter I have in hand; and I speak, therefore, as follows.

The Barons Attack Thibaut IV., Count of Champagne

After the king had foiled Count Peter of Brittany, all the barons of France were so wroth with Count Thibaut of Champagne that they settled to send for the Queen of Cyprus, who was the daughter of the eldest son of Champagne, so as to disinherit Count Thibaut, who was the son of the second son of Champagne.

But some took steps to reconcile Count Peter with Count Thibaut, and the matter was discussed to such effect that Count Thibaut promised to take to wife the daughter of Count Peter of Brittany. A day was fixed on which the Count of Champagne should espouse the damsel; and she was to be taken, for the marriage, to an abbey of Prémontré, near Château-Thierry, and called, as I believe, Val-Secret. The barons of France, who were nearly all related to Count Peter, undertook this duty, and conducted the damsel to Val-Secret to be married, and advised thereof the Count of Champagne, who was at Château-Thierry.

And while the Count of Champagne was coming for the marriage, my Lord Geoffry of la Chapelle came to him on the part of the king, with a letter of credence, and spoke thus: "My Lord Count of Champagne, the king has heard that you have covenanted with Count Peter of Brittany to take his daughter in marriage. Now the king warns you that, unless you wish to lose everything you possess in the kingdom of France, you will not do this thing, for you know that the Count of Brittany has done more evil to the king than any man living."

Then the Count of Champagne, by the advice of those he had with him, returned to Château-Thierry.

When Count Peter and the barons of France, who were expecting him at Val-Secret, heard this, they were all like men distraught, with anger at what he had done to them, and they at once sent to fetch the Queen of Cyprus. And as soon as she was come, they entered into a common agreement to gather together as many men-at-arms as they could, and enter into Brie and Champagne, from the side of France; and the Duke of Burgundy, who had to wife the daughter of Count Robert of Dreux, was to enter into Champagne from the side of Burgundy. And they fixed a day on which they should assemble before the city of Troyes, to take the city of Troyes if they could accomplish it.

The duke collected all the people he could, and the barons also. The barons came burning and wasting everything on one side, and the Duke of Burgundy on another, and the King of France came on yet another side to fight against them. The evil plight of the Count of Champagne was such that he himself burned his cities before the arrival of the barons, so that they might not find supplies therein. Among the other cities that the Count of Champagne burned, he burned Epernay, and Vertus, and Sézanne.

Simon of Joinville Defends Troyes—Peace Between the Count of Champagne and the Queen of Cyprus

The citizens of Troyes, when they perceived that they had lost the help of their lord, asked Simon, lord of Joinville, and father of the lord of Joinville that now is, to come to their help. And he, who had gathered together all his men-at-arms, moved from Joinville by night, so soon as the tidings were brought to him, and came to Troyes before it was day. And thus were the barons foiled of their intent to take the said city; wherefor the barons passed before Troyes without doing aught, and went and encamped in the meadow of l'Isle—there where the Duke of Burgundy already was.

The King of France, who knew they were there, at once I addressed himself to go thither and attack them; and the barons sent and begged him to withdraw in person from the field, and then they would go and fight against the Count of Champagne and the Duke of Lorraine and the rest of the king's people, with three hundred knights less than the count and duke had in their force.

But the king told them they should not so fight without him, for he would remain with his people in person. Then the barons sent back to the king and said that, if it so pleased him, they would willingly incline the Queen of Cyprus to make peace. The king replied that he would agree to no peace, nor suffer the Count of Champagne to agree to any peace, till they had retired from the county of Champagne.

They retired in such sort that from Isle, where they were, they went and encamped below Jully, and the king encamped at Isle, from which he had driven them. And when they knew that the king had come to Isle, they went and encamped at Chaource, and not daring to wait for the king, they went and encamped at Laignes, which belonged to the Count of Nevers, who was of their party.

So the king caused the Count of Champagne and the Queen of Cyprus to come to terms, and peace was made in such sort that the Count of Champagne gave to the Queen of Cyprus about two thousand *livres* (yearly) in land, and forty thousand *livres*, which latter sum the king paid for the Count of Champagne. And the Count of Champagne sold to the king, for the said forty thousand *livres*, the fiefs hereinafter named, viz.—the fief of the county of Blois, the fief of the county of Chartres, the fief of the county of Sancerre, the fief of the county of Châteaudun. Now there are certain people who say that the king only holds the said fiefs in pledge; but this is not so, for I asked our saintly king of it when we were oversea.

The land that Count Thibaut gave to the Queen of Cyprus is held by the Count of Brienne that now is, and by the Count of Joigny, because the great-grandmother of the Count of Brienne was daughter to the Queen of Cyprus and wife to the great Count Walter of Brienne.

Of Henry I., Called the Large-Hearted, Count of Champagne

In order that you may learn whence came the fiefs that the Count of Champagne sold to the king, you must know that the great Count Thibaut, who lies buried at Lagny, had three sons. The first was called Henry, the second Thibaut, and the third Stephen. The aforesaid Henry was Count of Champagne and of Brie, and was called Count Henry the Large-hearted; and rightly was he so called, for he was large-hearted both in his dealings with God and the world: large-hearted towards God as appears in the Church of St. Stephen of Troyes and the other fair churches which he founded in Champagne, and large-hearted towards the world as appeared in the case of Artaud of Nogent, and on many other occasions, of which I would tell you if I did not fear to interrupt my story.

This Artaud of Nogent was the citizen of all the world in whom the count had the greatest faith; and he became so rich that he built the castle of Nogent l'Artaud with his moneys. Now it happened that Count Henry was coming down from his halls at Troyes to go and hear mass at St. Stephen's on the day of Pentecost. At the foot of the steps there came before him a poor knight and knelt down before him and spoke thus: "Sire, I pray you, for the love of God, to give me of what is yours, so that I may marry my two daughters whom you see here."

Artaud, who went behind him, said to the poor knight: "Sir knight, it is not courteous on your part to beg of my lord, for he has given away so much that he has nothing left to give."

The large-hearted count turned towards Artaud and said: "Sir villain, you speak not sooth when you say I have nothing left to give; I have you left. There, take him, sir knight, for I give him to you, and moreover, I pledge myself for him."

The knight was not abashed, but took hold of Artaud's cloak, and said he would not leave him till they had done business together. And before he escaped, Artaud had done business with him to the tune of five hundred *livres*.

The second brother of Count Henry was called Thibaut and was Count of Blois. The third brother was called Stephen, and was Count of Sancerre. And these two brothers held from Count Henry all their heritages, and their counties, and the appurtenances thereof; and they held them afterwards from the heirs of

Count Henry who held the county of Champagne, until such time as Count Thibaut sold them to the King of France, as has been related above.

St. Louis Holds a Full Court at Saumur in 1241

Now let us return to our subject and tell how, after these things, the king held a full court at Saumur in Anjou, and I was there and can testify that it was the best-ordered court that ever I saw. For at the king's table ate, after him, the Count of Poitiers, whom he had newly made knight at the feast of St. John; and after the Count of Poitiers, ate the Count of Dreux, whom he had also newly made knight; and after the Count of Dreux the Count of la Marche; and after the Count of la Marche the good Count Peter of Brittany; and before the king's table, opposite the Count of Dreux, ate my lord the King of Navarre, in tunic and mantle of samite well bedight with a belt and a clasp, and a cap of gold; and I carved before him.

Before the king the Count of Artois, his brother, served the meat, and before the king the good Count John of Soissons carved with the knife. ,In order to guard the king's table there were there my Lord Imbert of Beaujeu, who was afterwards Constable of France, and my Lord Enguerrand of Coucy, and my Lord Archamband of Bourbon. Behind these three barons stood some thirty of their knights, in tunics of silken cloth, to keep guard over them; and behind these knights there were a great quantity of sergeants bearing on their clothing the arms of the Count of Poitiers embroidered in taffeta. The king was clothed in a tunic of blue satin, and surcoat and mantle of vermeil samite lined with ermine, and he had a cotton cap upon his head, which suited him very badly, because he was at that time a young man.

The king held these banquets in the halls of Saumur which had been built, so it was said, by the great King Henry of England (Henry II.) in order that he might hold his great banquets therein; and this hall is built after the fashion of the cloisters of the white monks of the Cistercian order.

But I think there is none other hall so large, and by a great deal. And I will tell you why I think so—it is because by the wall of the cloister, where the king ate, surrounded by his knights and sergeants who occupied a great space, there was also room for a table where ate twenty bishops and archbishops, and yet again, besides the bishops and archbishops, the Queen Blanche, the king's mother, ate near their table, at the head of the cloister, on the other side from the king.

And to serve the queen there was the Count of Boulogne, who afterwards became King of Portugal, and the good Count Hugh of St. Paul, and a German of the age of eighteen years, who was said to be the son of St. Elizabeth of Thuringia, for which cause it was told that Queen Blanche kissed him on the forehead, as an act of devotion, because she thought that his mother must ofttimes have kissed him there.

At the end of the cloister, on the other side, were the kitchens, the cellars, the pantries and the butteries; from this end were served to the king and to the queen meats, and wine, and bread. And in the wings and in the central court ate the knights, in such numbers, that I knew not how to count them. And many said they had never, at any feast, seen together so many surcoats and other garments, of cloth of gold and of silk; and it was said also that no less than three thousand knights were there present.

BATTLE OF TAILLEBOURG IN 1242

After this feast the king led the Count of Poitiers to Poitiers, so that his vassals might do homage for his fiefs. And when the king came to Poitiers, he would gladly have been back in Paris, for he found that the Count of la Marche, who had eaten at his table on St. John's Day, had assembled as many men-at-arms as he could collect, at Lusignan near Poitiers. The king remained at Poitiers nearly a fortnight, nor did he dare to depart therefrom till he had come to terms—how, I know not—with the Count of la Marche.

Ofttimes I saw the Count of la Marche come from Lusignan to speak to the king at Poitiers, and always he brought with him the Queen of England,[1] his wife, who was mother to the King of England. And many people said that the king and the Count of Poitiers had made an evil peace with the Count of la Marche.

No long time after the king had returned from Poitiers, the King of England came into Gascony to wage war against the King of France. Our saintly king rode forth to fight against him with as many people as he could collect. Then came the King of England and the Count of la Marche to do battle before a castle called Taillebourg, seated on an evil river called La Charente, at a point where one cannot pass except over a stone bridge, very narrow.

So soon as the king came to Taillebourg, and the hosts came in sight of one another, our people, who had the castle behind them,

---

1 Isabella of Angoulême, widow of John, and mother of Henry III.

bestirred themselves mightily and passed over the stream with great peril, in boats, and on pontoons, and fell upon the English. Then began a battle grim and fierce. When the king saw this, he put himself in peril, with the others; and for every man that the king had with him when he passed the stream, the English had, on their side, at least twenty. Nevertheless, as God willed, it so befell that when the English saw the king pass over, they fled, and took refuge in the city of Saintes, and several of our people entered into the city, mingled with them, and were taken prisoners.

Those of our people who were taken at Saintes reported that they heard great discord arise between the King of England and the Count of la Marche; and the King of England said that the Count of la Marche had sent for him on the plea that he would find great help in France. That very night the King of England left Saintes and went away into Gascony.

Submission of the Count of La Marche

The Count of la Marche, as one who could do no better for himself, came to the king's prison, and brought with him to the prison his wife and his children; and the king, in making peace with the count, obtained a great deal of his land, but how much I know not, for I had nothing to do with that matter, seeing I had never then worn a hauberk (*i.e.*, was not yet a knight). But I heard tell that besides the land which the king thus gained, the Count of la Marche made over to him ten thousand *livres parisis*, which were in the king's coffers, and the same sum every year.

When we were at Poitiers I saw a knight, my Lord Geoffry of Rancon by name, who, for some great wrong that the Count of la Marche had done him, so it was said, had sworn on holy relics that he would never have his head shorn, as knights are wont, but would wear his hair in woman's tresses until such time as he should see vengeance done on the Count of la Marche, either by himself or by some other. And when my lord Geoffry saw the Count of la Marche, his wife, and his children, kneeling before the king and crying for mercy, he caused a trestle to be brought, and his tresses cut off, and had himself immediately shorn in the presence of the king, of the Count of la Marche, and of all those there present.

In this expedition against the King of England, and against the barons, the king gave great gifts, as I have heard tell by those who returned thence. But neither on account of such gifts, nor of the expenses incurred in this expedition, nor in other expeditions, whether beyond the seas or this side of the seas, did he ever demand, or take, any (money) aid from his barons, or his knights, or his men, or his good cities, in such sort as to cause complaint. Nor is this to be wondered at; for he ruled himself by the advice of the good mother who was with him—and whose counsel he took—and of the right worthy men who had remained by him from the time of his father and of his grandfather.

St. Louis Falls Ill, and Takes the Cross in 1244

After the things related above, it happened, as God so willed, that a very grievous sickness came upon the king in Paris, and brought him to such extremity, so it was said, that one of the ladies who were tending him wished to draw the cloth over his face, saying he was dead; but another lady, who was on the other side of the bed, would not suffer it, and said the soul was still in his body.

And as he listened to the debate between these two ladies, our Lord wrought within him, and soon sent him health, for before that he had been dumb and could not speak. And as soon as he was in case to speak, he asked that they should give him the cross, and they did so. When the queen, his mother, heard say that speech had come back to him, she made as great joy thereof as ever she could. But when she knew that he had taken the cross—as also he himself told her—she made as great mourning as if she had seen him dead.

After he had taken the cross, so also took the cross, Robert, Count of Artois, Alfonse, Count of Poitiers, Charles, Count of Anjou, who afterwards was King of Sicily—all three brothers of the king;—and there also took the cross, Hugh, Duke of Burgundy, William, Count of Flanders, and brother of Count Guy of Flanders lately deceased, the good Hugh, Count of St. Paul, and my Lord Gaucher, his nephew, who did right well oversea, and would have done much good service if he had lived.

With them also took the cross, the Count of la Marche and my Lord Hugh Le Brun, his son, the Count of Sarrebruck and my Lord Gobert of Apremont, his brother—in whose company I, John, Lord of Joinville, passed over the sea in a ship which we hired, because we were cousins—and we passed over with twenty knights, of whom he was over ten, and I over ten.

Joinville Prepares to Join the Crusade

At Easter, in the year of grace that stood at 1248, I summoned my men, and all who held fiefs from me, to Joinville; and on the vigil of the said Easter, when all the people that I had summoned were assembled, was born my son John, Lord of Ancerville, by my first wife, the sister of the Count of Grandpré. All that week we feasted and danced, and my brother, the Lord of Vaucouleurs, and the other rich men who were there, gave feasts on the Monday, the Tuesday, the Wednesday and the Thursday.

On the Friday I said to them: "Lords, I am going oversea, and I know not whether I shall ever return. Now come forward; if I have done you any wrong, I will make it good, as I have been used to do, dealing, each in turn, with such as have any claim to make against me, or my people."

So I dealt with each, according to the opinions of the men on my lands; and in order that I might not weigh upon their debate, I retired from the council, and agreed, without objection raised, to what they recommended.

Because I did not wish to take away with me any penny wrongfully gotten, therefore I went to Metz, in Lorraine, and placed in pawn the greater part of my land. And you must know that on the day when I left our country to go to the Holy Land, I did not hold more than one thousand *livres* [2] a year in land, for my lady mother was still alive; and yet I went, taking with me nine knights and being the first of three knights-banneret. And I bring these things to your notice, so that you may understand that if God, who never yet failed me, had not come to my help, I should hardly have maintained myself for so long a space as the six years that I remained in the Holy Land.

As I was preparing to depart, John, Lord of Apremont and Count of Sarrebruck in his wife's right, sent to tell me he had settled matters to go oversea, taking ten knights, and proposed, if I so willed, that we should hire a ship between him and me; and I consented. His people and mine hired a ship at Marseilles.

Of a Clerk Who Killed Three of the King's Sergeants

The king summoned all his barons to Paris, and made them take oath that, if anything happened to him while away, they would give faith and loyalty to his children. He asked me to do the same; but I would not take the oath, because I was not his liegeman. While I

---
2. Say £800 of our money..

was on my way to Paris, I found three men dead upon a cart, whom a clerk had killed; and I was told they were being taken to the king. When I heard this, I sent one of my squires after, to know what befell. And my squire, whom I had sent, told me that the king, when he came out of his chapel, went to the entrance steps to look at the dead, and inquired of the provost of Paris how this thing had happened.

And the provost told him that the dead men were three of his sergeants of the Châtelet, who had gone into unfrequented streets to rob people.

"And they found," said he to the king, "this clerk, whom you see, here, and robbed him of all his clothes. The clerk, being only in his shirt, went to his lodging, and took his crossbow, and caused a child to bring his falchion. Then when he saw them again, he cried out upon them, and said they should die. So the clerk drew his crossbow, and shot, and pierced one of the men through the heart. The two others made off flying. And the clerk took the falchion which the child handed to him, and followed them in the moonlight, which was fine and clear. The one man thought to pass through a hedge into a garden, and the clerk struck him with his falchion," said the provost, "and cut right through his leg, in such sort that it only holds to the boot, as you may see here. The clerk then followed the other, who thought to go down into a strange house, where the people were still awake; but the clerk struck him in the middle of the head with his falchion, so that he clove his head to the teeth, as you may see here," said the provost to the king.

"Sire," continued he, "the clerk showed what he had done to the neighbours in the street, and then came and made himself your prisoner. And now, sire, I have brought him to you, to do with him what you will. Here he is."

"Sir clerk," said the king, "you have forfeited your priesthood by your prowess; and for your prowess I take you into my service, and you shall go with me overseas. And this thing I do for you, because I would have my men to fully understand that I will uphold them in none of their wickednesses."

When the people there assembled heard this, they cried out to our Saviour, and prayed God to give the king a good and a long life, and bring him back in joy and health.

Joinville Leaves his Castle

After these things I returned to our county, and we agreed, the

Count of Sarrebruck and I, that we should send our baggage in carts to Ausonne, thence to be borne on the river Saône, and to Arles by the Saône and the Rhône.

The day that I left Joinville I sent for the Abbot of Cheminon, who was held to be one of the most worthy of the order of the white monks (Cistercians). (I heard this witness regarding him given at Clairvaux on the festival of our Lady, when the saintly king was present, by a monk, who showed the abbot to me, and asked if I knew who he was; and I inquired why he asked me this, and he answered, "because I think he is the worthiest monk in all the white order. For listen," said he, "what I heard tell by a worthy man who slept in the same dormitory as the Abbot of Cheminon. The abbot had bared his breast because of the great heat; and this did the worthy man see who lay in the same dormitory: he saw the Mother of God go to the abbot's bed, and draw his garment over his breast, so that the wind might do him no hurt.")

This Abbot of Cheminon gave me my scarf and staff of pilgrimage; and then I departed from Joinville on foot, barefoot, in my shirt—not to re-enter the castle till my return; and thus I went to Blécourt, and Saint-Urbain, and to other places thereabouts where there are holy relics. And never while I went to Blécourt and Saint-Urbain would I turn my eyes towards Joinville for fear my heart should melt within me at thought of the fair castle I was leaving behind, and my two children.

I and my companions ate that day at Fontaine-l'Archevêque before Donjeux; and the Abbot Adam of Saint-Urbain—whom God have in His grace!—gave a great quantity of fair jewels to myself and the nine knights I had with me. Thence we went to Auxonne, and thence again, with the baggage, which we had placed in boats, from Auxonne to Lyons down the river Saône; and along by the side of the boats were led the great war-horses.

At Lyons we embarked on the Rhône to go to Arles the White; and on the Rhône we found a castle called Roche-de-Glun, which the king had caused to be destroyed, because Roger, the lord of the castle, was accused of robbing pilgrims and merchants.

THE CRUSADERS EMBARK, AUGUST 1248

In the month of August we entered into our ship at the Roche-de-Marseille. On the day that we entered into our ship, they opened the door of the ship and put therein all the horses we were to take oversea; and then they reclosed the door, and caulked it well, as when a cask is sunk in water, because, when the ship is on the high seas, all the said door is under water. --- When the horses were in the ship, our master mariner called to his seamen, who stood at the prow, and said: "Are you ready?" and they answered, "Aye, sir—let the clerks and priests come forward!"

As soon as these had come forward, he called to them, "Sing, for God's sake!" and they all, with one voice, chanted: "*Veni Creator Spiritus.*"

Then he cried to his seamen, "Unfurl the sails, for God's sake!" and they did so.

In a short space the wind filled our sails and had borne us out of sight of land, so that we saw naught save sky and water, and every day the wind carried us further from the land where we were born. And these things I tell you, that you may understand how foolhardy is that man who dares, having other's chattels in his possession, or being in mortal sin, to place himself in such peril, seeing that, when you lie down to sleep at night on shipboard, you lie down not knowing whether, in the morning, you may find yourself at the bottom of the sea.

At sea a singular marvel befell us; for we came across a mountain, quite round, before the coast of Barbary. We came across it about the hour of vespers, and sailed all night, and thought to have gone about fifty leagues; and, on the morrow, we found ourselves before the same mountain; and this same thing happened to us some two or three times. When the sailors saw tills, they were all amazed, and told us we were in very great peril; for we were nigh unto the land of the Saracens of Barbary.

Then spake a certain right worthy priest, who was caned the Dean of Maurupt; and he told us that never had any mischance occurred in his parish—whether lack of water, or overplus of rain, or any other mischance—but so soon as he had made three processions, on three Saturdays, God and His mother sent them deliverance. It was then a Saturday. We made the first procession round the two masts of the ship. I had myself carried in men's arms, because I was grievously sick. Never again did we see the mountain; and on the third Saturday we came to Cyprus.

Sojourn in Cyprus—Embassage From the Tartars—Joinville Takes Service With the King

When we came to Cyprus, the king was already there, and we found great quantities of the king's supplies, that is to say, the cellarage of the king, and his treasure, and his granaries. The king's cellarage was set in the middle of the fields, on the shore by the sea. There his people had stacked great barrels of wine, which they had been buying for two years before the king's arrival; and the barrels were stacked one upon the other in such sort that when you looked at them in front, the stacks seemed as if they were barns.

The wheat and the barley they had set in heaps in the midst of the fields, and when you looked at them, it seemed as if they were mountains, for the rain, which had long been beating on the grain, had caused it to sprout, so that the outside looked like green grass. Now it happened that when they wished to take the grain into Egypt, they took away the upper crust with the green grass, and found the wheat and barley within as fresh as if newly threshed.

The king himself, as I heard tell in Syria, would very willingly have gone on to Egypt, without stopping, had it not been for his barons, who advised him to wait for such of his people as had not yet arrived.

While the king was sojourning in Cyprus, the great king of the Tartars sent envoys to him, with many good and gracious words. Among other things, he signified that he was ready to help the king to conquer the Holy Land, and to deliver Jerusalem from the hands of the Saracens.

The king received the envoys in very friendly fashion, and sent other envoys in return, who remained away two years. And the king, by his envoys, sent to the King of the Tartars a tent made like a chapel, very costly, for it was all of fair, fine scarlet cloth. The king, moreover, to see if he could draw the Tartars to our faith, caused images to be graven in the said chapel, representing the Annuciation of our Lady, and all the other points of the faith. And these things he sent by two brothers of the order of Preachers, who knew the Saracen language, and could show and teach the Tartars what they ought to believe.

The two brothers came back to the king at the time when the king's brothers were returning to France; and they found the king, who had left Acre, where his brothers had parted from him, and had come to Cæsarea, which he was fortifying; nor was there at that time any truce or peace with the Saracens. How the king's envoys were received will I tell you, as they themselves told it to the king; and in what they reported you may hear much that is strange and marvellous; but I will not tell you of it now, because, in order to do so, I should have to interrupt matters already begun;—so to proceed.

I, who had not a thousand *livres* yearly in land, had undertaken, when I went oversea, to bear, beside my own charges, the charges of nine knights, and two knights-banneret; and so it happened, when I arrived in Cyprus, that I had no more left, my ship being paid for, than twelve score *livres tournois*; wherefore some of my knights apprised me that if I did not provide myself with moneys, they would leave me. But God, who never failed me yet, provided for me in such fashion that the king, who was at Nicosia, sent for me, and took me into his service, and placed eight hundred *livres* in my coffers; and thus I had more moneys than I required.

The Empress of Constantinople Arrives in Cyprus

While we were sojourning in Cyprus, the Empress of Constantinople[3] sent me word that she had arrived at Paphos, a city of Cyprus, and bade me go and seek her thence—I and my Lord Everard of Brienne. When we arrived at Paphos we were told how a stray wind had broken the ropes of the anchor that held her ship, and had driven it to Acre; and of all her baggage there was naught remaining save the mantle he had on, and a surcoat for meals. We brought her to Limassol, where the king and queen and all the barons of France and of the host received her very honourably.

On the morrow I sent her some cloth to make a dress, and fur of ermine with it; and I sent her some taffeta and cendal[4] to line the dress. My Lord Philip of Nanteuil, the good knight who was of the king's household, met my squire going to the empress. When this most worthy man saw what was toward, he went to the king and told him I had greatly shamed the king and the other barons, in that I had sent this dress to the empress, while they had never perceived what was lacking.

The empress had come to ask the king for help for her lord who had remained in Constantinople; and she wrought to such purpose that she took back with her a hundred couple of letters or more, as well from me as from the other friends she had there—by which let-

---

3. Mary, wife of Baldwin II. The Latin Empire of Constantinople was tottering to its fall.
4. A silken stuff.

ters we were bound on oath, if the king or the legate wished to send three hundred knights to Constantinople after the king returned from oversea, then, I say, we were bound by our oaths to go thither.

And I, to acquit myself of my oath, inquired of the king, when the time came for our departure to France—in presence of the Count of Eu, whose letter I have—and said that if the king desired to send the three hundred knights to Constantinople, I would go too, in order to fulfil my oath. And the king replied that he had not the wherewithal; and that however great his treasure might have been afore time, he had now drained it to the dregs. After we had arrived in Egypt, the empress went away to France, and took with her my Lord John of Acre, her brother, whom she married to the Countess of Montfort.

THE SOLDAN OF ICONIUM—THE KING OF ARMENIA—AND THE SOLDAN OF BABYLON

At the time when we came to Cyprus, the *Soldan* of Iconium was the richest king in all paynimry. And he had done a marvellous thing, for he had melted a great part of his gold in earthen jars, such as are used oversea to hold wine, and may contain three or four measures, and he had caused the jars to be broken, so that the ingots of gold remained uncovered in one of his castles, and everyone who entered the castle could see and handle them; and of these ingots there were at least six or seven.

His great wealth might well be seen from a pavilion which the King of Armenia sent to the King of France, and which was worth some five hundred *livres*; and the King of Armenia told the King of France that a *ferrais* of the *Soldan* of Iconium had given it him. Now a *ferrais* is he who has care of the *soldan's* pavilions and keeps his houses clean.

The King of Armenia, in order to deliver himself from subjection to the *Soldan* of Iconium, went to the King of the Tartars, and, to obtain his help, placed himself in subjection to the Tartars; and he brought back such a number of men-at-arms that he was in sufficient force to fight against the *Soldan* of Iconiurn. The battle lasted a long while, and the Tartars killed so many of the *soldan's* men that no one after had news of him. Because of the fame of this coming battle, which was very great in Cyprus, some of our sergeants passed into Armenia, both to take part in the battle and for the sake of booty; but not one of them ever came back.

The *Soldan* of Babylon expected that the king would arrive in

Egypt in spring, and bethought himself that he would, ere the spring, overthrow the *Soldan* of Emessa, who was his mortal enemy, and he went and besieged him in the city of Emessa. The *Soldan* of Emessa saw no way of deliverance from the *Soldan* of Babylon, for he perceived that the latter lived long enough, he would overthrow him. Therefore he bargained in such sort with the *ferrais* of the *Soldan* of Babylon that the *ferrais* poisoned him.

And the manner in which he poisoned him was this: The *ferrais* was aware that the *soldan* came every day, after dinner, to play chess on the mats that were at the foot of his bed; and the mat on which he knew that the *soldan* sat every day he put poison thereon. Now it happened that the *soldan*, who was unshod, turned himself about upon a sore that was on his leg. Immediately the poison struck into the open sore, and took away all power from the half of the body into which it had entered; and every time that the poison impinged upon his heart, the *soldan* remained for some two days unable to drink, or eat, or speak. So they left the *soldan* of Emessa in peace; and the people of the *Soldan* of Babylon carried him back into Egypt.

The Host Leaves Cyprus—1249

As soon as we entered into the month of March, by the king's command the king, the barons, and the other pilgrims ordered that the ships should be reladen with wine and provisions, so as to be ready to move when the king directed. And when the king saw that all had been duly ordered, the king and queen embarked on their ships on the Friday before Pentecost (21st May 1249), and the king told his barons to follow in their ships straight to Egypt.

On the Saturday the king set sail and all the others besides, which was a fair thing to look upon, for it seemed as if all the sea, so far as the eye could reach, were covered with the canvas of the ships' sails; and the number of the ships, great and small, was reckoned at eighteen hundred.

The king anchored at the head of a hillock which is called the Point of Limassol, and all the other vessels anchored round about him. The king landed on the day of Pentecost. After we had heard mass a fierce and powerful wind, coming from the Egyptian side, arose in such sort that out of two thousand eight hundred knights, whom the king was taking into Egypt, there remained no more than seven hundred whom the wind had not separated from the king's company and carried away to Acre and other strange lands; nor did they afterwards return to the king of a long while.

The day after Pentecost the wind had fallen. The king and such of us as had, according to God's will, remained with him, set sail forthwith, and met the Prince of Morea, and the Duke of Burgundy, who had been sojourning in Morea. On the Thursday after Pentecost the king arrived before Damietta, and we found there, arrayed on the seashore, all the power of the *soldan*—a host fair to look upon, for the *soldan's* arms are of gold, and when the sun struck upon them they were resplendent. The noise they made with their cymbals and horns was fearful to listen to.

The king summoned his barons to take counsel what they should do. Many advised that he should wait till his people returned, seeing that no more than a third part had remained with him; but to this he would by no means agree. The reason he gave was, that to delay would put the foe in good heart, and, particularly, he said that there was no port before Damietta in which he could wait for his people, and that, therefore, any strong wind arising might drive the ships to other lands, like as the ships had been driven on the day of Pentecost.

PREPARATION FOR DISEMBARKATION IN EGYPT

It was settled that the king should land on the Friday before Trinity and do battle with the Saracens, unless they refused to stand. The king ordered my Lord John of Beaumont to assign a galley to my Lord Everard of Brienne and to myself, so as that we might land, we and our knights, because the great ships could not get close up to the shore.

As God so willed, when I returned to my ship, I found a little ship that my Lady of Beyrout, who was cousin-german to my Lord of Montbéliard and to myself, had given me, and that carried eight of my horses.

When the Friday came I and my Lord Everard went, fully armed, to the king and asked for the galley; whereupon my Lord John of Beaumont told us that we should not have it. When our people saw that they would get no galley, they let themselves drop from the great ship into the ship's boat, pell-mell, and as best they could, so that the boat began to sink. The sailors saw that the boat was sinking, little by little, and they escaped into the big ship and left my knights in the boat.

I asked the master how many more people there were in the boat than the boat could hold. He told me twenty men-at-arms; and I asked him whether he could take our people to land if I relieved him of so many, and he said "Yes." So I relieved him in such sort that in three journeys he took them to the ship that had carried my horses.

While I was conducting these people a knight belonging to my Lord Everard of Brienne, and whose name was Plonquet, thought to go down from the great ship into the boat; but the boat moved away, and he fell into the sea and was drowned.

When I came back to my ship I put into my little boat a squire whom I made a knight, and whose name was my Lord Hugh of Vaucouleurs, and two very valiant bachelors—of whom the one had name my Lord Villain of Versey, and the other my Lord William of Dammartin—who were at bitter enmity the one against the other. Nor could anyone make peace between them, because they had seized each other by the hair in Morea. And I made them forgive their grievances and embrace, for I swore to them on holy relics that we should not land in company of their enmity.

Then we set ourselves to get to land, and came alongside of the barge belonging to the king's great ship, there where the king himself was. And his people began to cry out to us, because we were going more quickly than they, that I should land by the ensign of St. Denis, which was being borne in another vessel before the king. But I heeded them not, and caused my people to land in front of a great body of Turks, at a place where there were full six thousand men on horseback.

So soon as these saw us land, they came toward us, hotly spurring. We, when we saw them coming, fixed the points of our shields into the sand and the handles of our lances in the sand with the points set towards them. But when they were so near that they saw the lances about to enter into their bellies, they turned about and fled.

The Crusaders Disembark in Front of the Saracens

My Lord Baldwin of Rheims, a right good man, who had come to land, requested me, by his squire, to wait for him; and I let him know I should do so willingly, for that a right good man such as he ought surely to be waited for in like case of need, ☐ whereby I had his favour all the time that he lived. With him came to us a thousand knights; and you may be assured that, when I landed, I had neither squire, nor knight, nor varlet that I had brought with me from my own country, and yet God never left me without such as I needed.

At our left hand landed the Count of Jaffa, who was cousin-german to the Count of Montbéliard, and of the lineage of Joinville. It was he who landed in greatest pride, for his galley came all painted, within and without, with escutcheons of his arms, which arms are *or* with a cross of gules *patée*. He had at least three hundred rowers in his galley, and for each rower there was a targe with the count's arms thereon, and to each targe was a pennon attached with his arms wrought in gold.

While he was coming it seemed as if his galley flew, so did the rowers urge it forward with their sweeps; and it seemed as if the lightning were falling from the skies at the sound that the pennants made, and the cymbals, and the drums, and the Saracenic horns that were in his galley. So soon as the galley had been driven into the sand as far up as they could drive it, both he and his knights leapt from the galley, well armed and well equipped, and came and arrayed themselves beside us.

I had forgotten to tell you that when the Count of Jaffa landed he immediately caused his tents and pavilions to be pitched; and so soon as the Saracens saw them pitched, they all came and gathered before us, and then came on again, spurring hotly, as if to run in upon us. But when they saw that we should not fly, they shortly turned and went back again.

On our right hand, at about a long-crossbow-shot's distance, landed the galley that bore the ensign of St. Denis. And there was a Saracen who, when they had landed, came and charged in among them, either because he could not hold in his horse, or because he thought the other Saracens would follow him; but he was hacked in pieces.

St. Louis Takes Possession of Damietta

When the king heard tell that the ensign of St. Denis was on shore he went across his ship with large steps; and maugre the legate who was with him he would not leave from following the ensign, but leapt into the sea, which was up to his armpits. So he went, with his shield hung to his neck, and his helmet on his head, and his lance in his hand, till he came to his people who were on the shore.

When he reached the land, and looked upon the Saracens, he asked what people they were, and they told him they were Saracens; and he put his lance to his shoulder, and his shield before him, and would have run in upon the Saracens if the right worthy men who were about him would have suffered it.

The Saracens sent thrice to the *soldan*, by carrier-pigeons, to say that the king had landed, but never received any message in return, because the *soldan's* sickness was upon him. Wherefore they thought that the *soldan* was dead, and abandoned Damietta. The king sent a knight forward to know if it was sooth that Damietta was so abandoned.

The knight returned to the king and said it was sooth and that he had been into the houses of the *soldan*. Then the king sent for the legate and all the prelates of the host, and all chanted with a loud voice *Te Deum laudamus*. Afterwards the king mounted his horse, and we all likewise, and we went and encamped before Damietta.

Very unadvisedly did the Turks leave Damietta, in that they did not cut the bridge of boats, for that would have been a great hindrance to us;. but they wrought us very much hurt in setting fire to the bazaar, where all the merchandise is collected, and everything that is sold by weight. The damage that followed from this was as great as if—which God forbid!—someone were, tomorrow, to set fire to the Petit-Pont in Paris.

Now let us declare that God Almighty was very gracious to us when He preserved us from death and peril on our disembarkation, seeing that we landed on foot and affronted our enemies who were mounted. Great grace did our Lord also show us when He delivered Damietta into our hands, for otherwise we could only have taken it by famine, and of this we may be fully assured, for it was by famine that King John had taken it in the days of our fathers (in 1219).

Mistake of St. Louis—Disorder Among the Crusaders

Our Lord can say of us, as He said of the children of Israel—*et pro nihilo habuerunt terram desiderabilem*.[5] And what does He say afterwards? He says that they forgat God their Saviour. And so did we forget Him as I will shortly tell you.

But first I will tell you of the king who summoned his barons, the clerks, and the laymen, and asked them to help him to decide how the booty taken in the city should be divided. The patriarch was the first to speak, and he spoke thus: "Sire, methinks it were well that you should keep the wheat, and the barley, and the rice, and whatever is needed to sustain life, so as to provision the city; and that you should have it cried throughout the host that all other goods are to be brought to the legate's quarters, under pain of excommunication." To this advice all the other barons assented. Now, as it fell out, all the

---

5. "They despised the pleasant land." The references seem to be to Ps. cvi., ver. 21 and 24.

goods brought to the legate's quarters did not amount in value to more than six thousand *livres*.

When this had been done, the king and the barons summoned John of Valery, the right worthy man, and spoke to him thus: "Sir of Valery," said the king, "we are agreed that the legate should hand over to you the six thousand *livres*, so that you may divide them as may seem best to you."

"Sire," replied the right worthy man, "you do me much honour, and great thanks be yours! But, please God! that honour can I not accept, nor can I carry out your wish, for by so doing I should make null the good customs of the Holy Land, whereby, when the cities of the enemy are captured, the king takes a third of the goods found therein, and the pilgrims take two thirds. And this custom was well observed by King John when he took Damietta, and as old folk tell us, the same custom was observed by the kings of Jerusalem, who were before King John. If then it pleases you to hand over to me the two parts of the wheat, and the barley, and the rice, and the other provisions, then shall I willingly undertake to make division among the pilgrims."

The king did not decide to do this; so matters remained as they were; and many were ill-pleased that the king should set aside the good old customs. The king's people, who ought, by liberal dealing, to have retained the merchants, made them pay, so it was said, the highest rents they could exact for the shops in which to sell their goods; and the rumour of this got abroad to foreign lands, so that many merchants forbore to come and bring supplies to the host.

The barons, who ought to have kept what was theirs so as to spend it in fitting time and place, took to giving great feasts, and an outrageous excess of meats. The common people took to consorting with lewd women; whereby it happened, after we returned from captivity, that the king discharged a great many of his people.

And when I asked him why he had done this, he told me that he had found, of a certainty, that those whom he had discharged held their ill places of assemblage at a short stone's-throw from his pavilion, and that at a time when the host was in greatest distress and misery.

The Saracens Attack the Camp—Death of Walter of Autreche

Now let us go back to the matter in hand, and tell how, shortly after we had taken Damietta, all the horsemen of the *soldan* came before the camp, and attacked it from the land side. The king and all the horsemen armed themselves. I, being in full armour, went to speak to the king, and found him fully armed, sitting on a settle, and round him were the right worthy knights belonging to his own division, all in full armour. I asked if he desired that I and my people should issue from the camp, so that the Saracens should not fall upon our tents. When my Lord John of Beaumont heard my question, he cried to me in a very loud voice, and commanded me, in the king's name, not to leave my quarters till the king so ordered.

I have told you of the right worthy knights who were of the king's special following, for there were eight of them, all good knights who had won prizes for arms on the further or hither side of the seas, and such knights it was customary to call good knights. These are the names of the knights about the king:—my Lord Geoffry of Sargines, my Lord Matthew of Marly, my Lord Philip of Nanteuil, and my Lord Imbert of Beaujeu, Constable of France; but the last was not then present, he was outside the camp—he and the master of the crossbowmen, with most of the king's sergeants-at-arms—to guard the camp so that the Turks might not do any mischief thereto.

Now it happened that my Lord Walter of Autrèche got himself armed at all points in his pavilion; and when he was mounted upon his horse, with his shield at his neck and his helmet on his head, he caused the flaps of his pavilion to be lifted, and struck spurs into his horse to ride against the Turks; and as he left his pavilion, all alone, all his men shouted with a loud voice, "Chatillon." But so it chanced that or ever he came up to the Turks he fell, and his horse flew over his body; and the horse went on, covered with his arms, to our enemies, because the Saracens were, for the most part, mounted on mares, for which reason the horse drew to the side of the Saracens.

And those who looked on told us that four Turks came by Lord Walter, who lay upon the ground, and as they went by, gave him great blows with their maces there where he lay. Then did the Constable of France and several of the king's sergeants deliver him, and they brought him back in their arms to his pavilion. When he came there he was speechless. Several of the surgeons and physicians of the host went to him, and because it did not seem to them that he was in danger of death, they had him blooded in both arms.

That night, very late, my Lord Aubert of Narcy proposed. that we should go and see him, for as yet we had not seen him, and he was a man of great name and of great valour. We entered into his pavilion, and the chamberlain came to meet us, and asked us to move quietly, so as not to wake his master. We found him lying on coverlets of miniver, and went to him very softly, and found him dead. When this was told to the king, he replied that he would not willingly have a thousand such men acting contrary to his orders as this man had done.

Renewed Attacks on the Part of the Saracens—the King Decides to Await the Arrival of the Count of Poitiers

The Saracens entered every night into the camp on foot and killed our people there where they found them sleeping, whereby it chanced that they killed the sentinel of the lord of Courtenay, and left him lying on a table, and cut off his head, and took it away with them. And this they did because the *soldan* gave a *besant* of gold for every Christian man's head.

And we were at this disadvantage because the battalions guarded the camp, each one its night, on horseback; and when the Saracens wished to enter into the camp, they waited till the noise of the horses and of the battalions had passed, and then crept into the camp behind the horses, making their way out before it was day. So the king ordered that the battalion which had been used to keep guard on horseback should keep guard on foot, whereby all the camp was in safety, because of our men who kept guard and were spread out in such wise that one man touched the other.

After this was done, the king decided not to leave Damietta till his brother, the Count of Poitiers, had arrived with the remaining forces of France. And so that the Saracens might not charge on their horses into the midst of the camp, the king caused all the camp to be enclosed with great earthworks, and on the earthworks were set crossbowmen to watch every night, and sergeants; and such were set also at the entrance to the camp.

When the feast of St. Remigius had passed, and no news came of the Count of Poitiers—whereby the king and all those of the host were greatly troubled, for they feared lest some mischief had befallen him—then I reminded the legate how the Dean of Maurupt had caused us, when at sea, to go three times in procession, on three Saturdays, and how before the third Saturday we had arrived in Cyprus.

The legate put faith in what I said, and caused three processions, on three separate Saturdays, to be proclaimed throughout the host.

The first procession started from the legate's quarters, and they went to the church of our Lady in the city, which church had been the mosque of the Saracens, but the legate had dedicated it to the honour of the Mother of God. The legate preached the sermon on two Saturdays. Thither came the king and the honourable men of the host, to whom the legate gave full indulgences.

Before the third Saturday came the Count of Poitiers; nor would it have been well if he had come before, for between the three Saturdays there had been so great a tempest in the sea before Damietta, that at least twelve score ships, great and small, had gone to pieces and been lost, and all the people therein drowned. If therefore the Count of Poitiers had come before, both he and his people would have utterly perished.

When the Count of Poitiers arrived, the king summoned all the barons of the host to decide what course he should hold, whether to Alexandria or to Babylon. Now the good Count Peter of Brittany, and the main part of the barons of the host, were agreed that the king should go and besiege Alexandria, because there was before that city a good harbour to which the ships could bring provisions for the host.

But to this the Count of Artois was contrary, and said he would never agree that they should go anywhere except to Babylon, forasmuch as Babylon was the capital of Egypt; and if you wanted to kill the serpent, you must first crush its head. The king set aside the advice of his barons, and accepted the advice of his brother.

The Host Begins its March

At the beginning of Advent the king set out with his host to go towards Babylon, as the Count of Artois had advised. Pretty near to Damietta we found a stream that issued from the main stream, and it was decided that the host should remain there a day to dam up the said arm of the stream, so that we might pass. The thing was done pretty easily, for we dammed the said arm close to the main stream in such sort that the water flowed pretty easily along the main stream. At our passage over the arm, the *soldan* sent five hundred of his knights, the best mounted that he could find in all his host, to harass the host of the king, and delay our march.

On St. Nicholas Day (6th December 1249) the king commanded that we should prepare to ride forward, and forbade that anyone should be so bold as to attack the said Saracens.

Now it happened that when the host began to move forward, and the Saracens saw that no attack was to be made upon them—and they knew by their spies that the king had forbidden it—they waxed bold, and attacked the Templars who formed the van; and one of the Turks bore a knight of the Temple to the earth, right before the horse-hoofs of brother Renaud of Vichiers, who was then Marshal of the Temple. When the marshal saw this, he cried to his brother Templars: "Out on them for God's sake! I cannot brook this!" He struck his spurs into his horse, and all the host with him. The horses of our people were fresh, and the horses of the Turks already weary; and so, as I have heard tell, not one of them escaped, but all perished. Many of them had got into the river, and were drowned.

Of the Nile

It will now be convenient that I should tell you of the river that comes through Egypt, and of the earthly paradise. And these things I tell you so that you may understand certain matters on which I shall have to touch.

Now this river is different from all other rivers, for the further the other rivers flow down, the more little rivers and brooks fall into them, whereas no rivers or brooks fall into this' river, but, as it happens, it comes all in one channel into Egypt, and then throws out the seven branches that spread throughout the land.

And when the day of St. Remigius is past, the seven rivers spread over the land and cover the plain country; and when the waters withdraw the husbandmen go and plough, each in his own fields, with a plough that has no wheels, wherewith they turn over in the earth the wheat, the barley, the cumin, and the rice; and all these come up so well, that better could not be.

Nor does anyone know how these floods arise, save it be by the will of God; but if they did not arise, no good thing would grow, for the great heat of the sun would scorch it up, seeing that it never rains in the land. The water of the river is always troubled, so the people of the land, who wish to drink thereof, take it towards night and crush into it four almonds, or four beans, and the next day it is so good to drink that no fault can be found with it.

Before the river enters into Egypt, people who are accustomed so to do, cast their nets outspread into the river, at night; and when morning comes they find in their nets such goods as are sold by weight, and brought into the land, *viz.*, ginger, rhubarb, wood of aloes and cinnamon. And it is said that these things come from the earthly paradise; for the wind blows down the trees in paradise, just as the wind blows down the dry wood in the forests of our own land; and the dry wood of the trees in paradise that thus falls into the river is sold to us by the merchants.[6] The water of the river Is of such a nature, that when we had put it into white earthenware pots that are made in the land, and hung it to the ropes of our pavilions, it became, in the heat of the day, as cold as if drawn from a well.

They said in the country that the *Soldan* of Babylon had oftentimes tried to find out whence the river came; and he sent for this purpose people who carried with them a manner of bread called biscuit, because it is twice baked, and on this bread they lived until such time as they came back to the *soldan*. And they reported that they had explored the river, and had come to a great mass of rocks, sharp and sheer, which none could pass. From these rocks the river fell; and it seemed to them that there was a great foison of trees in the mountain above; and they said also that they had found marvellous savage beasts of divers sorts, as lions, serpents, elephants, that came and looked at them from the banks while they were going up against the stream.

Now let us go back to our first point, and say that when the river comes into Egypt it throws out its branches, as I said before. One of these branches goes to Damietta, another to Alexandria, a third to Tanis, a fourth to Rexi. And it was to this branch which goes to Rexi that the King of France came with all his host; and he encamped between the stream of Damietta and that of Rexi, and all the power of the *soldan* was encamped on the stream of Rexi, on the other side, over against our host, to defend the passage—which they could easily do, seeing that none could cross the said stream to go towards them, save he passed over swimming.

Building of a Causeway on the River

The king decided to build a causeway across the river so as to pass over against the Saracens. In order to protect those who were working at the causeway, the king caused two towers called cats-castles (*chats-châteaux*) to be constructed, for there were two towers before the "cats" (or covered ways) and two houses behind the towers, so as to preserve those who were on guard from the shot of the Saracens' engines, of which they had sixteen all set up.

---

6. Meaning of original a little obscure.

When we came there, the king caused eighteen engines to be built, and Jocelin of Cornaut was set over them as master engineer. Our engines threw against theirs, and theirs against ours; but never did I hear tell that ours had done very much damage. The king's brothers kept guard by day, and we, the other knights, kept guard by night at the covered ways. And thus we came to the week before Christmas.

So soon as the covered ways were finished, they began to build the causeway—but not before—because the king did not wish that the Saracens, who shot at us, aiming across the stream, should wound those who were bringing up earth. Now in building this causeway, the king and all the barons of the host were blinded and without foresight; for because they had, as I told you before, dammed up one of the arms of the stream—which thing they did easily, inasmuch as they set themselves to dam it up at the point where it left the larger stream— therefore they thought to dam up the stream of Rexi at a point where it had left the larger stream full half a league.

And in order to counteract the causeway that the king was making, the Saracens dug holes in front of their camp, and so soon as the stream came to the holes, it rushed into them, and made a great space of water. Thus it happened that they undid in one day all that we had done in three weeks; for when we had dammed up a part of the stream on our side, they enlarged it on their side by the holes that they made.

In the room of the *soldan* who had died of the sickness which he took before the city of Emessa, the Saracens had taken for chief a Saracen called Scecedin, who was the scheik's son. It was said that the Emperor Frederic had made him a knight. He ordered a part of his people to come and attack our camp before Damietta, and they did so; and came to a town called Sharmesah on the stream of Rexi.

On Christmas Day I and my knights were dining with my Lord Peter of Avallon, and while we dined the Saracens came, spurring hotly, up to our camp, and killed several poor folk who had gone into the fields on foot. We went to arm ourselves. But make what haste we could, we did not, on our return, find my Lord Peter, our host, for he was outside the camp, and had gone to meet the Saracens.

We spurred after, and rescued him from the Saracens, who had thrown him to the ground; and then brought him and his brother, the Lord of the Val, back to the camp. The Templars, who had come out on hearing the alarm, covered our retreat well and boldly. The Turks advanced, harassing us right up to the camp; wherefore the king commanded that the camp should be enclosed with trenches on the Damietta side, from the stream of Damietta to the stream of Rexi.

ATTACK OF THE SARACENS REPULSED

Scecedin, whose name I have already mentioned to you—the chief of the Turks—was the most highly esteemed of all paynimry. He bore on his banner the arms of the emperor who had made him a knight. His banner was barred; on one of the bars were the arms of the emperor who had made him a knight, on another were the arms of the *Soldan* of Aleppo, on the other were the arms of the *Soldan* of Babylon.

His name was Scecedin, the son of the scheik—or as one might say, "the aged one, the son of the aged one." This name was held as a great thing in paynimry; for they are the people in the world who most honour old people, if so be that God has preserved such from reproach and ill fame. Scecedin, this valiant Turk, had boasted, so the king's spies reported, that he would eat in the king's pavilion on the day of the feast of St. Sebastian.

The king, who knew of this, disposed of his host in such sort that the Count of Artois, his brother, should guard the covered ways and the engines; the king and the Count of Anjou—who afterwards was King of Sicily—were set to guard the camp on the side towards Babylon; and the Count of Poitiers, and we, the men of Champagne, were to guard the camp on the side towards Damietta. Now it happened that the afore-mentioned prince of the Turks caused his men to pass over into the island that lies between the stream of Damietta and the stream of Rexi—there where our host lay encamped—and he caused his forces to be set in line from the one stream to the other.

The King of Sicily attacked these people and discomfited them. Many were drowned in the one stream and in the other. Nevertheless a great part remained whom our people were afraid to attack, because the engines of the Saracens cast stones between the two streams. In the attack which the King of Sicily made against the Turks, Count Guy of Forez on his horse cut through the host of the Turks, and attacked, he and his knights, a body of Saracen sergeants, who bore him to the earth. His leg was broken, and two of his knights brought him back in their arms. With great difficulty was the King of Sicily extricated from the peril in which he stood; and much honour did he earn that day.

The Turks came against the Count of Poitiers, and against us, and we charged them, and drove them a great space. Some of their people were killed, and we returned without loss.

Greek Fire Hurled Against the Towers that Guarded the Covered Ways

One night when we were keeping guard over the towers that guarded the covered ways, it happened that the Saracens brought an engine called a petrary, which they had not hitherto done, and put Greek fire into the sling of the engine. When my Lord Walter of Ecurey, the good knight who was with me, saw it, he spoke thus:

> Lords, we are in the greatest peril that we have ever been in, for if they set fire to our towers and we remain here we are but lost and burnt up; while if we leave these defences which we have been set to guard, we are dishonoured. Wherefore none can defend us in this peril save God alone. So my advice and counsel is, that every time they hurl the fire at us, we throw ourselves on our elbows and knees, and pray to our Saviour to keep us in this peril

So soon as they hurled the first cast, we threw ourselves on our elbows and knees as he had taught us. That first cast fell between our two towers guarding the covered ways. It fell on the place in front of us, where the host had been working at the dam. Our firemen were ready to put out the fire; and because the Saracens could not shoot straight at them, because of two pavilion wings that the king had caused to be set up, they shot up into the clouds, so that the darts fell on the firemen's heads.

The fashion of the Greek fire was such that it came front-wise as large as a barrel of verjuice, and the tail of fire that issued from it was as large as a large lance. The noise it made in coming was like heaven's thunder. It had the seeming of a dragon flying through the air. It gave so great a light, because of the great foison of fire making the light, that one saw as clearly throughout the camp as if it had been day. Three times did they hurl Greek fire at us that night (from the petraries), and four times with the swivel crossbow.

Every time that our saintly king heard them hurling the Greek fire, he would raise himself in his bed, and lift up his hands to our Saviour, and say, weeping: "Fair Lord God, guard me my people!" And verily I believe that his prayers did us good service in our need. At night, every time the fire had fallen, he sent one of his chamberlains to ask how we fared, and whether the fire had done us any hurt.

Once when they hurled it at us, the fire fell near the tower which the people of my Lord of Courtenay were guarding, and struck the bank of the stream. Then, look you, a knight, whose name was l'Aubigoiz, came to me, and said, "Lord, if you do not come to our help we shall all be burned; for the Saracens have shot so many of their shafts that it is as if a great hedge were coming burning against our tower." We sprang up, and went thither, and found he spoke sooth. We put out the fire, and before we had put it out, the Saracens had struck us all with shafts that they shot across the stream.

The Towers Burned by the Greek Fire

The king's brothers kept guard over the towers by day, and went to the top of the towers to shoot bolts from the crossbows at the Saracens who were in the Saracens' camp; for the king had decided that the King of Sicily was to keep guard over the towers by day, while we were to keep guard over them by night; and now on a day when the King of Sicily was thus keeping guard, and we were to keep guard by night, we were in sore trouble of heart, because the Saracens had well-nigh shattered our towers.

And the Saracens brought out their petrary in full daylight, whereas they had so far only brought it out by night, and they threw Greek fire on to our towers. And they had brought their engines so near to the causeway which the host were building that no one dared to go to the towers because of the great stones that the engines cast, and that fell upon the causeway. Whence it happened that the two towers were burned, and the King of Sicily was so beside himself that he wished to throw himself there where the fire was, in order to put it out; and if he was incensed, why I and my knights could but praise God, seeing that if we had been on guard (in the towers) that night, we should all have been burned.

When the king saw this, he sent for all the barons of the host, and begged them each to give him wood from their ships to build a tower to help to dam up the stream; and he showed them clearly that there was no wood with which this could be done, save the wood of the vessels that had brought our goods up the river. Each brought according to his will, and when the tower was made, the wood was valued at ten thousand *livres* and more.

The king decided also that the tower should not be pushed forward on to the causeway until the day came when it was the turn of the king of Sicily to mount guard, so that he might thus repair the loss of the other towers that had been burned while he was on guard. As it had been decided, so was it done; as soon as the King of Sicily came on guard, he caused the tower to be pushed forward along the causeway, to the point where the other towers guarding the covered way had been burned.

When the Saracens saw this, they so arranged that all their sixteen engines should cast their shot upon the causeway, to the place whither the tower had been brought; and when they saw that our people feared to go to the tower because of the stones from the engines that fell on the causeway, they brought up the petrary, and cast Greek fire at the tower, and burned it utterly. Great was the courtesy that God showed to me and to my knights in this matter, for if we had mounted guard that night we should have done so in as great peril as on the former occasion, of which I have already spoken to you.

FORDING OF THE RIVER—DEATH OF THE COUNT OF ARTOIS

When the king saw this he called all his barons into council; and they agreed that they could not build a causeway on which to pass over against the Saracens, because our people were unable to dam up as much on our side as the Saracens could excavate on the other.

Then did constable my Lord Imbert of Beaujeu say to the king that a Bedouin had come to him and told him that he could show us a good ford, provided we gave him five hundred *besants*. The king agreed that the *besants* should be given him, provided he (on his part) proved the truth of what he promised. The constable thereon spoke to the Bedouin; but the Bedouin said he would not show the ford unless the moneys were first placed in his hands. So it was agreed that the *besants* should be given to him; and given to him they were.

The king decided that the Duke of Burgundy and the men of note from oversea who were with the host, should guard the camp, so that no harm might come to it; and that the king and his three brothers should pass the ford at the place which the Bedouin was to show them. So was the matter settled, and preparation made to pass over on Shrove Tuesday (8th February 1250), on which day we came to the Bedouin's ford. There, as the dawn of the day was appearing, we collected from all points; and when we were ready, we went to the stream and our horses began to swim. When we got to the middle of the stream, we touched ground and our horses found footing; and on the other bank of the stream were full three hundred Saracens, all mounted on their horses.

Then said I to my people:

Sirs, look only to the left hand, and let each draw thither; the banks are wet and soft and the horses are falling upon their riders and drowning them.

And it was sooth that some were drowned in the crossing, and among others was drowned my Lord John of Orleans, who carried a banner *vivré*.[7] Thereupon we moved in such sort that we turned up the stream, and found a dry way, and so passed over, praise God! that not one of us fell; and as soon as we had passed over, the Turks fled.

It had been so ordered that the Templars were to form the vanguard, and that the Count of Artois should have the second division after the Templars. Now it so happened that as soon as the Count of Artois had passed over the stream, he and all his people fell upon the Turks, who fled before them. The Templars notified to him that he was doing them great despite in that while his place was to come after them, he was going before; and they besought him to suffer them to go before, as had been arranged by the king.

Now it chanced that the Count of Artois did not venture to answer them, because of my Lord Foucand of Merle, who held the bridle of his horse; and this Foucand of Merle was a very good knight, but heard naught of what the Templars were saying to the count, seeing that he was deaf, and was crying, "Out on them, out on them!" Now when the Templars saw this, they thought they would be shamed if they suffered the count to outride them; so they struck spurs into their horses, helter-skelter, and chased the Turks, and the Turks fled before them, right through the town of Mansourah and into the fields beyond towards Babylon.

When they thought to return, the Turks threw beams and blocks of wood upon them in the streets, which were narrow. There were killed the Count of Artois, the Lord of Couci, who was called Raoul, and so many other knights that the numbers was reckoned at three hundred. The Temple, as the master has since told me, lost there fourteen score men-at-arms, and all mounted.

Joinville, Wounded and Surrounded by the Saracens, is Delivered by the Count of Anjou

I and my knights decided that we should attack some Turks who were loading their baggage in their camp to our left; and we fell upon

---

7. Term of heraldry—with waved lines..

them. While we were driving them through their camp, I perceived a Saracen, who was mounting his horse; one of his knights was holding the bridle. At the moment when he had his two hands on the saddle to mount, I gave him of my lance under the armpits and laid him dead.

When his knight saw that, he left his lord and the horse, and struck me with his lance as I passed, between the two shoulders, holding me so pressed down that I could not draw the sword at my belt. I had therefore to draw the sword attached to my horse; and when he saw that my sword was so drawn, he withdrew his lance and left me.

When I and my knights came out of the camp, we found some six thousand Turks, as we reckoned, who had left their quarters and retreated into the fields. When they saw us, they came running upon us, and killed my Lord Hugh of Trichâtel, Lord of Conflans, who was with me bearing a banner. I and my knights set spurs to our horses, and went to deliver my Lord Raoul of Wanou, who was with me, and whom they had struck to the ground.

While I was returning, the Turks pressed upon me with their lances. My horse knelt under the weight and I fell forward over the horse's ears. I got up as soon as ever I could, with my shield at my neck, and my sword in my hand; and my Lord Everard of Siverey—God have him in grace!—who was one of my people, came to me and said that we should draw off near to a ruined house, and there await the king, who was coming. As we were going thither, part on foot and part mounted, a great rout of Turks came rushing upon us, and bore me to the ground, and went over me, and caused my shield to fly from my neck.

When they had passed on, my Lord Everard of Siverey came back to me, and led me thence, and we went to the walls of the ruined house; and thither returned to us my Lord Hugh of Ecot, my Lord Frederic of Loupey, my Lord Renaud of Menoncourt. The Turks attacked us on all sides. Some of them entered into the ruined house and pricked us with their lances from above. Then my knights told me to hold their bridles, and so I did, for fear the horses should run away. And they defended themselves right manfully; and afterwards received great praise from all the right worthy men of the host, both those who were there and witnessed the deed, and those who heard tell thereof.

Then did my Lord Hugh of Ecot receive three lance wounds in the face, and my Lord Raoul; and my Lord Frederic of Loupey received a lance wound between the shoulders, and the wound was so large that the blood flowed from his body as from the bung-hole of a cask. My Lord Everard of Siverey was struck by a sword in the middle of the face in such sort that his nose fell over his lip. Then it came to my mind to think upon my Lord St. James, so that I prayed:

Fair Lord St. James, give me help and succour in this our need.

As soon as I had made this my prayer, my Lord Everard of Siverey said to me:

Lord, if you think that neither I nor my heirs will incur reproach therein, I will go and fetch you help from the Count of Anjou, whom I see in the midst of yonder field.

And I said to him:

My Lord Everard, meseems that you would earn for yourself great honour if you went for help to save our lives; and your own life too is in great jeopardy.

And I spoke sooth, for he died of that wound. He sought counsel of all the knights who were there, and all advised as I had advised. When he heard this, he asked me to let go my hold of his horse, which I held by the bridle, with the others, and I did so.

He came to the Count of Anjou, and begged him to succour me and my knights. A man of note who was with the Count of Anjou tried to dissuade him, but he said he would do what my knight asked of him; so he turned his bridle to come to our help, and several of his sergeants too set spurs to their horses. When the Saracens saw them coming, they left us. In front of the sergeants rode my Lord Peter of Auberive, with his sword in his fist, and when he saw that the Saracens had left us, he charged full into the Saracens who held my Lord Raoul of Wanou, and rescued him, sore wounded.

The King's Division Attacks the Saracens

As I was there on foot with my knights, wounded as I have said, the king came up with his battalions, and a great sound of shouting, and trumpets, and cymbals; and he halted on a raised causeway. Never have I seen so fair a knight! For he seemed by the head and shoulders to tower above his people; and on his head was a gilded helm, and in his hand a sword of Allemaine.

When he halted there, the good knights whom he had in his division, and whom I have already named to you, hurled themselves against the Turks; and with them several other valiant knights of his. And you must know that this was a very fine passage of arms, for in this battle no one drew bow or crossbow: it was a battle of mace and sword between the Turks and our people, all intermingled.

One of my squires, who had fled away with my banner, and had returned to me, gave me one of my Flemish horses, on which I mounted, and so drew up to the king, side by side.

While we were standing thus, my Lord John of Valery, the right worthy man, came to the king, and said he advised him to bear to the right towards the stream, so as to have the help of the Duke of Burgundy, and of those who were guarding the camp, and so also that his sergeants might obtain somewhat to drink, seeing that the day was already grown very hot.

The king commanded his sergeants to go and fetch the good knights of his council who were thereby, and named them all by their names. The sergeants went and summoned them from the midst of the fight, where the strife was very fierce between them and the Turks. They came to the king, and he asked counsel of them; and they said that my Lord John of Valery was advising him very well. Then the king commanded the great flag of St. Denis and his standard-bearer to move to the right towards the river. At the moving of the king's host there was again a mighty sound of trumpets, and cymbals, and horns.

The king had scarcely begun to move when he received several messages from the Count of Poitiers, his brother, and the Count of Flanders, and several other men of worth who had their forces there, all begging him not to move, because they were so hard pressed by the Turks that they could not follow him. The king summoned once more all the right worthy knights of his council, and all advised that he should wait. Shortly after, my Lord John of Valery came back, and blamed the king and his council for remaining where they were. On this all his counsellors advised that he should draw towards the river as the Lord of Valery advised.

At this moment the constable, my Lord Imbert of Beaujeu, came up to him and said that the Count of Artois, his brother, was defending himself in a house at Mansourah, and that he should go to his relief and succour him. And the king said, "Constable, go before, and I will follow." I said to the constable that I would be his knight, and he thanked me much. So we put ourselves in the way to go to Mansourah.

Then came to the constable a sergeant, a mace-bearer, all affeared, and told him that the king was stayed, and that the Turks had placed themselves between him and us. We turned, and saw that there were at least a thousand of them, and more, between him and us, and we were no more than six. Then I said to the constable,

> Lord, we cannot get to the king through these people, but let us go upward, and put this ditch that you see here between them and us, and so shall we be able to get back to the king.

The constable took my advice. And you may know that if the Turks had taken thought of us, they would certainly have killed us all; but they gave no thought to any save the king, and the big bodies of men; wherefore they fancied that we were on their side.

The Christians Driven Back on the River—Bridge Defended by Joinville—Retreat of the Count of Brittany From Mansourah

While we were returning down the bank of the river between the streamlet and the river, we saw that the king was come nigh to the river, and that the Turks were driving back the king's other battalions, slashing and striking with swords and maces; and they forced back the other battalions, with the king's battalions, upon the river.

The discomfiture was there so great that several of our people thought to pass over to the Duke of Burgundy, swimming; which they were unable to do, for their horses were weary, and the day had become very hot; so we saw, as we were coming down towards them, that the stream was covered with lances and shields, and with horses and men drowning and perishing.

We came to a little bridge that was over the streamlet, and I said to the constable,

> Let us stay here, and guard this little bridge, for if we abandon it the Turks will fall on the king from this side, and if our people are attacked from two sides, it will go hard with them.

And we did so. And it was told to us afterwards that we should all have been lost that day, save for the king. For the Lord of Courtenay and my Lord John of Saillenay told me that six Turks had come to the king's bridle and were leading him away captive, and that he alone delivered himself striking at them great strokes with his sword. And when his people saw how the king was defending himself, they took courage, and many of them abandoned thought of taking flight across the river, and drew to the king's side to help him.

Right straight upon us, who were keeping the little bridge, came the Count Peter of Brittany, riding from Mansourah, and he had been wounded with a sword across the face, so that the blood ran into his mouth. He rode upon a fine, well-limbed horse. He had thrown the reins on the pummel of the saddle, and held it with his two hands so that his people, who were behind, and pressed sorely upon him, might not hustle him out of the path to the little bridge.

Well did it seem how lightly he held them, for as he spat the blood out of his mouth, he said full often: "Ha, by God's head, have you ever seen such riff-raff!" Behind his men came the Count of Soissons, and my Lord Peter of Neuville, who was called "Caier," and they both had received blows enow during that day.

When they had passed, and the Turks saw that we were guarding the bridge, and turned our faces towards them, they ceased from following after Count Peter and his people. I came to the Count of Soissons, whose cousin-german I had married, and said:

> Lord, I think you would do well if you remained to keep this little bridge; for if we abandon the little bridge those Turks whom you see before you will rush over it, and so shall the king be assailed both in front and in rear.

And he asked whether, if he remained, I would remain with him?

And I replied, "Yes, right willingly." When the constable heard this, he told me not to move from thence till he returned, and that he would go and bring us help.

Joinville, Attacked by the Saracens, Continues to Hold the Bridge

There I remained on my thick-set stallion, and the Count of Soissons remained on my right, and my Lord Peter of Neuville on my left. Then behold there came a Turk from the direction of the king's troops, which were behind us, and struck my Lord Peter of Neuville from behind, with a mace, so that he laid him on his horse's neck with the blow that he gave, and then sprang across the bridge and rushed among his own people.

When the Turks saw that we would not abandon the little bridge, they passed over the streamlet and set themselves between the streamlet and the river, as we had done to go downwards; and we drew towards them in such manner as to be ready to charge them, whether they wished to go towards the king or to pass over the little bridge.

In front of us were two of the king's sergeants—of whom the one was called William of Boon, and the other John of Gamaches, and the Turks who had come between the streamlet and the river brought a large number of churls on foot, who pelted them with lumps of earth, but were never able to force them back upon us. At last they brought a churl on foot, who thrice threw Greek fire at them. Once William of Boon receive the pot of Greek fire on his targe, for if the fire had caught any of his garments he must have been burned alive.

We were all covered with the darts that failed to hit the sergeants. Now it chanced that I found a Saracen's gambeson (quilted tunic) lined with tow: I turned the open side towards me and made a shield of the gambeson, which did me good service, for I was only wounded by their darts in five places, and my horse in fifteen.

And it chanced again that one of my burgesses of Joinville brought me a pennon with my arms, and a lance head thereto, and every time we saw that the Turks pressed too hardly upon the sergeants, we charged them, and they went flying.

The good Count of Soissons, in that point of danger, jested with me and said:

"Seneschal, let these curs howl! By God's bonnet"—for that was his favourite oath—"we shall talk of this day yet, you and I, in ladies' chambers."

JOINVILLE REJOINS THE KING—THE SARACENS ARE DEFEATED, AND THE BEDOUINS PILLAGE THEIR CAMP

At night, as the sun was setting, the constable brought us the king's dismounted crossbowmen, and they placed themselves in rank before us; and when the Saracens saw them setting foot to the stirrup of their crossbows, they fled and left us there. Then the constable said to me:

Seneschal, this is well done. Now do you go to the king, and do not leave him at all until such time as he enters his pavilion.

So soon as I came to the king, my Lord John of Valery came to him and said:

Sire, my Lord of Châtillon asks you to give him the rearguard.

And the king did so right willingly, and then moved forward. And as we were going, I made him take off his helmet, and lent him my steel cap, so that he might have air.

When he had passed over the river there came to him brother Henry of Ronnay, Provost of the Hospitallers, and kissed his mailed hand. And the king asked if he had any tidings of the Count of Artois, his brother; and the provost said that he had news of him indeed, for he knew of a certainty that his brother, the Count of Artois, was in paradise.

"Ah, sire," said the provost, "be of good comfort herein, for never did King of France gain such honour as you have gained this day. For, in order to fight your enemies, you have passed over a river swimming, and you have discomfited them, and driven them from the field, and taken their engines, and also their tents, wherein you will sleep this night."

And the king replied: "Let God be worshipped for all He has given me!" and then the big tears fell from his eyes.

When we came to the camp we found that some Saracens on foot were pulling at the ropes of a tent which they were taking down, while people of ours of the lesser sort were tugging at the ropes on the other side. We ran in among these Saracens, the Master of the Temple and I, and they fled, and the tent remained in the hands of our people.

In this battle there were many people, and of great appearance, who came very shamefully flying over the little bridge of which I have already spoken to you, and they fled away panic-stricken; nor were we able at all to make any of them stop by us. I could tell some of their names, but shall forbear, for they are dead.

But of my Lord Guy Mauvoisin shall I not forbear to speak, for he came from Mansourah with honour. And all the way that the constable and I had followed up the river did he follow down; and in the same manner that the Turks pressed on the Count of Brittany and his men, so did they press on my Lord Guy Mauvoisin and his men; but as for my Lord Guy and his people, they gat themselves great honour. Nor is this to be marvelled at, that he and his people should approve themselves well on that day; for it was told to me, by those who had knowledge of his affairs, that all his company, save but a few, were knights of his own lineage or knights who were his liegemen.

When we had discomfited the Turks and driven them from their tents, and while none of our people remained in the camp, the Bedouins rushed into the camp of the Saracens, who were people of very high condition. Nothing in the world did they leave in the camp of the Saracens. They carried away everything that the Saracens had left. Nor did I ever hear tell that the Bedouins, though subject to the Saracens, were more lightly thought of because they had stolen and carried away these things—it being well known that the use and custom of the Bedouins is always to fall upon the weaker side.

THE BEDOUINS

As it pertains to my subject, I will here tell you what kind of people the Bedouins are. The Bedouins do not believe in Mahomet, but they believe in the law of Ali, who was uncle to Mahomet; and so also believes the Old Man of the Mountain, who entertains the Assassins. And they believe that when a man dies for his lord, or in any good cause, his soul goes into another body, better and more comfortable; and for this reason the Assassins are not greatly concerned if they are killed when carrying out the commands of the Old Man of the Mountain. But of the Old Man of the Mountain we will say no more at this present, but speak only about the Bedouins.

The Bedouins live neither in villages, nor cities, nor castles, but lie always out in the fields; and they establish their households, their wives and their children, at night, and by day when the weather is bad, in a sort of lodging that they make with the hoops of barrels tied to poles, like ladies' chariots; and over these hoops they throw sheepskins, called skins of Damascus, cured with alum. The Bedouins themselves wear great *pelisses* that cover the whole of their body, their legs, and their feet.

When it rains in the evening, or the weather is foul by night, they wrap themselves round in their cloaks, and take the bits out of their horses' mouths, and leave their horses to browse near. When the morrow comes, they spread out their cloaks to the sun, and rub and cure them; nor does it afterwards appear as if the cloaks had been wetted. Their belief is that no one can die save on the day appointed, and for this reason they will not wear armour; and when they wish to curse their children they say to them:

> Be thou accursed like a Frank, who puts on armour for fear of death!

In battle they carry nothing but sword and spear.

Nearly all are clothed in a surplice, like priests. Their heads are all bound round with cloths, that go beneath their chins, wherefore they are an ugly people, and hideous to behold, and the hairs of their heads and of their beards are all black.

They live on the milk of their beasts, and purchase, in the plains belonging to wealthy men, the pasturage on which their beasts subsist.

Their number no man can tell; for they are to be found in the kingdom of Egypt, in the kingdom of Jerusalem, and in all the other lands of the Saracens, and of the misbelievers—to whom they pay, every year, a great tribute.

I have seen in this country, since I came back from the land oversea, certain disloyal Christians, who hold the faith of the Bedouins, and say that no man can die save on the day appointed; and their belief is so disloyal that it amounts to saying that God has no power to help us. For those would indeed be fools who served God if we did not think he had power to prolong our lives, and to preserve us from evil and mischance. And in Him ought we to believe, seeing He has power to do all things.

The Camp Attacked During the Night—Joinville's Priest Puts Eight Saracens to Flight

Now let us tell that at nightfall we returned, the king and all of us, from the perilous battle aforementioned, and lodged in the place from which we had driven our enemies. My people, who had remained in the camp whence we started, brought me a tent which the Templars had given me, and pitched it before the engines taken from the Saracens; and the king set sergeants to guard the engines.

When I was laid in my bed—where indeed I had good need of rest because of the wounds received the day before,—no rest was vouchsafed to me. For before it was well day a cry went through the camp: "To arms! to arms!" I roused my chamberlain, who lay at my feet, and told him to go and see what was the matter.

He came back in terror, and said:

> Up, lord, up! for here are the Saracens, who have come on foot and mounted, and discomfited the king's sergeants who kept guard over the engines, and driven them among the ropes of our pavilions.

I got up, and threw a gambeson (quilted tunic) over my back, and a steel cap upon my head, and cried to our sergeants, "By St. Nicholas, they shall not stay here!"

My knights came to me, all wounded as they were, and we drove the Saracen sergeants from among the engines, and back towards a great body of mounted Turks who were over against the engines that we had taken. I sent to the king to give us succour, for neither I nor my knights could put on our hauberks because of the wounds we had received; and the king sent us my Lord Gaucher of Châtillon, who stationed himself in front of us, between the Turks and ourselves.

When the Lord of Châtillon had driven back the Saracen foot sergeants, they retreated on a great body of mounted Turks, who were drawn up before our camp so as to prevent us from surprising the host of the Saracens encamped behind them. Of this body of Turks, eight of the chiefs had dismounted, very well armed, and set up an intrenchment of hewn stone, so that our crossbowmen might not wound them. These eight Saracens shot volley after volley into our camp, and wounded several of our people and of our horses.

I and my knights consulted together, and we agreed that, when night came, we would take away the stones behind which they intrenched themselves. A priest of mine, named my Lord John of Voisey, assisted at this council, but made no such tarrying. He left our camp all alone and advanced towards the Saracens, clad in gambeson (quilted tunic), with his steel cap on his head, and dragging his spear from under his arm, with the point to the ground, so that the Saracens might not observe it.

When he came near the Saracens, who despised him because they saw he was alone, he quickly drew his spear from under his arm, and ran upon them. There was not one of the eight who thought of defence, but all turned and fled. When those on horseback saw that their lords came to them flying, they spurred forward to rescue them, and from our camp sprang forth some fifty sergeants. The mounted Saracens came on spurring, but they did not dare to attack our footmen, and wheeled about.

When they had done this two or three times, one of our sergeants took his spear by the middle, and hurled it at one of the mounted Turks, so that it struck him between the ribs; and he that was so struck, bore away the spear hanging by the point that was in his ribs. When the Turks saw this, they dared no longer to advance and fell back before us, and our sergeants took away the stones. From that time forward my priest was very well known throughout the host, and one and another would point him out, saying: "Look, that is my Lord of Joinville's priest, who discomfited the eight Saracens."

The Saracens Prepare for a General Attack Upon the Camp

These things happened on the first day of Lent (the 9th, February 1250). On that very day a valiant Saracen—made scheik by our enemies in the place of Scecedin, the scheik's son, whom they had lost in the battle on Shrove Tuesday—took the Count of Artois's coat of arms, and showed it to all the people of the Saracens, and told them it vas the king's coat of arms, and that the king was dead.

"And I show you these things," said he, "because a body without a head is not to be feared nor a people without a king. Therefore, if it so please you, we will attack them on Friday; and, meseems, you can but agree, for we cannot fail to take them all, seeing they have lost their chief." And all agreed that they would come and attack us on the Friday.

The king's spies, who were in the camp of the Saracens, came and told these tidings to the king. Then the king commanded all the chiefs of the divisions to cause their people to be armed by midnight, and to draw them up outside the pavilions and within the enclosure (which was made long stakes of wood so that the Saracens might not throw themselves into the camp; and the stakes were fixed in the ground in such manner that you could pass between them on foot). And as the king had commanded, so was it done.

Right at the sun-rising the Saracen before mentioned, whom they had made their chief, brought against us at least our thousand mounted Turks, and ordered them all round our camp, and round his own person—from the river that comes from Babylon to the river that went from our camp to a town called Rexi. When they had done this they brought against us such a great number of Saracens on foot that they surrounded all our camp as the mounted men surrounded it. Besides these two forces (mounted and dismounted) that I am telling you of, they arrayed all the power of the *Soldan* of Babylon, so as to give help if need were.

When they had done this, the chief came all alone, riding)n a little stallion, to see the disposal of our host; and according as he saw that our troops were more numerous in one place than another, he went back to fetch his men, and reinforced his battalions against ours. After this he caused the Bedouins, of whom there were at least three thousand, to pass towards the camp held by the Duke of Burgundy, which lay between the two rivers. And this he did, because he thought the king would send some of his people to help the duke against the Bedouins, whereby the king's host would be weakened.

Battle of the First Friday in Lent

It took him till midday to order these things; and then he caused the drums called *nacaires* to be beaten; and then they charged us, foot and horse. And first I will tell you of the King of Sicily—who was then Count of Anjou—because he was first on the side towards Babylon. The foe came against him as men play chess, for they first caused him to be attacked by their foot-men, and the foot-men assailed him with Greek fire; and the men, mounted and dismounted, pressed upon our people so sore that they discomfited the King of Sicily, who was on foot, among his knights.

And they came to the king, and told him of the great jeopardy in which his brother stood. And when the king heard this, he rode spurring amidst his brother's men, with his sword in his fist, and dashed so far among the Turks that they burnt the crupper of his horse with Greek fire. And by this charge that the king made he succoured the King of Sicily and his men, and drove the Turks from the camp.

After the troops of the King of Sicily came the troops of the barons oversea, of whom the Lord Guy of Ibelin and Lord Baldwin his brother were the chiefs. After their troops came the troops of my Lord Walter of Châtillon, full of right worthy men, and of good chivalry. These two divisions defended themselves so vigorously that the Turks were never able to pierce through them or drive them back.

After the troops of my Lord Walter came brother William of Sonnac, Master of the Temple, with the few brethren that remained to him after the battle of Tuesday. He had caused a work of defence to be erected in front of him with the engines that we had taken from the Saracens. When the Saracens came to attack him they threw Greek fire on to the hoardings he had erected, and these took fire easily, for the Templars had put into them a great quantity of pinewood planks. And you must know that the Turks did not wait till the fire had burned itself out, but ran in upon the Templars through the flames.

In this battle brother William, the Master of the Temple, lost an eye, and the other he had lost on Shrove Tuesday; and he died thereof, the said lord—on whom God have mercy! And you must know that behind the place where the Templars stood there was a space, the size of a journeyman's labour, so thickly covered with the Saracens' darts that the earth could not be seen by reason they were so many.

After the troops belonging to the Temple came the troops of my Lord Guy of Mauvoisin; and these troops the Turks were never able to overcome. Notwithstanding the Turks had so covered my Lord Guy of

Mauvoisin with Greek fire that his people could hardly extinguish it.

Starting from the place where my Lord Guy of Mauvoisin was stationed, the barriers that defended our camp went down about a stone's throw towards the river. Thence the barriers passed before the troops of Count William of Flanders and extended to the river that went towards the sea. In face of the barrier which came from the side of my Lord Guy Mauvoisin was our battalion; and because the troops of Count William of Flanders stood facing them, the Turks never dared to come and attack us; wherein God showed us great courtesy, for neither I nor my knights had our hauberks and shields, because we had all been wounded in the battle on Shrove Tuesday.

The Turks charged the Count of Flanders with great vigour and spirit, and on foot and horse. When I saw this I commanded our crossbowmen to shoot at those who were mounted. When those who were mounted saw they were being wounded from our side, then they took to flight; and when the count's people saw this, they left the camp, scrambled over the barriers, ran in among the dismounted Saracens, and discomfited them. Many were killed, and many of their targes taken. There acquitted himself right valiantly Walter of the Horgne, who carried the banner of my Lord of Apremont.

After the troops belonging to the Count of Flanders came the troops of the Count of Poitiers, the king's brother. These troops of the Count of Poitiers were on foot, and he alone mounted; and the Turks discomfited them immediately, and led away the Count of Poitiers captive. When the butchers, and the other camp followers, and the women who sold provisions, saw this, they raised the cry of alarm throughout the camp, and with God's help they succoured the count, and drove the Turks out of the camp.

After the troops of the Count of Poitiers came the troops of my lord Josserand of Brancion, who had come with the count into Egypt, and was one of the best knights that were in the host. He had so arranged his people that all his knights were on foot; and he himself was on horseback, as also his son my Lord Henry, and the son of my Lord Josserand of Nanton, and these he placed on horseback because they were but children. Several times the Turks discomfited his people.

Every time that he saw his people discomfited, he set spurs to his horse, and took the Turks in the rear; and oft, when he did this, the Turks left off attacking his people to set upon him.

Nevertheless this would not have availed to prevent the Turks from killing them all on the field of battle, had it not been for my Lord

Henry of Cône, who was in the Duke of Burgundy's division, a wise knight and valiant and of good counsel; for every time that he saw the Turks falling upon my Lord of Brancion, he caused the king's crossbowmen to shoot at the Turks across the river.

Thus did the Lord of Brancion escape from the peril of that day; but only in such sort that of the twenty knights he had about him he lost twelve, without counting the other men-at-arms; and he himself was so sorely mishandled that never afterwards could he stand upon his feet, and he died of that wound in the service of God.

And now will I speak to you somewhat of the Lord of Brancion. He had been, when he died, in thirty-six battles and skirmishes hand to hand, and always borne away the prize of valour. I saw him once in the host of the Count of Chalon, whose cousin he was, and he came to me and to my brother, and said to us, on a Good Friday: "My nephews, come and help me, you and your people, for the Germans are destroying the church."

We went with him, and ran upon them with our swords drawn, and with great labour and after a fierce struggle we drave them from the church. When this was done the right worthy man knelt before the altar, and called on our Saviour with a loud voice, and said:

> "Lord, I pray thee to have mercy upon me, and to take me out of these wars among Christians, in which I have lived a great while; and grant that I may die in Thy service, and so come to possess Thy kingdom of paradise.

And I have told you of these things, because I believe that God heard his prayer, as you may have seen from what has gone before.

After this battle, which was fought on the first Friday in Lent, the king summoned all his barons before him, and said to them:

> Great thanks do we owe to our Saviour, in that he has twice done us honour during this week: on Shrove Tuesday, when we drove the foe from their camp—where we are ourselves now lodged—and on the Friday following, which has just passed, when we have defended ourselves against them, we on foot, and they mounted.

And many other good and fair words did he speak for their recomforting.

The *Halca* or Guard of the *Soldan*

It is convenient, in pursuing our story, to disturb its course somewhat, at this point, for the purpose of showing how the *soldans* kept their forces ordered and conditioned. And it is sooth that they had formed the main part of their chivalry of foreigners, whom merchants had brought for sale out of strange lands, and whom they bought right willingly and at a high price. And these people that the merchants brought into Egypt were obtained in the East, because when one Eastern king defeated another, he took the poor people whom he had conquered, and sold them to the merchants, and the merchants came and sold them in Egypt.

As to the children, the *soldan* brought them up in his own house till their beards began to grow; and he would see that they had bows proportioned to their strength; and so soon as they waxed stronger, the weaker bows were cast into the *soldan's* arsenal, and the master artilleryman provided them with bows as strong as they could bend.

The arms of the *soldan* were *or*, and such arms as the *soldan* wore were worn by these young people also; and they were called *bahariz*.[8] So soon as their beards began to grow the *soldan* made them knights. And they wore the *soldan's* arms, save for one difference, *viz.*, that they added on to the arms or, crimson devices, roses, or crimson bends, or birds or other devices, according to their pleasure.

And these people, of whom I am speaking to you, were called *of the Halca*[9], because the *bahariz* slept in the tent of the *soldan*. When the *soldan* was in camp, those of the *Halca* were lodged about his quarters, and set to guard his person. At the entrance to his quarters were lodged, in a little tent, the porters of the *soldan*, and his minstrels, who had horns, and drums, and cymbals. And with these they made such a noise at the point of day and at nightfall, that those who were near could not hear one another speak; and clearly were they heard throughout the camp.

Nor would the minstrels have been rash enough to sound their instruments during the day, save by order of the master of the *Halca*,. whence it happened that if the *soldan* wished to give an order, he sent for the master of the *Halca*, and gave the order through him; and then the master caused the *soldan's* instruments to be sounded, and all the host assembled to hear the order of the *soldan*: the master of the *Halca*

---

8. Folk from the sea.
9. Guard.

spoke it, and all the host carried it out.

When the *soldan* went to war, the knights of the *Halca*, if so be that they approved themselves well in battle, were made *emirs* by the *soldan*, and he placed them in command of two hundred knights, or three hundred; and the better they approved themselves the more knights did he set them over.

The reward reserved for their deeds of chivalry is this: when they become famous and rich beyond question, and the *soldan* is afraid lest they should kill or disinherit him, then he causes them to be taken and put to death in his prison, and their wives deprived of all they possess. This is how the *soldan* dealt with those who captured the Count of Montfort, and the Count of Bar; and so did Bondocdar deal with those who had discomfited the King of Armenia.

For these latter, thinking to have some reward, dismounted and went to salute Bondocdar while he was hunting wild beasts; and he replied: "I salute you not," because they had disturbed his hunting; and he caused them to be beheaded.

Conspiracy of the *Emirs* Against the New *Soldan*

Let us now return to the matter in hand, and tell how the *soldan*, who was dead, had a son of the age of five and twenty years, wise, adroit, and crafty; and because the dead *soldan* feared that his son would dispossess him, he bestowed on him a kingdom which he had in the East. And now when the *soldan* was dead, the *emirs* sent to fetch the son, and so soon as the son was come into Egypt he took the golden rods from his father's seneschal, and constable, and marshal, and bestowed them upon those who had come with him from the East.

When the seneschal, constable, and marshal saw this they were very wroth, as were also those who had been of the father's council, and they felt that great shame had been put upon them. And because they doubted not that the son would do to them as the father had done to those who captured the Count of Bar, and the Count of Montfort (as you have been already told), they so practised with the men of the *Halca*, whose duty it was to guard the person of the *soldan*, that the men of the *Halca* agreed, at their request, to kill the *soldan*.

The Christians Begin to Suffer From Disease and Famine

After the two battles aforementioned, the host began to suffer very grievously; for at the end of nine days the bodies of our people, whom the Saracens had slain, came to the surface of the water; and this was said to be because the gall had putrefied. The bodies came floating to the bridge between our two camps, and could not pass under because the bridge touched the water. There was such great foison of them that all the river was full of corpses, from the one bank to the other, and, lengthwise, the cast of a small stone.

The king had hired a hundred vagabonds, who took full eight days to clear the river. They cast the bodies of the Saracens, who were circumcised, on the other side of the bridge, and let them go down with the stream; the Christians they caused to be put in great trenches, one with another. I saw there the chamberlains of the Count of Artois, and many others, seeking for their friends among the dead; but never did I hear tell that any was found (identified).

We ate no fish in the camp the whole of Lent save eels; and the eels ate the dead people, for they are a gluttonous fish. And because of this evil, and for the unhealthiness of the land—where it never rains a drop of water—there came upon us the sickness of the host, which sickness was such that the flesh of our legs dried up, and the skin upon our legs became spotted, black and earth colour, like an old boot; and with us, who had this sickness, the flesh of our gums putrefied; nor could anyone escape from this sickness, but he had to die. The sign of death was this, that when there was bleeding of the nose, then death was sure.

A fortnight afterwards the Turks, in order to starve us—which very much astonished our people—took several of their galleys that were above our camp, and caused them to be dragged by land and put into the river, a full league below our camp. And these galleys brought famine upon us; for no one, because of these galleys, dared to come up the stream from Damietta and bring us provisions.

We knew naught of these things till such time as a little ship, belonging to the Count of Flanders, escaped from them by force and told us of them, as also that the galleys of the *soldan* had taken full eighty of our galleys coming from Damietta, and put to death the people that were therein.

Thus there arose a great dearth in the camp, so that as soon as Easter was come an ox was valued at eighty *livres*, and a sheep at thirty *livres*, and a pig at thirty *livres*, and an egg twelve deniers, and a measure of wine ten *livres*.

The Host Recrosses the River—Six of Joinville's Knights Punished For Their Wickedness

When the king and the barons saw this, they agreed that the king should shift his camp, which was on the side towards Babylon, and move to the camping ground of the Duke of Burgundy, which was on the river that went to Damietta. In order to collect his people with greater safety, the king caused a barbican to be constructed before the bridge between our two camps, in such wise that one could enter the barbican from either side on horseback.

So soon as the barbican was ready, all the king's host gat to their arms, and the Turks made an attack in force upon the king's camp. Nevertheless, neither the king nor his people moved till all the baggage had been carried over, and then the king passed, and his body of troops after him, and after them all the other barons, save my Lord Walter of Châtillon, who had the rearguard. As they were entering into the barbican, my Lord Everard of Valery delivered my Lord John, his brother, whom the Turks were carrying away captive.

When all the host had passed, those who remained in the barbican were in great peril, for the barbican was not high, so that the mounted Turks shot full at them, and the Saracens on foot threw clods of earth right into their faces. All would have been lost had it not been for the Count of Anjou—afterwards King of Sicily—who went to their rescue, and brought them out safe and sound. Of that day did my Lord Geoffry of Mussambourc bear the prize—the prize of all who were in the barbican.

On the eve of Shrove Tuesday, I beheld a marvel, of which I will now tell you; for on that day was buried my Lord Hugh of Landricourt, who was with me, carrying a banner. There as he lay on a bier in my chapel, six of my knights were leaning on sacks full of barley; and because they were speaking loud in my chapel, and disturbing the priest, I went to them, and told them to hold their peace, and said it was a discourteous thing for knights and gentlemen to talk while mass was being sung.

And they began to laugh and told me, laughing, that they were remarrying the dead man's wife. And I spoke sharply to them, and told them that such words were neither good nor seemly, and that they had forgotten their companion over soon. And God took such vengeance upon them, that on the morrow was the great battle of Shrove Tuesday, in which they were all killed or mortally wounded, so that the wives of all six were in case to marry again.

Joinville Falls Sick—Death of His Priest

Owing to the wounds I had received on Shrove Tuesday, the sickness of the host took hold upon me, in my mouth and legs, as also a double tertian fever, and so great a cold in my head that the rheum flowed from the head through the nostrils; and because of the said sicknesses, I took to sickbed at mid-Lent; and thus it befell that my priest sang mass for me, before my bed, in my pavilion. And he had the same sickness as I. Now it chanced that at the consecration, he turned faint.

When I saw that he was about to fall, I, who had on my tunic, leapt from my bed barefoot, and took him in my arms, and told him to do all leisurely, and to proceed fairly with the consecration, for that I should not leave him till he had brought it to an end. He came to himself, and finished the consecration, and sang his mass fully to a close. But never did he sing mass again.

Attempt to Treat With the Saracens—Pitiful Condition of the Host

After these things the king's councillors and the councillors of the *soldan* appointed a set day on which to come to an agreement. The proposed conditions were these: that we should surrender Damietta to the *soldan*, and the *soldan* surrender to the king the kingdom of Jerusalem; and that the *soldan* should take charge of the sick that were at Damietta, and also of the salted meats—because they did not eat pork—and of the king's engines of war, until such time as the king was able to send and fetch all these things.

They asked the king's councillors what security would be given that the *soldan* should repossess Damietta. The king's councillors offered to deliver over one of the king's brothers, either the Count of Anjou, or the Count of Poitiers, to be kept until such time as Damietta was placed in the *soldan's* hands. The Saracens said they would consent to nothing unless the person of the king were left with them as a pledge; whereupon my Lord Geoffry of Sargines, the good knight, said he would rather that the Saracens should have them all dead or captive than bear the reproach of having left the king in pledge.

The sickness began to increase in the host in such sort, and the dead flesh so to grow upon the gums of our people, that the barber surgeons had to remove the dead flesh in order that the people might masticate their food and swallow it. Great pity it was to hear the cry throughout the camp of the people whose dead flesh was being cut away; for they cried like women labouring of child.

THE HOST ATTEMPTS TO RETREAT BY LAND AND WATER

When the king saw that he could only remain there to die, he and his people, he ordered and arranged that they should strike their camp, late on Tuesday (5th April 1250), at night, after the octave of Easter, to return to Damietta. He caused the mariners who had galleys to be told that they should get together the sick, and take them thither. He also commanded Josselin of Cornaut, and his brothers, and the other engineers, to cut the ropes that held the bridge between us and the Saracens; but of this they did nothing.

We embarked on the Tuesday, after dinner, in the afternoon, I and two of my knights whom I had remaining, and the rest of my followers. When the night began to fall, I told my mariners to draw up their anchor, and let us go down I the stream; but they said they dared not, because the *soldan's* galleys, which were between us and Damietta, would surely put us to death. The mariners had made great fires to gather the sick into their galleys, and the sick had dragged themselves to the bank of the river. While I was exhorting the mariners to let us begone, the Saracens entered into the camp, and I saw, by the light of the fires, that they were slaughtering the sick on the bank.

While my mariners were raising their anchor, the mariners appointed to take away the sick cut the ropes of their anchors and of their galleys, and came alongside our little ship, and so surrounded us on one side and the other that they well-nigh ran us down. When we had escaped from this peril, and while we were going down with the stream, the king, who had upon him the sickness of the host and a very evil dysentery, could easily have got away on the galleys, if he had been so minded; but he said that, please God, he would never abandon his people. That night he fainted several times; and because of the sore dysentery from which he suffered, it was necessary to cut away the lower part of his drawers, so frequent were his necessities.

They cried to us, who were floating on the water, that we should wait for the king; and when we would not wait, they shot at us with crossbow bolts; wherefor it behoved us to stop until such time as they gave us leave to fare forward.

THE KING MADE PRISONER—THE SARACENS REFUSE
TO BE BOUND BY TRUCE

Now I will leave off speaking of this matter, and tell you how the king was taken, as he himself related it to me. He told me how he had left his own division and placed himself, he and my lord Geoffry of Sargines, in the division that was under my Lord Gaucher of Châtillon, who commanded the rearguard.

And the king related to me that he was mounted on a little courser covered with a housing of silk; and he told me that of all his knights and sergeants there only remained behind with him my Lord Geoffry of Sargines, who brought the king to a little village, there where the king was taken; and as the king related to me, my Lord Geoffry of Sargines defended him from the Saracens as a good servitor defends his lord's drinking-cup from flies; for every time that the Saracens approached, he took his spear, which he had placed between himself and the bow of his saddle, and put it to his shoulder, and ran upon them, and drove them away from the king.

And thus he brought the king to the little village; and they lifted him into a house, and laid him, almost as one dead, in the lap of a *burgher*-woman of Paris, and thought he would not last till night. Thither came my Lord Philip of Montfort, and said to the king that he saw the *emir* with whom he had treated of the truce, and, if the king so willed, he would go to him, and renew the negotiation for a truce in the manner that the Saracens desired. The king begged him to go, and said he was right willing. So my Lord Philip went to the Saracen; and the Saracen had taken off his turban from his head, and took off the ring from his finger in token that he would faithfully observe the truce.

Meanwhile, a very great mischance happened to our people; for a traitor sergeant, whose name was Marcel, began to cry to our people:

Yield, lord knights, for the king commands you, and do not cause the king to be slain!

All thought that the king had so commanded, and gave up their swords to the Saracens. The *emir* saw that the Saracens were bringing in our people prisoners, so he said to my Lord Philip that it was not fitting that he should grant a truce to our people, for he saw very well that they were already prisoners.

So it happened to my Lord Philip that whereas all our people were taken captive, yet was not he so taken, because he was an envoy. But there is an evil custom in the land of paynimry that when the king sends envoys to the *soldan*, or the *soldan* to the king, and the king dies, or the *soldan*, before the envoys' return, then the envoys, from whithersoever they may come, and whether Christians or Saracen, are made prisoners and slaves.

Joinville Stayed on the River by a Contrary Wind

When this mischance befell our people, that they should be taken captive on land, so did it happen to us, to be taken captive on the water, as you shall shortly hear; for the wind blew from Damietta, and so counteracted the current of the river; and the knights, whom the king had placed in the lighter vessels to defend the sick, fled. Thus our mariners lost the current and got into a creek, and we had to turn back towards the Saracens.

We, who were going by water, came, a little before the break of dawn, to the passage where were the *soldan's* galleys that had prevented the coming of provisions from Damietta. Here there was great confusion and tumult; for they shot at us and at our mounted folk who were on the bank so great a. quantity of darts with Greek fire, that it seemed as if the stars of heaven were falling.

When our mariners had brought us out of the creek into which they had taken us, we found the king's light boats, that the king had appointed to defend our sick, and they went flying towards Damietta. Then arose a wind, coming from Damietta, so strong that it counteracted the current of the river.

By the one bank of the stream, and by the other, were a great quantity of boats belonging to our people who could not get down the stream, and whom the Saracens had taken and stayed; and the Saracens slew our people, and cast them into the water, and were dragging the coffers and baggage out of the boats that they had taken. The mounted Saracens on the bank shot at us with darts because we would not go to them. My people had put on me a jousting hauberk, so that I might not be wounded by the darts that fell into our boat.

At this moment my people, who were at the hinder point of the boat, cried out to me: "Lord, Lord, your mariners, because the Saracens are threatening them, mean to take you to the bank!" I had myself raised by the arms, all weak as I was, and drew my sword upon them, and told them I should kill them if they took me to the bank. They answered that I must choose which I would have: whether to be taken to the bank, or anchored in mid-stream till the wind fell. I told them I liked better that they should anchor in mid-stream than that they should take me to the shore where there was nothing before us save death. So they anchored.

Very shortly after we saw four of the *soldan's* galleys coming to us, and in them full a thousand men. Then I called together my knights and my people, and asked them which they would rather do, either yield to the *soldan's* galleys or yield to those on land. We all agreed that we would rather yield to the *soldan's* galleys, because so we should be kept together, than yield to those on land, who would separate us, and sell us to the Bedouins.

Then one of my cellarers, who was born at Doulevant, said: "Lord, I do not agree in this decision." I asked him to what he did agree; and he said to me: "I advise that we should all suffer ourselves to be slain, for thus we shall go to paradise." But we heeded him not.

JOINVILLE YIELDS HIMSELF A PRISONER—HIS LIFE IS THREATENED

When I saw that we must be taken, I took my casket and my jewels, and threw them into the river, and my relics also. Then said one of my mariners to me: "Lord, if you do not suffer me to say you are the king's cousin, they will kill you all, and us also."

And I told him I was quite willing he should say what he pleased. When the people on the first galley that came towards us to strike us amidships heard this, they threw down their anchors near to our boat.

Then did God send me a Saracen belonging to the emperor's[10] land. He had on drawers of unbleached linen, and came swimming across the stream to our vessel, and threw his arms about my waist, and said:

> Lord, if you do not take good heed, you are but lost; for it behoves you to leap from your vessel on to the beak that rises from the keel of that galley; and if you leap, these people will not mind you, for they are thinking only of the booty to be found in your vessel.

They threw me a rope from the galley, and I leapt on to the beak, so as God willed. And you must know that I tottered so that if the Saracen had not leapt after me, and held me up, I should have fallen into the water.

They set me in the galley, where there were full fourteen score men of their people, and he held me always in his arms. Then they threw me to the ground, and jumped upon my body to cut my throat, for anyone would have thought it an honour to kill me. But the Sara-

---

10. The Emperor Frederic II. of Germany, who had certain possessions in the East.

cen held me constantly in his arms, and cried: "Cousin to the king!" In this manner they bore me down to the ground twice, and once upon my knees, and then I felt the knife at my throat. In this extremity God saved me by the help of the Saracen, who took me to the castle of the ship, where the Saracen knights were assembled.

When I came among them, they took off my hauberk; and for the pity they had upon me, they threw over me a scarlet coverlet lined with miniver, which my lady mother had given me erewhile; and one of them brought me a white belt, and I girt myself over the coverlet; and in the coverlet I had made a hole, donning it as a garment.

And another brought me a hood which I put upon my head. And then, because of the fear in which I was, I began to tremble very much, and also because of the sickness. Then I asked for drink, and they brought me some water in a jar; and as soon as I set the water to my mouth to drink it down, it spurted out through my nostrils.

When I saw this, I sent for my people, and told them I was a dead man, seeing I had the tumour in my throat; and they asked how I knew it; and I showed them; and as soon as they saw the water spurting from my throat and from my nostrils, they took to weeping. When the Saracen knights who were there saw my people weeping, they asked the Saracen who had rescued us why they were weeping; and he replied that he understood I had the tumour in the throat, so that I could not recover. Then one of the Saracen knights told him to bid us be of good comfort, for he would give me somewhat to drink whereby I should be cured within two days; and this he did.

My Lord Raoul of Wanou, who was one of my following had been hamstrung in the great battle on Shrove Tuesday, and could not stand upon his feet; and you must know that an old Saracen knight, who was in the galley, would carry him, hanging from his neck, whenever the sick man's necessities so required.

Interview Between Joinville and the Admiral of the Galleys—the Sick Put to Death—Joinville Rejoins the Other Prisoners at Mansourah

The chief *emir* of the galleys sent for me and asked me if I were cousin to the king; and I said "No," and told him how and why the mariner had said I was the king's cousin. And he said I had acted wisely, for otherwise we should all have been put to death. And he asked me if I was in any manner of the lineage of the Emperor Frederic of Germany, who was then living. I replied that I thought my lady mother was the emperor's cousin-german. And he said that he loved me the more for it.

While we were at meat, he caused a citizen of Paris to be brought before us. When the citizen came in, he said to me: "Lord, what are you doing?"

"Why, what am I doing?" said I.

"In God's name," said he, "you are eating flesh on a Friday!"

When I heard that, I put my bowl behind me. And the *emir* asked my Saracen why I had done so, and he told him. And the *emir* replied that God would not take what I had done amiss, seeing I did it unwittingly. And you must know that this same reply was given to me by the Legate after we were out of prison; and yet, notwithstanding, I did not afterwards forbear to fast on bread and water, every Friday in Lent; wherefore the legate was very wroth with me, seeing that I was the only man of substance that had remained with the king.[11]

On the Sunday after, the *emir* caused me, and all the other prisoners taken on the water, to be landed on the bank of the river. While they were taking my Lord John, my good priest, out of the hold of the galley, he fainted, and they killed him and threw him into the river. His clerk fainted also, by reason of the sickness of the host that was upon him, and they threw a mortar on his head, so that he died, and they threw him into the river.

While the other sick people were being disembarked from the galleys in which they had been kept prisoners, there were Saracens standing by, with naked swords, who killed those that fell, and cast them all into the river. I caused them to be told, through my Saracen, that it seemed to me this was not well done; for it was against the teachings of Saladin, who said you ought never to kill a man after he has partaken of your bread and of your salt.

And the *emir* answered that the men in question were of no account, seeing they were helpless because of the sickness they had upon them.

He caused my mariners to be brought before me, and told me they had all denied their faith; and I told him never to place confidence in them, for lightly as they had left us so lightly, if time and opportunity occurred, would they leave their new masters. And the *emir* made answer that he agreed with me; for that Saladin was wont to say that never did one see a bad Christian become a good Saracen, or a bad Saracen become a good Christian.

---

11. The meaning is here a little obscure.

After these things he caused me to be mounted on a palfrey, and to ride by his side. And we passed over a bridge of boats and went to Mansourah, where the king and his people were prisoners; and we came to the entrance of a great pavilion, where the *soldan's* scribes were; and there they wrote down my name.

Then my Saracen said to me:

Lord, I shall not follow you further, for I cannot; but I pray you, lord, always to keep hold of the hand of the child that you have with you, lest the Saracens should take him from you.

And this child was called Bartholomew, and he was the bastard son of the Lord of Montfaucon. When my name had been written down, the *emir* led me into the pavilion where the barons were, and more than ten thousand persons with them. When I entered, the barons made such joy that we could not hear one another speak, and they gave thanks to our Saviour, and said they thought they had lost me.

The Prisoners, Threatened by the Saracens, are Told of the Treaty Concluded by the King

We had not been there long before they caused one of the chief men that were there to rise, and took us to another pavilion. Many of the knights and other people were kept by the Saracens in a court enclosed by mud walls. From this enclosed place they caused them to be taken, one after the other, and asked them, "Wilt thou abjure thy faith?" Those who would not abjure were set to one side, and their heads were cut off; and those who abjured were set on the other side.

At this point the *soldan* sent his council to speak with us, and they asked to whom they should give the *soldan's* message. And we told them to give it to the good Count Peter of Brittany. There were there certain people who knew the Saracen and French tongues, and are called dragomans, and they put the Saracen speech into French for the Count Peter. And the words were these: "Lord, the *soldan* sends us to you to know if you would be set free?"

The count answered "Yes."

"And what would you give the *soldan* for your deliverance?"

"What we can, so it be in reason," answered the count.

"And would you give," said they, "for your deliverance, any of the castles belonging to the barons oversea?"

The count replied that he had no power over these castles, for they were held from the emperor of Germany, then living. They then asked if we would surrender, for our deliverance, any of the castles belonging to the Temple or the Hospital? And the count replied that this could not be; for that when castellans were appointed to those castles, they were made to swear, on holy relics, never to surrender any of their castles for man's deliverance.

The council then replied that it seemed to them we had no mind to be delivered; and that they would go and send us such as would make sport of us with their swords, as they had done of the others belonging to our host. And they went their way.

So soon as they were gone, a great crowd of young Saracens rushed into our pavilion, having their swords girt; [12] and they brought with them a man of very great age,[13] very hairy, who caused us to be asked whether it was sooth that we believed in a God who had been taken for us, and wounded and put to death for us, and who on the third day had risen again?

And we answered "Yes." Then he told us that we should not be discomforted if we had suffered these persecutions for His sake; "for," said he, "you have not yet died for Him. as He died for you; and if He had power to rise again, rest assured that He will deliver you whensoever it so pleases Him."

Then he went away, and all the young men with him; whereat I was greatly rejoiced, for I thought most certainly that they had come to cut off our heads. And it was not long afterwards that the *soldan's* people came and told us that the king had procured our deliverance.

After the aged man who had given us comfort, was gone away, the counsellors of the *soldan* came back to us, and told us that the king had procured our deliverance, and that we must send four of our people to hear what he had done. We sent my Lord John of Valery, the right worthy man, my Lord Philip of Montfort, my Lord Baldwin of Ibelin, Seneschal of Cyprus, and my Lord Guy of Ibelin, Constable of Cyprus, one of the most accomplished knights I have ever seen, and one who most loved the people of that land. These four brought back to us word after what manner the king had procured our deliverance.

---

12. In Joinville's *Credo*, the swords are said to be "drawn."
13. "As old, seemingly, as a man could be," says the *Credo*,. and the *Credo* adds that the young Saracens "seemingly" held the old man to be mad. The whole scene is described, with a few additional details in the *Credo*.

St. Louis Threatened With Torture–He Negotiates With the Saracens

The counsellors of the *soldan* had tried the king in the same manner that they had tried us, in order to see if the king would promise to deliver over to them any of the castles of the Temple or the Hospital, or any of the castles belonging to the barons of the land; and, as God so wined, the king had answered after the very same manner that we had answered. And they threatened him, and told him that as he would not do as they wished, they would cause him to be put in the *bernicles*.

Now the *bernicles* are the most cruel torture that anyone can suffer. They are made of two pieces of wood, pliable, and notched at the ends with teeth that enter the one into the other; and the pieces of wood are bound together at the end with strong straps of ox-hide; and when they want to set people therein, they lay them on their side, and put their legs between the teeth; and then they cause a man to sit on the pieces of wood.

Hence it happens that, not half a foot of bone remains uncrushed. And to do the worst they can, at the end of three days, when the legs are swollen, they replace the swollen legs in the *bernicles*, and crush them all once more. To these threats the king replied that he was their prisoner, and that they could do with him according to their will.

When they saw that they could not prevail over the good king by threats, they came back to him and asked how much money he would give to the *soldan*, besides surrendering Damietta. And the king replied that if the *soldan* would accept a reasonable sum, he would advertise the queen to pay it for their deliverance. And they asked: "How is it that you will not tell us definitely that these things shall be done?"

And the king replied that he did not know if the queen would consent, seeing she was his lady and the mistress of her actions. Then the counsellors returned and spoke to the *soldan*, and afterwards brought back word to the king that if the queen would pay a million *besants* of gold, which are worth five hundred thousand *livres*,[14] the *soldan* would release the king.

And the king asked them, on their oath, whether the *soldan* would release them, provided the queen consented. So they went back once more and spoke to the *soldan*, and on their return, made oath that the

---

14. M. de Wailly estimates this at 10,132,000 *francs*, of modern French money, or, say, £405,000..

soldan would release the king on these conditions. And now that they had taken the oath, the king said and promised to the *emirs*, that he would willingly pay the five hundred thousand *livres* for the release of his people, and surrender Damietta for the release of his own person, seeing it was not fitting that such as he should barter himself for coin.

When the *soldan* heard this he said: "By my faith, this Frank is large-hearted not to have bargained over so great a sum! Now go and tell him," said he, "that I give him a hundred thousand *livres* towards the payment of the ransom."

THE CAPTIVES ARE TAKEN DOWN THE STREAM: AS FAR AS THE SOLDAN'S CAMP

Then the *soldan* caused the chief men to be put into four galleys and taken towards Damietta. In the same galley as I were the good Count Peter of Brittany, the Count William of Flanders, the good Count John of Soissons, my Lord Imbert of Beaujeu, the constable of France, the good knight my Lord Baldwin of Ibelin, and my Lord Guy, his brother.

Those who were in charge of us in the galley brought us to bank before an encampment which the *soldan* had established by the river; and it was of such a fashion as you shall presently hear. Before the encampment there was a tower, made of fir poles, and enclosed with dyed linen cloths, and here was the entrance to the encampment. And within this entrance was pitched a pavilion, where the *emirs* left their swords and armour when they went to speak to the *soldan*.

Beyond the pavilion was another entrance, like the first, and by this entrance you passed into a large pavilion, which was the *soldan's* hall. Beyond the hall was another tower, like the first, by which one entered into the *soldan's* chamber. Beyond the *soldan's* chamber there was a court; and in the midst of the court, a tower, higher than the rest, whither the *soldan* resorted when he wished to overlook the whole country and the camp. From the court an alley ran down to the river, and there the *soldan* had caused a pavilion to be pitched in the water, for bathing.

All the encampment was enclosed in trellises of wood, and on the outside the trellises were covered with blue cloths, so that those who were without should not be able to see in; and the towers, all four of them, were covered with cloth. We arrived, on the Thursday before Ascension Day (28th April 1250), at the place where this encampment was set up. The four galleys in which we were all together as prisoners, anchored before the *soldan's* encampment. The king was taken to a pavilion that stood nigh thereto. Matters had been so ordered by the *soldan* that on the Saturday before Ascension Day Damietta was to be surrendered to him, and he was to release the king.

The *Emirs* Conspire—The *Soldan* is Killed

The *emirs* whom the *soldan* had dismissed from his council in order to appoint thereto his own *emirs*, brought from foreign lands, now conferred together; and an astute Saracen I spake after this manner:

> Lords, you see the shame and dishonour that the *soldan* has put upon us, and how he has taken from us the dignity in which we had been established by his father. Now we may be sure that when he finds himself in the stronghold of Damietta he will cause us to be taken, and to die in prison, as his grandfather did to the *emirs* who captured the Count of Bar and the Count of Montfort. Therefore, so it seems to me, it would be better to cause him to be put to death before he escapes out of our hands.

They went therefore to those of the *Halca*, and demanded of them that they should kill the *soldan*, so soon as they had eaten with him, as he had invited them to do. Thus it befell that, after they had eaten, and the *soldan* had taken leave of his *emirs*, and was going to his chamber, one of the knights of the *Halca*, who bore the *soldan's* sword, struck the *soldan* therewith in the middle of the hand, between the four fingers, and clove the hand up to the arm.

The *soldan* turned to the *emirs*, who had caused this to be done to him, and said:

> Lords, I make appeal to you against these people of the *Halca*, who desire to slay me, as you can see!

Then the knights of the *Halca* made answer to the *soldan* with one voice, and said:

> As thou sayest that we desire to slay thee, better is it that we should slay thee than that thou shouldst slay us!

Then they caused the cymbals to be struck, and all the host came to ask what was the *soldan's* will. And they answered that Damietta was taken, and that the *soldan* was going thither, and that he ordered them to follow. So the host gat to their arms, and spurred towards Damietta.

And when we saw that they were going towards Damietta, we were in sore trouble of heart, for we thought that Damietta was lost. But the *soldan*, being young and active, fled into the tower that stood behind his chamber (as you have already heard), with three of his bishops, who had sat at meat with him; and he was there with them in the tower.

Those of the *Halca*, who were in number five hundred mounted men, threw down the *soldan's* pavilions, and swarmed round and about the tower, besieging him and the three bishops; and they cried to him to come down. And he said so he would if they promised him safety. They told him they would make him come down by force, for he was not in Damietta.

Then they threw at him Greek fire, and it caught the tower, which was made of pine planks and cotton cloth. The tower flared up quickly, nor have I ever seen finer nor straighter flame. When the *soldan* saw this, he gat down swiftly, and came flying towards the river, all along the way of which I have already spoken to you.

Those of the *Halca* had broken down all the enclosed way with their swords; and as the *soldan* fled along to go to the river, one of them gave him a spear-thrust in the ribs, and the *soldan* fled to the river, trailing the spear. And they followed after, till they were all swimming, and came and killed him in the river, not far from the galley in which we were. One of the knights, whose name was Faress-Eddin Octay, cut him open with his sword, and took the heart out of his body; and then he came to the king, his hand all reeking with blood, and said:

> What wilt thou give me? for I have slain thine enemy, who, had he lived, would have slain thee!

And the king answered him never a word.

THE LIFE OF THE PRISONERS IS AGAIN THREATENED— NEW TREATY OF THE KING WITH THE *EMIRS*

Full thirty of them came to our galley, with drawn swords in their hands, and Danish axes hanging at their necks. I asked my Lord Baldwin of Ibelin, who well knew the Saracen tongue, what these people said; and he answered that they said they had come to take off our heads.

Then were there a whole host of our people confessing to a brother of the Trinity whose name was John, and who belonged to the following of Count William of Flanders. But as for myself, I remembered no sin that I had committed, and only thought that the more I defended myself and the more I tried to escape, the worse I should fare.

Then I crossed myself, and knelt at the feet of one of them, who bore a Danish axe such as carpenters use, and I said: "Thus died St. Agnes."

My Lord Guy of Ihelin, Constable of Cyprus, knelt by my side, and confessed himself to me, and I said: "I absolve you, with such power as God has given me."

But when I rose from that place, I had no memory of aught that he had told me.

The Saracens made us rise from where we were, and set us in prison in the hold of the galley; and many of our people thought they had done this because they did not wish to fall upon us all together, but wished to kill us one after the other. There we lay in great misery that evening, and all through the night, and we were so pressed together that my feet came against the good Count Peter of Brittany and his came against my face.

On the morrow the *emirs* caused us to be taken from our prison in the hold; and the messengers told us we were to go and speak to the *emirs* in order to renew the covenant the *soldan* had made with us; and they also told us we might hold it for certain that if the *soldan* had lived he would have caused the king to be beheaded, and all of us likewise. Those who were able to go, went. The Count of Brittany, the constable and I, who were grievously sick, remained where we were. The Count of Flanders, the Count John of Soissons, the two brothers of Ibelin, and the rest who could help themselves, went.

These agreed with the *emirs* in such sort that, so soon as Damietta was delivered over to them, they would set free the king and the other men of rank who were there. As to the lesser folk, the *soldan* had caused them to be led away towards Babylon, such at least as he had not caused to be put to death. And this thing he had done contrary to the covenant made with the king, whereby it seemeth well that he would have put us to death also, so soon as he had come into possession of Damietta.

And the king was to swear further to gratify the Saracens with two hundred thousand *livres* before he left the river, and with two hundred thousand *livres* in Acre. The Saracens, by the covenant they made with the king, were to take charge of the sick in Damietta, and of the crossbows, the arms, the salted meats and the engines of war, until such time as the king sent for them.

The oaths which the *emirs* were to swear to the king were devised and set forth in writing, and were to this effect: that if they did not observe this covenant with the king they should be as dishonoured as a man who, for his sin, goes on pilgrimage to Mahomet, at Mecca, with his head uncovered; and as dishonoured as a man who leaves his wife, and then takes her again (for in that case, according to the law of Mahomet, if a man leaves his wife, he can never have her again, save after seeing her in the arms of another man).

The third oath was to this effect: that if they did not observe their covenant with the king, they should be as dishonoured as a Saracen who had eaten swine's flesh. The king was satisfied with the aforesaid oaths of the *emirs*, because Master Nicholas of Acre, who understood the Saracen tongue, said that, according to their law, they could devise no oaths stronger or more binding.

When the *emirs* had sworn they caused to be put in writing the oath they demanded of the king; and this oath was framed on the advice of the priests who had denied their faith and gone over to them, and the writing was to this effect: that if the king did not observe his covenants with the *emirs*, he should be as dishonoured as a Christian who denies God and His mother, and forfeits the fellowship of the twelve Companions of our Lord, and of all the saints. To this the king agreed right willingly.

The last point in the oath was to this effect: that if the king did not observe his covenants with the *emirs*, he should be as dishonoured as a Christian who denies God and His law, and who, in despite of God, spits upon the cross, and tramples upon it. When the king heard this he said that, please God, he would never take that oath!

The *emirs* sent Master Nicholas, who knew the Saracen tongue, to the king, and he spake to the king these words: "Sire, the *emirs* are greatly incensed, forasmuch as they have sworn what you required of them, whereas you will not swear what they require of you; and be assured that if you do not swear this oath they will cause your head to be cut off, as well as the heads of all your people."

The king replied that they could act in this matter as it seemed best to them; but that he liked better to die as a good Christian rather than to live under the wrath of God and of His mother.

The patriarch of Jerusalem, an old and reverend man of fourscore years, had obtained a safe conduct from the Saracens, and come to help the king to obtain his deliverance. Now it is the custom between the Christians and the Saracens that when the king or the *soldan* dies, those who are on an embassage, whether it be in a Christian or a pagan land, are made prisoners and slaves; and because the *soldan*, who had given the safe conduct to the patriarch, was now dead, the said patriarch was a prisoner like as we were.

When the king had given his answer, one of the *emirs* said that it was given by the advice of the patriarch, and he said to the pagans: "If you will believe me, I will make the king swear, for I will cause the head of the patriarch to fly into the king's lap."

They would not listen to this; but they took the patriarch from the side of the king, and tied him to the pole of the pavilion with his hands behind his back, and so straitly bound that the said hands swelled to the size of his head, and that the blood started from between the nails.

The patriarch cried to the king: "Sire, for the love of God, swear without fear; for seeing that you intend to hold to your oath, I take upon my own soul whatsoever there may be of sin in the oath that you take!" I know not how this matter of the oath was settled; but in the end the *emirs* held It themselves satisfied with the oath taken by the king, and by the other men of note there present.

Execution of the Treaty—Damietta Restored to the Saracens

As soon as the *soldan* was killed, they caused the instruments of the *soldan* to be brought before the king's tent; and it was told to the king that the *emirs* had had a great desire to make him Soldan of Babylon, and had held council thereon. And he asked me whether I thought he would have taken the kingdom of Babylon if it had been offered to him. And I told him that had he so taken it, he would have acted like a fool, seeing they had killed their lord; but he told me that in sooth he would not have refused it.

And you must know it was reported that this matter only remained where it was, and proceeded no further, because the Saracens said the king was the most steadfast Christian that could be found And they gave this as an example, that when he issued from his tent, he put himself cross-wise on the earth, and made the sign of the cross all over his body. And they said that if Mahomet had suffered them to be so maltreated, as the king had been, they would never have retained their belief in him; and they said further that if their people made the king to be *soldan*, they would have to become Christians, or else he would put them all to death.

After the covenants between the king and the *emirs* had been settled and sworn to, it was agreed that they should release us on the day after Ascension Day; and that so soon as Damietta was delivered over to the *emirs*, they would release the person of the king and of the men of note who were with him, as has been already said. On the Thursday at night (5th May 1250) those who were in charge of our four galleys came to anchor in the midst of the river, before the bridge of Damietta, and caused a pavilion to be pitched before the bridge, there where the king should land.

At sun-rising my Lord Geoffry of Sargines went into the city, and caused the city to be given up to the *emirs*. The *soldan's* flags were hoisted on all the towers of the city. The Saracen knights got into the city, and began to drink the wines, and were soon all drunken; whereupon one of them came to our galley, and drew his sword all reeking with blood, and said that for his part he had killed six of our people.

Before Damietta was surrounded, the queen had been received into our ships, together with all our people who were in Damietta, save the sick only. These last the Saracens, by their oath, were bound to keep and guard; but they killed them all. The king's engines of war, which they were also bound to preserve, they knocked to pieces. And the salted meat, which they were bound to keep for us, inasmuch as they do not eat pork, they did not keep. They made a pile of the engines, and a pile of the bacon, and another of the dead people, and they set fire thereto; and the fire was so great that it lasted the Friday, the Saturday, and the Sunday.

THE MASSACRE OF THE PRISONERS IS CONSIDERED

The king, and all we who were there, should have been set free at sunrise, but the Saracens kept us till sunset; and we had nothing to eat, nor the *emirs* either, and they were quarrelling the livelong day. And one of them spoke in this wise for those who belonged to his party:

> Lords, if you will listen to me, and to those who are of my party, you will kill the king and the men of note who are here; for then, for the space of forty years, we need fear nothing, seeing that their children are young, and that we hold Damietta; wherefore we can do this with the greater security.

Another Saracen, whose name was Sebreci, and who was a native of Mauritania, spoke contrariwise, and said this:

> If we kill the king, after we have killed the *soldan*, it will be said

that the Egyptians are the most evil people in the world, and the most disloyal

And those who desired that we should be killed, rejoined: "It is sooth that we have too wickedly rid ourselves of our *soldan*, whom we put to death; for we have therein gone counter to the commandments of Mahomet, in that he commanded us to guard our lord as the apple of our eye. And behold in this book, here is the commandment written. But listen," said he, "to this other commandment of Mahomet, that comes after."

And with that he turned over the leaf of a book that he held in his hand, and showed them another commandment, which was to this effect:

For the assurance of the faith, slay the enemy of the law.
Now have we disobeyed the commandments of Mahomet, in that we have killed our lord; but we shall do worse if we do not kill the king, whatever promise of safety has been given to him, seeing that he is the most powerful enemy of the pagan law.

Our death was nearly agreed to; whence it happened that one of the *emirs*, who was our adversary, thought we were an to be killed, and came on the river, and began to cry, in the Saracen tongue, to those who had the galleys in charge, and took his turban from his head, and made a sign to them with his turban. And now they lifted anchor, and took us back a full league up the stream towards Babylon. Then we gave ourselves up for lost, and many were the tears shed.

RELEASE OF THE CAPTIVES—JOINVILLE EMBARKS ON THE KING'S GALLEY—DEPARTURE OF SOME OF THE CRUSADERS FOR FRANCE

As God, who does not forget His own, so willed, it was agreed, at about the setting of the sun, that we should be released. So we were brought back, and our four galleys drawn to the bank. We demanded to be let go. They said they would not let us go till we had eaten, "for it would be a shame to our *emirs* if you left our prisons fasting."

So we told them to give us meat, and we would eat; and they said some had gone to fetch it in the camp. The food they gave us was fritters of cheese roasted in the sun so that worms should not come therein, and hard-boiled eggs cooked four or five days before; and these, in our honour, had been painted outside with divers colours.

They put us on land, and we went towards the king, whom they were leading to the river from the pavilion in which they had kept him; and there followed him full twenty thousand Saracens on foot, with their swords in their belts. On the river, before the place where the king stood, was a Genoese galley, and it seemed as if there were but one single man on board.

As soon as he saw the king on the bank of the river, he sounded a whistle; and at the sound of the whistle, eighty crossbowmen leapt from the hold of the galley, all fully equipped, with their crossbows wound up, and in a moment they had the bolts in socket. As soon as the Saracens saw them, they took to flight like sheep, so that none remained with the king save two or three.

A plank was thrown to the land, so that the king might go on board, as also the Count of Anjou, his brother, and my Lord Geoffry of Sargines, and my Lord Philip of Nemours, the Marshal of France, who was called of the Mez, and the Master of the Trinity, and I myself. The Count of Poitiers they kept in captivity, until such time as the king had paid the two hundred thousand *livres*, which he was to pay as a ransom before he left the river.

On the Saturday (7th May 1250) after Ascension Day—which Saturday was the day following the day of our deliverance—the Count of Flanders, and the Count of Soissons, and several other men of note who had been taken in the galleys, came to take leave of the king. The king told them he thought they would do well to wait till the Count of Poitiers, his brother, had been released.

But they said they could not wait, seeing their galleys were all ready for sea. So they embarked on board their galleys, and left for France; and they took with them the good Count Peter of Brittany, who was so sick that he lived no longer than three weeks, and died at sea.

Payment of the Ransom—Money Taken by Joinville from the Templars

They began to count[15] the money for the ransom on Saturday, in the morning; and they took for the counting the whole of Saturday, and Sunday until night; for they reckoned by weight in the balance, and each measure was worth ten thousand *livres*. When it came to the time of vespers on Sunday, the king's people who were counting the money sent to tell him that they still were short of the sum required by full thirty thousand *livres*. And the king had by him only the King of Sicily, and the Marshal of France, and the Minister of the Trinity,

---

15. Joinville says, "make the payment." But it seems clear from what follows that this was only the preliminary counting.

and I. All the rest were at the counting of the money for the payment of the ransom.

Then I said to the king that it would be well if he sent for the Marshal of the Temple—the master being dead—and asked them to lend him the thirty thousand *livres* for the release of his brother. The king sent to fetch the Templars and directed me to lay the matter before them.

When I had spoken to them, brother Stephen of Otricourt, who was Commander of the Temple, answered me thus: cc Lord of Joinville, this advice that you have given to the king is neither good nor reasonable. For you know that we receive funds in such sort, that we are bound, by our oaths, not to deliver them up, save to those who have entrusted them to us." Many were the hard and angry words that passed between him and me.

Then spoke brother Renaud of Vichier, who was Marshal of the Temple, and he said this:

> Sire, let us set to one side this quarrel between the Lord of Joinville and our commander; for indeed, as our commander says, we could not advance any of this money without being forsworn. And as to what the seneschal advises, *viz.*, that if we will not lend you the money, you had better take it—why, he says nothing that is very outrageous, and you must do as you think best; and if you do take what is ours here in Egypt, why, we have so much of what is yours at Acre, that you can easily indemnify us.

I said to the king that I would go and take the money, if he so ordered; and he ordered me accordingly. So I went to one of the galleys belonging to the Temple, the chief galley, and when I wished to go down into the hold of the galley, where the treasure was, I asked the Commander of the Temple to come and see what I took; but he did not deign to do so. The marshal said he would come and be a witness to the violence I should do him.

So soon as I had gone down to where the treasure was, I asked the Treasurer of the Temple, who was there, to give me the keys of a chest that lay before me; and he, seeing I was thin and emaciated with sickness, and had on only such clothes as I had worn in prison, said he would give me none of them. Then I perceived a hatchet lying there, and lifted it and said I would make of it the king's key. When the marshal saw this, he took me by the fist, and said:

Lord, we see right well that you are using force against us, and we will cause the keys to be handed over to you.

Then he ordered the treasurer to give me the keys, which he did. And when the marshal told the treasurer who I was, he was greatly astonished.

I found that the chest that I opened belonged to Nicholas of Choisi, a sergeant of the king. I threw out the silver I found therein, and went and sat on the prow of our little vessel that had brought me. And I took the Marshal of France, and left him with the silver in the Templar's galley, and on the galley I put the Minister of the Trinity.

On the galley the marshal handed the silver to the minister, and the minister gave it over to me on the little vessel where I sat. When we had ended and came towards the king's galley, I began to shout to the king: "Sire, sire, see how well I am furnished!" And the saintly man received me right willingly and right joyfully. We gave over what I had brought to those who were counting the money for the ransom.

LOYALTY OF THE KING IN CARRYING OUT THE TREATY

When the counting was over, the king's councillors, who had effected the counting, came to the king, and said that I the Saracens would not deliver his brother until the money I was actually in their possession. There were those of the I council who thought that the king should not hand over the moneys until he had received his brother back. But the king replied that he would hand them over, seeing he had covenanted with the Saracens to do so, and as for the Saracens, if they wished to deal honestly, they would also hold to the terms of their covenant.

Then my Lord Philip of Nemours told the king that they had miscounted, by a measure of ten thousand *livres*, to the prejudice of the Saracens. At this the king was very wroth, and said it was his will that the ten thousand *livres* should be restored, seeing he had covenanted to pay two hundred thousand *livres* before he left the river.

Then I touched my Lord Philip with my foot, and told the king not to believe him, seeing that the Saracens were the wiliest reckoners in the whole world. And my Lord Philip said I was saying sooth, for he had only spoken in jest; and the king said such jests were unseemly and untoward. "And I command you," said the king to my Lord Philip, "by the fealty that you owe to me as being my liegeman—which you are—that if these ten thousand *livres* have not been paid you will cause them to be paid without fail."

Many people had advised the king to withdraw to his ship, which waited for him at sea, so as to be no longer in the hands of the Saracens. But he would never listen to them, saying he should not depart from the river, as he had covenanted, until such time as he had paid the two hundred thousand *livres*. So soon, however, as the payment had been made, the king, without being urged thereto, said that henceforth he was acquitted of his oaths, and that we should depart thence, and go to the ship that was on the sea.

Then our galley was set in motion, and we went a full great league before one spoke to another, because of the distress in which we were at leaving the Count of Poitiers in captivity.[16] Then came my Lord Philip of Montfort in a galleon, and cried to the king: "Sire, sire! speak to your brother, the Count of Poitiers, who is in this other ship!"

Then cried the king: "Light up! light up!" And they did so. Then was there such rejoicing among us that greater could not be. The king went to the count's ship, and we went too. A poor fisherman went and told the Countess of Poitiers that he had seen the Count of Poitiers released, and she caused twenty *livres parisis* to be given to him.

Of Gaucher of Chatillon—of the Bishop of Soissons, Who Was Martyred—and of a Renegade

I ought not to forget certain things that happened in Egypt while we were there. First I will tell you of my Lord Gaucher of Châtillon. Now a knight, whose name was my Lord John of Monson, told me that he saw my Lord of Châtillon in a street of the village where the king was taken; and this street ran straight through the village, so that you could see the open fields at the one end and the other; and in this street was my Lord Gaucher of Châtillon, with his naked sword in his fist.

When he saw that the Turks came into the street he ran upon them, sword in hand, and sent them flying out of the village; and the Turks as they fled before him—or they could shoot behind as well as before—covered him all with darts. When he had driven them out of the village, he pulled out the darts that he had upon him, and then replaced his coat of armour, and rose in his stirrups, and lifted up his sword-arm, and cried: "Châtillon, knight, Châtillon, where are my good men?" When he turned and saw that the Turks had entered the street at the other end, he ran upon them again, sword in hand, and sent them flying; and this he did three times in the manner aforesaid.

---

16. Literally, "at the captivity of the Count of Poitiers."

When the *emir* of the galleys took me to join those who had been captured on land, I inquired for the Count of Châtillon among those who had been about him; but could find no one to tell me how he was taken; save that my Lord John Fouinon, the good knight, told me that when he was himself taken prisoner to Mansourah, he found a Turk mounted on the horse of my Lord Gaucher of Châtillon; and the horse's crupper was all covered with blood. And my Lord John inquired of the Turk what he had done to the man to whom that horse belonged? And the Turk replied that he had cut his throat, riding upon that horse, as might well be seen from the crupper that was covered with blood.

There was a very valiant man in the host, whose name was my Lord James of Castel, Bishop of Soissons. When he saw that our people were retreating towards Damietta, he—who had a great desire to be with God—felt no wish to return to the country where he was born; so he made haste to be with God, and set spurs to his horse, and fell single-handed upon the Turks, who killed him with their swords, and thus set him in God's companionship, and among the number of the martyrs.

While the king awaited the payment that was being made for the release of his brother, the Count of Poitiers, a Saracen very well apparelled, and a very handsome man of his body, came to the king and presented him with milk taken in jars, and flowers of divers colours and kinds, on behalf of the children of Nasac, who had been *Soldan* of Babylon; and he presented these gifts, speaking in French.

The king asked him where he had learnt French; and he said that he had aforetime been a Christian. Then the king said: "Away, I will speak to you no further!" I drew him apart, and asked what was his story. He told me he was born at Provins, and that he had come to Egypt with King John, and that he was married in Egypt, and a man of great note.

And I said: "Do you not know very well that if you die in this condition you will be damned, and go to hell?"

And he said "Yes," for he was assured no religion was as good as the Christian religion; "but I dare not face the poverty in which I should be, and the shame, if I returned to you. Every day they would say to me: 'Look at that renegade!' So I like better to live here rich and at ease rather than put myself in such a position as I foresee."

And I told him he would have to suffer greater shame in the day of judgment, when his sin would be made manifest to all, than the shame of which he spoke. Many good words did I speak to him, but little did they avail. So he left me, and I never saw him more.

The Sufferings of the Queen at Damietta

Now you have heard, in what has gone before, of the great tribulations which the king and all of us endured. From such tribulations the queen did not escape, as you shall presently be told. For, three days before she was brought to bed, came the news that the king was taken; with which news she was so affrighted that, as oft as she slept in her bed, it seemed to her that the chamber was full of Saracens, and she cried out, "Help! help!"

And so that the child she bore in her body should not perish, she caused an ancient knight, of eighty years, to lie near her bed, and hold her by the hand; and every time she so cried out, he said: "Lady, have no fear, for I am here."

Before she was brought to bed she caused everyone to leave her chamber, save this knight only, and knelt before him, and besought him to do her a service; and the knight consented, and gave her his oath. And she said:

I ask of you, by the troth you have now pledged me, that if the Saracens take this city, you will cut off my head before I fall into their hands.

And the knight replied:

Be assured that I shall do so willingly; for I was already fully minded to kill you or ever you should be taken.

The queen was brought to bed of a son, who had for name John; and they called him Tristram for the great sorrow and anguish that were about his birth. On the very day that she was brought to bed, she was told that those of Pisa, and Genoa, and the other free cities, were minded to flee away; and on the day following she had them all called before her bed, so that the chamber was quite full, and said to them:

"Lords, for God's sake do not leave this city; for you see that if this city were lost, my lord the king would be utterly lost, and all those who have been taken captive with him and if this moves you not, yet take pity upon the poor weak creature lying here, and wait till I am recovered.

And they replied: "Lady, what can we do? For we are dying of hunger in this city."

And she told them that for famine they need not depart, "for," said she, "I will cause all the food in this city to be bought, and will keep you all from henceforth at the king's charges."

They advised together, and came back to her, and said they consented to remain right willingly. Then the queen—whom may God have in His grace!—caused all the food in the city to be bought at a cost of three hundred and sixty thousand *livres* and more. Ere due time she had to rise from her bed, because the city must needs be surrendered to the Saracens. Then the queen came to Acre to await the king.

The King Adjourns His Claims Against the Saracens—Passage to Acre

While the king was waiting for the deliverance of his brother, he sent brother Raoul, a preaching brother, to an *emir*, whose name was Faress-Eddin Octay, one of the most loyal Saracens I have ever seen. And the king notified to the *emir* that he greatly marvelled how he and the other *emirs* could have suffered the treaty to be so villainously broken; for they had killed the sick whom they were bound to entertain, and made litter of his engines of war, and had burned the sick, as well as the salted swine's flesh that they were bound to preserve.

Faress-Eddin Octay answered brother Raoul, and said: "Brother Raoul, tell the king that because of my law I am unable to help him in this matter, which is grievous to me. And tell him also, from me, to show no outward seeming of discontent so long as he remains in our hands; for that would be his death." And the *emir* was of opinion that so soon as he king came to Acre, he might bear the thing in mind. [17]

When the king came to his ship, he found that his people had prepared nothing for him, neither bed nor clothing. So he had to lie, until we came to Acre, upon the mattresses the *soldan* had given him, and to wear the garments that the *soldan* had caused to be made and given to him, and these were of black samite lined with minever and grey squirrel's fur, and round the said garments were a great quantity of buttons made all of fine gold.

While we were on the sea, for six days, I, who was sick sat always beside the king. And he told me then how he had been taken, and how, with the help of God, he had negotiated for his ransom and ours. And he made me tell how I had been taken on the water; and afterwards he told me I owed great thanks to God for having delivered me

---

17. Or "remind him." Meaning obscure.

from so great perils. Much did he sorrow over the death of the Count of Artois, his brother; and he said that the Count of Artois would very unwillingly have refrained from coming to see him as the Count of Poitiers had done, and would certainly have come to see him on board his galleys.

He also complained to me of the Count of Anjou, who was on board the same ship, because the Count of Anjou gave him but little of his company. One day he asked what the Count of Anjou was doing; and they told him he was playing at tables with my Lord Walter of Nemours. And he went thither tottering, for he was weak by reason of sickness; and he took the dice and the tables, and threw them into the sea and he was very wroth with his brother because he had so soon taken to playing at dice. But my Lord Walter came off best, for he threw all the moneys on the table into his own lap—and they were very many—and carried them away.

Troubles of Joinville at Acre

Hereinafter you shall be told of many tribulations and troubles that I had at Acre, from which God, in Whom trusted, and still do trust, delivered me. And these thing: I shall cause to be written, so that those who hear them may have trust in God in their tribulation and troubles; and God will give them His help as also He did to me.

Let us relate then how, when the king came to Acre, all the clergy and people of Acre came down to the sea, in procession, to meet and receive him with very great rejoicings They brought me a palfrey. So soon as I was mounted, my heart failed me, and I said to him who had brought the palfrey that he should hold me up, lest I should fall. With great trouble was I taken up the steps of the king's hall.

I went and sat at a window, with a child near me: he was about ten years of age, and called Bartholomew, and was the bastard son of my lord Ami of Montbéliard, Lord of Montfaucon. While I was sitting there, and no man taking heed of me, there came to me a varlet wearing a red tunic, with two yellow stripes, and he saluted me and asked whether I knew him?—and I said nay. And he told me he came from Oiselay, my uncle's castle. And I asked him whose man he was; and he said he had no master, and that he would remain with me, if I so desired. And I said I desired it right well. Then he went and fetched me white coifs, and combed me right well.

Then the king sent for me to eat with him; and I went in the vest that had been made for me while I was a prisoner, out of the clippings of my coverlet; and my coverlet I left to the child Bartholomew, together with four ells of camlet that had been given me, for the love of God, while I was a prisoner. Guillemin, my new varlet, came and carved before me, and obtained food for the child while we were eating.

My new varlet came and told me he had obtained a lodging for me near the baths, where I might wash myself from the filth and sweat I had brought from prison. When night came, and I was in the bath, my heart failed me, and I swooned; and with great trouble was I taken out of the bath and carried to my bed. The next day an old knight, whose name was my Lord Peter of Bourbonne, came to see me, and I retained him by me; he stood surety for me in the city as regards what was wanted for my clothing and equipment.

When I was fittingly arrayed, full four days after we came thither, I went to see the king; and he reproved me, and said I had not done well in delaying so long to come and see him; and he commanded me, as I valued his love, to eat with him every day, night and morning, until such time as he had decided what we should do: whether go back to France or remain there.

I told the king that my Lord Peter of Courtenay owed me four hundred *livres* of my wages, which he would not pay to me. And the king replied that he would soon cause me to be paid out of the coin he owed to the Lord of Courtenay; and so he did. By the advice of my Lord Peter of Bourbonne, we took forty *livres* for our expenses, and the rest we gave into the keeping of the commander of the palace of the Temple. When the time came that I had expended the forty *livres*, I sent the father of John Caym of Sainte-Menehould, whom I had engaged in my service overseas, to fetch another forty *livres*. The commander answered him that he had no moneys of mine, and did not know me.

I went thereon to brother Renaud of Vichiers, who had by the king's help, and on account of the courtesy he had shown to the king when a prisoner—as I have already told you—been made Master of the Temple, and I complained to him of his commander of the palace, who would not give me back the moneys I had entrusted to him. When he heard this, he was greatly moved, and said:

> Lord of Joinville, love you well; but be assured if you will not desist from urging this claim, I shall love you no more; for you wish to make people believe that our brethren are robbers.

And I told him that, please God, I should not desist.

Four days was I in this trouble of heart, as one who is altogether without money to spend. After these four day the master came to me laughing, and said he had found my moneys. As to the manner in which they were found, it was because he had changed the commander of the palace, and sent him to a village called Sephouri; and this man returned me my moneys.

Sickness of Joinville—Generosity of the Count of Anjou

The Bishop of Acres who then was—he was a native of Provins—caused the house of the priest of St. Michael to be lent to me. I had retained in my service Caym of Sainte Menehould, who served me well by the space of two years—better than any man I had with me in the land oversea—and I had retained several other people in my service. And it chanced that there was at my bed's head a closet through which one went into the church.

Now it happened that a continuous fever laid hold upon me, so that I took to my bed, and all my people also. And never a day, at that time, had I anyone to help me, or to lift me up, and I looked forward to nothing but death, because of a warning that was in mine ear continually; for every day they brought into the church twenty dead men or more, and from my bed, each time they were brought in, I heard the chant: "*Libera me, Domine.*"

Then would I weep, and render thanks to God, and speak to Him thus:

> Lord, I render to Thee worship for this suffering that Thou hast sent me; for much pride and display has there been my downlying and uprising. And I pray Thee, Lord, to deliver me from this sickness.

And so the Lord did, both me and my people.

After these things I required Guillemin, my new squire, to render me an account, and he did so; and I found that he had done me wrong to the extent of ten *livres tournois*, and more. And when I demanded them of him, he said he would return them to me when he could. I dismissed him, and told him I forgave him what he owed me, for he had deserved it well.

I afterwards learned from the knights of Burgundy, when they returned from captivity—for they had brought him to the lands oversea—that he was the most courteous thief that ever was; for whenever a knight wanted a knife, or a strap, gloves or spurs, or any other thing, he went and stole it, and then gave it to him.

At the time when the king was in Acre, the king's brothers took to playing at dice; and the Count of Poitiers played so courteously that, when he had won he caused the hall to be thrown open, and the gentlemen to be called in, and the ladies, if there were any, and gave away handfuls, as well of his own money as of what he had won.

And when he had lost, he purchased, by estimate, the money of those with whom he had been playing, whether it were his brother the Count of Anjou, or others, and gave away all, his own money and that of the other people.

The King's Return is Discussed

At the time when we were at Acre, the king sent, one Sunday, for his brother the Count of Flanders and the other men of note, and spoke to them thus: "Lords, my lady the queen, my mother, has sent to me, and beseeches me, as urgently as she can, to return to France, because my kingdom is in great peril, seeing that I have neither peace nor truce with the King of England. Those belonging to this land, with whom I have spoken, tell me that, if I depart, this land is but lost for all those who are in Acre will follow after me, none daring to remain when the people are so few.

So I pray you," said he, "to think well upon this matter; and because it is of great import, I will give you time, and you shall answer me according as you think right, eight days from today."

During these eight days the legate came to me and said that he did not see how the king could remain oversea; and he besought me, very instantly, to return with him in his ship. And I told him this was not within my power; for was without means, having, as he knew, lost all my possessions on the water, when I was taken prisoner.

And I gave him this answer, not because I would not very willingly have gone with him, but because of a word which my Lord of Bourlemont, my cousin-german—God rest his soul!—spoke to me when I was going oversea. "You are going oversea," said he, "now take heed how you come back for no knight, be he poor or be he rich, can come back without dishonour if he leaves in the hands of the Saracens the meaner folk of our Lord, in whose company he went forth." The legate was wroth with me, and told me I should not have refused his proposal.

Divers Opinions Expressed in the Council—
Joinville Opposes the Return to France

On the Sunday after, we came again before the king; and the king asked his brothers, and the other barons, and the Count of Flanders, what advice they gave, whether to go or to remain. They all replied, that they had charged my Lord Guy of Mauvoisin to state the advice they wished to give to the king. The king commanded the Lord Guy to state this advice accordingly; and he spake as follows:

> Sire your brothers, and the men of note here present, have looked to your estate, and seen that you cannot remain in this land to your own honour, and that of your realm; for of all the knights that came in your company—of whom you led two thousand eight hundred into Cyprus—there are not now, in this city, one hundred remaining. So they advise you, sire that you go to France, and there procure men and money whereby you may hastily return to this land, and take vengeance upon the enemies of God, who have had you in captivity.

The king would not rest satisfied with what my Lord Guy Mauvoisin had said; but he inquired of the Count of Anjou, the Count of Poitiers, and the Count of Flanders, and several other men of note who sat near them. And all agreed with my Lord Guy Mauvoisin. The legate asked Count John of Jaffa, who sat behind them, what he thought.

The Count of Jaffa begged that they would suffer him not to reply to this question, "for," said he, "my castle is on the marches, and if I advised the king to remain, men would think I did so to my own profit."

Then the king asked him, as urgently as he could, to say what he thought. And the count said that if the king could but hold the field for a year, he would do himself great honour by remaining. Then the legate inquired of those who were sitting by the Count of Jaffa, and all agreed with my Lord Guy Mauvoisin.

I was sitting about the fourteenth in front of the legate. He asked me what I thought; and I replied that I agreed with the Count of Jaffa. And the legate asked me, all in wroth, how the king could hold the field with so few men as he had? And I replied, all in wroth also, because methought that he said this to anger me:

Sir, I will tell you, as you seem to desire it. It is said, sir, but I know not if it be true, that the king has not yet spent any of his own moneys, but only the moneys of the clergy. So let the king bring his moneys to the spending, and let the king send to obtain knights from Morea, and from oversea; and when they hear tell that the king is paying well and largely, the knights will come from all parts, whereby, if God so pleases, he will be able to hold the field for a year. And by his so remaining, he will cause to be delivered the poor captives who have been taken in the service of God, and in his service, and who will ever go free if he departs hence.

There was no one in that place who had not near friends in captivity; so no one reproved me, and all began to weep.

After me, the legate asked my Lord William of Beaumont, rho was then Marshal of France, what he thought; and he said that I had spoken very well, "and I will tell you," said he, "the reason why."

(At this) my Lord John of Beaumont, the good knight, who was his uncle and had a great desire to return to France, cried out upon him in foul terms and said: "What have you got to say, son of the filthy tongue? Sit down and keep quiet!"

The king said: —"My Lord John, you do wrong. Let him speak."

"*Certes*, sir I shall not do so." The marshal however thought it well to keep silence; nor did anyone afterwards agree with me save the Lord of Chatenai.

Then the king said: "Lords, I have heard you duly; and I will give you my answer as to what it pleases me to do eight days from today."

REPROACHES ADDRESSED TO JOINVILLE—HIS SECRET INTERVIEW WITH THE KING

When we came away from thence they began to flout me on all sides.

> Now, Lord of Joinville, the king must indeed be crazy if he does not listen to you in preference to the council of all the realm of France!

When the tables were set, the king made me sit beside him during the meal, where he was always used to make me sit if his brothers were not present. Never a word did he say to me as long as the meal lasted, which was not according to his custom, for he always took note of me when we were eating. And indeed I thought he was wroth with me because I said he had not yet spent any of his moneys, and should spend largely.

While the king was hearing grace, I went to a barred window that was in an embrasure towards the head of the king's bed, and I passed my arms through the bars of the window, and thought that if the king went back to France, I should go to the Prince of Antioch, who held me for his kinsman, and had asked me to come to him (and there remain) until such time as another expedition came out to the land oversea, whereby the captives might be delivered, according to the counsel the Lord of Boulaincourt had given me.

And while I was there, the king came and leant upon my shoulders, and placed his two hands upon my head; and I thought it was my Lord Philip of Nemours, who had already tormented me too much that day because of the advice I had given, and I spoke thus: "Leave me in peace, my Lord Philip!"

By chance, as I was turning my head, the king's hand fell upon my face, and I knew it was the king because of an emerald that he had on his finger.

And he said

Keep quite quiet, for I want to ask how you came to be so bold, you who are but a young man, as to advise me to remain here, against the advice of all the great men and wise of France, who counselled me to depart?

"Sire," said I, "even if I had so ill a thought in my heart, should by no means so counsel you."

"Do you mean to say," he replied, "that I should be doing wrong if I departed?"

"So God help me, sire, yes," said I.

And he said to me: "If I remain, will you remain also?"

And I told him yes, "if I can, either at my own charges or the charges of another."

"Now be quite easy in your mind," said he, "for I am very well pleased with you for the counsel you have given; but do not tell this to anyone till the week; out."

I was more at ease after hearing these words, and defended myself with the greater boldness against those who attacked me. Now the peasants of that land are called *colts*, and Master Peter of Avallon, who lived at Sur, heard tell that I was being called a *colt*, because I had advised the king to remain among the *colts*, so Master Peter of Avallon sent to tell me I should defend myself against those who called me *colt*, and say to them that I liked better to be a *colt* than a broken-down hack, such as they were.

THE KING ANNOUNCES THAT HE WILL REMAIN IN THE HOLY LAND

The following Sunday we all came back again before the king; and when the king saw we were all assembled, he made the sign of the cross upon his mouth (invoking thereby, as I think, the aid of the Holy Spirit, for my lady mother once told me that every time I wished to say aught, I should invoke the aid of the Holy Spirit, and make the holy sign upon my mouth). And the words which the king spoke were these:

> Lords, I greatly thank those who have advised me to return to France, and I thank also those who have advised ne to remain here. But I bethink me that if I remain there will be no danger of loss to my realm; for my lady the queen has people enough to defend it; and I consider also that the barons of this land tell me that if I depart hence, the kingdom of Jerusalem is lost, for none will dare to remain after I have left. I have therefore decided that I will by no means abandon the kingdom of Jerusalem, which I came hither to guard and reconquer. So my conclusion is, that for the present I remain here. And I say to you all, you men of note that are here, as also to such other knights as may wish to remain with me, that you come and speak to me boldly and I will give you so much that the fault will not be mine but yours, if you be not willing to remain.

Many that heard these words were filled with amazement, and many there were that wept.

ST. LOUIS DECIDES TO SEND AWAY HIS BROTHERS—HE KEEPS JOINVILLE IN HIS SERVICE

The king ordered, so it is said, that his brothers should return to France. Whether this was at their own request or by the king's will, I know not. The words that the king had spoken with regard to his remaining oversea were spoken about the feast of St. John. Now it happened that on the day of the feast of St. James,[18]—whose pilgrim I was, and who had conferred great benefits upon me—the king went back to the chamber in which his mass was said, and called together

---
18 The 25th July 1250.

his council, who had remained with him, *viz.*, my Lord Peter the chamberlain, who was the most loyal and upright man I ever saw in the king's household; my Lord Geoffrey of Sargines, the good knight and right worthy man my Lord Giles le Brun, good knight and right worthy man to whom the king had given the constableship of France after the death of my Lord Imbert of Beaujeu, the right worthy man.

To these the king spoke after the following manner, in a loud voice, and as one not well pleased: "Lords, it is already a month past that men know I have settled to remain here, and I have not yet heard tell that you have retained any knights in my service."

"Sire," said they, "we can none other; for all rate their services so high, because they wish to return to their own land, that we dare not give them what they ask."

"And whom," said the king, "would you be able to obtain cheapest?"

"Certainly," they replied, "the Seneschal of Champagne, "but we dare not give him what he asks."

I was in the king's chamber, and heard these words. Then the king said: "Call me the seneschal." I went to him, and knelt before him.

He caused me be seated, and spoke thus: "Seneschal, you know that I have loved you much; and my people tell me they find you hard to deal with. How is this?"

"Sire," I replied, "I can none other; for as you know, I was taken prisoner on the water, and none of my possessions were then left to me; I lost all."

And he asked me what I demanded; and I said I demanded two thousand *livres* till Easter, for the two-thirds of the year.

" Now tell me," said he, "have you tried to make a bargain with any knights?"

And I said, "Yes, with my Lord Peter of Pontmolain, the third of three knights-banneret, who would each cost four hundred *livres* till Easter."

He reckoned on his fingers: "That makes twelve hundred *livres* that your new knights will cost you."

"Now bethink you, sire," said I, "if it will not cost me full eight hundred *livres* to procure horse and armour for myself, and to get food for my knights; for you would not have us eat in your house."

Then he said to his people: "In truth, I see nothing outrageous in this: and I retain your services," said he to me.

THE KING'S BROTHERS EMBARK—ENVOYS OF THE EMPEROR FREDERICK II., AND THE *SOLDAN* OF DAMASCUS

After these things the king's brothers got their ships ready, as did also the other men of note and wealth that were in Acre. At the time of their departing, the Count of Poitiers borrowed jewels from those who were going back to France; and to us, who remained, he gave of them freely and liberally. Much did the one and the other brother beseech me to have good care of the king; and they told me there was none other remaining with him on whom they placed such reliance. When the Count of Anjou saw the time had come when he must embark, he showed such sorrow that all were astonished. Nevertheless he went back to France.

Not long after the king's brothers had left Acre, there came envoys to the king from the Emperor Frederic, bringing letters of credence, and saying to the king that the emperor had sent them to effect our deliverance. They showed the king the letter which the emperor was sending to the *soldan* who was dead—for the emperor did not know of his death—and telling the *soldan* to give ear to what the envoys had to say with regard to the deliverance of the king.

Many said it would not have been well for us if the envoys had found us in captivity; for they thought the emperor had sent the envoys rather to embarrass us than to set us free. The envoys found us free, so they went their way.

While the king was at Acre, the *Soldan* of Damascus sent envoys to the king, and complained greatly of the *emirs* of Egypt, who had killed his cousin; and he promised the king that, if he would help him, he would deliver up to him the kingdom of Jerusalem, which was in his—the *soldan's*—hand. The king decided to make answer to the *Soldan* of Damascus through envoys of his own, whom he sent to the *soldan*. With these envoys went Brother Yves le Breton, of the order of the Preaching Brothers, who knew the Saracen tongue.

While they were going from their hostel to the palace of the *soldan*, Brother Yves saw an old woman going across the street, and she bore in her right hand a dish full of fire, and in her left a phial full of water. Brother Yves asked her: 'What are you doing with these?"

And she answered that with the fire she was minded to burn up paradise, so that there should be none remaining; and with the water to quench hell, so that there should be none remaining.

And he asked: "Why wilt thou do this?"

"Because I would that none should do good to have the guerdon of paradise, or because of the fear of hell, but solely for the love of God, who is all-worthy and can do for us whatsoever is best."

JOHN THE ARMENIAN, THE KING'S ARTILLERYMAN

John the Armenian, who was artilleryman to the king, went at that time to Damascus, to buy horn and glue for the making of crossbows; and he saw an old man, very aged, seated in the bazaar of Damascus. This aged man called to him and asked him if he were a Christian; and he said "Yes."

And the aged man said to him:

> Much must you Christians hate one another; for once upon a time I saw King Baldwin of Jerusalem, who was a leper, discomfiting Saladin, and Baldwin had with him but three hundred men-at-arms, whereas Saladin had three thousand; but now you have been brought to so low estate by your sins that we take you in the fields as if you were wild beasts.

Then John the Armenian said he would do well to hold his peace with regard to the sins of the Christians, seeing that the sins committed by the Saracens were far greater. And the Saracen replied that he had answered foolishly. And John asked why? And the Saracen said he would tell him why; but first he would ask him a question. So he asked him if he had any child?

And John said: "Yes a son." And he asked which would annoy him most, if he received a buffet—that that buffet should be administered by his son, or by him, the Saracen? And John said, he would be more angry with his son, if he did this thing, than with the Saracen.

> "Then I will tell thee why," said the Saracen; "it is after this manner: you Christians hold yourselves to be sons of God, and after His name of Christ you are called Christians; and such has been His courtesy towards you, that He has given you teachers by whom you may know when you do well and when you do evil. Therefore God is more wroth with you for a little sin that you may commit than with us for a great sin, seeing we commit it in ignorance, and are so blind that we think we shall be free of all our sins if we wash ourselves with water before we die; because Mahomet told us that by water we shall be saved at our deaths."

John the Armenian was once in my company, after I returned from overseas and was going to Paris. While we were at meat in the pavilion, a great crowd of poor folk came to beg of us for God's sake, and made a great clamour. One of our people who was there gave orders to a varlet, saying: "Up, up, and drive out these wretches!"

"Ah!" said John the Armenian, "you have spoken very ill; for if the King of France were presently to send to each one of us by his messengers one hundred marks of silver, we should not drive those messengers away; and yet you drive away these messengers who offer the utmost than can be given. For they ask you to give to them for God's sake, which means that you will give them what is yours, and they (in return) will give you God Himself. For God has said out of His own mouth that the poor have power to make gift of Himself to us, and the saints say that the poor can bring us into agreement with Him; for like as water extinguishes fire, so do alms extinguish sin. Let it never therefore happen," said John, "that you drive away the poor thus. But give unto them, and God will give unto you."

Envoys From the Old Man of the Mountain—Their Threats Treated With Contempt

While the king was sojourning at Acre, envoys came to him from the Old Man of the Mountain. When the king returned from his mass, he caused them to be brought before him. The king had them seated in such manner that there was, in front, an *emir* well clothed and well appointed, and behind the *emir*, a young bachelor, well appointed, who held in his fist three knives, of which the one entered into the handle of the other; and these knives, if the *emir's* proposals were rejected, he was to present to the king in token of defiance.

Behind the bachelor who held the three knives, was another, and he had a strong (winding) sheet wound round about his arm, and this he was to present to the king for his burial, if he refused the demands of the Old Man of the Mountain.

The king told the *emir* to say what was his will; and the *emir* presented his letters of credence, and spoke thus: "My lord sends me to ask if you know him?" And the king answered that he did not know him, for he had never seen him; but that he had often heard tell of him.

"And seeing that you have heard tell of my lord," said the *emir*, "I marvel greatly that you have not sent him so much of your substance as would keep him for your friend—like as the Emperor of Germany, the King of Hungary, the *Soldan* of Babylon, and the rest do year by year, because they know of a certainty that they can only keep their lives as long as my lord pleases. And if it does not suit you to do this, then cause him to be acquitted of the tribute that he owes to the Hospital and to the Temple, and he will cry quits with you."

(Now at that time the Old Man of the Mountain paid a tribute to the Temple and to the Hospital, for the Templars and Hospitallers stood in no fear of the Assassins, seeing that the Old Man had nothing to gain by the death of the Master of the Temple or of the Hospital, inasmuch as he knew very well that if he caused one to be killed, another, equally good, would be put in his place. Wherefore he had no wish to sacrifice his Assassins in a service where there was nothing to be gained.)

The king answered the *emir* that he would see him again in the afternoon.

When the *emir* returned, he found the king seated so that the Master of the Hospital was on the one side of him and the Master of the Temple on the other.

Then the king told the *emir* to say again what he had said in the morning. And the *emir* replied he had no intention of repeating what he had said save in the presence of those who had been with the king in the morning. Then the two masters said: "We command you to repeat what you said."

And he answered that as they commanded it he would do so. Then the two masters caused him to be told, in the Saracen tongue, that he should come on the morrow and speak to them at the Hospital.

When he came to them on the morrow the two masters caused him to be told that his lord was very rash in daring to address such rude words to the king; and they caused him to be told further, that if it were not for the king's honour, to whom they had come as envoys, they should have been drowned in the foul sea of Acre, in their lord's despite.

And we command you to return to your lord, and to come back here within fifteen days, bringing to the king, on the part of your lord, such letters, and such jewels, that the king may hold himself appeased, and have you in his good grace.

The Envoys of the Old Man of the Mountain Return with Words of Peace—Brother Yves Le Breton Sent to the Old Man

Within fifteen days the envoys of the Old Man of the Mountain returned to Acre, and brought to the king the Old Man's shirt; and they told the king, on the Old Man's part, that this signified that as the shirt is nearer to the body than any other garment, so did the Old Man hold the king to be nearer to himself in love than any other king. And the Old Man sent to the king his ring, which was of very fine gold, with his name written thereon; and he sent word that with this ring he espoused the king, wishing that henceforward they should be as one.

Among the other jewels that he sent to the king, he sent an elephant of crystal, very well fashioned, and a beast called a giraffe, of crystal also, and apples of divers kinds of crystal, and games of tables and chess. And all these things were embowered in ambergris, and the ambergris was tied to the crystal with delicately wrought fastenings of good fine gold. And you must know that when the envoys opened the caskets containing these things, it seemed as if the whole chamber were full of balm, so sweet was the odour that came therefrom.

The king sent back the envoys to the Old Man, and with them a great foison of jewels, cloths of scarlet, cups of gold, and horses' bits of silver; and with the envoys the king sent Brother Yves le Breton, who knew the Saracen tongue. And Brother Yves found that the Old Man of the Mountain did not believe in Mahomet, but believed in the law of Ali, who was uncle to Mahomet.

This Ali raised Mahomet to the place of honour which he held; and when Mahomet had obtained lordship over the people, he despised his uncle, and withdrew himself from him. And when Ali saw this, he gathered to him as many people as he could, and taught them another belief than Mahomet had taught; whence it still comes that all who believe in the law of Ali say that those who believe in the law of Mahomet are miscreants; while contrariwise those who believe in the law of Mahomet say that those who believe in the law of Ali are miscreants.

One of the points taught by the law of Ali is, that when a man gets himself killed doing the commands of his lord, his soul goes into a pleasanter body than before; and therefore the Assassins do not hesitate to get themselves killed when their lord so orders, because they believe they will then be in better case after they are dead.

Another point is this: that they believe no man can die until the day appointed for him; and this belief no man should hold, seeing that God has power to prolong our lives, or to shorten them. And on this point the Bedouins accept the law of Ali, for which reason they will not put on armour when they go into battle, since by so doing they think they would be acting contrary to the commandment of their law. And when they curse their children they say:

> Let there be upon thee the curse of the Frank, who puts on armour for fear of death.

Brother Yves found a book by the head of the Old Man's bed, and in that book were written many words that our Lord when on earth had said to St. Peter. And Brother Yves said to him: "Ah! for God's sake, sire, read often in this book, for these are very good words." And the Old Man said he ofttimes did so.

> "Since our Lord St. Peter," said he, "is very dear to me: for at the beginning of the world the soul of Abel, when he was killed, went into the body of Noah; and when Noah died it returned into the body of Abraham; and from the body of Abraham, when he died, it came into the body of St. Peter, at that time when God came on earth."

When Brother Yves heard this, he showed him that his creed was not sound, and taught him with many good words; but the Old Man would not listen to him. And these things Brother Yves told to the king, when he came back to us.

When the Old Man rode abroad, a crier went before him bearing a Danish axe, with a long haft all covered with silver, and many knives affixed to the haft; and the crier cried: "Turn aside from before him who bears in his hands the death of kings!"

REPLY OF THE *SOLDAN* OF DAMASCUS—JOHN OF VALENCIENNES BEING SENT TO EGYPT OBTAINS THE RELEASE OF MANY PRISONERS

I had forgotten to tell you of the reply that the king made to the *Soldan* of Damascus—which was this: that he had no intent to join with the *soldan* until such time as he knew whether the *emirs* of Egypt would do him right for the treaty they had broken; and that he would send to the *emirs*, and if they would not do him right for the broken treaty, then he would willingly help the *soldan* to avenge his cousin, the *Soldan* of Babylon, whom they had slain.

While the king was at Acre he sent my Lord John of Valenciennes into Egypt, who demanded of the *emirs* that they should make reparation for the outrages and wrongs they had done to the king. And they said they would do so willingly, provided the king would enter into an alliance with them against the *Soldan* of Damascus. My Lord John of Valenciennes blamed them greatly for the wrongs done to the king, which have been stated above; and he advised that it would be well, in order to dispose the heart of the king to kindness towards them, if they sent him all the knights they held in captivity. And this they did; and, of further courtesy, they sent all the bones of Count Walter of Brienne, so that they might be buried in holy earth.

When my Lord John of Valenciennes was come back to Acre, with two hundred knights that he brought from captivity, not counting the other people, my Lady of Sayette, who was cousin to Count Walter and sister to my Lord Walter, Lord of Reynel—whose daughter John, Lord of Joinville, took to wife after his return from overseas—then my Lady of Sayette, I say, took the bones of Count Walter and caused them to be buried in the Church of the Hospitallers in Acre. And she caused the service to be done in such manner that each knight offered a taper and a *denier* of silver, and the king offered a taper and a *besant* of gold, and all at the charges of my Lady of Sayette. And much the people marvelled when the king did this, for he had never before been seen to offer money not his own. But this he did of his courtesy.

THE KING ENGAGES FORTY KNIGHTS OF CHAMPAGNE— HIS REPLY TO THE EGYPTIAN ENVOYS

Among the knights that my Lord John of Valenciennes had brought back, I found full forty who belonged to the court of Champagne. I caused tunics and surcoats of green cloth to be fashioned for them, and led them before the king, and begged him to deal with them in such sort that they should remain in his service. The king heard what they asked for, and held his peace.

And one of the knights of his council said I did not well when I brought such proposals to the king, seeing that the king had already full seven thousand men too many wearing his livery.[19] And I told him

---

19. M. de Wailly translates *livrée* into modern French as *livre*, the coin. I agree, however, with Miss Wedgwood in thinking that Joinville used the term as meaning—what indeed it is—*livrée*, a livery.

it was great pity he should speak thus; and that among us, the men of Champagne, we had lost at least thirty-five knights, all bannerets, and of the court of Champagne; and I said further: "The king will not do well if he listens to you, seeing in what need he is of knights."

After these words I began to weep very bitterly; and the king told me to hold my peace, and that he would give these knights all I had asked. So the king engaged them as I wished, and placed them in my battalion.

The king gave answer to the envoys from Egypt that he would make no treaty with them, unless they sent him all the heads of Christians that they had hung round the walls of Cairo since the time when the Count of Bar and the Count of Montfort were taken prisoners; and unless they delivered up all the children who had been taken young and had denied their faith; and unless they gave him quittance for the two hundred thousand *livres* that he still owed them. Together with the envoys of the *emirs* of Egypt, the king sent to Babylon my Lord John of Valenciennes, a wise man and a valiant.

At the beginning of Lent the king prepared, with all the forces he had, to go and fortify Cæsarea, which the Saracens had destroyed, and which was twelve leagues from Acre, on the way towards Jerusalem. My Lord Raoul of Soissons, who had remained sick in Acre, went with the king to fortify Caesarea. I know not how it was, save that such was God's will, but the Saracens never did us harm during the whole year. While the king was fortifying Cæsarea, the envoys of the Tartars returned, and we will now tell you of the news they brought.

How the Tartars Chose a Chief to Shake off the Yoke of Prester John, and of the Emperor of Persia

As I have told you before, while the king was sojourning in Cyprus, envoys came from the Tartars and gave him to understand that they would help him to conquer the kingdom of Jerusalem from the Saracens. The king sent back these envoys, and sent with him, by his own envoys, a chapel which he had caused to be fashioned all in scarlet; and in order to draw the Tartars to our faith, he had caused all our faith to be imaged in the chapel: the Annunciation of the angel, the Nativity, the baptism that God was baptised withal, and all the Passion, and the Ascension, and the coming of the Holy Ghost; and with the chapel he sent also cups, books, and all things needful for the chanting of the mass, and two Preaching Brothers to sing the mass before the Tartars.

The king's envoys arrived at the port of Antioch; and from Antioch it took them full a year's journeying, riding ten leagues a day, to reach the great King of the Tartars. They found all the land subject to the Tartars, and many cities that they had destroyed, and great heaps of dead men's bones.

They inquired how the Tartars had arrived at such authority, and killed and utterly confounded so many people; and this was how, as the envoys reported it to the king: The Tartars came, being there created, from a great plain of sand where no good thing would grow. This plain began from certain rocks, very great and marvellous, which are at the world's end, towards the East; and the said rocks have never been passed by man, as the Tartars testify. And they said that within these rocks are enclosed the people of Gog and Magog, who are to come at the end of the world, when Antichrist shall come to destroy all things.

In this plain dwelt the people of the Tartars; and they were subject to Prester John, and to the Emperor of Persia, whose land came next to his, and to several other misbelieving kings, to whom they rendered tribute and service every year, for the pasturage of their beasts, seeing they had no other means of livelihood. This Prester John, and the King of Persia, and the other kings, held the Tartars in such contempt that when they brought their rents they would not receive them face-wise, but turned their backs upon them.

Among the Tartars was a wise man, who journeyed over all the plains, and spoke with the wise men of the plains, and of the different places, and showed them in what bondage they stood, and prayed them all to consider how best they might find a way of escape from the bondage in which they were held. He wrought so effectually that he gathered them all together at the end of the plain, over against the land of Prester John, and explained matters to them. And they answered that whatever he desired, that they would do. And he said that they would achieve nothing unless they had a king and lord over them. And he taught them after what manner they might obtain a king: and they agreed.

And this was the manner: out of the fifty-two tribes that there were, each tribe was to bring an arrow marked with its name; and by consent of all the people it was agreed that the fifty-two arrows so brought should be placed before a child aged five years; and the arrow that the child took first would mark the tribe from which the king would be chosen. When the child had so lifted up one of the arrows, the wise men caused all the other tribes to draw back; and it was settled that the tribe from which the king was to be chosen should select among themselves fifty-two of the wisest and best men that they had.

When these were elected, each one brought an arrow marked with his name. Then was it agreed that the man whose arrow the child lifted up should be made king. And the child lifted up one of the arrows, and it was that of the wise man by whom the people had been instructed. Then were the people glad, and each rejoiced greatly. And the wise man bade them all be silent, and said: "Lords, if you would have me to be your king, swear to me by Him who made the heavens and the earth, that you will keep my commandments." And they swore it.

The ordinances that he established had for purpose the maintenance of peace among the people; and they were to this effect: that none should steal another man's goods, nor any man strike another, on penalty of losing his fist; that no man should have company with another's wife or daughter, on penalty of losing his fist, or his life. Many other good ordinances did he establish among them for the maintenance of peace.

Victory of the Tartars Over Prester John—Vision of One of Their Princes—His Conversion

After he had established order and arrayed them, the king spoke in this wise:

Lords, the most powerful enemy that we have is Prester John. And I command you to be all ready, on the morrow, to fall upon him; and if it so happens that he defeats us—which God forbid!—let each do as best he can. And if we defeat him, I order that the slaying last three days and three nights, and that none, during that space, be so rash as to lay hand on the booty, but all be bent on slaying the people; for after we have obtained the victory, I will distribute the booty, duly and loyally, so that each shall hold himself well paid.

To this they all agreed.

On the morrow they fell upon their enemies, and, as God so willed, discomfited them. All those whom they found in arms, and capable of defence, they put to the sword; and those whom they found in religious garb, the priests and other religiouses, they slew not. The other people belonging to Prester John's land, who were not in that battle, made themselves subject unto the Tartars.

One of the princes of the tribes spoken of above, was lost for three months, so that no one had news of him; and when he came back he was neither athirst nor an hungered, for he thought he had remained away no more than one night at the most. The news that he brought back was this: that he had gone to the top of a tall hillock and had found thereon a great many folk, the fairest folk that he had ever seen, the best clothed and the best adorned; and at the end of the hillock he saw sitting, a king, fairer than the rest, and better clothed, and better adorned; and this king sat upon a throne of gold.

At his right sat six kings, crowned, richly adorned with precious stones, and at his left six kings. Near him, at his right hand, was a queen kneeling, and she prayed and besought him to think upon her people; at his left hand knelt a man of exceeding beauty, and he had two wings resplendent as the sun. And round the king were a great foison of fair folk with wings.

Then the king called the prince to him, and said: "Thou art come from the host of the Tartars."

And he replied: "Sire, that is so, truly."

And the king said:

Thou shalt go to thy king and tell him that thou hast seen me, who am lord of heaven and earth; and thou shalt tell him to render thanks to me for the victory I have given him over Prester John, and over his people. And thou shalt tell him also, as from me, that I give him power to bring the whole earth under his subjection.

"Sire," said the prince, "how will he then believe me?"

Thou shalt tell him to believe thee by these signs: that thou shalt go and fight against the Emperor of Persia, with three hundred of thy people, and no more; and in order that your great king may believe that I have power to do all things, I shall give thee the victory over the Emperor of Persia, who will do battle against thee with three hundred thousand armed men, and more; and before thou goest to do battle against him, thou shalt ask of thy king to give thee the priests and men of religion whom he has taken in the (late) battle; and what these teach, that thou shalt firmly believe, thou and all thy people.

"Sire," said the prince, "I cannot go hence, if thou dost not cause me to be shown the way."

Then the king turned towards a great multitude of knights, so well armed that it was a marvel to see them; and he called one of them, and said: "George, come hither." And the knight came and knelt before him.

Then the king said to him: "Rise, and lead me this man safe and sound to his tent." And this the knight did at the dawning of a certain day.

As soon as all his people saw the prince, they made such joy of him, as did all the host likewise, that it was past the telling. He asked the great king to give him the priests, and he gave them to him; and then the prince and all his people received the priests' teaching so favourably that they were all baptised. After these things the prince took three hundred men-at-arms, and caused them to be confessed and to make ready for battle, and then went and fought against the Emperor of Persia, and defeated him, and drove him from his kingdom, so that the said emperor came flying to the kingdom of Jerusalem; and this was the same emperor who discomfited our people, and took Count Walter of Brienne prisoner, as shall be told to you hereinafter.

Manners of the Tartars—Pride of Their King—St. Louis Repents of Having Sent an Envoy to Him

The people of this Christian prince were so numerous that the king's envoys told us that he had in his camp eight hundred chapels on waggons. Their manner of living is such that they eat no bread, and live on meat and milk. The best meat they have is horseflesh; and they put it to lie in brine and dry it afterwards, so that they can cut it as they would black bread. The best beverage they have, and the strongest, is mare's milk, flavoured with herbs. There was presented to the great king of the Tartars a horse laden with flour, who had come a three-months journey's distance; and he gave it to the envoys of the king.

There are among them a great many Christian folk who hold the creed of the Greeks, and there are, besides, the Christians of whom we have already spoken, and others. These Christians the Tartars send against the Saracens when they wish to make war on the Saracens; and contrariwise they use the Saracens in any war against the Christians.

All manner of childless women go with them to war, and they give pay to such women as they would do to men, according to their strength and vigour. And the king's envoys told us that the men and women soldiers ate together in the quarters of the chiefs under whom they served; and that the men dared not touch the women in any sort, because of the law that their first king had given them.

The flesh of all manner of beasts dying in the camp is eaten. The women who have children see after them, and take care of them; and also prepare the food of the people who go to battle. They put the raw meat between their saddles and the lappets of their clothing, and when the blood is well pressed out, they eat it quite raw. What they cannot eat, there and then, they throw into a leather bag; and when they are hungry they open the bag and always eat the oldest bits first.

Thus I saw a Khorasmin, one of the Emperor of Persia's people, who guarded us in our imprisonment, and when he opened his bag we held our noses, for we could not bear it, because of the stink that came out of his bag.

But now let us go back to the matter in hand, and tell how the great King of the Tartars, after he had received the king's envoys and presents, sent to gather together, under safe conduct, several kings who had not as yet submitted to him; and when they were come he caused the king's chapel to be pitched, and spoke to them after this manner: "Lords, the King of France has sued for mercy, and submitted himself to us, and behold here is the tribute he has sent us; and if you do not submit yourselves to us we will send and fetch him for your destruction." Many there were who, through fear of the French king, placed themselves in subjection to that Tartar king.

With the king's envoys returned other envoys from the great King of the Tartars, and these brought letters to the King of France, saying:

> "A good thing is peace; for in the land where peace reigns those that go about on four feet eat the grass of peace; and those that go about on two feet till the earth—from which good things do proceed—in peace also. And this thing we tell thee for thy advertisement; for thou canst not have peace save thou have it with us. For Prester John rose up against us, and such and such kings"—and he named a great many—"and we have put them all to the sword. So we admonish thee to send us, year by year, of thy gold and of thy silver, and thus keep us to be thy friend; and if thou wilt not do this, we will destroy thee and thy people, as we have done to the kings already named."

And you must know that it repented the king sorely that he had ever sent envoys to the great King of the Tartars.

Certain Knights Arrive From Norway

Now let us return to the matter in hand, and tell how, while the king was fortifying Caesarea, there came to the camp my Lord Alenard of Senaingan, and he told us he had built his ship in the realm of Norway, which is at the world's end, towards the west, and how, in coming to the king, he had gone all round Spain, and passed through the Straits of Morocco. Great perils had he undergone before he came to us. The king retained him in his service and nine of his knights.

And this lord Alenard told us that, in the land of Norway, the nights were so short in summer that every night you saw at one time the light of the day that was passing and the light of the day that was dawning.

And he betook himself, he and his people, to the hunting of lions; and they took several very perilously; for they would go forward to shoot at the lions, spurring as hard as they could; and when they had shot their shafts, the lions sprang at them; and now would they have been seized and devoured if they had not let fall a piece of ragged cloth, which the lion leapt upon, tore and devoured, thinking he had hold of a man.

While the lion was thus tearing the cloth, another hunter went and shot at him, and the lion left tearing the cloth, and sprang after this hunter; and he in turn let fall another piece of cloth, and again the lion pounced upon it. And thus they killed the lion with their arrows.

Philip of Toucy Engaged by the King—Customs of the Comans

While the king was fortifying Caesarea, my Lord Philip of Toucy came to him. And the king said he was his cousin, because he was descended from one of the sisters of King Philip—which sister the Emperor (of Constantinople) had to wife. The king retained him in his service, with nine of his knights, for a year; and afterwards he departed, and went back to Constantinople, whence he had come. He told the king that the Emperor of Constantinople, and the other men of note in Constantinople, had allied themselves with a people that were called Comans, so as to have their help against Vataces, the Emperor of the Greeks.

And in order that the one party should help the other in all good faith, the emperor and the other men of note that were with him suffered themselves to be bled, and put their blood into a great bowl of silver. And the King of the Comans, and the other men of note that were with him, did likewise, and mingled their blood with the blood of our people, and mixed therewith wine and water, and drank thereof, and our people also; and then they said they were brothers in blood.

Then they caused a dog to pass between their people and our people, and cut the dog in pieces with their swords, our people doing the same; and they said that whoso failed the other in this alliance on either side should thus be cut in pieces.

Again my Lord Philip told us of a great marvel that he had seen when in the camp of the Comans; for one of their rich knights being dead, they had made a very large and wide grave in the earth, and had seated him therein, very nobly apparelled, in a chair; and with him they put into the grave the best horse that he had, and best sergeant, both alive.

The sergeant, before he was put in the grave with his lord, took leave of the King of the Comans and of the other rich lords; and while he was taking leave of them, they put into his scarf a great foison of gold and silver, and said: "When I come into the other world, thou shalt give me back what I here entrust to thee."

And the sergeant said: "That shall I do right willingly."

The great King of the Comans then gave him a letter, addressed to the first of their kings, notifying that the right worthy sergeant had lived well, and served him right well, and ought to be duly rewarded. When this was done, they placed the sergeant in the grave with his lord, and with the live horse; and then they threw over the mouth of the grave boards, closely fitted, and all the host ran for stones and for earth, and ere they slept that night they had made a great mound in memory of those whom they had thus buried.

NEW ENGAGEMENT OF JOINVILLE—HOW HE LIVED OVERSEAS

While the king was fortifying Caesarea, I went upon a day into his quarters, to see him. He was talking to the legate, and as soon as he saw me enter into his chamber he rose, and took me aside, and said:

You know that I only retained your services till Easter, so I pray you to tell me what I shall give you to remain with me for a year beyond Easter.

And I told him I did not wish him to give me more of his moneys than he had already given me; but that I wished to make with him another bargain.

"Because," said I, "you wax wroth when one asks you for anything; so I wish you to make a covenant with me, that if I ask you for anything during the whole of the year, you will not be wroth, and if you refuse it, I on my side will not be wroth either."

When the king heard this he began to laugh aloud, and said he would keep me in his service on this covenant; and he took me by the hand, and led me to the legate and to his councillors, and told them of the bargain we had made; and they were greatly rejoiced, because I was the man of most note and substance in the host.

Hereinafter will I tell you how I planned and arranged my affairs during the four years that I remained in the land oversea, after the king's brothers had departed. I had two chaplains, who said my hours to me. The one chanted my mass as soon as the dawn of day appeared; the other waited till my knights, and the knights belonging to my division, had risen.

When I had heard my mass, I went to the king. If the king wished to ride abroad, I kept him company. Sometimes it chanced that messengers came, so that we had much business during the morning.

My bed was laid in my pavilion after such a manner that none could enter in without seeing me as I lay in my bed; and this I did so that there should be no ill suspicion as concerning women. When it came to the feast of St. Remigius, I caused pigs to be bought for my styes, and sheep for my sheepfolds, and flour and wine for the provisioning of my quarters during the whole winter; and this I did because provisions became dearer in winter, seeing that the sea is more treacherous in winter than in the summer.

And I bought full a hundred tuns of wine, and always caused the best to be drunk first; and the wine of the varlets I caused to be mixed with water, and the wine of the squires with less water. At my own table were served before each knight a large phial of wine and a large phial of water, and each mixed according to his will.

The king had given me for my battalion fifty knights. Every time that I ate, I had ten knights at my table with my own ten knights; and they ate, one fronting the other, according to the custom of the land, and sat upon mats on the ground. Every time that there was a call to arms, I sent thither fifty-four knights, who were called *dizeniers*, because each commanded ten men. Every time that we rode out armed, all the fifty knights ate in my quarters on their return. At all the annual festivals I asked to my table all the men of note in the host, whereby it sometimes happened that the king had to borrow some of my guests.

SOME OF THE JUDGMENTS PRONOUNCED AT CÆSAREA

Hereinafter you shall hear tell of the justice and judgments that I saw rendered at Cæsarea while the king was sojourning there. First we will tell of a knight who was taken in a brothel, and to whom a certain choice was left, according to the customs of the country. And the choice was this: that either the wanton woman should lead him through the camp, in his shirt, and shamefully bound with a rope, or that he should lose his horse and arms and be driven from the host.

The knight gave up his horse to the king, and his arms, and left the host. Then I went and asked the king to give me the horse for a poor gentleman who was in the host. And the king answered me that this request was not reasonable, seeing that the horse was still worth eighty *livres*.

And I replied: "Now have you broken our covenant, for you are wroth with me for my request."

And he said to me, laughing merrily: "Say what you like, I am not wroth with you." Nevertheless I did not get the horse for the poor gentleman.

The second judgment was this: the knights of our battalion were hunting a wild animal that is called a gazelle, and is like a deer. The brethren of the Hospital leapt out upon our knights, and hustled them and drove them away. So I complained to the Master of the Hospital; and the Master of the Hospital answered that he would do me right according to the customs of the Holy Land, which were such that he would cause the brethren who had committed the outrage, to eat sitting on their mantles, until such time as those on whom the outrage had been committed should raise them up.

The master dealt with them according to his promise; and when we saw that they had eaten for a while sitting on their mantles, I went to the master, and found him at meat, and asked him to cause the brethren to rise who were eating before him sitting on their mantles; and the knights on whom the outrage had been committed begged him also. He answered that he would do nothing of the kind, for he would not suffer it that the brethren should evil entreat those who came on pilgrimage to the Holy Land.

When I heard this I sat down with the brethren and began to eat with them, and I told him I should not rise till the brethren had risen. And he told me this was forcing his hand, and granted my request; and he caused me and the knights that were with me to eat with him, while the brethren went and ate with the others at a table.

The third judgment that I saw rendered at Cæsarea was this: A certain sergeant of the king, whose name was Le Goulu, laid his hand on one of the knights in my battalion. I went and complained to the king. The king said that, as it seemed to him, I might well leave the matter where it stood, seeing that the sergeant had given my knight no more than a push. And I said I would not leave the matter where it stood; and if he did not do me right, I should leave his service, seeing that his sergeants were suffered to push knights.

Then he caused right to be done to me, and in this wise, according to the customs of the land: the sergeant came to my quarters, barefoot, clothed only in his shirt and drawers, and with a naked sword in his hand; and he knelt before the knight, took the sword by its point and handed the pommel to the knight, and said:

> Lord, I make amends for that I laid my hand upon you, and I have brought you this sword so that you may cut off my fist, if such is your pleasure.

And I asked the knight to forgive him his offence, and he did so.

The fourth penalty was as follows: Brother Hugh of Jouy, who was Marshal of the Temple, was sent to the *Soldan* of Damascus by the Master of the Temple to negotiate an agreement respecting a large tract of land which the Temple had been used to hold, but which the *soldan* wished to divide, so that the Temple should have one half and the *soldan* the other. The agreement was made accordingly, subject to the king's consent. And Brother Hugh brought back with him an *emir* from the *Soldan* of Damascus, together with the agreement in writing, duly executed.

The master told these things to the king; and the king was greatly surprised, and said the master had been over-bold in holding speech or negotiating with the *soldan* without first speaking to him, the king; and the king added that reparation should be made. And the reparation was made in this wise: The king caused the flaps of three of his pavilions to be raised; and all the commonalty of the host who would, had leave to assemble there and see what was toward.

And thither came the Master of the Temple, and all his brotherhood of knights, all barefoot, right through the camp, because their quarters were outside. And the king caused the Master of the Temple to sit in front of him, and also the *soldan's* envoy; and the king said to the master, in a loud voice:

> Master, you will tell the *soldan's* envoy that it repents you that you have made any treaty with the *soldan* without first speaking to me; and because you did not first so speak to me, you must hold the *soldan* discharged from what he has covenanted, and return him all his covenants.

Thereupon the master took the written agreements and gave them to the *emir*; and then the master said: "I give you back the agreements that I entered into wrongfully; whereof it repenteth me."

Then the king told the master to rise, and to cause all the brethren to rise; and he did so. And the king said: "Now kneel, and make reparation, because you have gone to the *soldan* against my will."

The master knelt, and handed the end of his mantle to the king, and gave over to the king all that they possessed to take therefrom such fine and penalty as the king might determine. "And I declare in the first place," said the king, "that Brother Hugh, who made these agreements, shall be banished from all the realm of Jerusalem."

Neither the master, who was godfather with the king to the Count of Alençon, born at Castle Pilgrim, nor even the queen, nor any other, was able to do aught on behalf of Brother Hugh, and he had to avoid the Holy Land and the kingdom of Jerusalem.

Treaty With the Egyptian Emirs—St. Louis Fortifies Jaffa

While the king was fortifying the city of Cæsarea, his envoys returned from Egypt, and brought with them the treaty, as devised by the king, in the manner already told. And the covenants between the king and the *emirs* were such that the king was to go, on a day therein named, to Jaffa; and on the day that the king went to Jaffa the Egyptian *emirs* were bound by their oaths to be at Gaza to deliver up to the king the kingdom of Jerusalem. The treaty, such as the envoys brought it, was sworn to by the king, and by the men of note in the host; and by our oaths we were bound to help the *emirs* against the *Soldan* of Damascus.

When the *Soldan* of Damascus knew that we had allied ourselves with those in Egypt, he sent full four thousand Turks, well appointed, to Gaza, whither those from Egypt were to come; and this he did because he knew full well that if the host from Egypt could join us, it would be to his loss. Nevertheless the king did not desist from marching on Jaffa. When the Count of Jaffa saw that the king was coming, he prepared his castle in such wise that it seemed to be a town well capable of defence; for at each of the battlements—of which there were full five hundred—he set a shield, with his arms, and a pennon; and this thing was fair to see, for his arms were or with a cross of gules *patté*.

We encamped in the fields round the castle, and surrounded the castle, which lies on the sea, from the one sea to the other. Forthwith the king betook himself to fortify a new burgh, all round the old castle, and going from the one sea to the other. Oftentimes I saw the king himself carrying a hod to the trenches so as to gain the promised indulgence.

The Egyptian *emirs* failed us in their covenants; for they did not dare to come to Gaza because of the people of the *Soldan* of Damascus who were there.

Nevertheless they observed their covenant in so far that they sent to the king all the heads of the Christians hung on the walls of the castle of Cairo, at the time when the Count of Bar and the Count of Montfort were taken; and these the king caused to be buried in holy ground. And they also sent the children who had been taken when the king was taken; which thing they did regretfully, for the children had already denied their faith. And with these they sent to the king an elephant, which the king sent to France.

While we sojourned at Jaffa an *emir*, belonging to the party of the *Soldan* of Damascus, came to reap the corn at a village three leagues from the camp. It was agreed that we should attack him. When he saw us coming he took to flight. While he was flying, a young gentleman varlet took to chasing after him, and bore two of his knights to the earth without breaking his spear, and then struck the *emir* in such sort that the lance broke in his body.

Envoys from the Egyptian *emirs* besought the king to appoint a day on which they might come to him; when they would come without fail. The king decided that he would not refuse, and appointed them a day: and they made a covenant with him, on oath, that on the day appointed they would be at Gaza.

Of the Count of Eu—the Prince of Antioch—and the Three Armenian Gleemen

While we were waiting for the day that the king had appointed for the meeting with the Egyptian *emirs*, the Count of Eu, who was a squire, came to the camp; and he brought with him my Lord Arnoul of Guines, the good knight, and his two brothers, he being in command of nine knights. The Count of Eu remained in the service of the king, and the king made him a knight.

At this point the Prince of Antioch returned to the camp, and the princess his mother; and the king did him great honour, and made him a knight very honourably. His age was not more than sixteen years; but never have I seen a child of such discernment. He asked the king to give him hearing before his mother; and the king consented. And the words that he spoke to the king before his mother were these:

> Sire, it is no doubt true that my mother should still keep me for four years in her tutelage; but that is no reason why she should suffer my land to be lost, and go to decay. And this I say, sire, because the city of Antioch is perishing in her hands. Wherefore I beseech you, sire, that you ask her to grant me money and men, so that I may go and succour my people who are there and give them help. And, sire, rightly should she do this; for if I remain with her in the city of Tripoli, needs is it that great expense should be incurred; and the great expense I shall so incur will be incurred for nothing.

The king heard him right willingly, and did all in his power to bring his mother to give him as much as could be extracted from her. As soon as he parted from the king, he went to Antioch, and there obtained favour. With the king's consent he quartered his arms, which are gules, with the arms of France, because the king had made him a knight.

With the prince came three gleemen from Great Armenia. They were brothers and were going to Jerusalem on pilgrimage; and they had three horns, and these horns were so devised that the sound came from the side of their faces. When they began to sound their horns, you would have said it was the voice of swans coming from a mere; for they made the sweetest music and the most melodious, so that it was marvellous to hear them.

They all three also leapt marvellously; for a mat was put under their feet, and they made a somersault standing, so that their feet came back upon the mat. Two made the somersault with their heads backwards, and the eldest also; and when they caused him to jump with his head forward, he signed himself with the cross, for he was affeared lest he should break his neck as he turned.

BREAK IN THE NARRATIVE—OF WALTER, COUNT OF BRIENNE AND JAFFA, AND HOW HE WAS MADE PRISONER BY THE EMPEROR OF PERSIA—AND OF OTHER MATTERS THERETO PERTAINING

Because it is a good thing that the memory of the Count of Brienne, who was Count of Jaffa, should not be forgotten, we will speak of him here, for he held Jaffa for many years, and defended it a long while by his prowess; and he lived, for the most part, by what he gained from the Saracens and the enemies of the faith.

Thus it happened on a time that he discomfited a great number of Saracens who were conveying a great foison of cloth of gold and silk; and he captured it all. And when he had brought it to Jaffa he divided it among his knights, so that none was left over for himself. His manner of life was such that, when he parted from his knights, he shut himself up in his chapel, and was long at his orisons or ever he went at night to sleep with his wife, who was a very good lady, and a wise, and sister to the King of Cyprus.

The Emperor of Persia, whose name was Barbaquan, and whom one of the Tartar princes had discomfited, as I have already told you, came with all his host into the kingdom of Jerusalem, and took the Castle of Tabarie, which had been fortified by my Lord Odo of Montbeliard, the constable, who was Lord of Tabarie through his wife.

Much evil did the Emperor of Persia work upon our people, for he destroyed whatever he could find outside Castle-Pilgrim, and outside Acre, and outside Safad, and outside Jaffa also. And when he had wrought this destruction, he betook himself to Gaza, there to join himself to the *Soldan* of Babylon, who was to come thither to harry and oppress our people.

The barons of the land decided, and the patriarch, that they would go and attack the emperor before the *Soldan* of Babylon arrived. And in order to obtain help, they sent to fetch the *Soldan* of la Chamelle, one of the best knights in all paynimry, to whom they showed such great honour in Acre that they spread cloths of gold and silk before him wheresoever he was to pass. Thus they came to Jaffa, our people and the *soldan* with them.

The patriarch had excommunicated Count Walter because he

would not give up a tower that he held in Jaffa, and that was called the patriarch's tower. Our people besought Count Walter to go with them and fight against the Emperor of Persia; and he said he would do so willingly provided the patriarch would give him absolution till their return.

The patriarch would none of it; nevertheless Count Walter went with them. Our people formed three divisions, of which one was under Count Walter, another under the *Soldan* of la Chamelle, while the patriarch and those belonging to the land formed the third. In the division of the Count of Brienne were the Hospitallers.

They rode forward until they came within sight of their enemies. As soon as our people saw them, they halted, and their enemies formed themselves in three divisions likewise. While the Khorasmins were setting their division in array, Count Walter came to our people, and cried: "Lords, for God's sake, let us fall upon them, for we are giving them time, in that we have halted." But no one would listen to him.

When Count Walter saw this, he came to the patriarch, and begged for absolution, in the manner aforesaid; but the patriarch would none of it. Now with the Count of Brienne was a valiant clerk, who was Bishop of Ramleh, and had done many fine deeds of chivalry in company of the count, and he said to Count Walter:

> Be not troubled in conscience because the patriarch will not give you absolution, for he is in the wrong, and you are in the right; and I absolve you in the name of the Father, and of the Son, and of the Holy Ghost. Let us at them!

So they dug their spurs into their horses and fell upon the division of the Emperor of Persia, which was the last. Very many were the people killed on the one side and on the other; and there was Count Walter taken, for all our people fled so shamefully that many in their despair drowned themselves in the sea. And they were thus panic-stricken because one of the battalions of the Emperor of Persia attacked the *Soldan* of la Chamelle, and though the *soldan* defended himself right well, yet of two thousand Turks that he led into battle, only fourteen score remained when he left the field. [20]

The emperor decided that he would besiege the *soldan* in the castle of la Chamelle, because he thought the *soldan* could not long hold out after he had lost so many of his people. When the *soldan* saw this, he came to his people and told them that he would go out and fight

---

20. This battle took place in 1244..

against the emperor, for if he suffered himself to be besieged, he would be lost. He so arranged matters that he sent out all his people who were ill armed by a hidden valley; and as soon as they heard the *soldan's* drums beating, they fell upon the emperor's camp from behind, and began to slay the women and children.

Now the emperor had gone into the field to fight the *soldan*, whom he saw there before his eyes; but when he heard the cry raised in the rear by his own people, he returned into his camp to succour the women and children.

Then the *soldan* fell upon him and upon his people, and that so well and to such good purpose, that out of the twenty-five thousand there present of the emperor's people neither man nor woman remained; all were either killed in fight or given to the sword.

Before the Emperor of Persia came to la Chamelle, he had taken Count Walter prisoner before Jaffa; and they hung him by the arms to a forked pole, and told him they would not take him down till the Castle of Jaffa was theirs. While he was thus hanging by the arms he cried to those in the castle not to surrender for any hurt that might be done to him, and that if they did surrender, he would slay them with his own hands.

When the emperor saw this, he sent Count Walter to Babylon, as a present to the *soldan*, and likewise the Master of the Temple and several other prisoners whom he had taken. Those who led the count into Babylon were full three hundred men, and these were not killed when the emperor was slain before la Chamelle.

And these three hundred men, who were Khorasmins, were among those who afterwards attacked us on the Friday, when we were on foot. Their banners were red and indented up towards the lance; and on their lances they had fashioned heads with hair, that seemed like the heads of devils.

Several of the merchants of Babylon cried to the *soldan* that he should do them justice against Count Walter for the great losses they had suffered at his hands, and the *soldan* suffered them to go and take vengeance upon him. So they went and slew him in prison, where he was killed for the Lord's sake; whence we may well believe that he is in heaven, and among the number of the martyrs.

Narrative Resumed—Return to the History of St. Louis—*Soldan* of Damascus and Egyptian *Emirs* Make Peace—Defeat of Master of St. Lazarus

The *Soldan* of Damascus took his people that were at Gaza and entered into Egypt. The *emirs* came and fought against him. The division immediately under the *soldan* defeated the *emirs* with whom they engaged, and on the other side the division of the *emirs* of Egypt defeated the rear division of the *Soldan* of Damascus. So the *Soldan* of Damascus went back to Gaza, wounded in the head and in the hand.

And before he left Gaza the *emirs* of Egypt sent their envoys and made peace with him, and failed in all the covenants they had made with us; and thenceforward we had neither truce nor peace either with those of Damascus or those of Babylon. And you must know that the greatest number of men-at-arms that ever we had was no more than fourteen hundred.

While the king was encamped before Jaffa, the Master of St. Lazarus espied, towards Ramleh, at three great leagues' distance, certain beasts, and various things whereof he thought to make great booty; and so he, who held no rank in the host, and thus did what seemed best in his own eyes, went thither without speaking to the king. When he had gathered together his spoils, the Saracens fell upon him, and discomfited him in such sort that of all the people he had in his company, no more than four escaped.

So soon as he came back into the camp, he began to cry to arms. I went and armed myself, and begged the king to suffer me to go to the place; and he gave me leave, and ordered that I should take with me the knights of the Temple and of the Hospital.

When we came thither, we found that certain stranger Saracens had come down into the valley where the Master of St. Lazarus had been discomfited. While these stranger Saracens were looking upon the dead, the master of the king's crossbowmen ran upon them; and before we came up, our people had discomfited them and killed several.

One of the king's sergeants and one of the Saracens bore each the other to the earth at one stroke with their lances. Another of the king's sergeants, when he saw this, took their two horses, and was leading them away to steal them; and so that no one might see him, he got between the walls of the city of Ramleh.

While he was leading the horses away, an old cistern, over which he passed, gave way under him. The three horses, and he himself, fell to the bottom, and I was told of it. I went to see, and found that the cistern was still falling in upon them, and that, with a little more, they would have been all buried. So we returned without loss, except such loss as had been incurred by the Master of St. Lazarus.

ENGAGEMENT BETWEEN THE CROSSBOWMEN AND THE MEN OF THE *SOLDAN* OF DAMASCUS, NEAR JAFFA

So soon as the *Soldan* of Damascus had made peace with the *emirs* of Egypt, he ordered such of his people as were at Gaza to return to him. They passed before our camp at less than two leagues' distance, nor did they ever venture to attack us, though they were, in number, full twenty thousand Saracens, and ten thousand Bedouins. Before they came over against our camp the master of the king's crossbowmen and his division observed them for three days and three nights, lest they should fall upon us unawares.

On St. John's Day (6th May 1253), that was after Easter, the king heard his sermon. During the sermon a sergeant, belonging to the master of the crossbowmen, entered the king's chapel, fully armed, and told him that the Saracens had surrounded the master crossbowmen. I begged the king to let me go thither, and he granted my request, and told me to take with me four or five hundred men-at-arms, and named those whom he wished me to take.

As soon as we issued from the camp, the Saracens, who had put themselves between the master of the crossbowmen and the camp, went off to join an *emir* who was on a hillock in front of the master of the crossbowmen, with full a thousand men-at-arms.

Then began a fight between the Saracens and the master of the crossbowmen's sergeants, of whom there were full fourteen score. And as soon as the *emir* saw that his people were hard pressed, he sent them help, and in such numbers that they drove our sergeants back upon the master's troops. When the master saw that his people were being hard pressed, he sent to their help a hundred or six score men-at- arms, who drove back the assailants upon the troops of the *emir*.

While we were there, the legate and the barons of the land, who had remained with the king, told the king that he had acted very foolishly in putting me in danger; and by their advice the king sent to recall me, and the master of the crossbowmen also. The Turks departed, and we returned to the camp. Many people wondered why they did not come to attack us, and certain people said that if they did not do so, it was because they and their horses had been famished at Gaza, where they had sojourned nearly a year.

The Host of the Soldan of Damascus Passes Before Acre—Fine Feat of Arms of John Le Grand

When these Saracens had departed from before Jaffa and came before Acre, they sent word to the Lord of Assur, who was constable of the kingdom of Jerusalem, that they would destroy the gardens of the city if he did not send them fifty thousand besants; and he made answer that he would send them none. Then they arrayed their battalions, and came all along the sands of Acre, and so near to the city as to be well within the shot of a swivel-crossbow. The Lord of Assur issued from the town, and set himself on Mount St. John, there where the cemetery of St. Nicholas is, to defend the gardens. Our foot sergeants issued from Acre, and began to harass the Saracens with bows and crossbows.

The Lord of Assur called to him a knight of Genoa, whose name was my Lord John le Grand, and ordered him to go and recall the lesser people who had issued from the town of Acre, so that they should not put themselves in peril. While he was bringing them back, a Saracen began to cry out to him, in the Saracen tongue, that he would joust with him, if that were his pleasure; and my Lord John told him he would do so willingly.

While my Lord John was going towards the Saracen to joust, he looked to his left hand, and saw a little troop of Turks, full eight in number, who had halted to see the joust. He left the jousting with the Saracen, and went towards the little troop of Turks, who were stopping quite still, to see the joust, and ran one of them through the body with his lance, and laid him dead.

When the others saw this, they ran upon him as he was returning towards our people, and one of them struck him a great blow with his mace on his steel cap; and as this Turk passed, my Lord John with his sword struck him on the turban that was wrapped round his head, and caused the turban to fly off into the field. (They wear turbans when they fight, because the turbans will ward off the heavy blow of a sword.)

Another Turk spurred upon him, and would have thrust his spear between his shoulders: but my Lord John saw the spear coming and inclined to the left; then as the Saracen passed, my Lord John gave him a back-handed stroke with the sword across the arm, so that his spear flew into the midst of the field. And so my Lord John returned, and brought back his foot people. And these fine strokes were struck before the Lord of Assur, and the men of note that were in Acre, and before all the women who were looking on upon the walls.

Sack of Sayette

When this great foison of Saracens, who were before Acre, and had not dared to fight against us, as you have heard, nor against those at Acre,—when they heard tell—and it was sooth—that the king was fortifying the city of Sayette, and with very few good men, they set themselves to draw thither. My Lord Simon of Montbeliard, who was master of the king's crossbowmen, and chief of the king's people in Sayette, heard that the Saracens were coming, and he retreated into the castle of Sayette, which is very strong and surrounded by the sea on all sides; and this he did because he saw right well that he had no power to resist the coming Saracens. He took with him into the castle as many people as he could, but these were only a few, seeing that the castle was too small.

The Saracens threw themselves into the town, and found no resistance, for it was not all enclosed. They killed more than two thousand of our people; and with the booty there gained went off to Damascus. When the king heard these tidings he was greatly angered. Ah! could he only redress what had been done! And the barons of the land turned this feeling of his to their advantage; because the king had before been minded to go and fortify a hillock on the way from Jaffa to Jerusalem—on which hillock there had stood an ancient stronghold in the days of the Maccabees.

Now the barons of oversea were not of opinion that this old castle should be rebuilt, because it was five leagues from the sea, so that no provisions could be sent thither from the sea without falling into the hands of the Saracens, who were stronger than we were. When therefore the news came to the camp that the burgh of Sayette had been destroyed, the barons of the land came to the king, and told him it would be more honourable to refortify Sayette, which the Saracens had destroyed, than to build a new fortress; and the king agreed thereto.

Why St. Louis, Taking Example of King Richard of England, Refused to Behold Jerusalem—and Matters Thereto Relating

While the king was at Jaffa, it was told him that the *Soldan* of Damascus would be willing that he should go to Jerusalem, and under a sure and safe conduct. The king held a great council thereon; and the conclusion of the council was that no one advised the king to go, since he would have (in the end) to leave the city in the hands of the Saracens.

They gave the king an example as follows: When the great King Philip departed from Acre to go to France, he suffered all his people to remain in the host with Duke Hugh of Burgundy, the grandsire of the duke lately deceased. While the duke sojourned at Acre, and King Richard of England also, news came to them that they could take Jerusalem on the morrow, if they so desired, seeing that all the chivalry of the *Soldan* of Damascus had gone to rejoin him elsewhere, because of a war that he had with another *soldan*.

So they arrayed their people, and the King of England formed the first division of the forces, and the Duke of Burgundy, with all the people belonging to the King of France, the second division.

While they were thus thinking to take the city, word came to the King of England from the duke's camp that he should proceed no further, because the duke was retreating, and retreating for this reason and none other, so that it might not be said that the English had taken Jerusalem. While they were speaking of this, one of his knights cried: "Sire, sire, come so far hither, and I will show you Jerusalem!"

And when the king heard this he threw his coat-armour before his eyes, all in tears, and said to our Saviour:

> Fair Lord God, I pray Thee suffer me not to see Thy Holy City since I cannot deliver it from the hands of Thine enemies!

This example they showed to the king; for if he, the greatest Christian king, went on pilgrimage without delivering the city from God's enemies, then would all other kings and pilgrims, coming thereafter, rest content with going on pilgrimage after the same manner as the King of France, and give no thought to the deliverance of Jerusalem.

King Richard did so many doughty deeds when he was overseas that when the horses of the Saracens were afraid of any bush, their master would say: "Do you think"—so would they say to their horses—"Do you think that is King Richard of England?"

And when the children of the Saracen women cried, they said to them: "Wisht, wisht! or I will go and fetch King Richard, and he will kill thee!"

The Duke of Burgundy, of whom I have just spoken to you, was a very good knight with his hands, but he was never accounted wise, either towards God or towards this world. And this may well appear from what has just been related. And because of this, the great King Philip, when they told him that Count John of Chalon had a son, who had been called Hugh after the Duke of Burgundy, said he hoped that God would make him as valiant (*preux*) a man as the duke. And they asked him why he had not said as right worthy a man (*prud'-homme*).

"Because," said he, "there is a great difference between a valiant man (*preux-homme*) and a right worthy man (*prud'-homme*). For there are many valiant knights in Christian lands, and in the lands of the Saracens, who never believed in God nor in His mother. Whence I tell you," said he, "that God grants a great gift, and a very special grace, to the Christian knight whom He suffers to be valiant of body, and at the same time keeps in His service, guarding him from mortal sin. And the knight who thus governs himself should be called right worthy (*prud'-homme*) because that prowess comes to him by the gift of God. And those of whom I spoke before may be called valiant (*preux-homme*) because they are valiant of their body, and yet neither fear God nor are afraid of sin."

Fortifications of Jaffa—Departure of St. Louis For Sayette—Pilgrims From Great Armenia—Joinville Sends as Envoy One of His Knights

Of the great sums which, the king spent in fortifying Jaffa it is not convenient that I should speak, for they cannot be counted. He fortified the burgh from the one sea to the other, and set there full twenty-four towers, and the fosses were puddled with mud within and without. There were three gates, of which the legate built one, together with a portion of the wall.

And to show you the cost that the king incurred, you must know that I inquired of the legate how much this gate and the portion of wall had cost. And he asked me how much I thought? and I reckoned that the gate had cost full five hundred *livres*, and the portion of the wall three hundred *livres*. And he told me—so might God help him!—that gate and wall together had cost him full thirty thousand *livres*.

When the king had finished fortifying the burgh of Jaffa, he decided to go and refortify the city of Sayette, which the Saracens had destroyed. He started on the day of the feast of the Apostles St. Peter and St. Paul (29th June 1253); and that night the king and his host lay before the castle of Assur, which was very strong. The same night the king called his people together and told them that if they agreed he would go and take a city of the Saracens called Naplouse; which city the ancient Scriptures called Samaria.

The Templars and the Hospitallers and the barons of the land answered him, with one accord, that it would be well to try and take the city; but that he ought not to go thither in person, because, if anything happened to him, all the land would be lost. And he said that they should not go unless he went with them. Therefore this enterprise remained unachieved, because the lords of the land would not consent that he should go in person.

Journeying day by day we came to the sands of Acre, where the king and the host encamped. At that place came to me a great troop of people from Great Armenia, who were going on pilgrimage to Jerusalem, having paid a great tribute to the Saracens, by whom they were conducted. By an interpreter, who knew their language and ours, they besought me to show them the sainted king.

I went to the king there where he sat in a pavilion, leaning against the pole of the pavilion; and he sat upon the sand, without a carpet, and without anything else under him. I said to him:

> Sire, there is here outside a great troop of people from Great Armenia, going to Jerusalem; and they pray me, sire, to cause the sainted king to be shown to them; but I have no desire as yet to kiss your bones.

He laughed aloud, and told me to go and fetch them; and so I did. And when they had seen the king they commended him to God, and the king commended them to God likewise.

On the following day the host lay at a place called the "Colt's Crossing," where the water is very good, and therewith they water the plants from which sugar comes. When we were encamped, one of my knights came to me and said: "Lord, I have lodged you in a fairer place than you were lodged in yesterday."

Another knight, who had chosen my yesterday's camping-ground, sprang upon him in wrath, and cried: "You are over-bold in speaking of anything I may have done!"

And he sprang upon him and took him by the hair. Then I sprang upon him in turn, and hit him with my fist between the two shoulders, and he let go.

And I said to him: "Quick, out of my quarters, for, so help me God, you shall never again be follower of mine."

The knight went away, showing great dole and sorrow, and brought to me my Lord Giles le Brun, the Constable of France; and for the great repentance that my Lord Giles saw in the knight on account of the folly he had wrought, he besought me, as instantly as he could, to take him back into my household. And I replied that I would not take him back unless the legate released me from my oath.

To the legate they went, and told him of the matter; and the legate answered that he had not power to release me, because the oath was reasonable; for the knight had well deserved his punishment. And these things I relate to you so that you may keep from taking any oath which in reason it were not convenient to take; for, as the wise man says, *Who swears lightly, lightly forswears himself.*

Expedition Against Belinas and Joinville in Peril

On the following day the king went and encamped before the city of Assur, which in the Bible is called Tyre. There the king called together the men of note in the host, and asked them if it would be well to go and take the city of Belinas before he went to Savette. We all thought it would be well if the king sent his people thither; but no one advised that he should go thither himself; and with great difficulty was he dissuaded therefrom.

Finally it was decided that the Count of Eu should go, and my Lord Philip of Montfort, the Lord of Assur, my Lord Giles le Brun, Constable of France, my Lord Peter the Chamberlain, the Master of the Temple and his brethren, and the Master of the Hospital and his brethren also.

We armed ourselves at nightfall, and came, a little after daybreak, to a plain lying before the city which is called Belinas; and the ancient Scriptures call it Cæsarea Philippi. In this city there springs up a fountain which is called Jor; and in the midst of the plain that lies before the city springs up another very beautiful fountain which is called Dan. And it is so, that when the two rivulets issuing from these two fountains come together, they call the river Jordan; and it is in that river that God was baptised.

By agreement between the Templars, Count Eu, the Hospitallers, and the barons of the land there present, it was decided that the king's division—in which division I then was, because the king had retained in his service the forty knights that were in my division—and my Lord Geoffry of Sargines, the right worthy man also, should set ourselves between the castle and the city; that the barons of the land should enter into the city by the left, and the Hospitallers by the right, and that the Templars should enter the city straight in front of us by the road from which we had come.

We then moved forward so far, that we came before the city; and we found that the Saracens that were in the city had discomfited the king's sergeants, and driven them from the city. When I saw this I came to the right worthy men who were with the Count of Eu, and said to them:

> Lords, if you do not go where we have been ordered to go, between the city and the castle, the Saracens will slay all our people who have entered into the city.

Our way was very perilous, and the place to which we had to go was fraught with danger; there were three pairs of dry walls that must needs be passed, and the slope was so steep that the horses could scarcely keep their footing; and the hillock we had to gain was crowded with Turks on horseback.

While I was speaking to the Count of Eu and his knights, I saw that our foot sergeants were breaking down the walls. When I saw this, I said to those I was addressing that it had been ordered that the king's division should go thither, where the Turks were; and that as this had been ordered, I should go. I turned, I and my two knights, towards those who were pulling down the walls, and I saw a mounted sergeant who thought to pass over the wall, and his horse fell upon him.

When I saw this I dismounted, and took my horse by the bridle. But, as God willed, when the Turks saw us coming, they abandoned the position we had to occupy. From this position the rock went down sheer into the city.

When we got there, and the Turks had gone, the Saracens who were in the city held themselves for beaten, and abandoned the city to our people without resistance. While I stood in that place, the Marshal of the Temple heard tell that I was in peril, and he came up to the top of the mound towards me. The Germans, who were in the division of the Count of Eu, also came after me; and when they saw the Turks on horseback flying towards the castle, they moved to go after them, and

I said: "Lords, you are not doing well; for we are here where we have been ordered to be, and you are going beyond your orders."

The castle that stands above the city is called Subeibe, and it is full half a league up in the mountains of Lebanon; and the slope that leads up to the castle is bestrewn with great rocks as big as hutches. When the Germans saw that their pursuit was but folly, they turned back, and when the Saracens saw that they thus turned back, they attacked them on foot, and gave them from the tops of the rocks great blows with their maces, and dragged away the housings from their horses.

The sergeants who were with us, seeing how the Germans were mishandled, began to be affrighted; so I told them that if they went off I would have them struck off the king's wages for ever. And they said to me:

Lord, the game is not equal between us; for, if it comes to flight, you are on horseback, while we are on foot; and the Saracens will kill us.

And I said to them: "Lords, I swear to you that I will not fly, for I will remain with you on foot." So I dismounted, and sent away my horse to the Templars, who were a full crossbow shot behind.

During the retreat that the Germans were making, the Saracens shot one of my knights, whose name was my Lord John of Bussey, with a quarrel, in the throat; and he fell dead right before me. My Lord Hugh of Escot, whose nephew he was. and who approved himself right well in the Holy Land, said to me: "Lord, come and help us to carry my nephew back here."

"Ill befall whomsoever helps you!" said I, "for you went up there without my orders; and if mischance has come upon you, you have deserved it. Carry him down there into the ditch. I shall not depart hence till they send to fetch me."

When my Lord John of Valenciennes heard of the peril in which we were, he came to my Lord Oliver of Termes, and to the other chiefs of Languedoc, and said: "Lords, I beseech and command you, in the king's name, to help me to bring back the seneschal"

While he was exerting himself thus, my Lord William of Beaumont came to him and said: "You are troubling yourself in vain, for the seneschal is dead."

And he answered: "Whether he be dead or alive I will carry news of him to the king!" Then he started, and came to us, there where we had gone up on the mountain; and as soon as he drew near to us, he sent word that I should come and speak to him; and so I did.

Then Oliver of Termes said to me that we were there in great peril, for if we went down by the way we had gone up we must needs suffer very great loss, because the hill was too steep, and the Saracens would fall upon us; "but if you will listen to me," said he, "I will show you a way of escape without loss."

And I told him to say on, and I would do as he wished.

"I will tell you," said he, "how we may escape. We will go all along this slope, as if we were going towards Damascus; and the Saracens you see before you will think we wish to take them in the rear. And so soon as we are in those plains we will spur round the city; and we shall have passed over the brook before they can come up with us; and withal we shall do them great harm, for we will set fire to the threshed corn that is lying in yon fields."

We did as he proposed; and he caused canes to be taken, such as are used for the making of flutes, and live coals to be set therein, and the canes to be thrust in among the threshed corn. And thus, by the counsel of Oliver of Termes, God brought us back in safety. And you must know that when we came back to the camp where our people were, we found that all had put off their armour; for none there had given us a thought. So we returned on the following day to Sayette, where the king was.

SAINT LOUIS BURIES THE CORPSES OF THE CHRISTIANS OF SAYETTE—FRIENDSHIP BETWEEN JOINVILLE AND THE COUNT OF EU

We found that the king in person had caused the bodies of the Christians whom the Saracens had killed (at Sayette)—as has been told above—to be duly buried; and he himself, in person, bore the decayed and evil-smelling corpses to the trenches in which they were to be buried; and he did this without ever holding his nostrils, as others did. He also caused workmen to come from all parts, and set himself to fortify the city with high walls and great towers. And when we came to the camp we found that he, in person, had meted out the places where we were to be quartered. My place he had set near to that of the Count of Eu, because he knew that the Count of Eu loved my company.

I will tell you of the jests that the Count of Eu played upon us. I had made a house in which I was wont to eat, I and my knights, by the light of the door. Now the door stood towards the Count of Eu's quarters; and he, who was very ingenious, made a little engine with which he could throw (stones) into my house; and he would spy out when we sat down to meat, and arrange his engine so as to command the length of our table, and then throw (stones) therewith, and so break our pots and our glasses.

Again I had furnished myself with fowls and capons, and some one, I know not who, had given him a young bear: and this bear he suffered to get at my fowls, and it had killed a dozen of them before any one came to the place; and the woman who kept the fowls beat the bear with her distaff.

Capture of Bagdad by the Tartars

While the king was fortifying Sayette, certain merchants came to the camp and related to us how the King of the Tartars had taken the city of Bagdad, as also the pope of the Saracens, who was lord of the city, and called the *Caliph* of Bagdad. The merchants told us in what manner the king had taken the city of Bagdad and the *caliph*, and it was in this wise:

When they had besieged the *caliph's* city, the king made known to the *caliph* that he would willingly arrange for a marriage between their children; and the *caliph's* counsellors advised him to agree to the marriage. Then the King of the Tartars desired the *caliph* to send as many as forty persons of his council, and of his men of most note, to swear to the marriage; and the *caliph* did so.

Again the King of the Tartars desired him to send forty of the richest and most notable men that he had; and the *caliph* did so. The third time he desired him to send forty of the best men in his company; and he did so. When the King of the Tartars saw that all the chief men of the town were in his power, he bethought himself that the lesser people in the town could not defend themselves without leaders; so he caused the heads of these six score men of note to be smitten off, and then caused the town to be assaulted, and took it, and the *caliph* also.

In order to cover his treachery, and to throw on the *caliph* the blame for the capture of the city, he caused the *caliph* to be taken and put into a cage of iron, and to be made to fast so far as a man can fast without dying; and then he asked him if he were hungry. And the *caliph* said "Yes;" nor was that to be wondered at.

Then the King of the Tartars caused a great charger of gold, loaded with jewels and precious stones, to be brought to him, and said: "Dost thou know these jewels?"

And the *caliph* said, "Yes, they were mine."

And he asked him if he loved them well? And he answered "Yes."

"As thou lovest them so much," said the King of the Tartars, "now take such a portion as seemeth good to thee, and eat."

The *caliph* replied that he could not, since these were not meats that could be eaten. Then the King of the Tartars said to him: "Now mayest thou see what were thy means of defence; for if thou hadst bestowed thy treasure—which, at this hour, is of no use to thee—upon thy men-at-arms, then, by so spending thy treasure thou mightest have defended thyself against us; whereas now it faileth thee in thy very direst need."

Of a Clerk Whom Joinville took to be an Assassin

While the king was fortifying Sayette, I went to his mass at the point of day, and he told me to wait for him, as he wished to ride abroad; and I did so. When we were in the fields we came before a little church, and saw, being on horseback, a priest singing mass. The king told me that this church had been built in honour of the miracle that God performed upon the Devil, when He drove him out of the body of the widow's daughter; and he said to me that, if I were willing, he would hear the mass that the priest had begun; and I told him that meseemed this were a good thing to do.

When it came to the giving of the "peace," I saw that the clerk who helped at the singing of the mass was big, black, lean and shaggy, and I feared that if he brought the "peace" to the king, he might perchance prove to be an Assassin, a wicked man, and kill the king. So I went and took the "peace," and brought it to the king. When the mass was sung, and we had remounted, we found the legate in the fields; and the king went to him, and called me, and said to the legate:

> I complain to you of the seneschal, who brought me the 'peace,' and would not suffer the poor clerk to bring it me.

And I told the legate the reason why I had so done; and the legate said I had done right well. And the king replied, "Truly, no!" Great debate was then between them; and I held my peace. And this story have I told you so that you may see the great humility of the king.

Of this miracle that God performed on the widow's daughter does the Gospel speak, which says that God was, when he performed the miracle, *in parte Tyri et Sidonis*; for then the city which I have called Sur was called Tyre, and the city that I have herein called Sayette was called Sidon.

Envoys of the Lord of Trebisond—Arrival of the Queen at Sayette

While the king was fortifying Sayette there came to him envoys from a great lord in the depths of Greece, who called himself the great Comnenus and the Lord of Trebisond. They brought to the king divers jewels as a present. Among other things they brought to the king bows of cornel-wood; and the notches of the bolts were screwed into the bows, and when the bolts were shot out, one saw that they were very sharp, and very well fashioned. [21]

These envoys asked the king to send a maiden from his palace so that their lord might take her to wife. And the king replied that he had brought none from oversea; and he advised them to go to Constantinople, to the emperor, who was the king's cousin, and ask him to give them for their lord a wife of the king's lineage and of the emperor's lineage. And this the king advised so that the Emperor of Constantinople might have the alliance of this great and wealthy man against Vataces, who was then the Emperor of the Greeks.

The queen, who had but lately recovered after the birth of the Lady Blanche—of whom she had been confined at Jaffa—arrived at Sayette; and she had come by sea. When I heard tell that she was come, I rose from before the king, and went to meet her, and led her to the castle. And when I came back to the king, who was in his chapel, he asked me if the queen and his children were well; and I told him, yes.

And he said:

I knew when you rose from before me that you were going to meet the queen, and so I have caused the sermon to wait for you.

And these things I tell you because I had then been five years with the king, and never before had he spoken to me, nor, so far as ever I heard, to anyone else, of the queen and of his children; and, so it appears to me, it was not seemly to be thus a stranger to one's wife and children.

---

21. This passage is probably corrupt in the MSS. and very obscure, and it has given rise to much disquisition. The "cornel-wood" may be horn, and my impression is that the bows were crossbows; nor is it easy to understand the mechanism suggested.

Of a Poor Knight and His Four Sons

On All Saints' Day (1st November 1253), I invited all the men of note in the camp to my quarters, which were by the sea. And while we were at meat there came in a ship a poor knight with his wife, and four children that they had. I caused them to partake of food in my quarters.

When we had eaten, I called together the men of note who were there, and said to them:

> Let us do here a great alms, and relieve this poor man of his children, and each take one, and I will take one.

So each took one, and quarrelled to have him. When the poor knight saw this, he and his wife, they began to weep for joy.

Now it so happened that when the Count of Eu returned from eating in the king's quarters, he came to see the men of note who were in my quarters, and he took away my child, who was of the age of twelve years.

This child served the count so well and loyally that when we returned to France the count saw to his marriage and made him a knight.

And every time I was there where the count was, this knight could scarce keep away from me, and would say: "Lord, may God reward you!

For this honour that I enjoy I owe it to you." As to his other three brothers, I know not what became of them.

Pilgrimage of Joinville—Mistake on the Part of the Queen—Marvellous Stone

I asked the king to suffer me to go on pilgrimage to our Lady of Tortosa: a very great place of pilgrimage, because it was there that the first altar had been made on earth in honour of the Mother of God. And our Lady performed there many great miracles; and the following among others: There was a man, out of his wits, who had the devil in his body. While his friends, who had brought him thither, were praying to the Mother of God to give him health, the Enemy, who was within him, answered them:

> Our Lady is not here. She is in Egypt affording help to the King of France, and to the Christians, who will come to land this day, they on foot against the paynim who are on horseback.

The day was set in writing, and the writing brought to the legate, who himself, with his own mouth, told me of it. And be assured that our Lady did help us that very day, and would have helped us more if we had not angered her, her and her Son, as I have told you before.

The king gave me leave to go, and told me, in full council, to buy a hundred pieces of camlet of divers colours, to be given to the Franciscans when we returned to France. Then was my heart comforted, for I thought he would not tarry oversea much longer.

When we came to Tripoli, my knights asked me what I intended to do with the camlets, and prayed me to tell them. "Perchance," said I, "I have stolen them for profit." The Prince of Tripoli—whom God have in His grace!—received us with great joy, and did us all the honour he could; and he would have given to me and to my knights great gifts, if so be that we would have taken them. But we would take nothing save some of his relics, whereof I took some to the king, together with the camlet I had bought for him.

Moreover I sent to my lady the queen four pieces of camlet. The knight who presented them to her carried them wrapped up in a white cloth. When the queen saw him enter the chamber where she was, she knelt before him, and he knelt before her; and the queen said: "Rise up, sir knight; you ought not to kneel, who are the bearer of relics."

But the knight said: "Lady, these are not relics; these are pieces of camlet that my lord sends you."

When the queen heard this, and her ladies, they began to laugh; and the queen said to my knight: "Tell your lord that I wish him an evil day, since he has caused me to kneel to his camlet."

While the king was at Sayette they brought him a stone that broke in flakes, the most marvellous stone in the world; and when you scaled off one of the flakes, you found, between the two stones, the form of a sea-fish. The fish was of stone; but it wanted nothing in form, eyes, bones, nor colour, nor anything else, to make it otherwise than if it were alive. The king gave me one of these stones, and I found therein a tench, brown of colour, and of such fashion as a tench ought to be.

The King Hears of the Death of His Mother—Harshness of the Queen Blanche Towards the Queen Margaret

To Sayette came news to the king that his mother was dead. He made such lamentation that, for two days, no one could speak to him. After that he sent one of the varlets of his chamber to summon me.

When I came before him in his chamber, where he was alone, and he saw me, he stretched out his arms, and said: "Ah, seneschal, I have lost my mother!"

"Sire," said I, "I do not marvel at that, since she had to die; but I do marvel that you, who are a wise man, should have made such great mourning; for you know what the sage says: that whatever grief a man may have in his heart, none should appear on his countenance, because he who shows his grief causes his enemies to rejoice and afflicts his friends."

He caused many fine services to be held for the queen overseas; and afterwards sent to France a chest full of letters to the churches, asking them to pray for her.

My Lady Mary of Vertus, a very good lady and a saintly woman, came to tell me that the queen was making great lamentation, and asked me to go to her and comfort her. And when I came there, I found her weeping; and I told her that he spake sooth who said that none should put faith in woman. "For," said I, "she that is dead is the woman that you most hated, and yet you are showing such sorrow."

And she told me it was not for the queen that she was weeping, but because of the king's sorrow in the mourning that he made, and because of her daughter, afterwards the Queen of Navarre, who had remained in men's keeping.

The unkindness that the Queen Blanche showed to the Queen Margaret was such that she would not suffer, in so far as she could help it, that her son should be in his wife's company, except at night when he went to sleep with her. The palace where the king and his queen liked most to dwell was at Pontoise, because there the king's chamber was above and the queen's chamber below; and they had so arranged matters between them that they held their converse in a turning staircase that went from the one chamber to the other; and they had further arranged that when the ushers saw the Queen Blanche coming to her son's chamber, they struck the door with their rods, and the king would come running into his chamber so that his mother might find him there; and the ushers of Queen Margaret's chamber did the same when Queen Blanche went thither, so that she might find Queen Margaret there.

Once the king was by his wife's side, and she was in great peril of death, being hurt for a child that she had borne. Queen Blanche came thither, and took her son by the hand, and said: "Come away; you have nothing to do here!"

When Queen Margaret saw that the mother was leading her son away, she cried: "Alas! whether dead or alive, you will not suffer me to see my lord!" Then she fainted, and they thought she was dead; and the king, who thought she was dying, turned back; and with great trouble they brought her round.

The King Decides to Return to France—Interview Between Joinville and the Legate

When the city of Sayette was nearly all fortified, the king caused several processions to be made throughout the camp; and after the processions the legate caused prayers to be made that God should, according to His will, so order the king's matters that the king should do what was most agreeable to God, either in returning to France or remaining where he was.

After the processions had been made the king called me, as I was sitting with the men of note of the land, and took me into a courtyard, and made me turn my back towards them. Then the legate said to me:

> Seneschal, the king is greatly pleased with your services, and would right willingly procure you profit and honour; and in order to set your heart at rest, he desires me to tell you that he has settled to go to France at this coming Easter.

And I replied: "God grant that he may carry out his wish."

Then the legate rose, and told me to go with him to his quarters; which I did. Then he shut me into his privy chamber—he and I, and none other—and put my two hands between both his, and began to weep very bitterly; and when he could speak, he said:

> Seneschal, I am greatly rejoiced, and I give thanks to God that the king, and you, and the other pilgrims should escape from the great peril in which you have been in this land. And much am I in distress of heart that I shall have to leave your saintly company, and go to the court of Rome, amid the treacherous people who are there. But I will tell you what I think to do. I think to remain here a year after you have left, and to spend all that I have in fortifying the suburbs of Acre. So will I show them clearly that I bring back no monies with me; and then, my hands being empty, they will not pursue me.

I once told the legate of two sins that one of my priests had related to me; and he answered me in this manner:

> No one knows as I do of all the treacherous sins committed in Acre: wherefore it behoves that God avenge them in such sort that the city of Acre be washed clean in the blood of its inhabitants, and that other people come hereafter to dwell there.

This prophecy of the right worthy man has in part been brought to pass, for the city has been well washed in the blood of its inhabitants;[22] but those have not yet come who are to dwell there; and when they do come, God grant that they be righteous, and govern themselves according to the will of the Lord!

JOINVILLE CONDUCTS THE QUEEN TO SUR—THE KING SETS SAIL

After these things the king sent for me and ordered me to arm myself, I and my knights. I asked him why: and he told me I was to conduct the queen and his children to Sur, some seven leagues distant. I answered him not a word; and yet his command was fraught with peril, for we had then neither truce nor peace with the Saracens of Egypt or those of Damascus. God be thanked, we gat to Sur all peacefully, and without hindrance, at nightfall, though we had twice to dismount, in our enemies' land, for the purpose of making a fire and cooking our meat, and of feeding the children and causing them to take suck.

When the king departed from the city of Sayette, which he had fortified with great walls and great towers, and with great fosses puddled within and without, the patriarch and barons came to him, and spoke in this wise:

> Sire, you have fortified the city of Sayette, and that of Cæsarea, and the *burgh* of Jaffa—all to the very great advantage of the Holy Land; and you have greatly strengthened the city of Acre with the walls and towers that you have built. Sire, we have considered among ourselves, and we do not see that henceforward your sojourn here will bring profit to the kingdom of Jerusalem: wherefore we advise and counsel you to go to Acre in the coming Lent, and prepare for your passage, so that you may be able to return to France after Easter.

By the advice of the patriarch and of the barons, the king departed

---

22. It was sacked by the Saracens in 1291.

from Sayette, and came to Sur, where the queen was; and from thence they came to Acre at the beginning of Lent.

All during Lent the king caused his vessels to be made ready to return to France; and there were thirteen of them, as well ships as galleys. The ships and galleys were got ready in such sort that the king and queen embarked on board their ships on the vigil of St. Mark, after Easter (24th April 1254); and we had a fair wind for our departing. On St. Mark's day the king told me that on that day he had been born; and I told him that henceforward he might well say that on that day he had been reborn, for certes he was well reborn when he escaped from that perilous land.

The King's Ship Strikes Against a Sandbank

On the Saturday we came in sight of the isle of Cyprus, and of a mountain in Cyprus which is called the Mountain of the Cross. That Saturday a mist rose from the land, and descended from the land to the sea; and by this our mariners thought we were further from the isle of Cyprus than we were, because they did not see the mountain above the mist. Wherefore they sailed forward freely, and so it happened that our ship struck a reef of sand below the water; and if we had not found that little sandbank where we struck, we should have struck against a great mass of sunken rocks, where our ship would have been broken in pieces, and we all shipwrecked and drowned.

As soon as our ship struck, a great cry rose in the ship, for each one cried "Alas!" and the mariners and the rest wrung their hands, because each was in fear of drowning. When I heard this, I rose from my bed, where I was lying, and went to the ship's castle with the mariners. As I came there, Brother Raymond, who was a Templar and master of the mariners, said to one of his varlets: "Throw down the lead." And he did so.

And as soon as he had thrown it he cried out, and said: "Alas! we are aground!"

When Brother Raymond heard that he rent his clothes to the belt, and took to tearing out his beard, and to crying: "Ay me! Ay me!"

At this point one of my knights, whose name was my Lord John of Monson, the father of the Abbot William of St. Michael, did me a great kindness, for he brought me, without a word, a lined surcoat of mine, and threw it on my back, because I had donned my tunic only. And I cried out to him and said: "What do I want with your surcoat, that you bring me, when we are drowning?"

And he said to me: "By my soul, lord, I should like better to see us all drowned than that you should take some sickness from the cold, and so come to your death."

The manners cried: "Ho! galleys, come and take the king!" But of the four galleys that the king had there, never a galley came near; and in this they acted wisely, for there were full eight hundred persons on board the ship who would have jumped into the galleys to save their lives, and thus have caused the galleys to sink.

The varlet who had the lead threw it a second time, and came back to Brother Raymond, and told him that the ship was no longer aground. Then Brother Raymond went and told it to the king, who was lying crosswise on the deck of the ship, barefoot, in his tunic only, and all dishevelled—before the body of our Lord which was on the ship—and he lay there as one who fully thought to be drowned.

So soon as it was day, we saw before us the rock on which we would have struck if the ship had not caught the end of the sand-reef.

In the morning the king sent to fetch the master mariners of the ships; and they sent four divers to the bottom of the sea. And these dived into the sea; and when they came out, the king and the master mariners heard them one after the other separately, so that one diver did not know what the other had said. Nevertheless they learned from the four divers that, in the scraping of our ship against the sand, the sand had knocked off full four fathoms of the keel on which the ship was built.

Then the king called the master mariners before us, and asked them what advice they gave as concerning the blow the ship had received. They consulted together, and advised the king to leave his ship and go into another ship.

> "And we give you this advice," said they, "because we believe for certain that all the timbers of your ship are dislocated: wherefore we are in doubt whether, when your ship gets into the high sea, she will be able to stand the blows of the waves, and not go to pieces. For so it chanced, when you came from France, a ship struck in like manner; and when she came into the high seas she was unable to stand the blows of the waves, and broke up, and all perished, so many as were in the ship, save one woman and her child, who were saved upon a piece of the ship."

And I can bear you witness that he spoke sooth, for I saw the woman and the child at Baffe, in the quarters of the Count of Joigny; and the count entertained them for the love of God.

Then the king asked my Lord Peter the Chamberlain, and my Lord Giles le Brun, Constable of France, and my Lord Gervais of Escraines, who was master cook to the king, and the archdeacon of Nicosia, who bore his seal, and was afterwards cardinal, and myself, what we advised concerning these things. And we replied that as regards all worldly matters one ought to believe those who are most conversant with them. "Therefore," said we, "we counsel you, for our parts, to do what the seamen advise."

Then the king said to the mariners: "I ask you, on your fealty, whether if the ship were your own, and freighted with your own merchandise, you would leave her?"

And they replied, all together, "No," for they liked better to put their bodies in peril of drowning rather than to buy a new ship at a cost of four thousand *livres* and more. "And why do you then advise me to leave the ship?"

"Because," said they, "the stakes are not equal. For neither gold nor silver can be set against your person, and the persons of your wife and children, who are here; therefore we advise you not to put yourself, or them, in jeopardy."

Then the king said to them:

> Lords, I have heard your opinion, and that of my people; and now I will tell you mine, which is this: If I leave the ship, there are in her five hundred people and more who will land in this isle of Cyprus, for fear of peril to their body—since there is none that does not love his life as much as I love mine—and these peradventure, will never return to their own land. Therefore I like better to place my own person, and my wife, and my children in God's hands than do this harm to the many people who are here.

The great harm that the king would have done to the people in his ship may be plainly seen by what happened to Oliver of Termes, who was in the king's ship. Now he was one of the boldest men I have ever seen, and had so approved himself in the Holy Land; but he did not dare to stay with us for fear of drowning, and remained in Cyprus: and he was there so let and hindered that he did not return to the king for a year and a half; and yet he was a man of note, and a wealthy man, and could well pay for his passage. Now bethink you how the lesser folk would have fared who had not the wherewithal to pay for their passages, when such a man was so hindered and delayed!

STORM ON THE COAST OF CYPRUS—VOW MADE BY THE QUEEN AND JOINVILLE

Out of this danger, from which God caused us to escape, we fell into another; for the wind, which had driven us on to the coast of Cyprus, where we had thought to drown, now arose, so strong and violent, that it beat us back upon the island once more. The manners threw out their anchors against the wind, but were never able to stop the ship till they had thrown out five. It became necessary to take down the sides of the king's chamber;[23] nor was there any one who ventured to remain therein, for fear lest the wind should carry him into the sea. At this moment the Constable of France, my Lord Giles le Brun, and I were lying in the king's chamber, and the queen opened the door of the chamber, and thought to find the king there.

And I asked her what she came seeking. And she said she had come to speak to the king, to ask him to make promise to God, or to His saints, of some pilgrimage, so that God might deliver us from the peril in which we were; for the mariners had said we were like to drown. And I said:

Lady, promise to make a journey to the shrine of my Lord St. Nicholas of Varangeville, and I will be warrant for him that God will bring you back to France, you and the king, and your children.

"Seneschal," she said, "I would do so right willingly; but the king is so strange that if he knew I had made this promise without his privity, he would never let me go."

"At least," I said, "you will do one thing: If God brings you back to France, you will promise to give a ship of silver, worth five marks, for the king, for yourself, and for your three children; and I will be warrant that God will bring you back to France; for I made a vow to St. Nicholas that if he saved us from the peril in which we were last night, I should go from Joinville, on foot and unshod, to seek him at Varangeville."

---

23. The passage is obscure. I translate as the words stand. The "chamber," I take it, was a kind of deck cabin.

And she said that, as for the ship of silver, of the value of five marks, she promised it to St. Nicholas, and that I was to be his warrant; and I replied: "That shall I be right willingly."

So she departed and stayed away but a little while; and then she came back to us and said to me: "St. Nicholas has saved us from this peril; for the wind has fallen."

When the queen—whom God have in His mercy!—was come back to France, she caused the ship of silver to be fashioned in Paris. And there were in the ship the king, the queen, and the three children, all in silver; and the mariners, the mast, the rudder, the cordage, all of silver; and the sails were all sewn with silver thread. And the queen told me that the fashioning of it had cost one hundred limes. When the ship was made, the queen sent it to me at Joinville, so that I might cause it to be taken to St. Nicholas; which also I did. And I saw it still at St. Nicholas when we conducted the king's sister [24] to (be married to the son of) the King of Germany, at Haguenau.

Profit to be Derived From the Threatenings of God

Now let us return to our subject, and proceed. After we had escaped from these two perils, the king sat himself on the bulwark of the ship, and made me sit at his feet, and spoke thus: "Seneschal, our God has shown us His great power in this: that a little wind—not one of the four great master winds!—has come near to drowning the King of France, his wife, and his children, and all his company. Now are we bound to give Him grace and thanks for the peril from which he has delivered us.

"Seneschal," said the king, "such tribulations, when they come to people, or great sicknesses, or great presecutions, are, as the saints tell us, the threatenings of our Saviour. For just as God says to those who escape from great sicknesses: 'Now see how I might have brought your life to an end, had such been My will,' even so could

"He now say to us: 'You see how I might have drowned you all, had such been My will.' Now ought we," continued the king. "to look to ourselves, and see if there is anything in us that displeases Him, and on account whereof He has thus placed us in fear and jeopardy; and if we find anything in us that displeases Him, we should cast it out. For if we do otherwise, after the

---

24. The present king, *i.e.*, Philip the Fair, whose sister Blanche married Rudolph, the son of the King or Emperor of Germany..

warning He has given us, He will smite us with death, or with some other great tribulation, to the destruction of our bodies and of our souls."

And the king added:

Seneschal, the saint says: 'Lord God, why dost thou threaten us? For if thou destroyest us all, Thou wilt be none the poorer; and if Thou savest as alive Thou wilt he none the richer. Whereby we may see,' says the saint, 'that the warnings that God gives us can neither be to His advantage, nor save Him from harm; and that it is only out of His great love that He sends His warnings to awaken us, so that we may see our defects clearly, and remove from us all that is displeasing to Him.' Now let us do this," said the king, "and we shall be acting wisely.

The Isle of Lampedousa

We left the island of Cyprus after we had watered there, and taken in such other things as we required. Then we came to an isle called Lampedousa, where we took a great quantity of conies; and we found an ancient hermitage in the rocks, and found the garden that the hermits who dwelt there had made of old time: where were olives, and figs, and vines, and other trees. The stream from the fountain ran through the garden.

The king, and we all, went to the end of the garden, and found an oratory in the first cave, whitewashed with lime, and there was there a cross of red earth. We entered into the second cave, and found two bodies of dead men, with the flesh all decayed; the ribs yet held all together, and the bones of the hands were on their breasts, and they were laid towards the East, in the same manner that bodies are laid in the earth.

When we got back to our ship, we found that one of our mariners was missing; and the master of the ship thought he had remained there to be a hermit: wherefore Nicholas of Soisi, who was the king's master sergeant, left three bags of biscuit on the shore, so that the mariner might find them, and subsist thereon.

The Isle of Pentelaria—the King is Inexorable

When we came away from thence, we saw a great island in the sea, called Pentelaria, and it was peopled by Saracens who were subject to the King of Sicily and the King of Tunis. The queen begged the king to send thither three galleys to get fruit for the children; and the king consented, and ordered the masters of the galleys to go thither, and be ready to come back to him when his ship passed before the island. The galleys entered into a little port that was in the island; and it chanced that when the king's ship passed before the port, we got no tidings of our galleys.

Then did the mariners begin to murmur among themselves. The king caused them to be summoned, and asked them what they thought of the matter. The mariners said it seemed to them that the Saracens had captured his people and his galleys. "But we advise and counsel you, sire, not to wait for them; for you are between the kingdom of Sicily and the kingdom of Tunis, which—both the one and the other of them—love you not at all; if, however, you suffer us to sail forward, we shall, during the night, have delivered you from peril; for we shall have passed through this strait."

"Truly," said the king, "I shall not listen to you, and leave my people in the hands of the Saracens without at least doing all in my power to deliver them. I command you to turn your sails, and we will fall upon them." And when the queen heard this, she began to make great lamentation, and said: "Alas! this is all my doing!"

While they were turning the sails of the king's ship, and of the other ships, we saw the galleys coming from the island. When they came to the king, the king asked the mariners why they had tarried; and they replied that they could not help themselves, but that the fault lay with certain sons of *burgesses* of Paris, of whom there were six, who stayed eating the fruit of the gardens; wherefore they had been unable to get them off, nor could they leave them behind.

Then the king commanded that the six *burghers'* sons should be put into the barge astern; at which they began to cry and to howl, saying: "Sire, for God's sake, take for ransom all that we have; but do not put us there where murderers and thieves are put; for we shall be shamed to all time."

The queen and all of us did what we could to move the king; but the king would listen to none of us. So they were put into the barge, and remained there till we came to land. And they were there in such danger and distress that when the sea rose, the waves flew over their heads, and they had to sit down lest the wind should carry them into the sea. And it served them right; for their gluttony caused us such mischief that we were delayed for eight good days, because the king had caused the ships to turn right about.

Fire in the Queen's Chamber

Another adventure befell us at sea, before we came to land, and it happened thus: One of the queen's bedeswomen, when she had put the queen to bed, was heedless, and taking the kerchief that had been wound about her head, threw it on to the iron stove on which the queen's candle was burning; and when she had gone to bed in the cabin where the women slept, below the queen's chamber, the candle burnt on, till the kerchief caught fire, and from the kerchief the fire passed to the cloths with which the queen's garments were covered.

When the queen awoke, she saw her cabin all in flames, and jumped up quite naked, and took the kerchief, and threw it all burning into the sea, and took the cloths and extinguished them. Those who were in the barge behind the ship cried, but not very loud: "Fire! fire!" I lifted up my head and saw that the kerchief still burned with a clear flame on the sea, which was very still. I put on my tunic as quickly as I could, and went and sat with the mariners.

While I sat there my squire, who slept before me, came to me and said that the king was awake, and asked where I was.

"And I told him," said he, "that you were in your cabin; and the king said to me, 'Thou liest.'"

While we were thus speaking, behold the queen's clerk appeared, Master Geoffry, and said to me: "Be not afraid; nothing has happened."

And I said: "Master Geoffry, go and tell the queen that the king is awake, and that she should go to him and set his mind at ease."

On the following day the Constable of France, and my Lord Peter the chamberlain, and my Lord Gervais, the master of the pantry, said to the king: "What happened in the night that we heard mention of fire?"

And I said not a word.

Then said the king: "What happened was by mischance, and the seneschal is more reticent than I. Now I will tell you," said he, "how it came about that we might all have been burned this night."

And he told them what had befallen, and said to me: "I command you henceforward not to go to rest till you have put out all fires, except the great fire that is in the hold of the ship. And take note that I shall not go to rest till you come back to me." And I did so as long as we were at sea; and it was only after I had gone back to the king that he would go to rest.

A Miracle Performed by the Virgin Mary

Another adventure befell us at sea. My Lord Dragonet, a man of note of Provence, was asleep one morning in his ship, which was a full league in front of ours; and waking he called to a squire of his and said to him: "Go and stop up that opening, for the sun strikes on my face." The squire saw that he could not stop up the opening unless he got outside the ship, so he got outside.

While he was going to stop up the opening, his foot slipped, and he fell into the water. Now the ship had no barge in tow, for it was small; and very soon he was left behind, a long way from the ship. We who were on the king's ship saw him, and fancied it was a bundle or a barrel, because he who had fallen into the water made no effort to help himself.

One of the king's galleys picked him up, and brought him to our ship, where he told us how this had befallen him. I asked him how it was he had taken no thought to save himself, either by swimming, or in any other manner.

He answered me that there was no reason, or need, why he should thus take thought, because, so soon as he began to fall, he commended himself to our Lady of Vauvert, and she held him up by the shoulders from the time that he fell until the king's galley picked him up. In honour of this miracle, I have caused it to be depicted in my chapel at Joinville, and in the glass windows at Blecourt.

The King Decides Reluctantly to Disembark at Hyeres

After we had been six weeks at sea, we came to a port at two leagues' distance from a castle called Hyeres, which belonged to the Count of Provence, who afterwards became King of Sicily. The queen and all the council were agreed that the king should disembark there, because the land belonged to his brother.

The king answered us that he would not leave his ship till we came to Aigues-Mortes, which was in his own land. On this point the king held firm against us on the Wednesday and the Thursday, nor could we prevail against him to decide otherwise.

In the Marseilles ships there are two rudders attached to two tillers in such marvellous fashion that you can turn the ship to the right hand, or to the left, as quickly as you can turn a saddle horse. On the Friday the king was sitting upon one of these tillers, and he called me to him, and said: "Seneschal, what do you think of this matter?"

And I said to him:

Sire, it would be but right if that chanced to you that chanced to my Lady of Bourbon, who would not disembark at this port, but set out to sea again to go to Aigues-Mortes, and remained at sea for six weeks."

Then the king called his council together, and told them what I had said, and asked what they advised; and they all advised that he should disembark presently, since it would not be wise on his part if he again put his own person, his wife, and his children, in peril by the sea after having escaped therefrom. The king accepted the advice we gave him; whereby the queen was greatly rejoiced.

Advice Given to the King by Joinville

The king and his wife and children disembarked therefore at the castle of Hyeres. While the king was waiting at Hyeres in order to obtain horses to come into France, the Abbot of Cluny, who afterwards was Bishop of Olive, presented him with two palfreys, which would today be well worth five hundred *livres*—one for the king himself, and the other for the queen.

When the abbot had presented them, he said to the king: "Sire, I will come again tomorrow to speak to you about my affairs." When the morrow came, the abbot returned. The king heard him with great diligence and at great length.

When the abbot had departed, I came to the king, and said: "I should like to ask, if it so pleases you, whether you have given ear to the Abbot of Cluny with the more favour because of those two palfreys that he gave you yesterday?"

The king thought a long time, and then said: "Truly, yes."

"Sire," I continued, "do you know why I have asked you this question?"

"Why? "said he.

"Because, sire," I replied, "I advise and counsel that, when you return to France, you forbid all your sworn councillors to accept aught from those who have matters to bring before you; for you may rest assured that, if they accept aught, they will listen more willingly, and with greater diligence, to those who have bestowed somewhat upon them; like as you have done to the Abbot of Cluny."

The king called all his council together, and incontinently told them what I had said; and they answered that the advice I had given him was good.

Of Brother Hugh the Franciscan

The king heard tell of a Franciscan whose name was Brother Hugh; and because of the great fame of this Franciscan, the king sent to summon him, for he desired to see him and hear him speak. The day on which Brother Hugh came to Hyeres, we looked out upon the road by which he was coming, and saw that a great crowd of people were following him on foot, both men and women. The king caused him to preach. The beginning of his sermon was on the religiouses, and he spoke thus: "Lords, I see too many religiouses in the king's court, and in his company."

And to these words he added:

And in the first place I myself am one too many here; and this I say because the religiouses. here are in no condition to be saved—unless the Holy Scriptures lie to us, which cannot be. For the Holy Scriptures tell us that a monk cannot live out of his cloister without mortal sin, any more than a fish can live out of water. And if the religiouses who are with the king say that his court is a cloister, then I say unto them that it is the very largest cloister that ever I saw, for it extends from this side of the sea to the other.

And if they say that in that cloister they can lead a hard life for the salvation of their souls, then I do not believe them; for I tell you that I have eaten with them here of divers meats in great foison, and drunk good wines both strong and clear. Wherefore I am certain that if they had been in their cloisters, they would not have lived in such ease as they now live with the king."

In his sermon he told the king how he should govern for the good of his people; and at the end of the sermon he said that he had read the Bible and the books that go with the Bible, and that he had never seen, neither in the books of believers nor in the books of unbelievers, that any kingdom, or lordship, was lost, or passed from one lord to another, or one king to another, unless there had first been default of right and justice.

"Now let the king," said he, "have a care, since he is going into France, that he execute right and justice among his people, and remain thereby in the love of God, so that God do not take from him both his kingdom and his life."

I said to the king that he should keep Brother Hugh in his company as long as he could. He told me he had already so besought the brother, but that he would not remain at his bidding. Then the king took me by the hand and said: "Let us go and beseech him."

We came to him, and I said: "Sir, do what my lord asks you, and stay with him so long as he is in Provence."

And he answered me angrily: "Of a truth, sir, I shall not do so. I shall go whither God will love me better than in the king's company." One day he stayed with us, and the next he went his way. It has since been told me that he lies buried in the city of Marseilles, and there works many fair miracles.

Counsels Given by Philip Augustus to St. Louis

On the day that the king left Hyeres, he went down from the castle on foot, because the hill was steep; and he went so far on foot, not being able to come at his own palfrey, that he had to mount on mine. And when his own palfrey came up, he turned very angrily on Ponce, the squire; and after he had mis-said him well, I said: "Sire, you ought to forgive much to Ponce, the squire; for he has served your grandfather, and your father, and yourself."

> "Seneschal," said he, "he has not served us, but we have served him, in suffering him to remain near our persons considering his evil qualities. For King Philip, my grandfather, told me that we ought to reward our servants, one more and the other less, according to their service; and he used to say again that none can govern a country well if he does not know how to refuse as boldly, and with as much hardihood, as he knows how to give. And I teach you these things," said the king, "because the world is so eager to ask and acquire, that there are few people who look to the salvation of their souls, and their personal honour, provided they can draw to themselves the goods of others, whether rightfully or wrongfully."

Joinville Parts from the King—He Comes to Him Again Later at Soissons—Marriage Between Isabel of France and Thibaut II., King of Navarre

The king passed through the county of Provence to a city called Aix in Provence, where it was said that the body of the Magdalen lay; and we went to a very high cave in a rock, where, so it was related, she had lived in hermitage for seventeen years. When the king came to Beaucaire, and I saw him in his own land, and his own dominions, I took leave of him, and went to the Dauphiness of Vienne, my niece, and to the Count of Chalon, my uncle, and to the Count of Burgundy, his son.

And when I had sojourned a space at Joinville, and had arranged my affairs, I went back to the king, whom I found at Soissons; and he made such joy of me that all who were there marvelled. There I found Count John of Brittany, and his wife, the daughter of King Thibaut, who offered to do homage to the king for all such rights as she might have in Champagne; and the king adjourned the matter, and referred her, as also King Thibaut II., to the parliament of Paris, where they might be heard, and justice done to the parties.

To this parliament came the King of Navarre and his council, and the Count of Brittany also. At this parliament King Thibaut asked for my Lady Isabel, the king's daughter, to have her to wife. Notwithstanding the words that our people of Champagne spoke behind my back, because of the love they had seen the king show to me at Soissons, I did not forbear to go to the king and speak to him about this marriage.[25] "Go," said the king, "and get the Count of Brittany to agree, and then we will conclude our marriage."

And I told him that he ought not to give up the marriage on that ground (*i.e.*, if the count objected). But he said that on no account would he conclude the marriage until such time as an agreement had been come to; for no one should ever say that he had married his children by depriving his barons of their heritage.

I reported these words to Queen Margaret of Navarre, and to the king her son, and to their other counsellors; and when they heard them they hastened to come to an agreement. And so soon as they were agreed, the King of France gave his daughter to King Thibaut; and the nuptials were celebrated at Melun, largely and with full pomp; and from thence King Thibaut led his bride to Provins, where they made their entry amid a great number of barons.

Habits and Customs of St. Louis—He Refuses the Unjust Demands of His Bishops

After the king returned from overseas, he lived in such devotion that never did he wear fur of beaver or grey squirrel, nor scarlet, nor gilded stirrups and spurs. His clothing was of camlet and blue cloth; the fur on his coverlets and clothing was deer's hide, or the skin from the hare's legs, or lambskin. He was so sober in his eating that he never ordered special meats outside what his cook prepared: what was set

---

25. Sense a little obscure, and MSS. not quite agreed.

before him that did he eat.

He put water to his wine in a glass goblet, and according to the strength of the wine he added water thereto by measure; and would hold the goblet in his hand while they mixed water with his wine behind his table. He always caused food to be given to his poor, and after they had eaten, caused money to be given to them.

When the minstrels of the men of note came in after he had eaten, and brought their viols, he would wait before he heard grace until the minstrel had ended his song; then he would rise, and the priests stand before him to say grace. When we were private with him, he would sit at the foot of his bed; and when the Preaching Brothers and Dominicans who were there brought to his mind some book which he might like to hear read, he would say: "You shall not read it to me; for there is no book so good after eating as to talk freely, that is to say, so to talk that everyone says what best pleases him." When strangers of note ate with him, he made them very good company.

Of his wisdom will I now speak to you. There were times when people bore witness that no one of his council was as wise as he. And this appeared in that when people spoke to him of any matter, he did not say: "I will take advice thereon;" but if he saw the right clearly and evidently he answered without appeal to his councillors, and at once. In this wise I heard that he gave answer to all the prelates of the kingdom of France regarding a petition they made to him in the following case.

The Bishop Guy of Auxerre spake to him for all of them, and said:

> Sire, these archbishops and bishops here present have charged me to tell you that Christendom decays and melts in your hands, and that it will decay still further unless you give thought thereto, because no man stands in fear of excommunication. We require you therefore to command your bailiffs and your sergeants to compel all excommunicate persons who have been under sentence for a year and a day, to make satisfaction to the Church.

And the king replied, without taking any advice, that he would willingly order his bailiffs and sergeants to constrain excommunicate persons in the manner desired, provided full cognisance of the sentence were given to him in each case, so that he might judge whether the sentence were righteous or not.

And they consulted together, and answered the king that they would not give him such cognisance, because the matters involved were spiritual. And the king replied in turn that he would not give them cognisance of such matters as pertained to him, nor order his sergeants to constrain excommunicate persons to obtain absolution, whether such excommunication were rightful or wrongful.

"For if I did so," said the king, "I should be acting contrary to God and against right. And I will give you an example, which is this: that the bishops of Brittany held the Count of Brittany for seven years under sentence of excommunication; and then the count obtained absolution from the court of Rome; and if I had constrained him at the end of the first year, I should have constrained him wrongfully."

OTHER EXAMPLES OF ST. LOUIS'S FIRMNESS AND JUSTICE

It happened, after we had returned from overseas, that the monks of St. Urban elected two abbots. The Bishop Peter of Chalons,—on whom God have mercy!—drove them both out, and consecrated as abbot my Lord John of Mymeri, and gave him the crozier. I would not acknowledge the said John of Mymeri as abbot, because he had wronged the Abbot Geoffry, who had appealed against him, and gone to Rome.

I held the abbey so long in my hands that the said Geoffry won the crozier, and the monk to whom it had been given by the bishop did not get it; and while the contention lasted, the bishop caused me to be excommunicated. Therefore there was, at a parliament held in Paris, much quarrelling between me and the Bishop Peter of Chalons, and between the Countess Margaret of Flanders and the Archbishop of Rheims, to whom she gave the lie.

At the following parliament, all the prelates besought the king to come and speak to them privily. When he returned from speaking to the prelates, he came to us, who were waiting for him in the judgment chamber, and told us, laughing heartily, of the trouble he had had with the prelates; for, in the first place, the Archbishop of Rheims had said to the king:

> Sire, what will you do for me on account of the wardship of St. Remigius of Rheims, which you are taking from me? For by the relics that are here before us, I swear I would not have upon my conscience such a sin as there is upon yours, for all

the kingdom of France.

"By the relics that are here before us," said the king, "I swear that for Compiègne alone you would take that sin upon your conscience, because of the covetousness that is in you. So now one of us two is foresworn! Then the Bishop of Chartres demanded of me," said the king, "that I should cause what I had of his in my possession to be returned to him. And I told him I should not do it, until such time as my dues had been paid. And I told him too that he had done me homage with his hands in mine, and that he was dealing with me neither well nor loyally when he endeavoured to deprive me of what was mine by inheritance. The Bishop of Chalons," continued the king, "said to me: 'Sire, what do you propose to do for me as concerning the Lord of Joinville who deprives that poor monk of the abbey of St. Urban?' "Sir bishop," the king had replied, "you have settled it among you that no excommunicate person is to be heard in a lay court; and I have seen a letter, sealed with thirty-two seals, to the effect that you are excommunicate: therefore I will not hear you till you have got yourself absolved."

And these things I tell you so that you may see clearly how the king could settle such matters as he had to settle, alone, and by his own good counsel.

The Abbot Geoffry of St. Urban, after I had settled this matter for him, returned me evil for good, and lodged an appeal against me. He gave the saintly king to understand that he was in the king's wardship. I thereon asked the king to cause enquiry to be made whether the wardship of the abbey was the king's or mine.

"Sire," said the abbot, "please God you shall not do this; but so arrange that the question between us and the Lord of Joinville be settled by due process of law; for we to whom the abbey belongs by inheritance would rather have it in your wardship than in his."

Then the king said to me: "Do they speak sooth that the wardship of the abbey is mine?"

"Certainly not, sire," I replied, "it is mine."

Then the king said to the abbot:

It may be that the inheritance is yours; but as to the wardship, from what you tell me, and from what the seneschal tells me, that is a matter between him and me only. Nor shall I forbear, for aught that you have said, to endeavour to arrive at the truth of the matter, for if I compelled him to plead at law, I should be doing a wrong to him, who is my liegeman, for I should put his right to the issue of law, whereas he offers to let me know the truth clearly.

So he caused the truth to be enquired into, and when the truth was made clear, he handed over to me the wardship of the abbey, and gave me sealed letters thereto. [26]

St. Louis's love of peace

Now it happened that the saintly king laboured so effectually that the King of England,[27] his wife, and his children, came to France to treat of a peace between them and him. To this peace his council were strongly opposed, and they spoke to him thus:

Sire, we marvel greatly that you are minded to give to the King of England a great portion of the land which you and your predecessors have won from him, and which he has forfeited by misfeasance. Now it seems to us that if you believe you have no right to the land, you are not making full restitution unless you restore all the conquests that you and your predecessors have made; while if you believe that you have a right to the land, it seems to us that whatever you restore is restored to your loss.

To this the saintly king replied after the following manner:

Lords, I am convinced that the King of England's predecessors were rightfully dispossessed of all the conquered land that I hold; and the land that I am giving him I do not give as a thing that I am bound to give either to himself or to his heirs; but I give it so that there may be love between my children and his, who are cousins-german. And meseems that what I give him is given to good purpose, since he has not hitherto been my liegeman, but will now have to do me homage.

No man in the world laboured more to maintain peace among his

---

26. This passage is in parts obscure, and the text may be corrupt. I agree with Miss Wedgwood as to the sense given in her version, which seems to me to render Joinville's intention better than the version (into relatively modern French) of M. de Wailly.
27. Henry III.

subjects, and specially among the great men who were neighbours, and the princes of the realm; as, for instance, between the Count of Chalon, uncle of the Lord of Joinville, and his son the Count of Burgundy, who were at war when we came back from overseas. And in order to make peace between the father and the son he sent men of his council, at his own charges, into Burgundy; and by his efforts peace was established between the father and the son.

There was at that time war between King Thibaut the Second, of Champagne, and Count John of Chalon, and the Count of Burgundy, his son, regarding the abbey of Luxeuil. To appease this war my lord the king sent Gervais of Escraines, who was then master of the meats in France; and by his efforts he reconciled them.

After this war, which the king appeased, arose another war between the Count Thibaut of Bar and Count Henry of Luxemburg, who had the sister of Count Thibaut to wife. And so it happened that they fought together near Preny, and Count Thibaut of Bar made Count Henry of Luxemburg prisoner, and took the castle of Ligny, which belonged to the Count of Luxemburg in right of his wife. In order to appease this war the king sent, at his own charges, my Lord Peter the chamberlain, the man in the world in whom he had greatest faith; and the king laboured so effectually that they were reconciled.

As to the foreigners whom the king had reconciled, there were some of his council who said he would have done better to let them fight; for if he suffered them to impoverish themselves, they would attack him less readily than if they were rich. And to this the king made answer, and said that they spoke unwisely.

> For if the neighbouring princes saw that I let them fight together, they might consult and say: 'It is from malice that he lets us fight together thus.' And so, perchance, out of hatred, they would come and fall upon me, which might be greatly to my loss, to say nothing of the enmity of God that I should incur, who has said: 'Blessed are the peacemakers.'

Whence it also came that the people of Burgundy and Lorraine, whom he had pacified, loved and obeyed him so well that I have seen them come and plead their suits before him at his courts of Rheims, Paris and Orleans.

HORROR OF ST. LOUIS AND OF JOINVILLE FOR ALL BLASPHEMY

The king so loved God and His sweet Mother that he caused all those to be grievously punished who were convinced of speaking of them evilly or lightly, or with a profane oath. Thus I saw him cause a goldsmith, at Caesarea, to be bound to a ladder, in his drawers and shirt, with a pig's gut and haslet round his neck, and in such quantity that they reached up to his nose. I heard tell that, since I came from overseas, he caused, on this account, a citizen of Paris to be burned in the nose and lip; but this I did not myself witness. And the saintly king was used to say: "I would consent to be branded with a hot iron on condition that all profane oaths were removed out of my realm."

I was full twenty-two years in his company, and never heard him swear by God, nor His Mother, nor His saints. When he wished to affirm anything, he would say: "Truly that was so," or "Truly that is so."

Never did I hear him name the Devil, unless the name came in some book, where it was right that it should come, or in the life of the saints where the book made mention thereof. And great shame it is to the realm of France, and to the king who suffers it, that scarcely can anyone speak without saying: "May the Devil take it!"

And it is a great sin of speech to devote to the Devil men or women who were given to God as soon as they were baptised. In the house of Joinville whosoever speaks such a word receives a buffet or pummel, and bad language is nearly outrooted.

St. Louis's Love for the Poor—How He Taught His Children—His Alms and Pious Foundations—His Scruples in the Collation to Benefices

He asked me if I washed the feet of the poor on Holy Thursday; and I answered him "No," for such an act appeared to me unseemly. And he told me I should not hold the act in disdain, seeing that God had so done. "Very unwillingly then would you do what the King of England does—who washes the feet of lepers, and kisses them."

Before he lay down in his bed he would cause his children to come to him, and bring to their minds the deeds of good kings and good emperors, telling them it was of such men they should take example. And he would bring to their minds also the deeds of great men who were wicked, and by their ill-living, and their rapine, and their avarice, had brought their kingdoms to ruin.

"And these things," he would say, "I bring to your minds, so that you may avoid them, and that God's anger be not kindled against you."

He made them learn the hours of our Lady, and say before him the hours of the day, so as to accustom them to hear the hours when they ruled over their own lands.

The king was such a large alms-giver that wherever he went in his kingdom he caused money to be given to the poor churches, to the lazar houses, to the alms-houses, to the hospitals, and to the poor gentlemen and gentlewomen. Every day he gave food to a great number of poor folk, beside those who ate in his chamber; and ofttimes have I seen him cutting their bread and giving them drink.

Many abbeys were built in his time, *viz.*, Royaumont, the abbey of St. Anthony, by Paris, the abbey of the Lis, the abbey of Maubuisson, and many other religious houses of Preachers and Franciscans. He built the almshouse of Pontoise, the alms-house of Vernon, the house of the blind in Paris, the nunnery of the Franciscan sisters at Saint-Cloud, which his sister, my Lady Isabel, founded by his sanction.

When any benefice in holy Church fell to the king's gift, he first, before bestowing it, consulted good men of religion and others; and when he had fully informed himself, he bestowed the benefices of holy Church, in good faith, loyally, and as in the sight of God. In every town of his realm, where he had never been before, he went to the Preachers and Franciscans, if there were any there, to ask for their prayers.

How the King Reformed His Bailiffs, Provosts, and Mayors—and How He Instituted New Ordinances—and How Stephen Boileau was His Provost of Paris

After King Lewis had returned to France from overseas, he bore himself very devoutly towards our Saviour, and very justly towards his subjects; wherefore he considered and thought it would be a fair thing, and a good, to reform the realm of France. First he established a general ordinance for all his subjects throughout the realm of France, in the manner following:—

> We, Louis, by the grace of God King of France, ordain that Our bailiffs, viscounts, provosts, mayors, and all others, in whatever matter it may be, and whatever office they may hold, shall make oath that, so long as they hold the said office, or perform the functions of bailiffs, they shall do justice to all, without acceptation of persons, as well to the poor as to the rich, and to strangers as to those who are native-born; and that they shall observe such uses and customs as are good and have been approved.

And if it happens that the bailiffs, or viscounts, or others, as the sergeants or foresters, do aught contrary to their oaths, and are convicted thereof, we order that they be punished in their goods, or in their persons, if the misfeasance so require; and the bailiffs shall be punished by Ourselves, and others by the bailiffs.

Henceforward the other provosts, the bailiffs and the sergeants shall make oath to loyally keep and uphold Our rents and Our rights, and not to suffer Our rights to lapse or to be suppressed or diminished; and with this they shall swear not to take or receive, by themselves or through others, gold, nor silver, nor any indirect benefit, nor any other thing, save fruit, or bread, or wine, or other present, to the value of ten *sous*, the said sum not being exceeded.

And besides this, they shall make oath not to take, or cause to be taken, any gift, of whatever kind, through their wives, or their children, or their brothers, or their sisters, or any other persons connected with them; and so soon as they have knowledge that any such gifts have been received, they will cause them to be returned as soon as may be possible. And, besides this, they shall make oath not to receive any gift, of whatever kind, from any man belonging to their bailiwicks, nor from any others who have a suit or may plead before them.

Henceforth they shall make oath not to bestow any gift upon any men who are of Our council, nor upon their wives, or children, or any person belonging to them; nor upon those who shall receive the said officers' accounts on Our behalf, nor to any persons whom we may send to their bailiwicks, or to their provostships, to enquire into their doings. And with this they shall swear to take no profit out of any sale that may be made of Our rents, Our bailiwicks, Our coinage, or aught else to Us belonging.

And they shall swear and promise, that if they have knowledge of any official, sergeant, or provost, serving under them, who is unfaithful, given to robbery and usury, or addicted to other vices whereby he ought to vacate Our service, then they will not uphold him for any gift, or promise, or private affection, or any other cause, but punish and judge him in all good faith.

Henceforward Our provosts, Our viscounts, Our mayors, Our foresters, and Our other sergeants, mounted and dismounted, shall make oath not to bestow any gift upon their superiors, nor upon their superiors' wives, nor children, nor upon any one belonging to them.

And because We desire that these oaths be fairly established, We order that they be taken in full assize, before all men, by clerks and laymen, knights and sergeants, notwithstanding that any such may have already made oath before Us; and this We ordain so that those who take the oaths may avoid the guilt and the sin of perjury, not only from the fear of God and of Ourselves, but also for shame before the world.

We will and ordain that all Our provosts and bailiffs abstain from saying any word that would bring into contempt God, or our Lady, or the saints; and also that they abstain from the game of dice and keep away from taverns. We ordain that the making of dice be forbidden throughout Our realm, and that lewd women be turned out of every house; and whosoever shall rent a house to a lewd woman shall forfeit to the provost, or the bailiff, the rent of the said house for a year.

Moreover, We forbid Our bailiffs to purchase wrongfully, or to cause to be purchased, either directly, or through others, any possession or lands that may be in their bailiwick, or in any other, so long as they remain in Our service, and without Our express permission; and if any such purchases are made, We ordain that the lands in question be, and remain, in Our hands.

We forbid Our bailiffs, so long as they shall be in Our service, to marry any sons or daughters that they may have, or any other person belonging to them, to any other person in their bailiwick, without Our special sanction; and moreover We forbid that they put any such into a religious house in their bailiwick, or purvey them with any benefice of holy Church, or any other possession; and moreover We forbid that they obtain provisions or lodgings from any religious house, or nearby, at the expense of the religouses. This prohibition as concerns marriages and the acquisition of goods, as stated above, does not apply to provosts, or mayors, nor to others holding minor offices.

We order that no bailiff, provost, or any other, shall keep too many sergeants or beadles, to the burdening of our people; and We ordain that the beadles be appointed in full assize, or else be not regarded as beadles. When sergeants are sent to a distant place, or to a strange county, We ordain that they be not received without letters from their superiors.

We order that no bailiff or provost in Our service shall burden the good people in his jurisdiction beyond what is lawful and right; and that none of Our subjects be put in prison for any debt save in so far as such debt may be due to Ourselves only.

We ordain that no bailiff levy a fine for a debt due by any of Our subjects, or for any offence, save in full and open court, where the amount of such fine may be adjudged and estimated, with the advice of worthy and competent persons, even when the fine has already been considered by them (informally? passage obscure). And if it happens that the accused will not wait for the judgment of Our court, which is offered him. but offers for the fine a certain sum of money, such as has been commonly received aforetime, we ordain that the court accept such sum of money if it be reasonable and convenient; and, if not, we ordain that the fine be adjudicated upon, as aforesaid, even though the delinquent place himself in the hands of the court.

We forbid that the bailiffs, or the mayors, or the provosts, should compel Our subjects, either by threats, or intimidation, or any chicanery, to pay a fine in secret or in public, or accuse any save for reasonable cause.

And We ordain that those who hold the office of provost, viscount, or any other office, do not sell such office to others without Our consent; and if several persons buy jointly any of the said offices, We order that one of the purchasers shall perform the duties of the office for all the rest, and alone enjoy such of its privileges in respect of journeyings, taxes, and common charges, as have been customary aforetime.

And We forbid that they sell the said offices to their brothers, nephews, or cousins, after they have bought them from Us; and that they claim any debts that may be due to themselves, save such debts as appertain to their office. As regards their own personal debts, they will recover them by authority of the bailiff, just as if they were not in Our service.

We forbid Our bailiffs and provosts to weary our subjects, in the causes brought before them, by moving the venue from place to place. They shall hear the matters brought before them in the place where they have been wont to hear them, so that Our subjects may not be induced to forego their just rights for fear of trouble and expense.

From henceforth we command that Our provosts and bailiffs dispossess no man from the seisin which he holds, without full enquiry, or Our own especial order; and that they impose upon Our people no new exactions, taxes and imposts; and that they compel no one to come forth to do service in arms, for the purpose of exacting money from him; for We order that none who owes Us service in arms shall be summoned to join the host without sufficient cause, and that those who would desire to come to the host in person should not be compelled to purchase exemption by money payment.

Moreover, we forbid Our bailiffs and provosts to prevent corn, wine and other merchandise from being taken out of Our kingdom, save for sufficient cause; and when it is convenient that these goods should not be taken out of the kingdom, the ordinance shall be made publicly, in the council of worthy and competent elders, and without suspicion of fraud or misdoing. Similarly We ordain that all bailiffs, viscounts, provosts, and mayors do remain, after they have left office, for the space of forty days in the land where such office has been exercised—remaining there in person, or by deputy—so that they may answer to the new bailiffs in respect of any wrong done to such as may wish to bring a complaint against them.

By these ordinances the king did much to improve the condition of the kingdom.

Reform of the Provost-ship of Paris

The provostship of Paris was at that time sold to the citizens of Paris, or indeed to any one; and those who bought the office upheld their children and nephews in wrongdoing; and the young folk relied in their misdoings on those who occupied the provostship. For which reason the mean people were greatly downtrodden; nor could they obtain justice against the rich, because of the great presents and gifts that the latter made to the provosts.

Whenever at that time any one spoke the truth before the provost, and wished to keep his oath, refusing to perjure himself regarding any debt, or other matter on which he was bound to give evidence, then the provost levied a fine upon that person, and he was punished. And because of the great injustice that was done, and the great robberies perpetrated in the provostship, the mean people did not dare to sojourn in the king's land, but went and sojourned in other provostships and other lordships. And the king's land was so deserted that when the provost held his court, no more than ten or twelve people came thereto.

With all this there were so many malefactors and thieves in Paris and the country adjoining that all the land was full of them. The king, who was very diligent to enquire how the mean people were governed and protected, soon knew the truth of this matter. So he forbade that the office of provost in Paris should be sold; and he gave great and good wages to those who henceforward should hold the said office.

And he abolished all the evil customs harmful to the people; and he caused enquiry to be made throughout the kingdom to find men who would execute good and strict justice, and not spare the rich any more than the poor.

Then was brought to his notice Stephen Boileau, who so maintained and upheld the office of provost that no malefactor, nor thief, nor murderer dared to remain in Paris, seeing that if he did, he was soon hung or exterminated: neither parentage, nor lineage, nor gold, nor silver could save him. So the king's land began to amend, and people resorted thither for the good justice that prevailed. And the people so multiplied, and things so amended, that sales, seisines, purchases, and other matters were doubled in value, as compared with what the king had received aforetime.

"In all these matters which We have ordained for the advantage of Our subjects, and of Our realm, we reserve to Ourselves the right to elucidate, amend, adjust, or diminish, according as We may determine."

By this ordinance also the king did much to reform the kingdom of France, as many wise and ancient persons bear witness.

Love of St. Louis for the Poor—of His Alms and Pious Foundations

From the time of his childhood, the king had pity on the poor and suffering; and the custom was that, wherever the king went, six score poor persons were always fed every day, in his house, with bread and wine, and meat or fish. In Lent and Advent the number of the poor was increased; and ofttimes it happened that the king served them, and set their food before them, and carved the meat before them, and gave them money with his own hand at their departing.

Particularly at the great vigils, before the solemn festivals, he served the poor in all matters as aforesaid, before he himself either ate or drank. Besides all this he had, every day, to dine or sup near him, old and broken men, and caused them to be fed with the same meats of which he himself partook; and when they had eaten they took away a certain sum of money.

Besides all this the king gave, day by day, large and great alms to the poor religiouses, to the poor in hospitals, to the poor sick, and to poor communities, also to poor gentlemen and ladies, and girls, and to fallen women, and to poor widows, and to women who were lying in, and to poor work men, who through age or sickness could no longer work at their crafts; so that hardly would it be possible to number his alms.

Therefore may it well be said that he was more fortunate than Titus, the Emperor of Rome, of whom old writings tell that he was sad and discomforted for any day on which he had not been able to confer some benefit.

From the first that he came to his kingdom and knew where he stood he began to erect churches, and many religious houses, among which the abbey of Royaumont bears the palm for honour and magnificence. He caused many almshouses to be erected: the almshouse of Paris, that of Pontoise. that of Compiègne and of Vernon, and assigned to them large rents.

He founded the abbey of St. Matthew at Rouen, where he set women of the order of the Preaching Brothers; and he founded that of Longchamp, where he set women of the order of the Minorist Brothers, and assigned to them large rents for their livelihood.

And he allowed his mother to found the abbey of the Lis near Melun-sur-Seine, and the abbey near Pontoise, which is called Maubuisson, and there assigned to them large rents and possessions. And he caused to be built the House of the Blind, near Paris, for the reception of the poor blind of the city; and caused a chapel to be built for them, so that they might hear the service of God. And the good king caused the house of the Carthusians, which is called Vauvert, to be built outside Paris, and assigned sufficient rents to the monks who there served our Saviour.

Pretty soon after he caused another house to be built outside Paris, on the way to St. Denis, and it was called the house of the *Filles-Dieu*; and he caused to be placed there a great multitude of women who, through poverty, had lapsed into the sin of incontinence; and he gave them, for their maintenance, four hundred *livres* a year. And in many places of his kingdom he instituted houses for *beguines*,[28] and gave them rents for their livelihood, and commanded that any should be received therein who were minded to live in chastity.

There were some of his familiars who murmured at his giving such large alms, and because he expended so much; and he would say: "I like better that the great and excessive expenditure which I incur should be incurred in almsgiving for the love of God, than in pomp and splendour and for the vainglory of this world." Yet, notwithstanding that the king spent so largely in almsgiving, he did not forbear to incur daily great expenditure in his household. Largely and liberally did the king behave to the parliaments and assemblies of his barons and knights; and he caused his court to be served courteously, and largely, and without stint, and in more liberal fashion than aforetime in the court of his predecessors.

OF THE RELIGIOUS ORDERS THAT THE KING ESTABLISHED IN FRANCE

The king loved all people who set themselves to serve God, and took on them the religious habit; nor did any come to him but he gave them what they needed for a living. He provided for the brothers of Carmel, and bought them land on the Seine, towards Charenton, and caused a house to be built for them, and purchased for them vestments, chalices, and such other things as are needful for the service of our Saviour. And after he provided for the brothers of St. Augustine, and bought them the grange of a citizen of Paris, and all its appurtenances, and caused a church to be built for them outside the gate of Montmartre.

The brothers of the "Sacks" he provided for, and he gave them a site on the Seine, towards Saint-Germain des Prés, where they established themselves; but they remained there no long time, for they were shortly suppressed. After the brothers of the "Sacks "had been lodged came another kind of brothers, who were called the order of the "White Mantles," and they begged the king to give them help so that they might remain in Paris. The king bought them a house and certain old buildings lying round where they might lodge near the old gate of the Temple in Paris, rather near to the Weavers' house. These "White Mantles" were suppressed at the Council of Lyons, held by Gregory X.

---

28. Women living by rule, but without religious vows. I imagine that, in this passage, Joinville attached an idea of repentance to these particular *beguines*.

Afterwards came yet another kind of brothers, who had themselves called brothers of the Holy Cross, and wore a cross upon their breasts; and they asked the king to help them. The king did so willingly, and lodged them in a street called the Cross-roads of the Temple, and now called the street of the Holy Cross.

Thus did the good king surround the city of Paris with people of religion.

St. Louis Assumes the Cross for the Second Time

After the things above stated, it happened that the king summoned all his barons to Paris during a certain Lent (1267). I excused myself on account of a quartan fever which I then had, and begged him to suffer me to remain away. But he sent me word that he insisted that I should come, because he had with him good physicians who well knew how to cure quartan fever.

To Paris I went. When I came thither on the night of the vigil of our Lady in March, I found no one, neither the queen nor any other, who could tell me why I had been summoned by the king. Now it chanced, as God so willed, that I slept during matins; and meseemed, while I slept, that I saw the king before an altar, on his knees; and meseemed further that many prelates, duly vested, were vesting him with a red chasuble of Rheims serge.

After seeing this vision I called my Lord William, my priest, who was very wise, and told him of the vision. And he said to me: "Lord, you will see that the king will take the cross tomorrow." I asked him why he thought so.

And he told me he thought so because of the dream that I had dreamed; for the chasuble of red serge signified the cross, which was red with the blood that God shed from His side, and His feet, and His hands. "And for that the chasuble is of Rheims serge," said he, "that signifies that the Crusade shall be of little profit, as you shall see if God gives you life."

When I had heard mass at the Magdalen in Paris, I went to the king's chapel and found the king, who had gone up the scaffolding where were the relics, and was causing the true cross to be taken down. While the king was coming down, two knights, who were of his council, began to speak to one another; and the one said: "Never believe me if the king is not crossing himself here."

And the other made answer: "If the king crosses himself, this will be one of the most dolorous days that ever were in France. For if we do not take the cross, we shall lose the king's favour; and if we take the cross we shall lose God's favour, because we shall not take it for His sake, but for the sake of the king."

So it happened that on the following day the king took the cross, and his three sons with him; and afterwards it befell that the Crusade was of little profit, according to the prophecy of my priest.

Much was I pressed by the King of France, and the King of Navarre, to take the cross. To this I replied that while I was in the service of God and of the king overseas, and since I had returned, the sergeants of the King of France and of the King of Navarre had ruined and impoverished my people, so that, to all time, I and they would be the poorer for it. And I told them this, that if I wished to do what was pleasing to God, I should remain here, to help and defend my people; and if I put my body in danger in the pilgrimage of the cross, while seeing quite clearly that this would be to the hurt and damage of my people, I should move God to anger, Who gave His body to save His people.

I held that all those who advised the king to go on this expedition committed mortal sin; for at the point at which France then was, all the kingdom was at good peace with itself and with its neighbours, while ever since he departed, the state of the kingdom has done nothing but go from bad to worse.

Great was the sin of those who advised the king to go, seeing how weak he was of his body, for he could bear neither to be drawn in a chariot, nor to ride. So great was his weakness that he suffered me to carry him in my arms from the mansion of the Count of Auxerre, where I took leave of him, to the abbey of the Franciscans. And yet, weak as he was, if he had remained in France he might have lived longer, and done much good, and many good works.

St. Louis Falls Sick—His Instructions to His Son

Of the king's journey to Tunis will I say and tell nothing, forasmuch as, thank God! I was not there, and have no wish to put in my book anything of which I am not certain. So we will speak only of our saintly king, and tell how, after he had landed at Tunis, before the castle of Carthage, he fell sick of a flux in the stomach, and Philip, his eldest son, was sick of a quartan fever, and of the same flux in the stomach as the king; and the king took to his bed, and felt that he must shortly pass out of this world into the other.

Then he called my Lord Philip, his son, and commanded him, as if by testament, to observe all the teachings he had left him, which are hereinafter set down in French, and were, so it is said, written with the king's own saintly hand:

> Fair son, the first thing I would teach thee is to set thine heart to love God; for unless he love God none can be saved. Keep thyself from doing aught that is displeasing to God, that is to say, from mortal sin. Contrariwise thou shouldst suffer every manner of torment rather than commit a mortal sin.
>
> If God send thee adversity, receive it in patience, and give thanks to our Saviour, and bethink thee that thou hast deserved it, and that He will make it turn to thine advantage. If He send thee prosperity, then thank Him humbly, so that thou become not worse from pride, or any other cause, when thou oughtest to be better. For we should not fight against God with His own gifts.
>
> Confess thyself often, and choose for confessor a right worthy man who knows how to teach thee what to do, and what not to do; and bear thyself in such sort that thy confessor and thy friends shall dare to reprove thee for thy misdoings. Listen to the services of holy Church devoutly, and without chattering; and pray to God with thy heart and with thy lips, and especially at mass when the consecration takes place. Let thy heart be tender and full of pity towards those who are poor, miserable and afflicted; and comfort and help them to the utmost of thy power.
>
> Maintain the good customs of thy realm, and abolish the bad. Be not covetous against thy people: and do not burden them with taxes and imposts save when thou art in great need.
>
> If thou hast any great burden weighing upon thy heart, tell it to thy confessor or to some right worthy man who is not full of vain words. Then shalt thou be able to bear it the more easily.
>
> See that thou hast in thy company men, whether religious or lay, who are right worthy, and loyal, and not full of covetousness, and confer with them oft; and fly and eschew the company of the wicked. Hearken willingly to the Word of God, and keep it in thine heart; and seek diligently after prayers and indulgences. Love all that is good and profitable, and hate all that is evil wheresoever it may be.
>
> Let none be so bold as to say before thee any word that would

draw and move to sin, or so bold as to speak evil behind another's back for pleasure's sake; nor do thou suffer any word in disparagement of God and of His saints to be spoken in thy presence. Give often thanks to God for all the good things He has bestowed upon thee, so that thou be accounted worthy to receive more.

In order to do justice and right to thy subjects, be upright and firm, turning neither to the right hand nor to the left, but always to what is just; and do thou maintain the cause of the poor until such time as the truth is made clear. And if anyone has an action against thee, make full inquisition until thou knowest the truth; for thus shall thy counsellors judge the more boldly according to the truth, whether for thee or against.

If thou holdest aught that belongeth to another, whether by thine own act or the act of thy predecessors, and the matter be certain, make restoration without delay. If the matter be doubtful, cause enquiry to be made by wise men, diligently and promptly.

Give heed that thy servants and thy subjects live under thee in peace and uprightness. Especially maintain the good cities and commons of thy realm in the same estate and with the same franchises as they enjoyed under thy predecessors: and if there be aught to amend, amend and set it right, and keep them in thy favour and love. For because of the power and wealth of the great cities, thine own subjects, and specially thy peers and thy barons, and foreigners also, will fear to undertake aught against thee.

Love and honour all persons belonging to holy Church, and see that no one take away, or diminish, the gifts and alms made to them by thy predecessors. It is related of King Philip, my grandfather, that one of his counsellors once told him that those of holy Church did him much harm and damage, in that they deprived him of his rights, and diminished his jurisdiction, and that it was a great marvel that he suffered it; and the good king replied that he believed this might well be so, but he had regard to the enefits and courtesies that God had bestowed upon him, and so thought it better to abandon some of his rights than to have any contention with the people of holy Church.

To thy father and mother thou shalt give honour and reverence, and thou shalt obey their commandments. Bestow the benefices of holy Church on persons who are righteous and of a clean life, and do it on the advice of men of worth and uprightness.

Beware of undertaking a war against any Christian prince without great deliberation; and if it has to be undertaken, see that thou do no hurt to holy Church, and to those who have done thee no injury. If wars and dissensions arise among thy subjects, see that thou appease them as soon as thou art able.

Use diligence to have good provosts and bailiffs, and enquire often of them, and of those of thy household, how they conduct themselves, and if there be found in them any vice of inordinate covetousness, or falsehood, or trickery. Labour to free thy land from all vile iniquity, and especially strike down with all thy power evil swearing and heresy. See to it that the expense of thy household be reasonable.

Finally, my very dear son, cause masses to be sung for my soul, and prayers to be said throughout thy realm; and give to me a special share and full part in all the good thou doest. Fair dear son, I give thee all the blessings that a good father can give to his son. And may the blessed Trinity and all the saints keep and defend thee from all evils; and God give thee grace to do His will always, so that He be honoured in thee, and that thou and I may both, after this mortal life is ended, be with Him together, and praise Him everlastingly. Amen.

Death of St. Louis

When the good king had so taught his son, my Lord Philip, the infirmity that was upon him began to grow apace; and he asked for the sacraments of holy Church, and received them, being clear of thought and of sound understanding, as appeared duly, for when they anointed him with oil and said the seven Psalms, he repeated the verses in turn.

And I heard my Lord, the Count of Alençon, his son, tell that when the king came near to death he called upon the saints to help and succour him, and especially upon my Lord St. James, saying St. James's orison, which begins:

> "*Esto, Domine*" that is to say, "O God, be the sanctifier and guardian of thy people." Then he called to his aid my Lord St. Denis of France, saying St. Denis's orison, which is to this effect: "Lord God, grant that we may despise the prosperity of this world, and not stand in fear of any adversity."

And I then heard my Lord of Alençon—on whom God have mercy!—relate how his father called on my Lady St. Genevieve. After that, the saintly king caused himself to be laid on a bed covered with ashes, and put his hands across his breast, and, looking towards heaven, rendered up his spirit to our Creator; and it was at the same hour that the Son of God died upon the cross for the world's salvation.

A piteous thing, and worthy of tears, is the death of this saintly prince, who kept and guarded his realm so holily and loyally, and gave alms there so largely, and set therein so many fair foundations. And like as the scribe who, writing his book, illuminates it with gold and azure, so did the said king illuminate his realm with the fair abbeys that he built, and the great number of almshouses, and the houses for Preachers and Franciscans, and other religious orders, as named above.

On the day after the feast of St. Bartholomew the Apostle did the good King Louis pass out of this world, and in the year of the Incarnation of our Saviour, the year of grace 1270 (the 25th August). And his bones were put in a casket, and borne thence, and buried at St. Denis in France, where he had chosen his place of sepulture; and in the place where they were buried God has sithence performed many fair miracles in his honour, and by his merit.

Canonisation of St. Louis

After this, at the instance of the King of France, and by command of the Pope, [29] came the Archbishop of Rouen, and Brother John of Samois, who has since been made bishop, they came to St. Denis in France, and there remained a long space to make inquisition into the life, the works, and the miracles of the saintly king. And I was summoned to come to them, and they kept me two days. And after they had questioned me and others, what they had ascertained and set down was sent to the court of Rome; and the Pope and the cardinals looked diligently into what had been sent to them, and according to what they saw there they did right to the king, and set him among the number of the confessors.

Hence was there, and ought there to be, great joy in all the realm of France; and great honour to those of his lineage who are like him in doing well, and equal dishonour to those of his lineage who will not follow him in good works: great dishonour, I say, to those of his lineage who would do evil; for men will point a finger at them, and say that the saintly king, from whom they sprang, would have scorned

---

29. Martin IV.

to commit so foul an act.

After the good news had come from Rome, the king appointed a day, on the morrow of St. Bartholomew (25th August 1298), when the holy body should be raised. When the body was raised, the Archbishop of Rheims that then was—on whom God have mercy!—and my Lord Henry of Villers, my nephew, who was then Archbishop of Lyons, bore it first in hand; and afterwards it was borne by many others, as well archbishops as bishops, more than I can name: they bore it to a platform that had been erected.

Then preached Brother John of Samois; and among the other great feats that our saintly king had performed, he related one of the worthy deeds to which I had borne testimony in my sworn declaration, and of which I had been witness; and he spoke thus:

> So that you may see that he was the most loyal and upright man in his time, I will tell you that he was so loyal that he held a covenant he had made with the Saracens, though he had made it by simple word of mouth only, and if so be that he had not held it, he would have gained ten thousand *livres* and more." He told them all the story as I have already told it above. And when he had told them all, he said: "Do not think I am lying to you, for I see before me such a man as testified to us of this thing, and did so on oath.

After the sermon was ended the king and his brothers bore back the holy body to the church, with the help of their lineage—to whom this honour was due; for a great honour had been done them, if so be that they approve themselves worthy of it, as I have said above. Let us pray to the sainted king to ask God to give us what is needful for our souls and bodies. Amen!

Joinville Sees St. Louis in a Dream, and Erects an Altar to Him

I will tell you yet again of things that are to the honour of our saintly king, *viz.*, what I saw when I was in my bed asleep; and it seemed to me, in my dream, that I beheld him before my chapel at Joinville; and he was, so I thought, marvellously joyous and glad at heart, and I myself was right glad to see him in my castle; and I said to him: "Sire, when you go hence, I will lodge you in a house of mine, that is in a city of mine called Chevillon."

And he answered me, laughing, and said to me: "Lord of Joinville, by the faith I owe you, I have no wish so soon to go hence."

When I awoke I set myself thinking; and meseemed it would be pleasing both to God and to the king if I lodged him in my chapel; and so I did, for I built him an altar, to the honour of God, and to his honour, and there masses shall be sung in his honour forever; and a rent has been established in perpetuity that this may be done.

And these things have I told to my Lord King Louis, who is the inheritor of his name; and methinks he would do what is agreeable to God, and agreeable to our sainted King Louis, if he procured relics of the true holy body, and sent them to the said chapel of St. Lawrence at Joinville, so that those who come hereafter to the saintly king's altar may have the greater devotion.

Conclusion

I would make known to all that I myself saw and heard a great portion of what is here related concerning the saintly king; and that a great portion I found in a book,[1] written in French—which latter portion I have caused to be written in this book. And I tell you of these things, so that those who hear this book read may give full credence to what the book says that I myself saw and heard; while as to the other things here written, I do not certify to you that they are true, because I myself, in person, neither saw nor heard them.

This was written in the year of grace 1309, in the month of October.

---

1 Joinville seems to have had knowledge of certain books relating to St. Lewis, and it is difficult to identify the one to which he here refers. The question is discussed by M. de Wailly—see pp. 488-491 of his edition. See also M. Viollet's paper, *Les Enseignements de Saint Louis à son fils*, Bibliothèque de l'Ecole des Charles, tome 35., 1874. There is, however, little practical difficulty, when reading the Chronicle, in distinguishing between what Joinville relates as an eyewitness and what he relates on the authority of others.

ALSO FROM LEONAUR
AVAILABLE IN SOFTCOVER OR HARDCOVER WITH DUST JACKET

CAPTAIN OF THE 95th (Rifles) by *Jonathan Leach*—An officer of Wellington's Sharpshooters during the Peninsular, South of France and Waterloo Campaigns of the Napoleonic Wars.

BUGLER AND OFFICER OF THE RIFLES by *William Green & Harry Smith* With the 95th (Rifles) during the Peninsular & Waterloo Campaigns of the Napoleonic Wars

BAYONETS, BUGLES AND BONNETS by *James 'Thomas' Todd*—Experiences of hard soldiering with the 71st Foot - the Highland Light Infantry - through many battles of the Napoleonic wars including the Peninsular & Waterloo Campaigns

THE ADVENTURES OF A LIGHT DRAGOON by *George Farmer & G.R. Gleig*—A cavalryman during the Peninsular & Waterloo Campaigns, in captivity & at the siege of Bhurtpore, India

THE COMPLEAT RIFLEMAN HARRIS by *Benjamin Harris as told to & transcribed by Captain Henry Curling*—The adventures of a soldier of the 95th (Rifles) during the Peninsular Campaign of the Napoleonic Wars

WITH WELLINGTON'S LIGHT CAVALRY by *William Tomkinson*—The Experiences of an officer of the 16th Light Dragoons in the Peninsular and Waterloo campaigns of the Napoleonic Wars.

SURTEES OF THE RIFLES by *William Surtees*—A Soldier of the 95th (Rifles) in the Peninsular campaign of the Napoleonic Wars.

ENSIGN BELL IN THE PENINSULAR WAR by *George Bell*—The Experiences of a young British Soldier of the 34th Regiment 'The Cumberland Gentlemen' in the Napoleonic wars.

WITH THE LIGHT DIVISION by *John H. Cooke*—The Experiences of an Officer of the 43rd Light Infantry in the Peninsula and South of France During the Napoleonic Wars

NAPOLEON'S IMPERIAL GUARD: FROM MARENGO TO WATERLOO by *J. T. Headley*—This is the story of Napoleon's Imperial Guard from the bearskin caps of the grenadiers to the flamboyance of their mounted chasseurs, their principal characters and the men who commanded them.

BATTLES & SIEGES OF THE PENINSULAR WAR by *W. H. Fitchett*—Corunna, Busaco, Albuera, Ciudad Rodrigo, Badajos, Salamanca, San Sebastian & Others

---

AVAILABLE ONLINE AT **www.leonaur.com**
AND OTHER GOOD BOOK STORES

NAP-1

www.ingramcontent.com/pod-product-compliance
Lightning Source LLC
Chambersburg PA
CBHW030227170426
43201CB00006B/137